AF262822

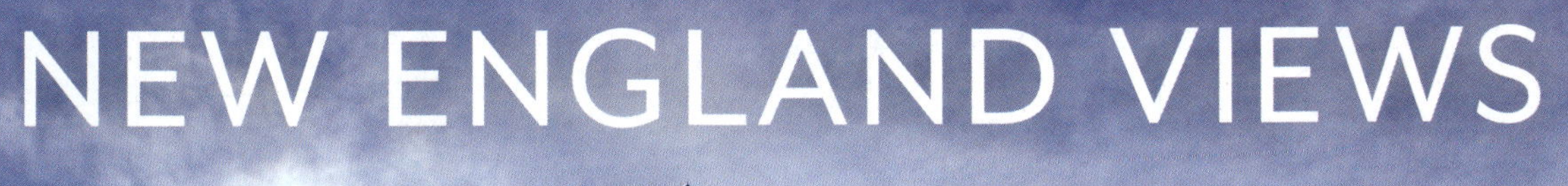

NEW ENGLAND VIEWS

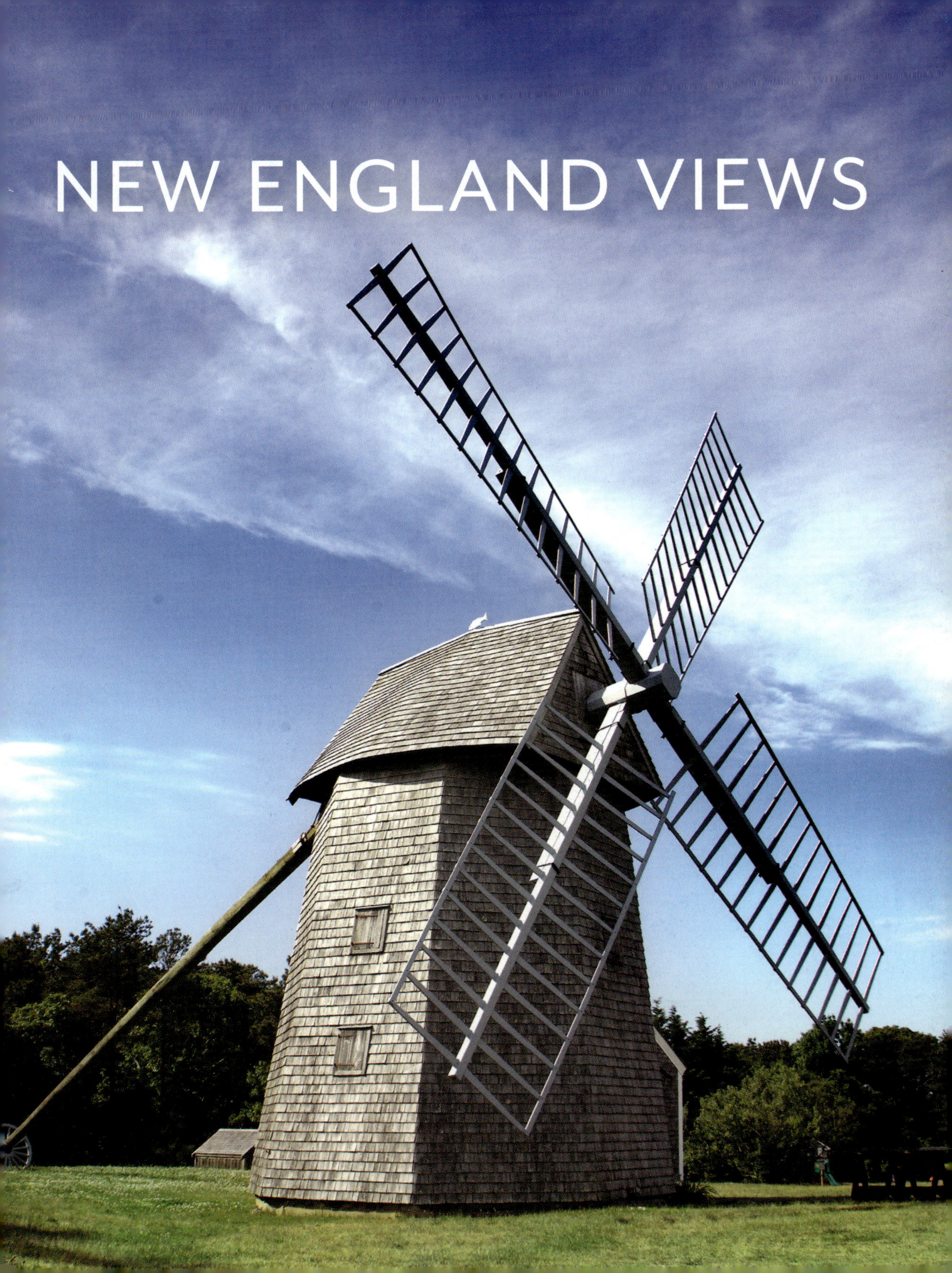

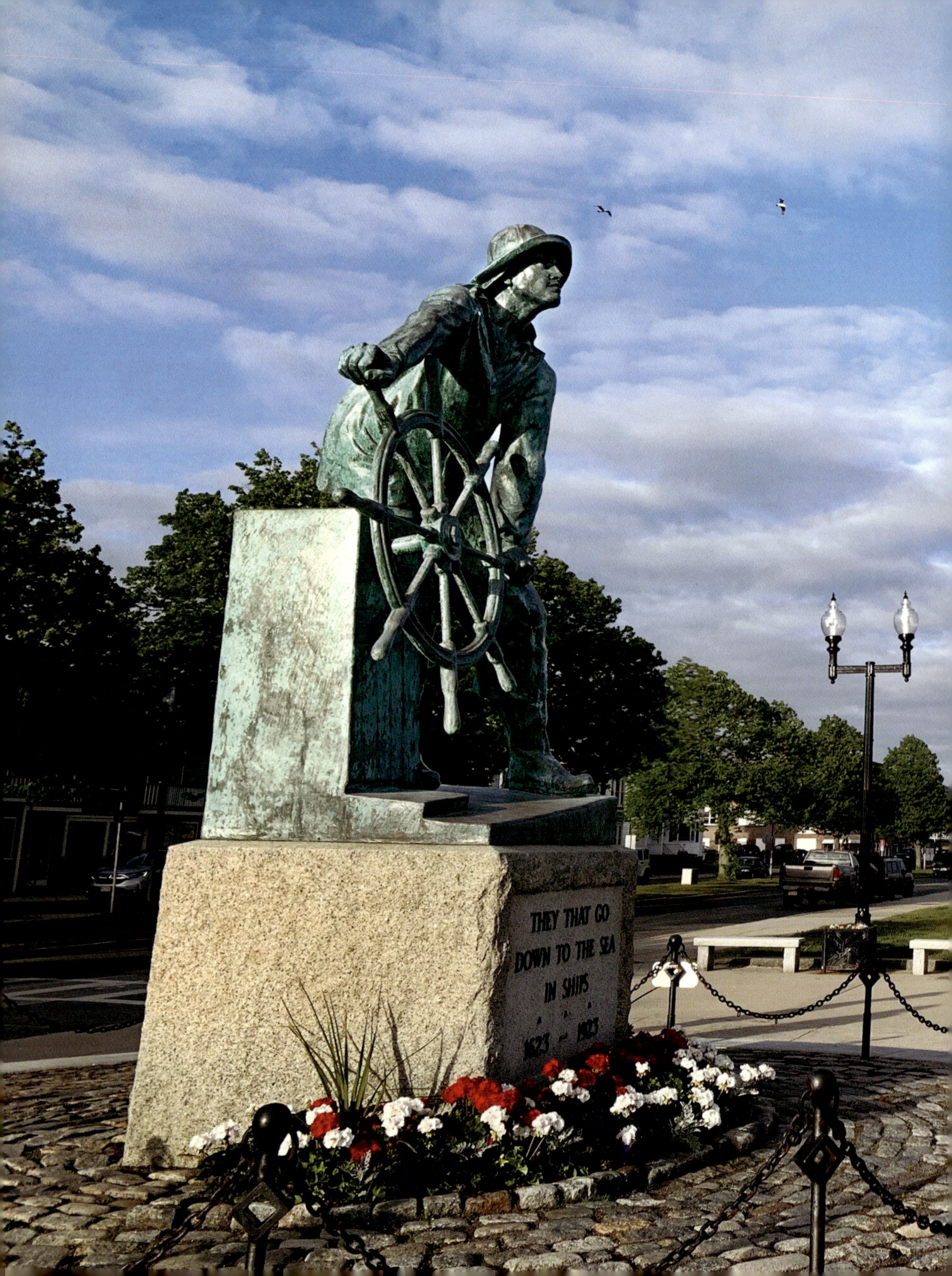

THEY THAT GO
DOWN TO THE SEA
IN SHIPS
1623 — 1923

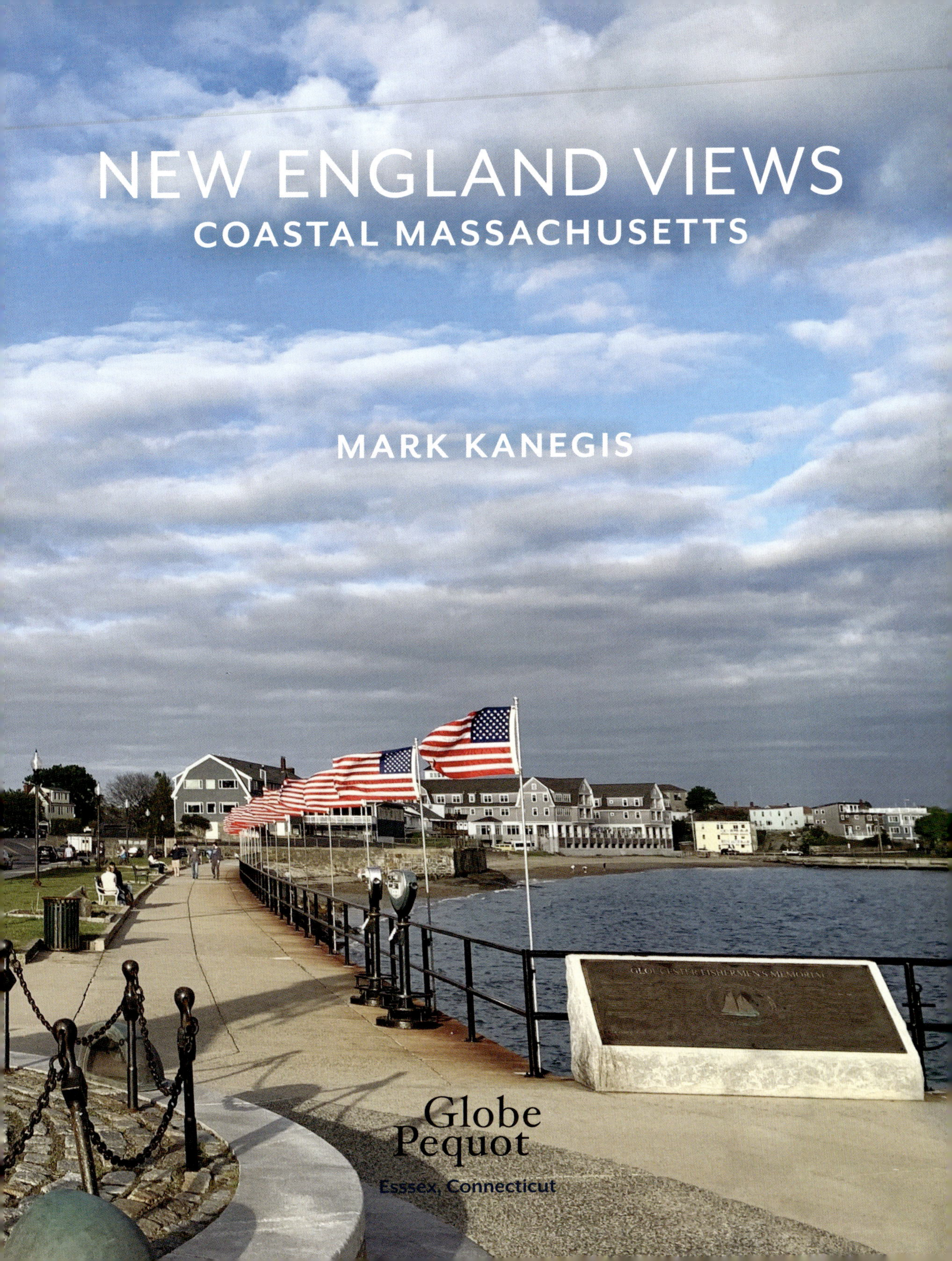

NEW ENGLAND VIEWS
COASTAL MASSACHUSETTS

MARK KANEGIS

Globe
Pequot

Esssex, Connecticut

Globe
Pequot

An imprint of Globe Pequot, the trade division of
The Rowman & Littlefield Publishing Group, Inc.
4501 Forbes Blvd., Ste. 200
Lanham, MD 20706
www.rowman.com

Distributed by NATIONAL BOOK NETWORK

British Library Cataloguing in Publication Information available
Library of Congress Cataloging-in-Publication Data available
ISBN 978-1-4930-5524-1 (cloth : alk. paper)
ISBN 978-1-4390-5525-8 (electronic)

Printed in India

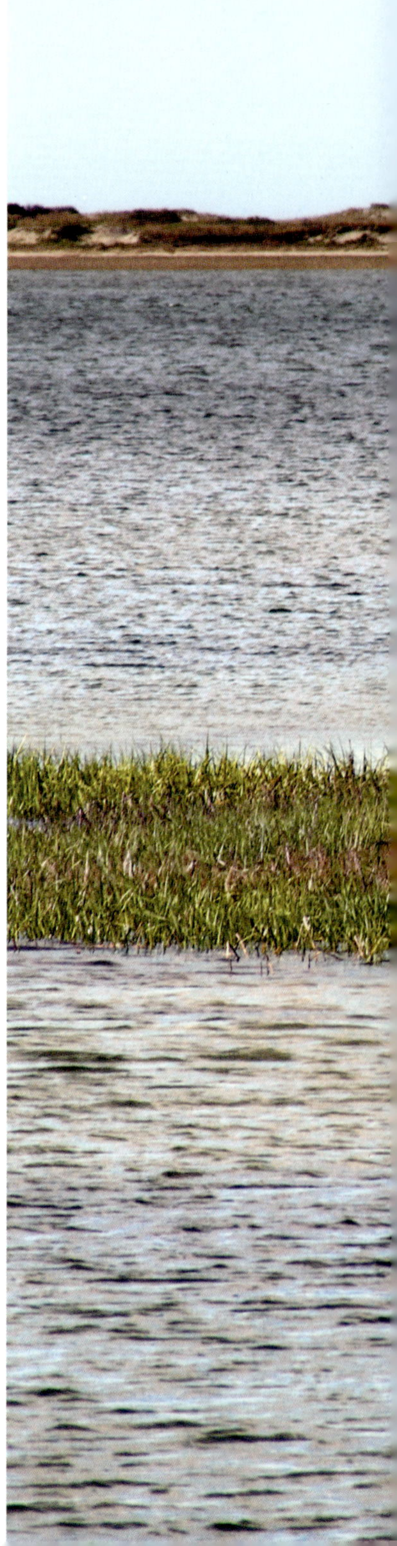

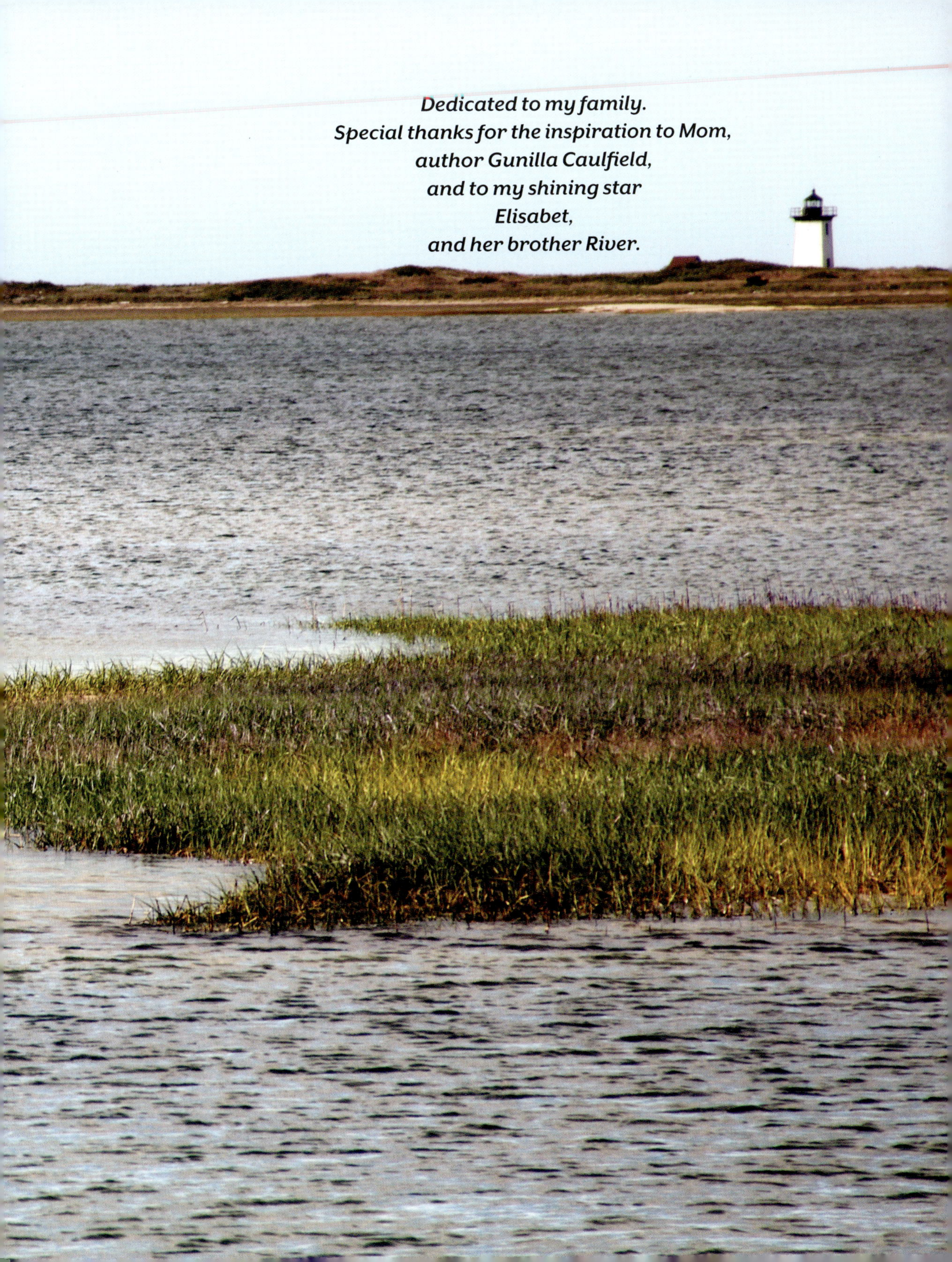

Dedicated to my family.
Special thanks for the inspiration to Mom,
author Gunilla Caulfield,
and to my shining star
Elisabet,
and her brother River.

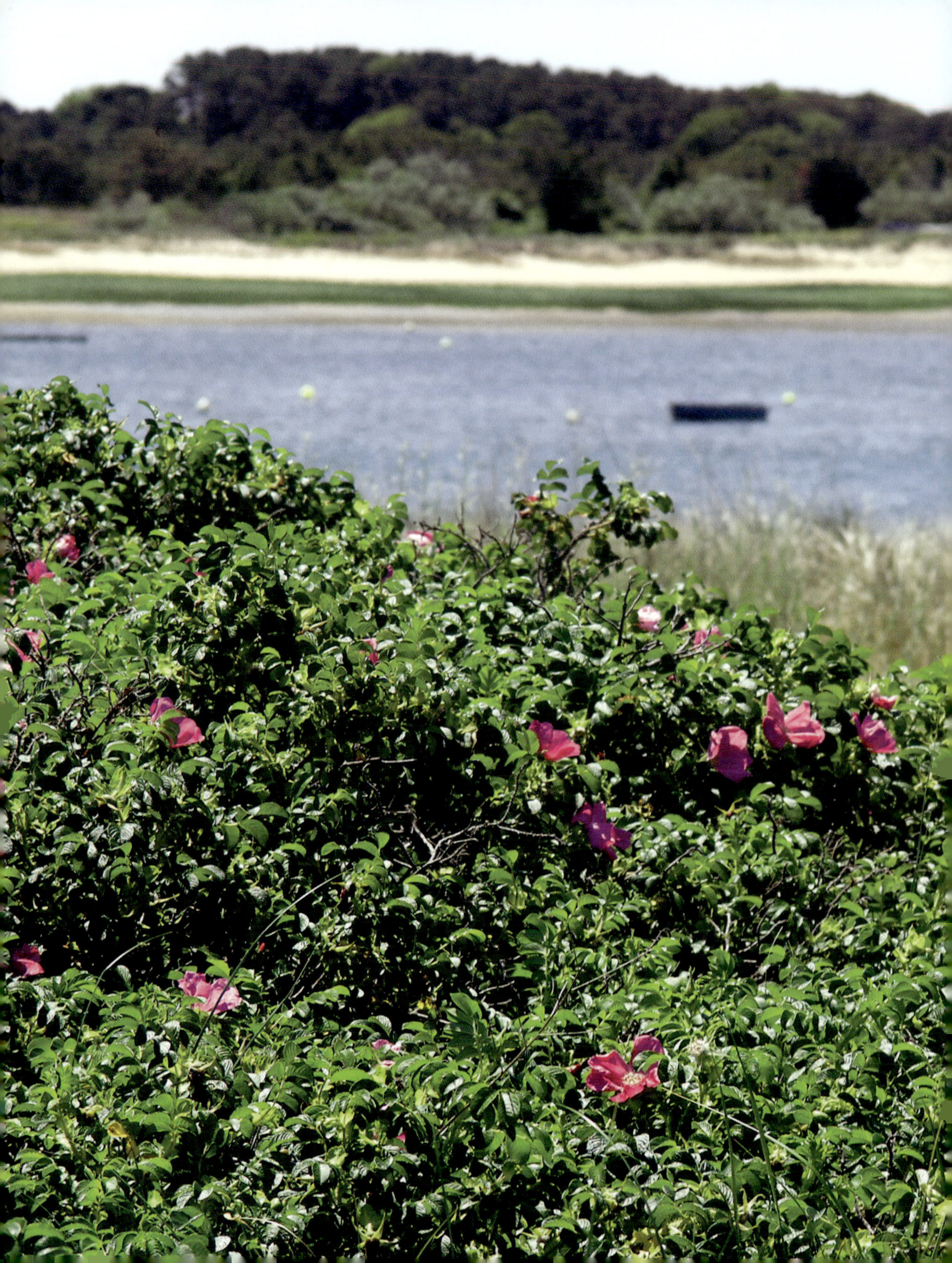

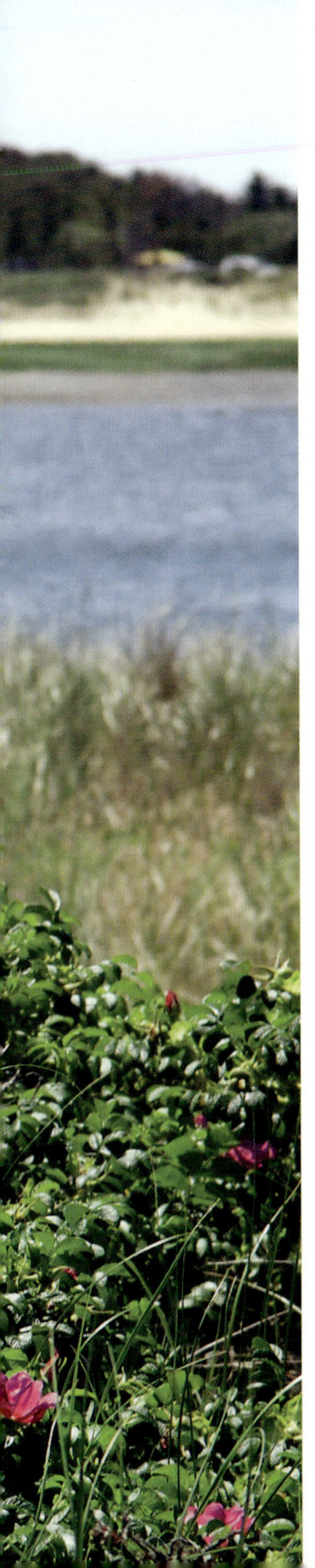

Contents

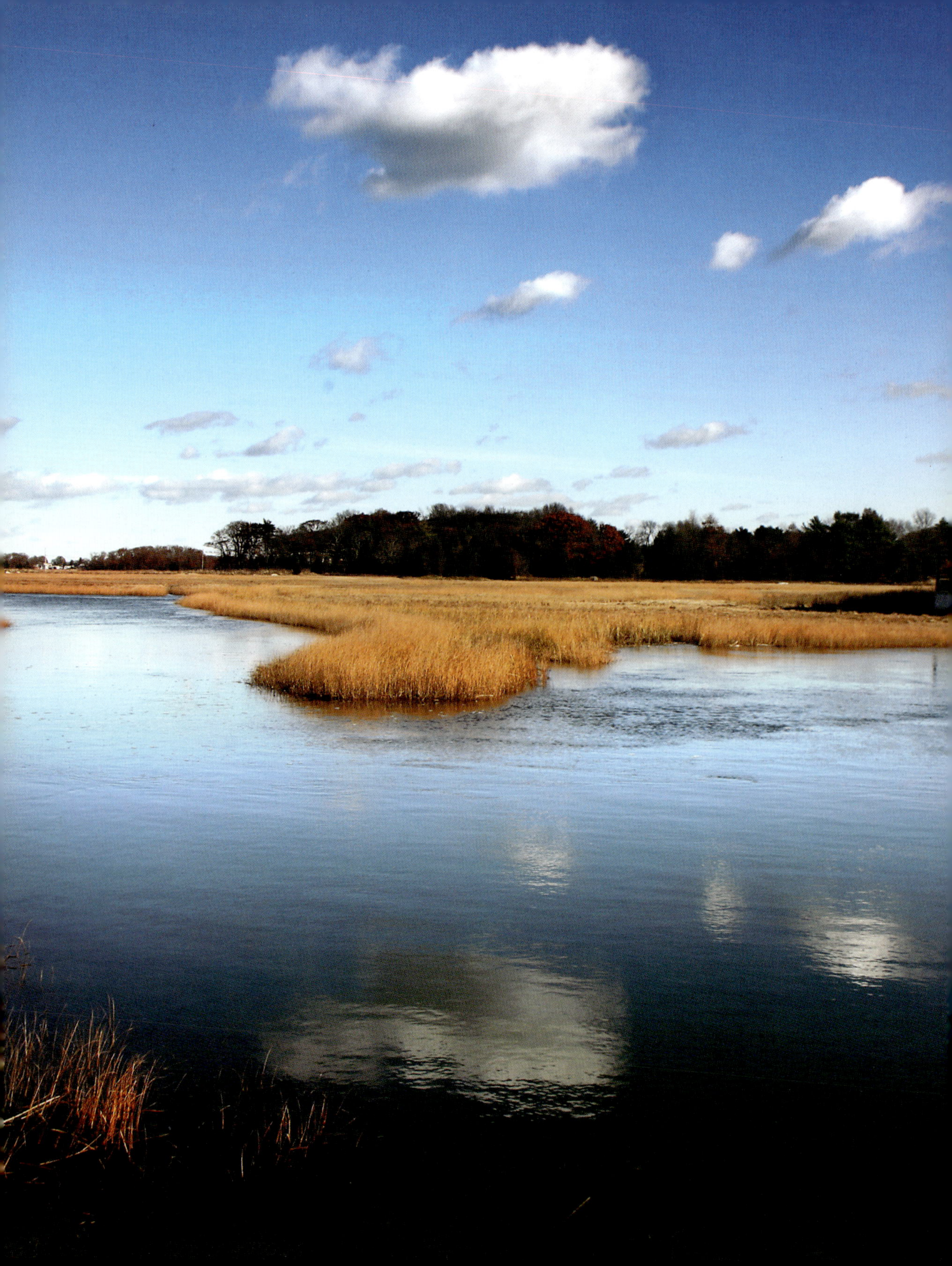

Introduction

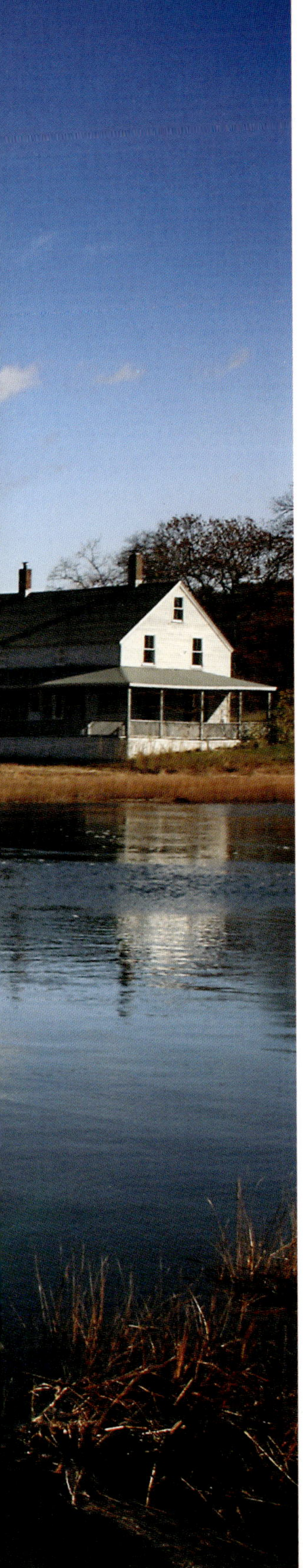

"We cannot live only for ourselves. A thousand fibers connect us with our fellow men."

—Herman Melville

Traveling on various adventures around our beautiful region, it's clear that New Englanders have a strong sense of pride and resiliency. Locals, and local businesses, know they can count on the support and encouragement of friends and neighbors. It's that strength of character and community, coupled with a zest for life and the outdoors, that helps us thrive, while enduring the whimsical nature of the weather . . . not to mention the whimsical nature of tourism. It's an honor to meet so many great locals, and see so many enchanting places.

In this book you'll join us on a tour to see an amazing collection of imagery that defines the characteristics of our unique region. Fascinating coastal villages with unrivaled landscapes and seascapes, majestic lighthouses, beaches, and even a castle. Historic landmarks, harbors filled with fishing boats, and the rugged folks who work them. The colorful blend of seasons and destinations creates a tapestry that is uniquely New England.

Note: The term "settlers" in this book refers to the European voyagers who arrived here on the *Mayflower* in 1620, and those who came after them. There were already Indigenous Peoples living in the region for more than 10,000 years before the settlers.

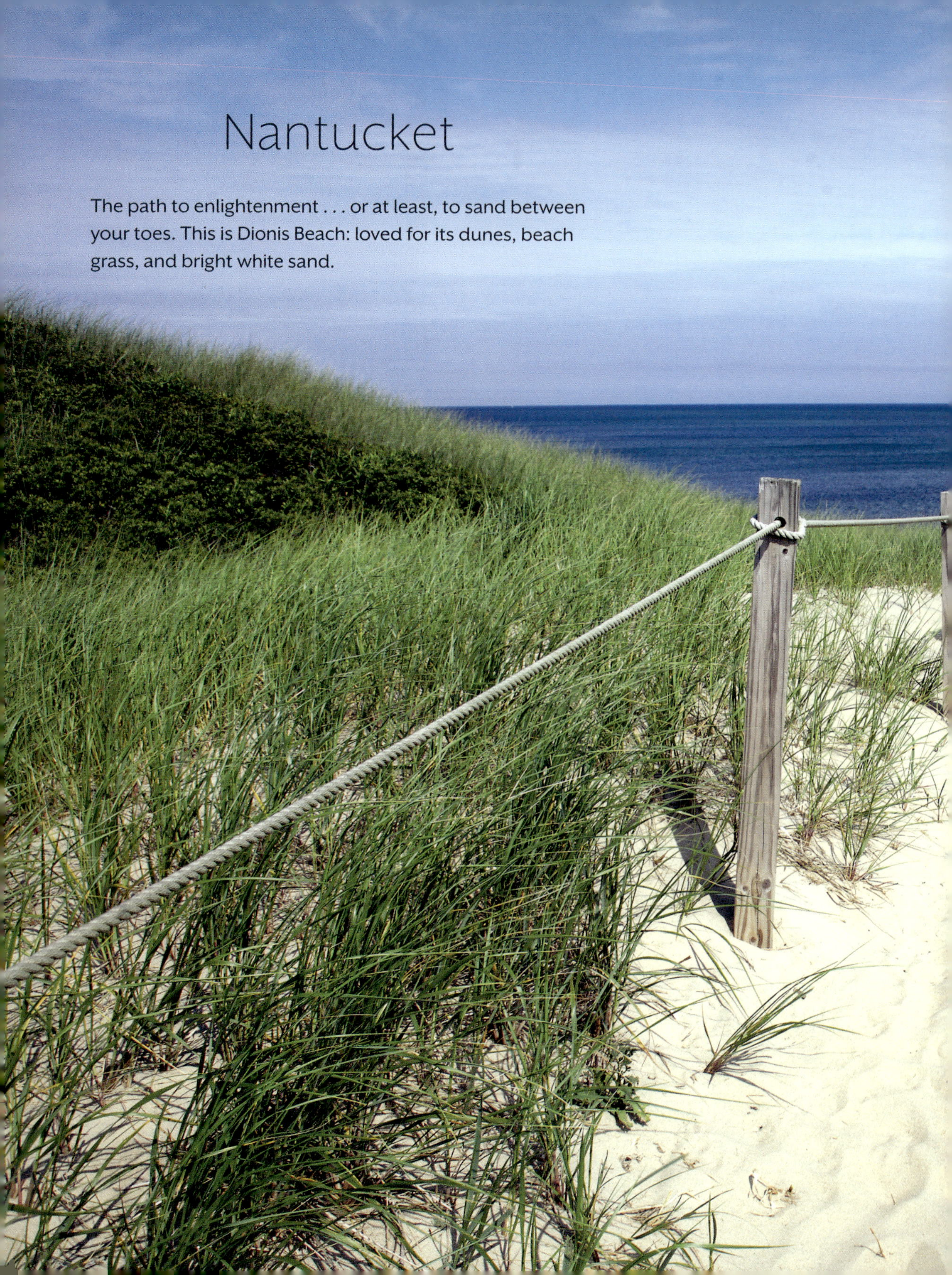
Nantucket

The path to enlightenment . . . or at least, to sand between
your toes. This is Dionis Beach: loved for its dunes, beach
grass, and bright white sand.

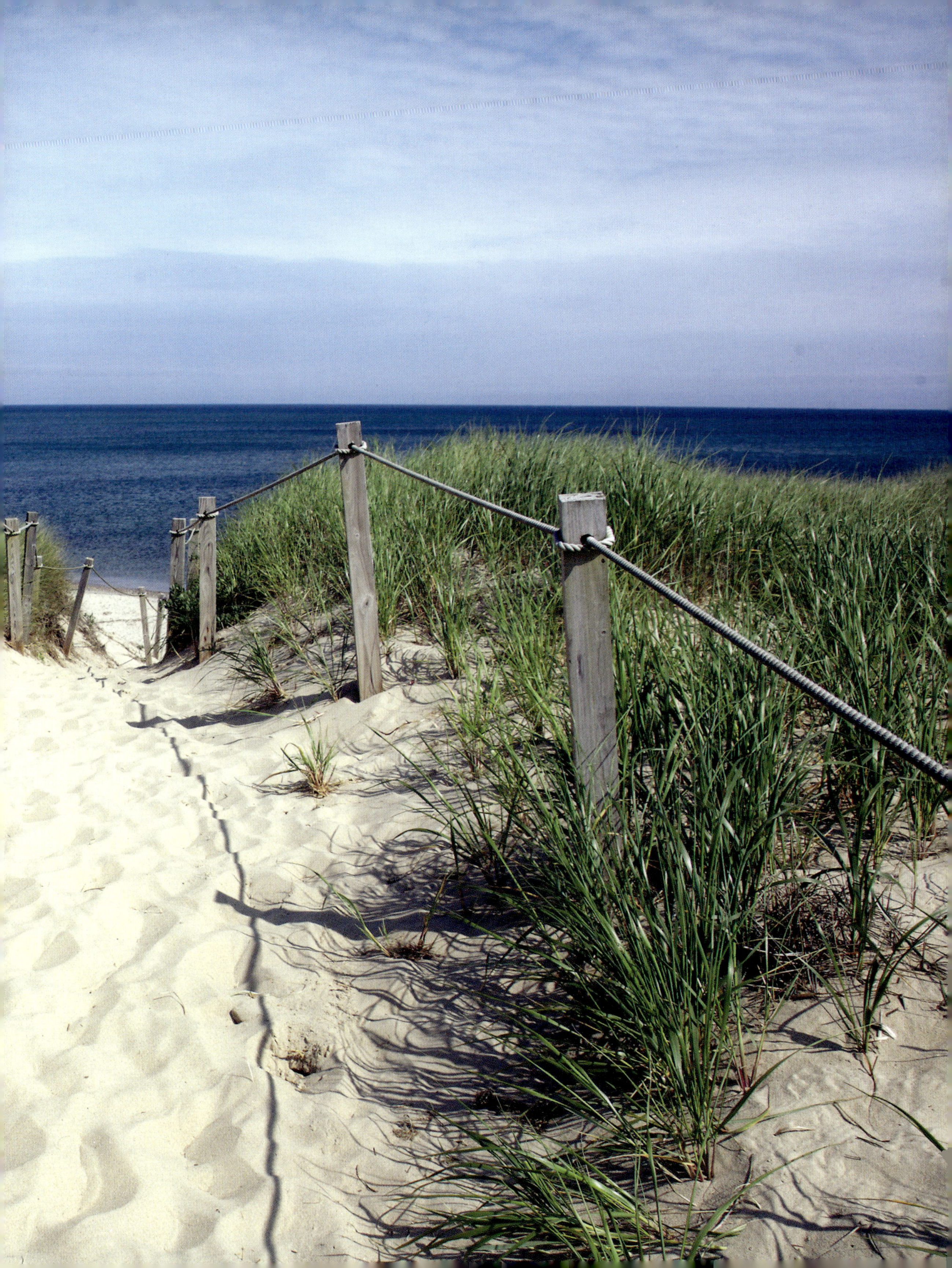

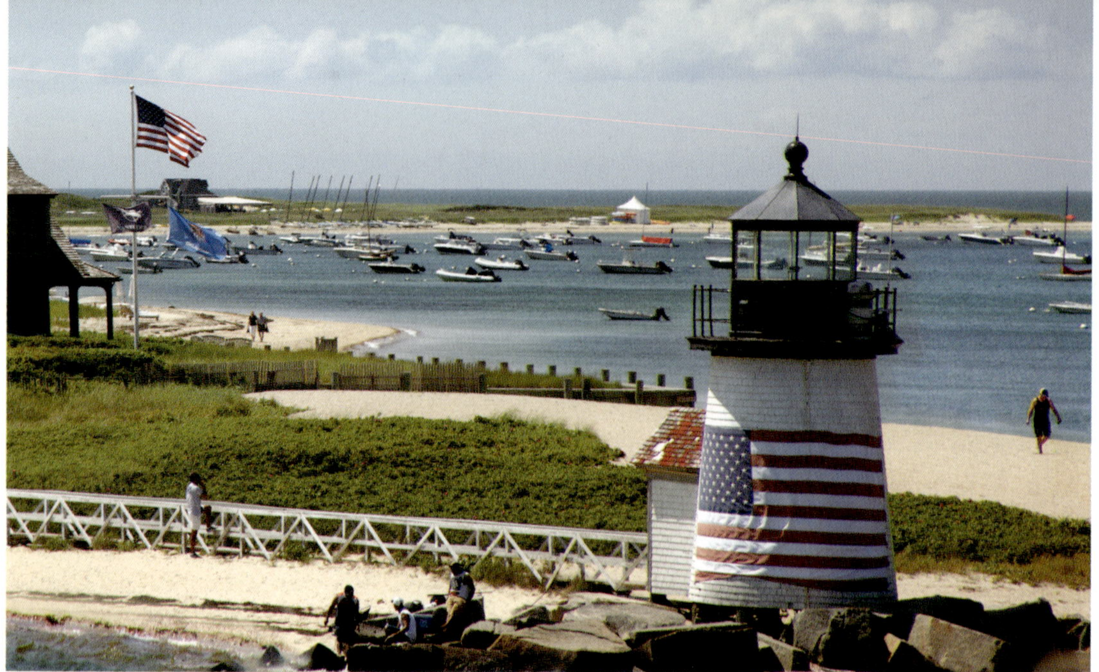

Your first sight upon entering beautiful Nantucket Harbor is Brant Point Light. It's perched at the tip of a sandy peninsula that juts out into the harbor. The current tower was constructed in 1901, but there have been nine other towers here since 1746.

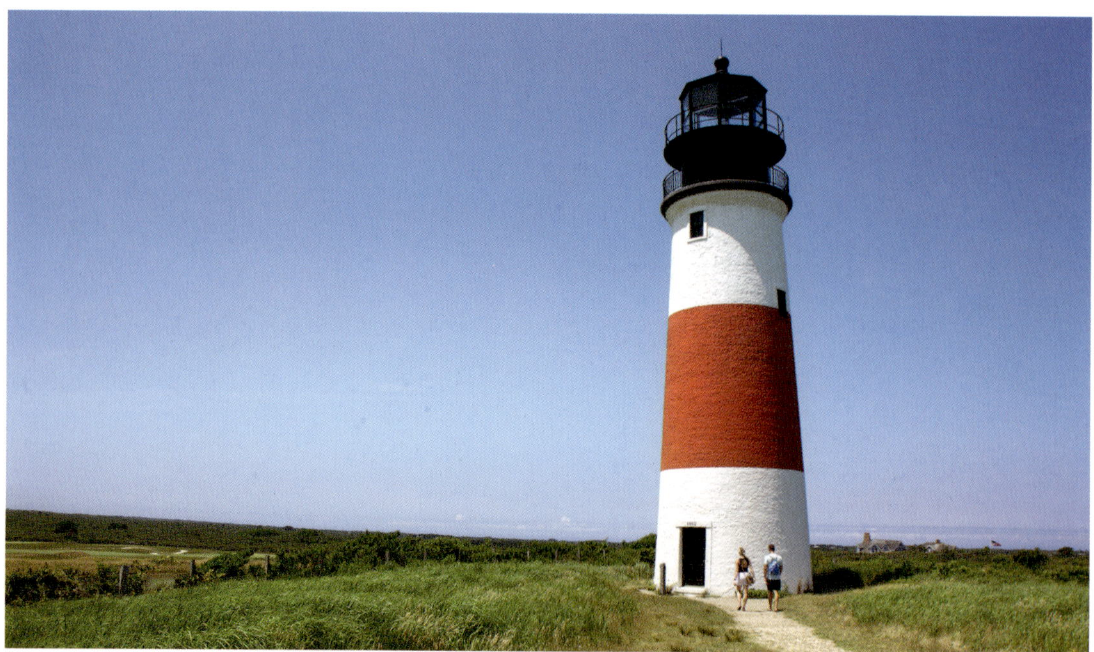

A couple strolls down the sandy path to iconic Sankaty Head Light. This heavenly scene plays out on the eastern edge of the island, overlooking the ocean and Sankaty Head Golf Club. The lighthouse was built in 1850, and is still operational.

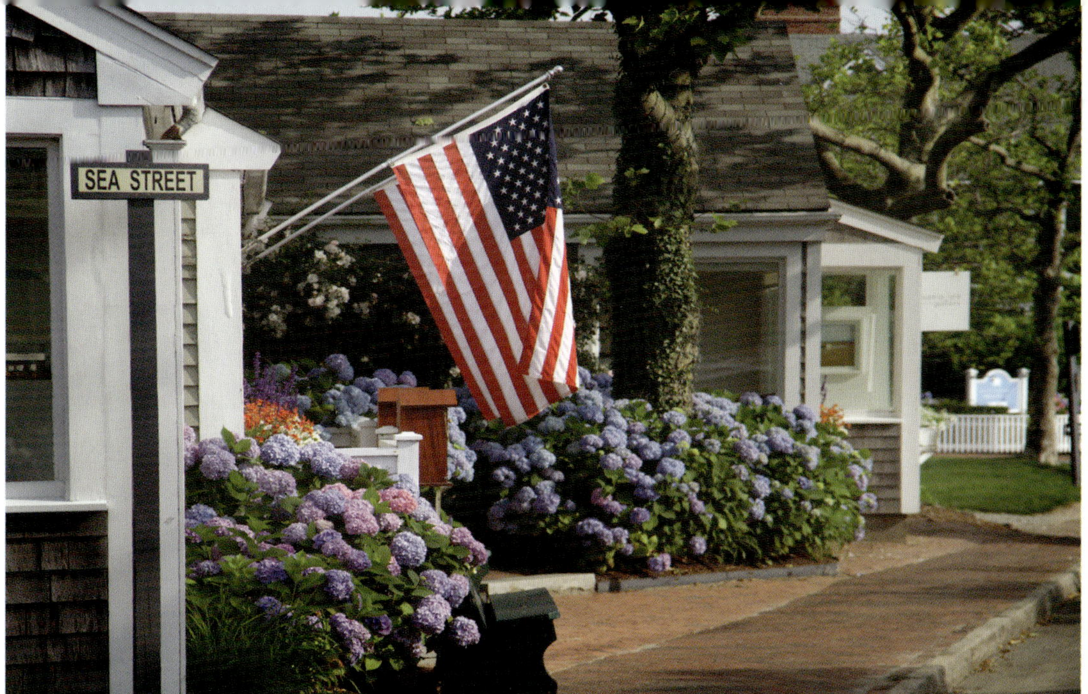

Nantucket doesn't allow any chain stores, and downtown has great New England charm, with flower-lined streets and brick sidewalks.

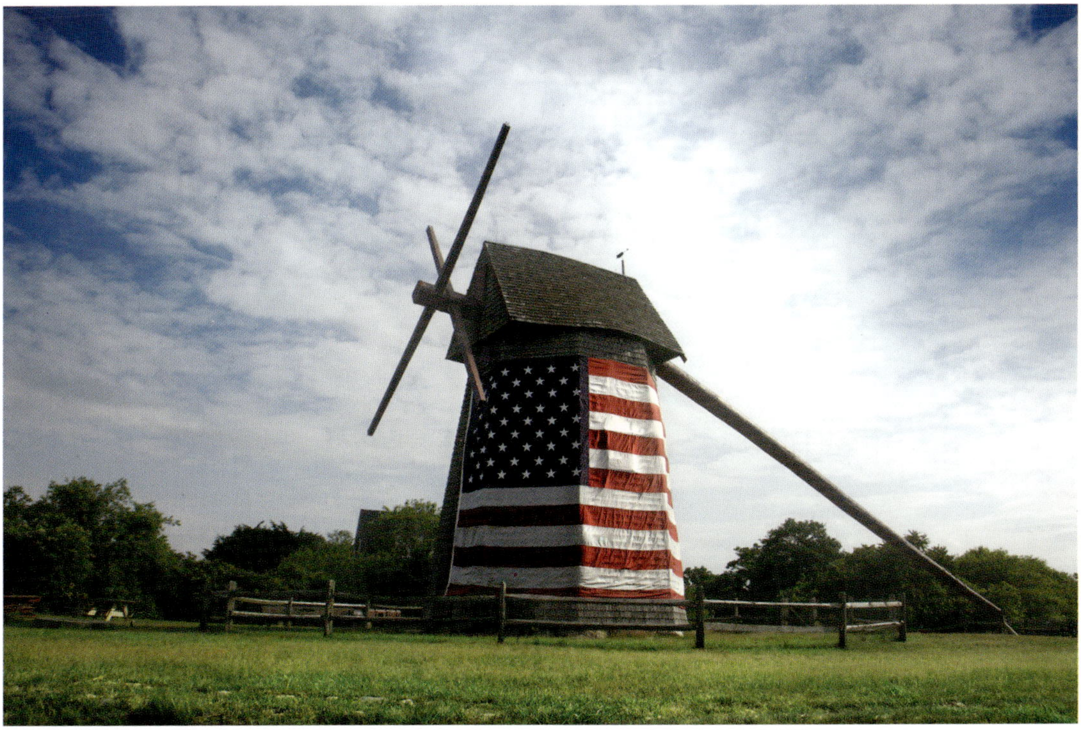

The historic Old Mill in Nantucket is the earliest working mill in America, built in 1746.

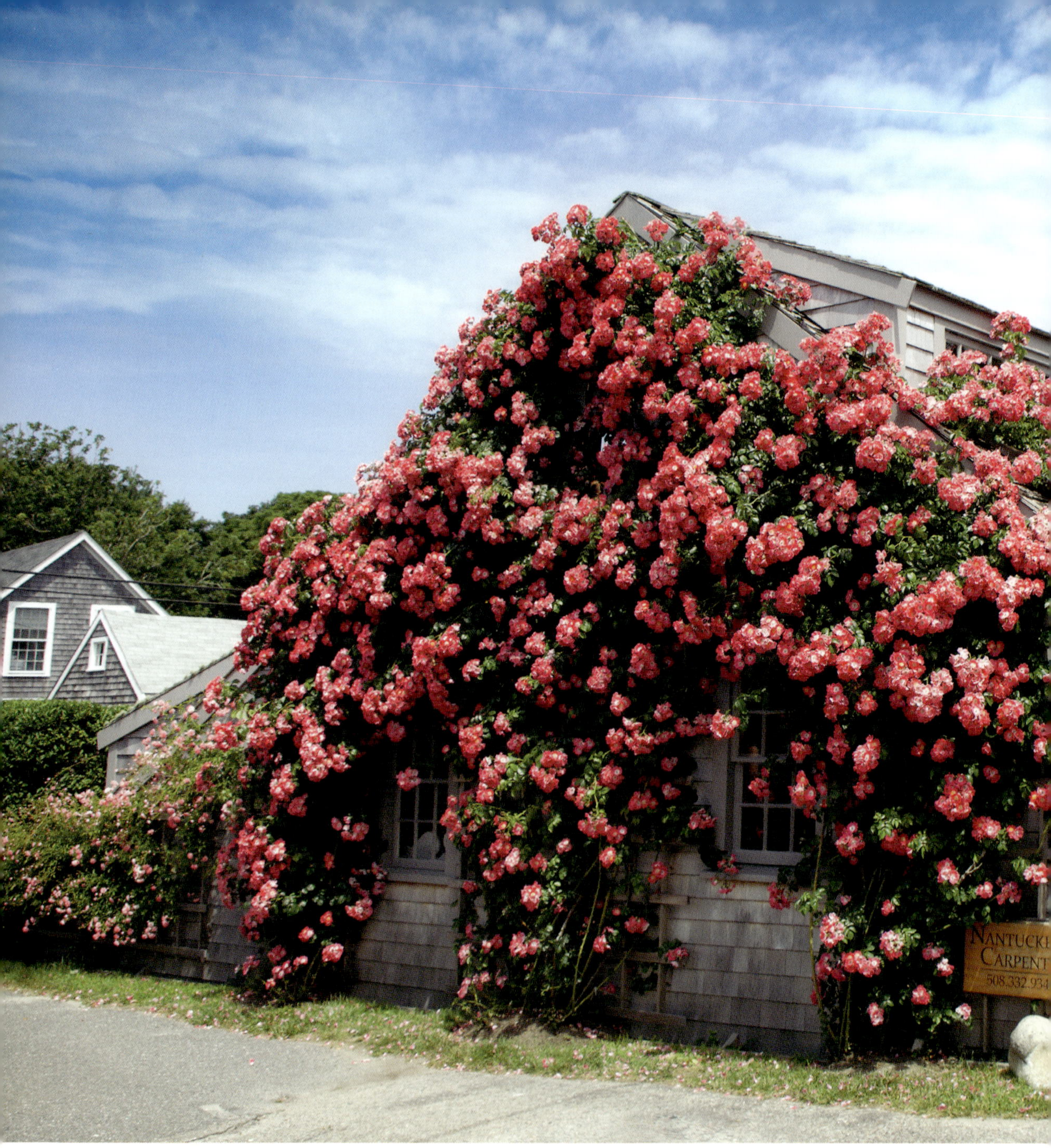

NANTUCKE
CARPENT
508.332.934

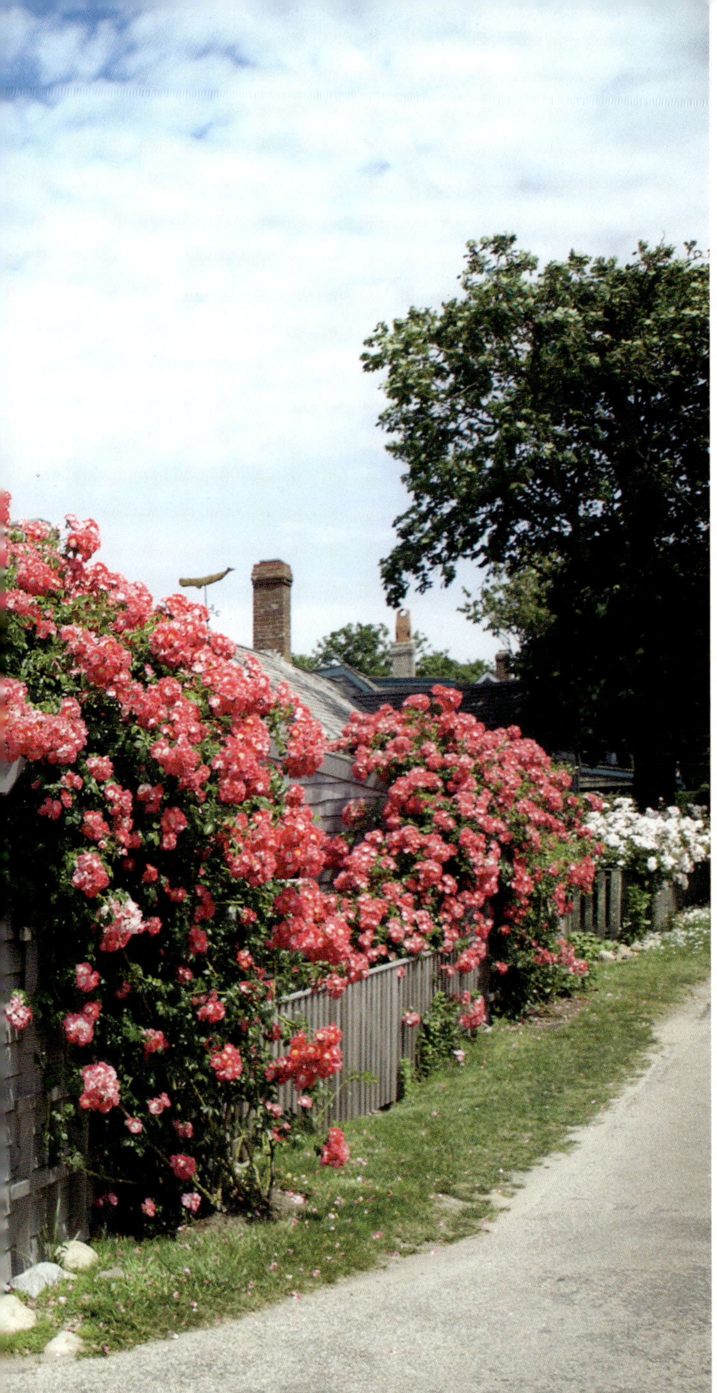

Early summer in Sconset village means roses. The homes here have gardens with riots of flowers competing for sunshine, and perhaps camera clicks. This one got to me . . . it's like something from a fairytale.

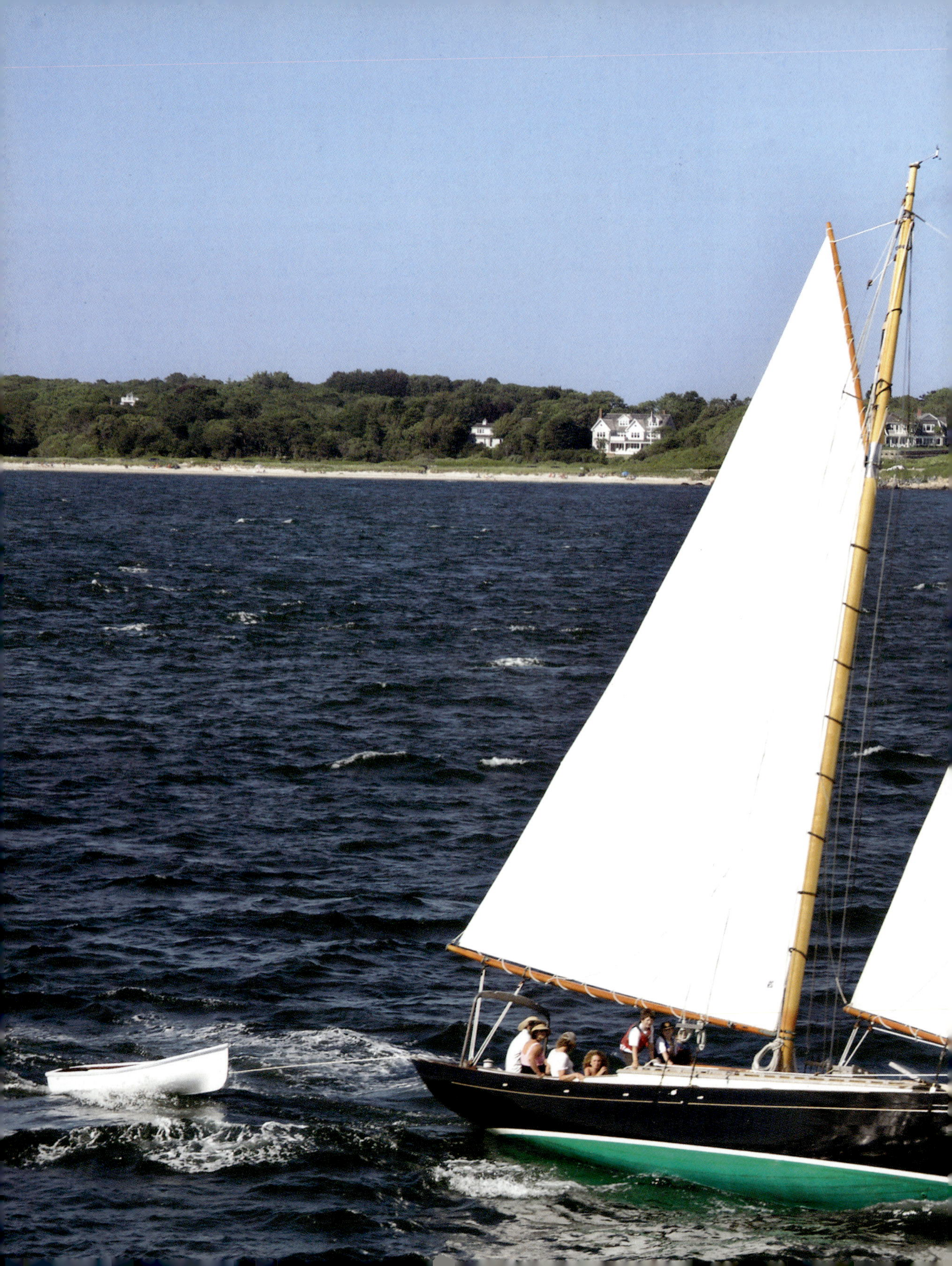

Martha's Vineyard

On the ferry ride to Martha's Vineyard we had the great fortune to encounter this beautiful schooner, as we passed Nobska Point Lighthouse in Woods Hole. The ferry ride to the Vineyard is a perfect sightseeing opportunity if you like boats and lighthouses.

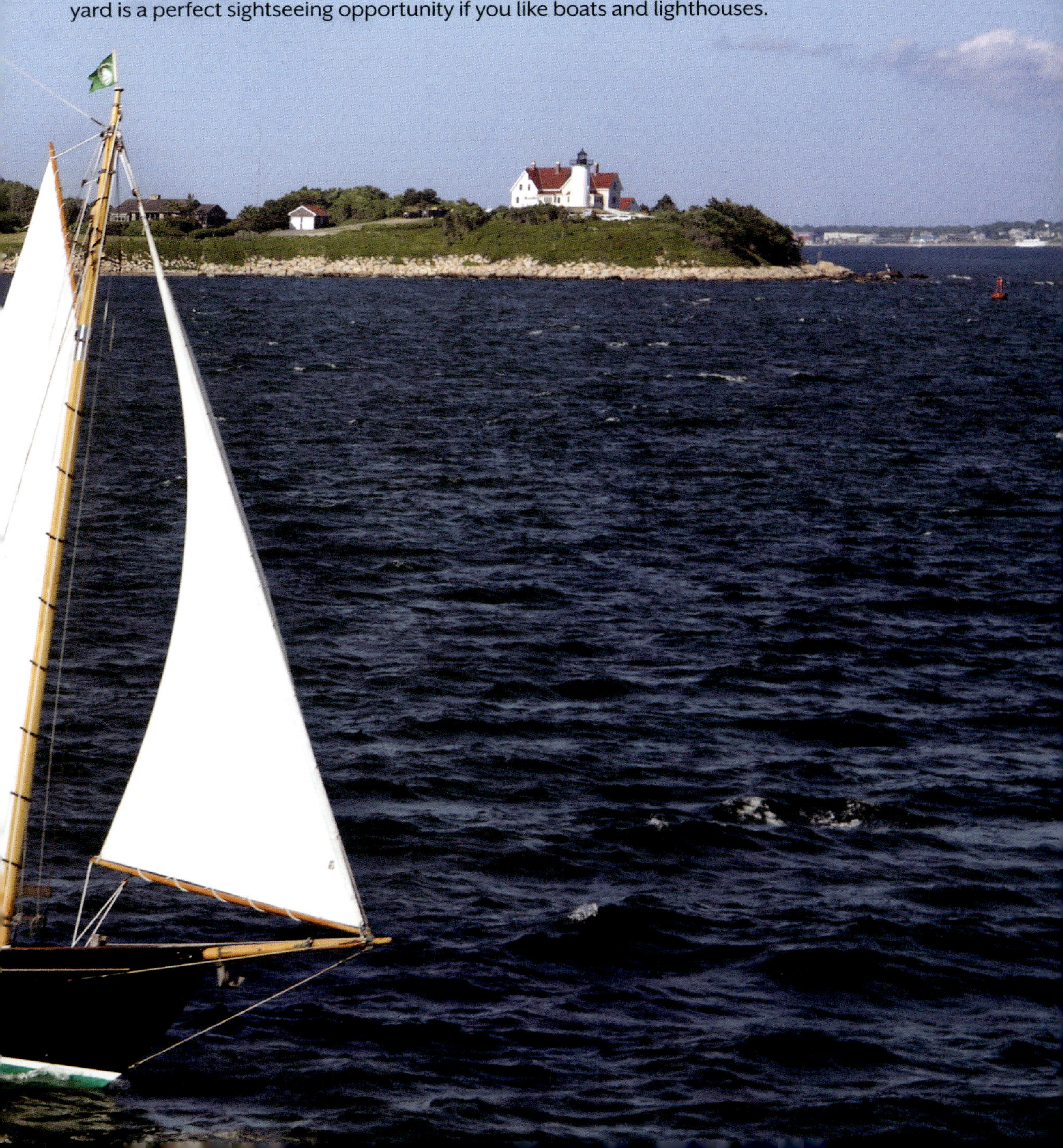

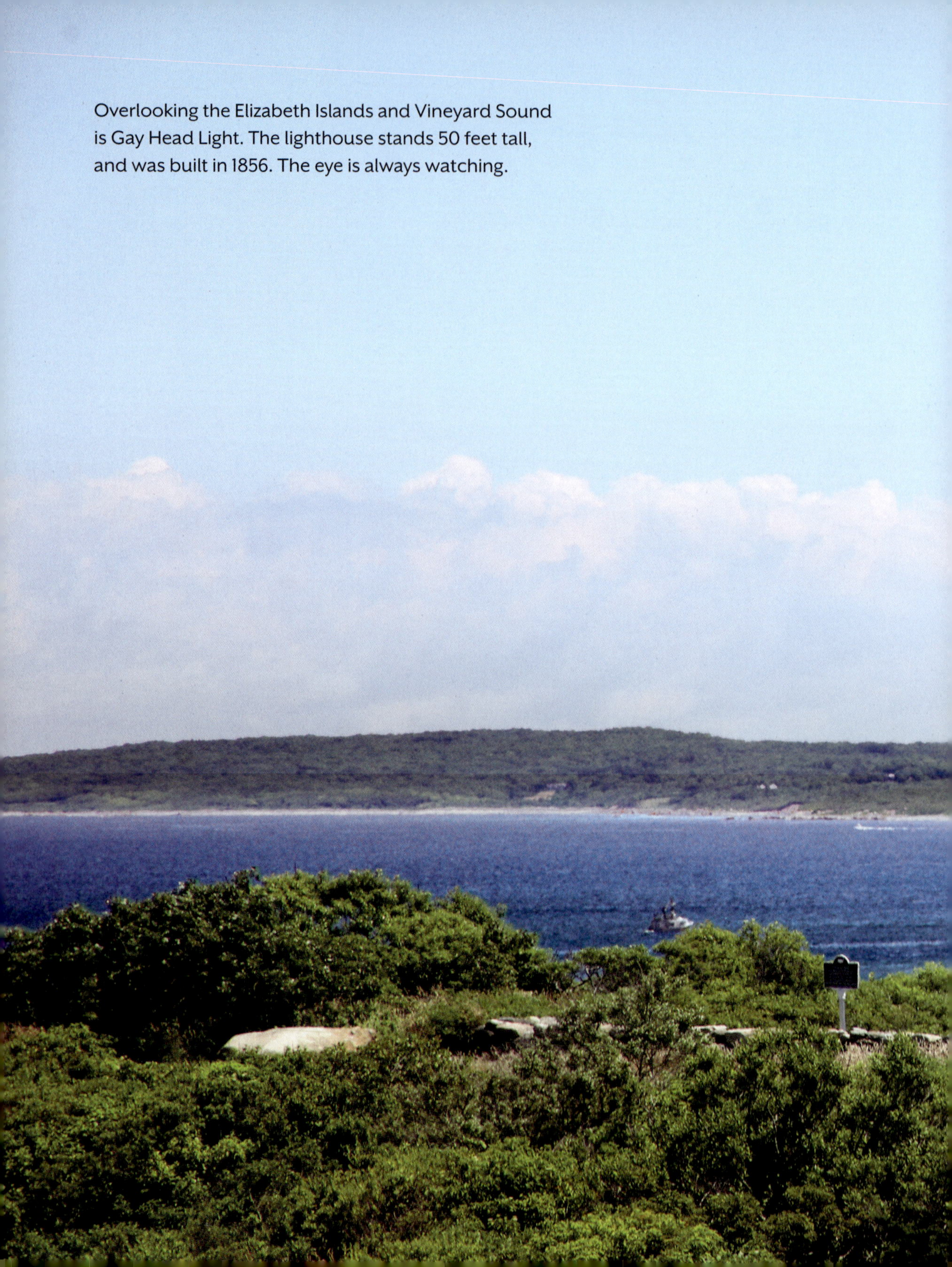

Overlooking the Elizabeth Islands and Vineyard Sound
is Gay Head Light. The lighthouse stands 50 feet tall,
and was built in 1856. The eye is always watching.

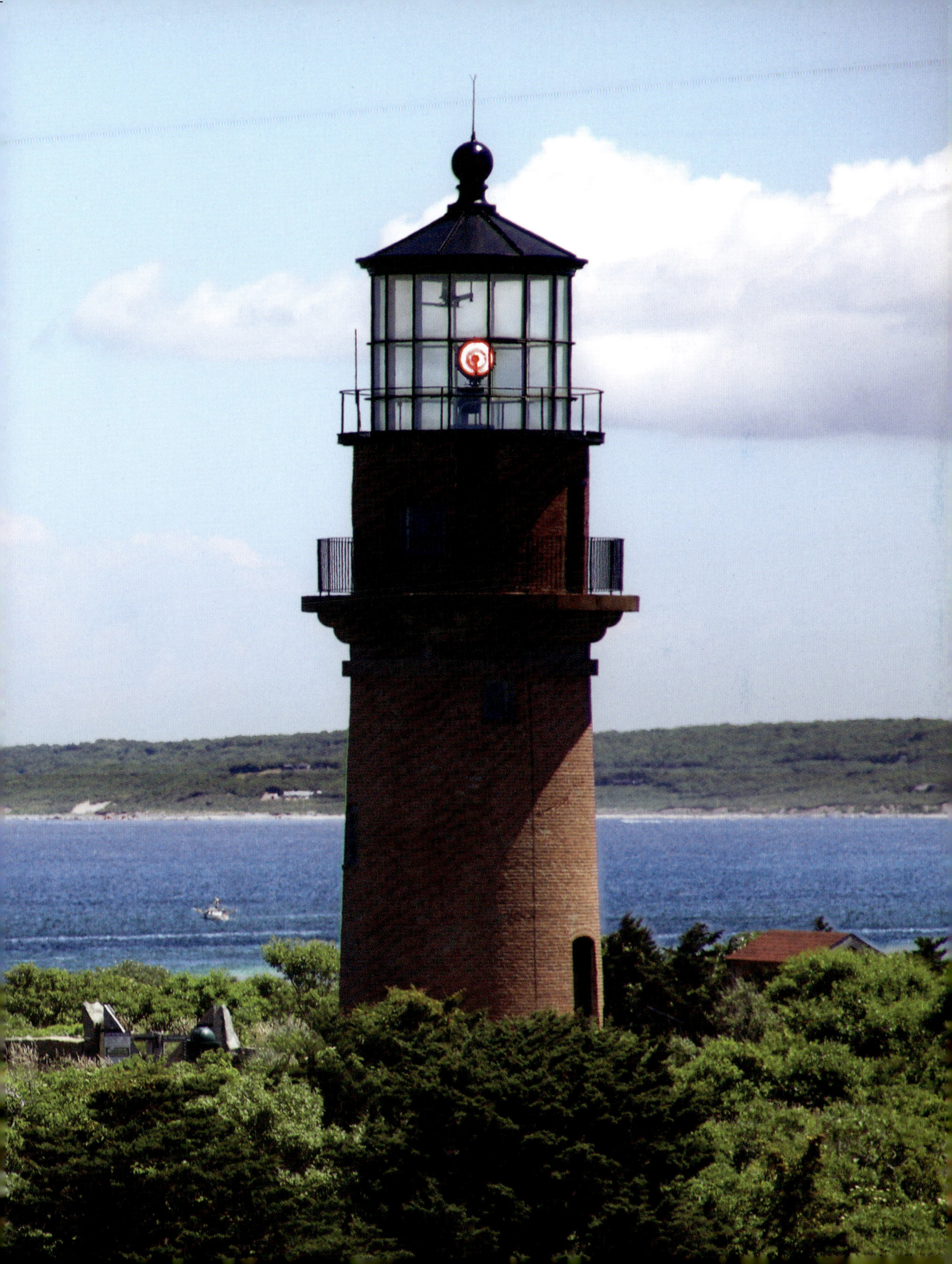

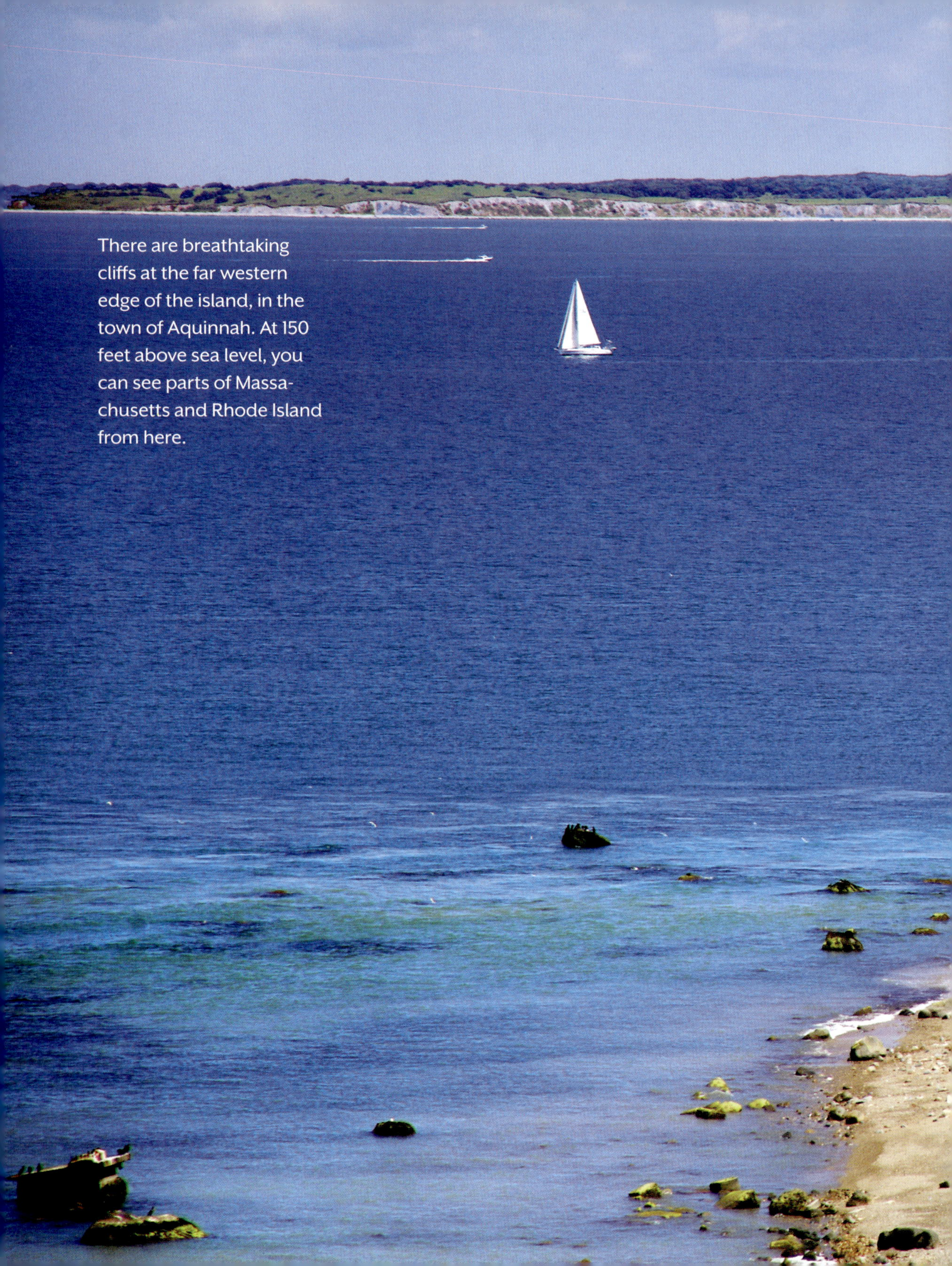

There are breathtaking cliffs at the far western edge of the island, in the town of Aquinnah. At 150 feet above sea level, you can see parts of Massachusetts and Rhode Island from here.

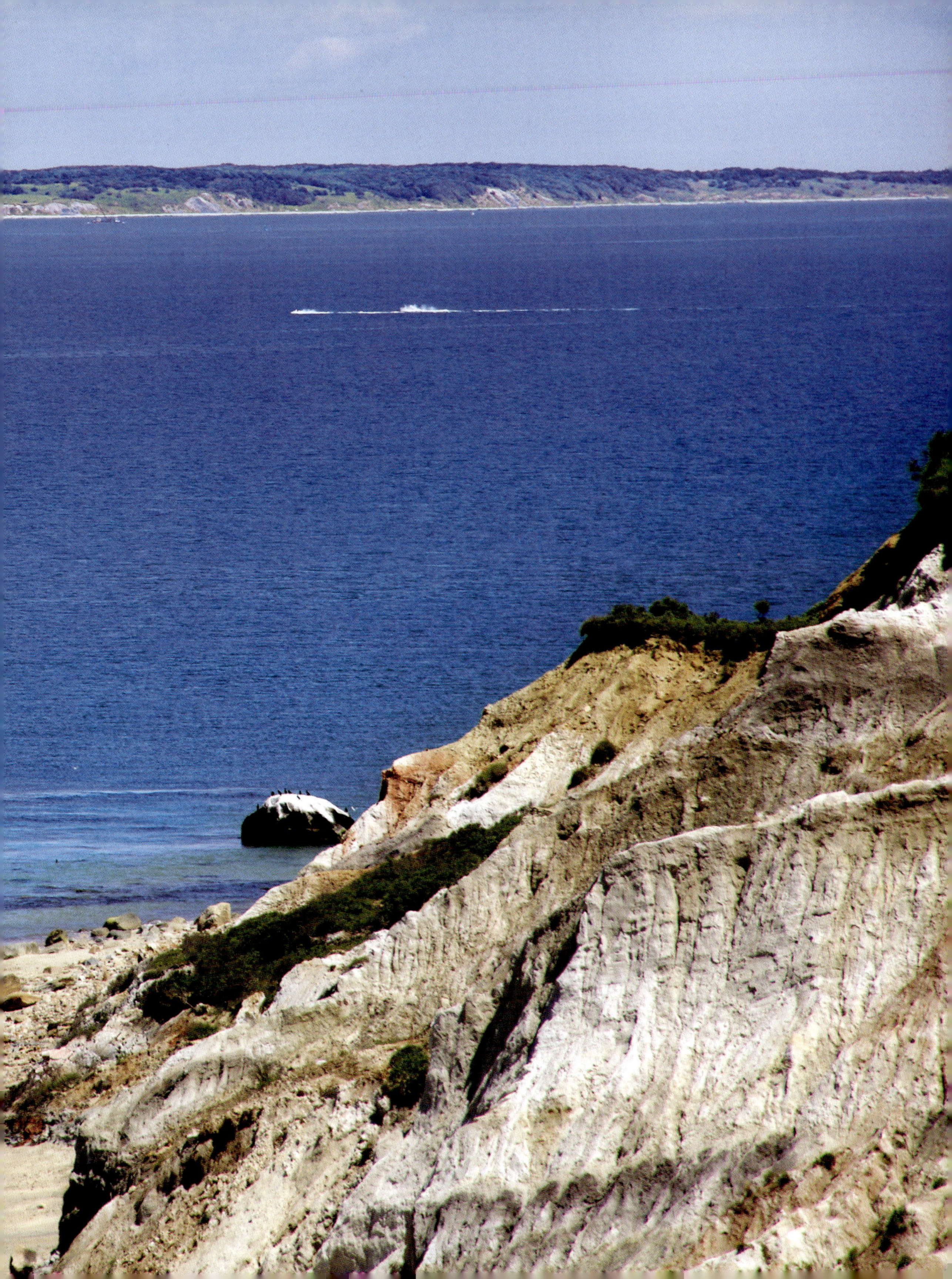

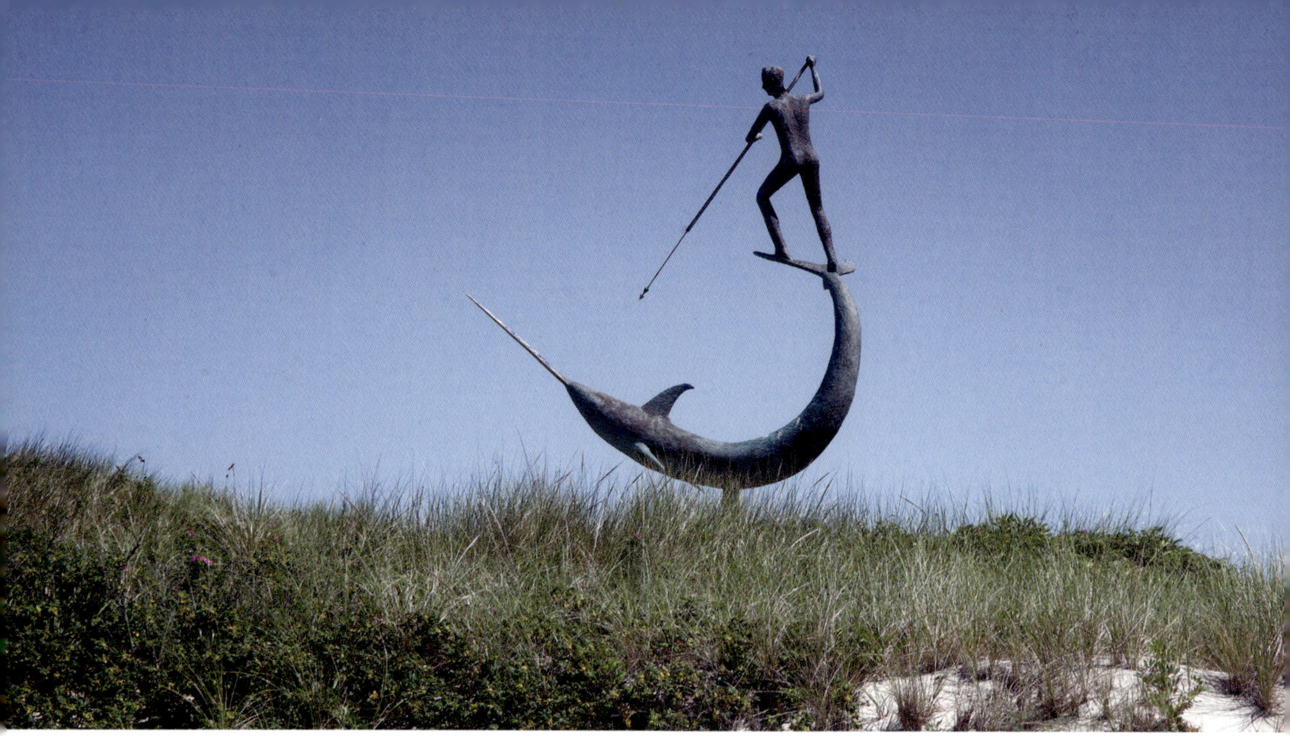

High upon the marsh in the village of Menemsha is an amazing bronze statue that commemo-rates harpoon sword–fishermen. Jay Lagemann designed it.

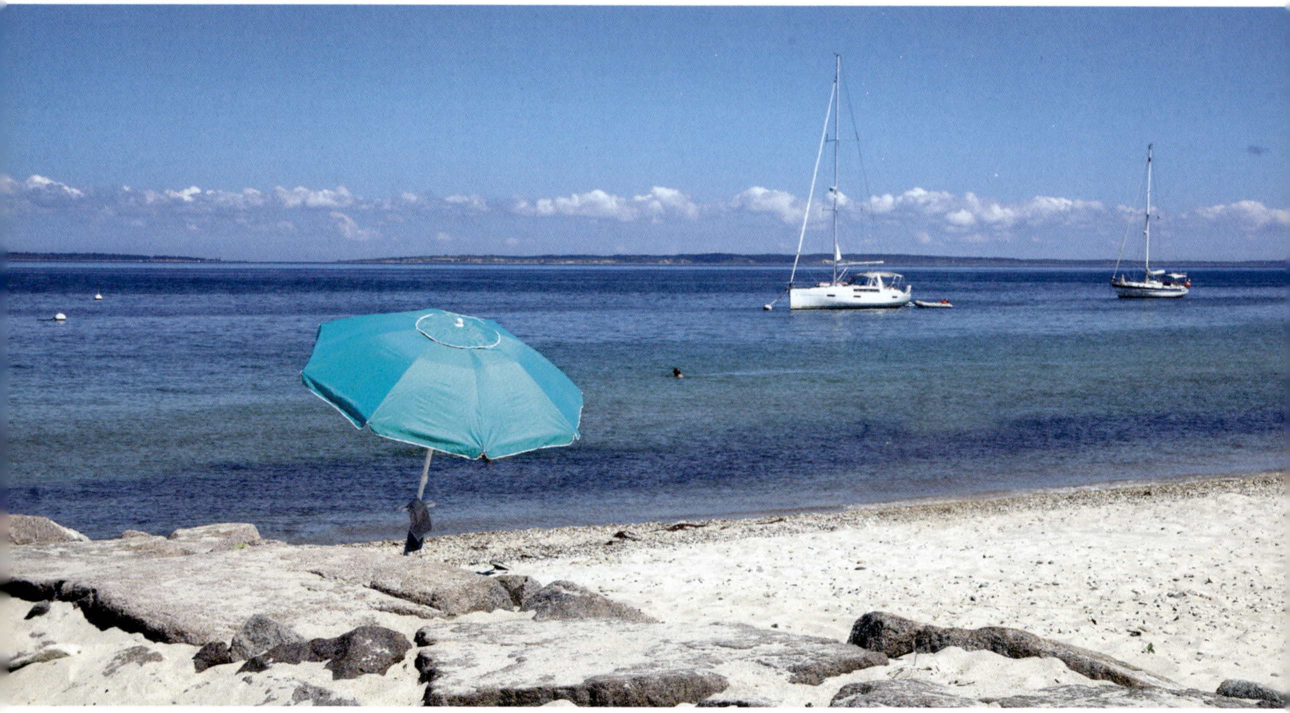

It's a tropical scene of aquamarine, at Menemsha Beach.

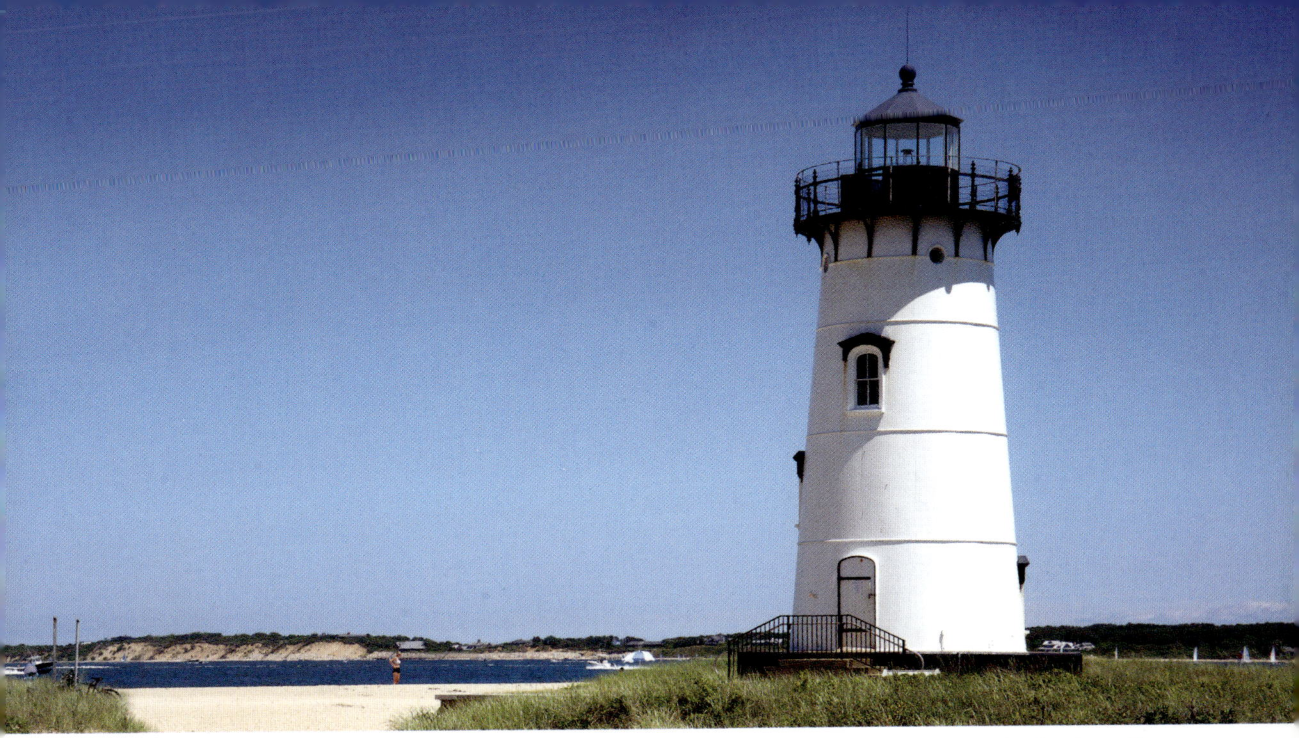

Edgartown Harbor Light sitting pretty on Lighthouse Beach by the entrance to the harbor. The current lighthouse tower was built in 1939, and it stands 45 feet tall.

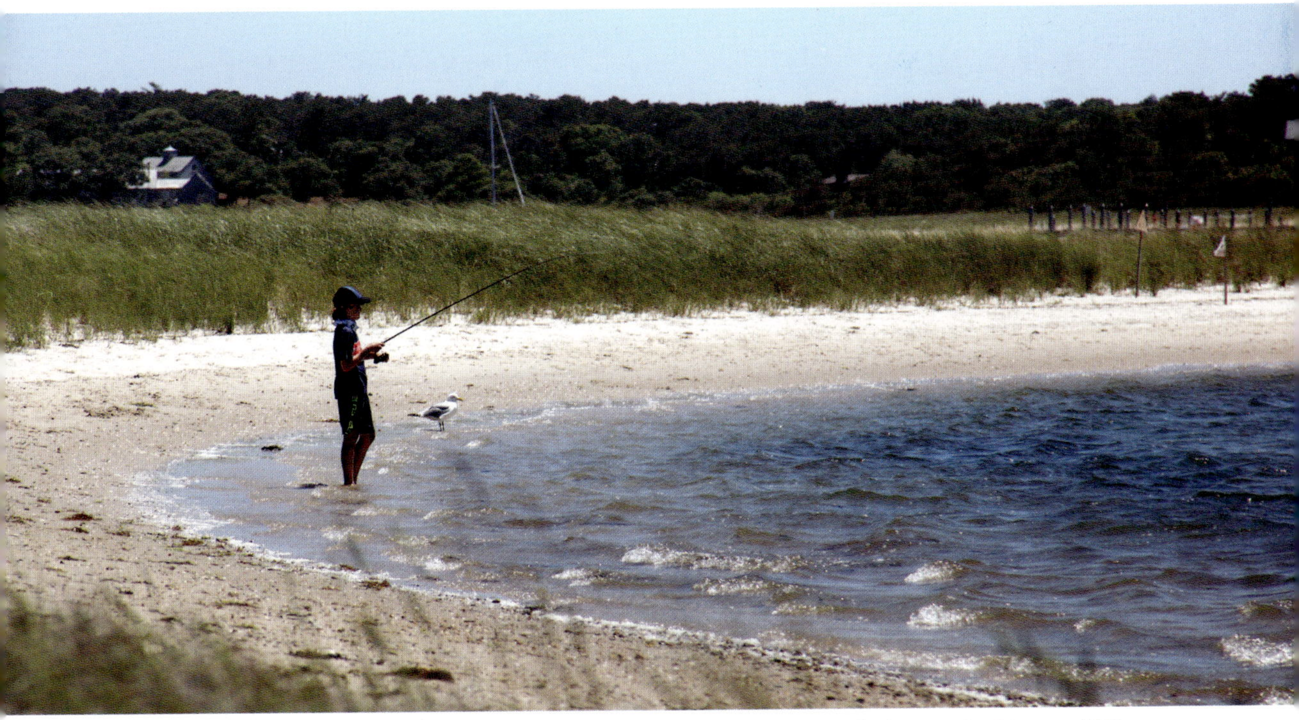

On the beach next to the lighthouse, a person and a gull are equally interested to see if the fish are biting today.

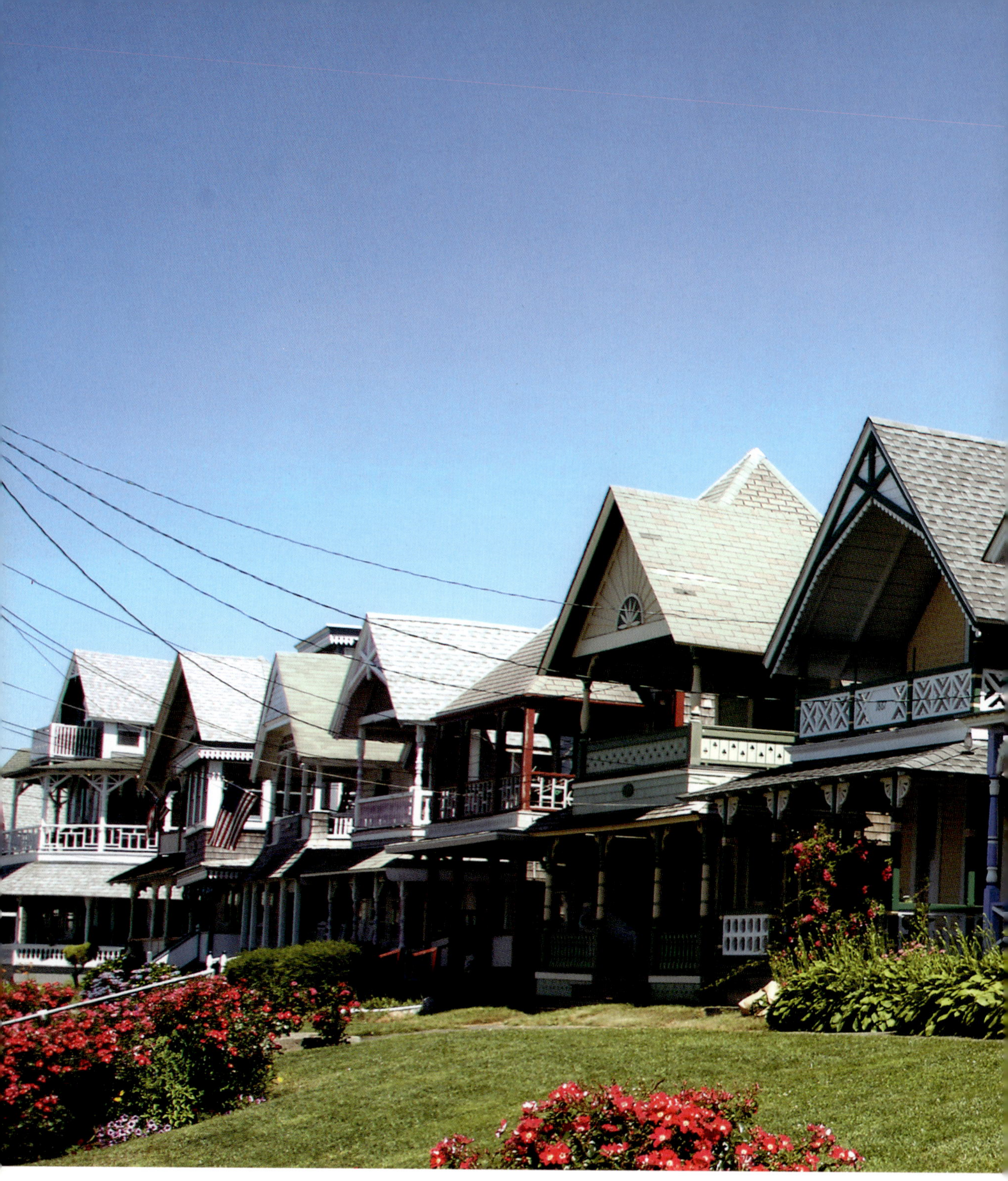

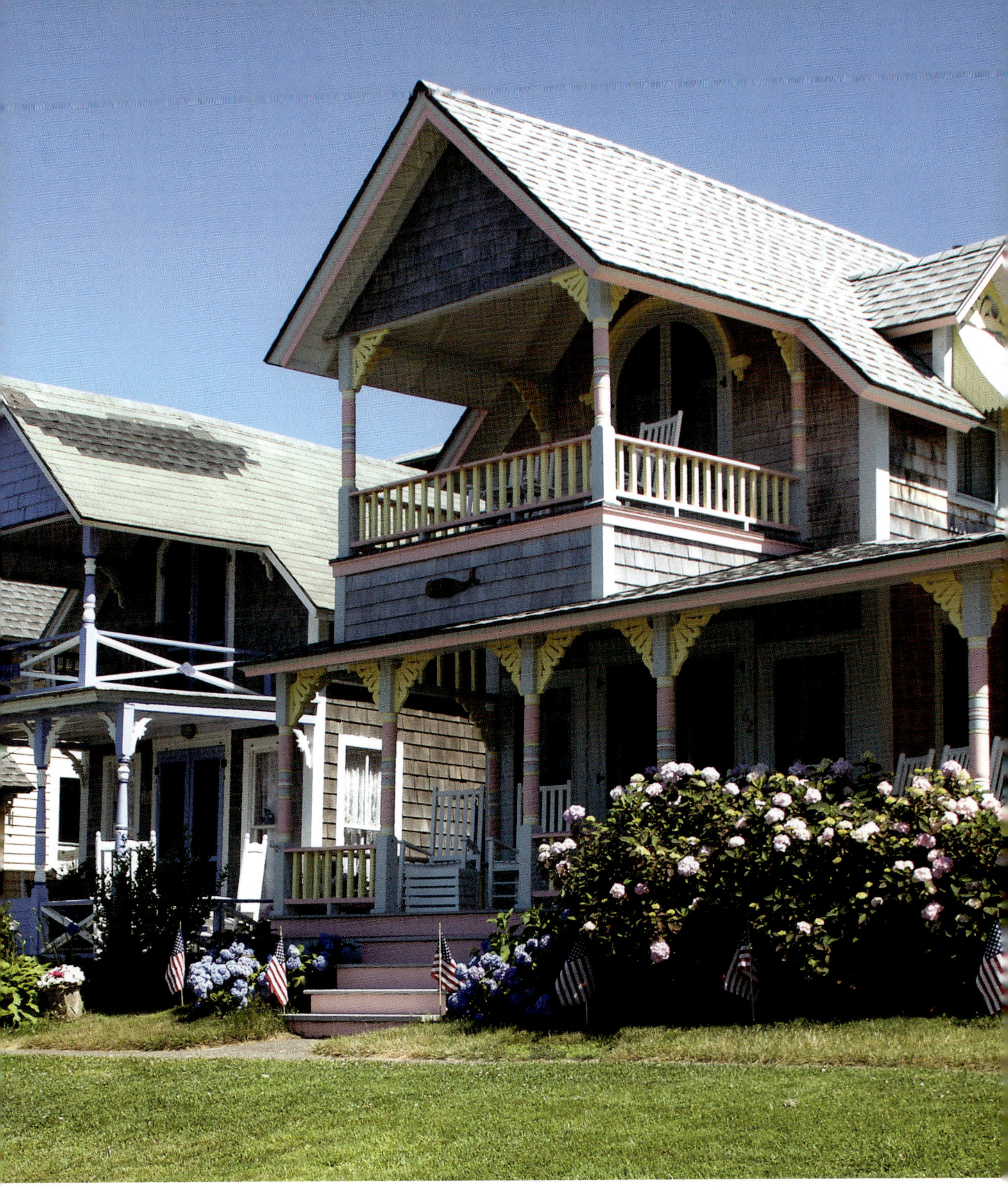

A row of Gingerbread Houses in Oak Bluffs.

Cape Cod

A fine day in June at Saints Landing Beach. This narrow beach with light sand is in the sheltered area of Cape Cod Bay, so the surf is usually light and tranquil.

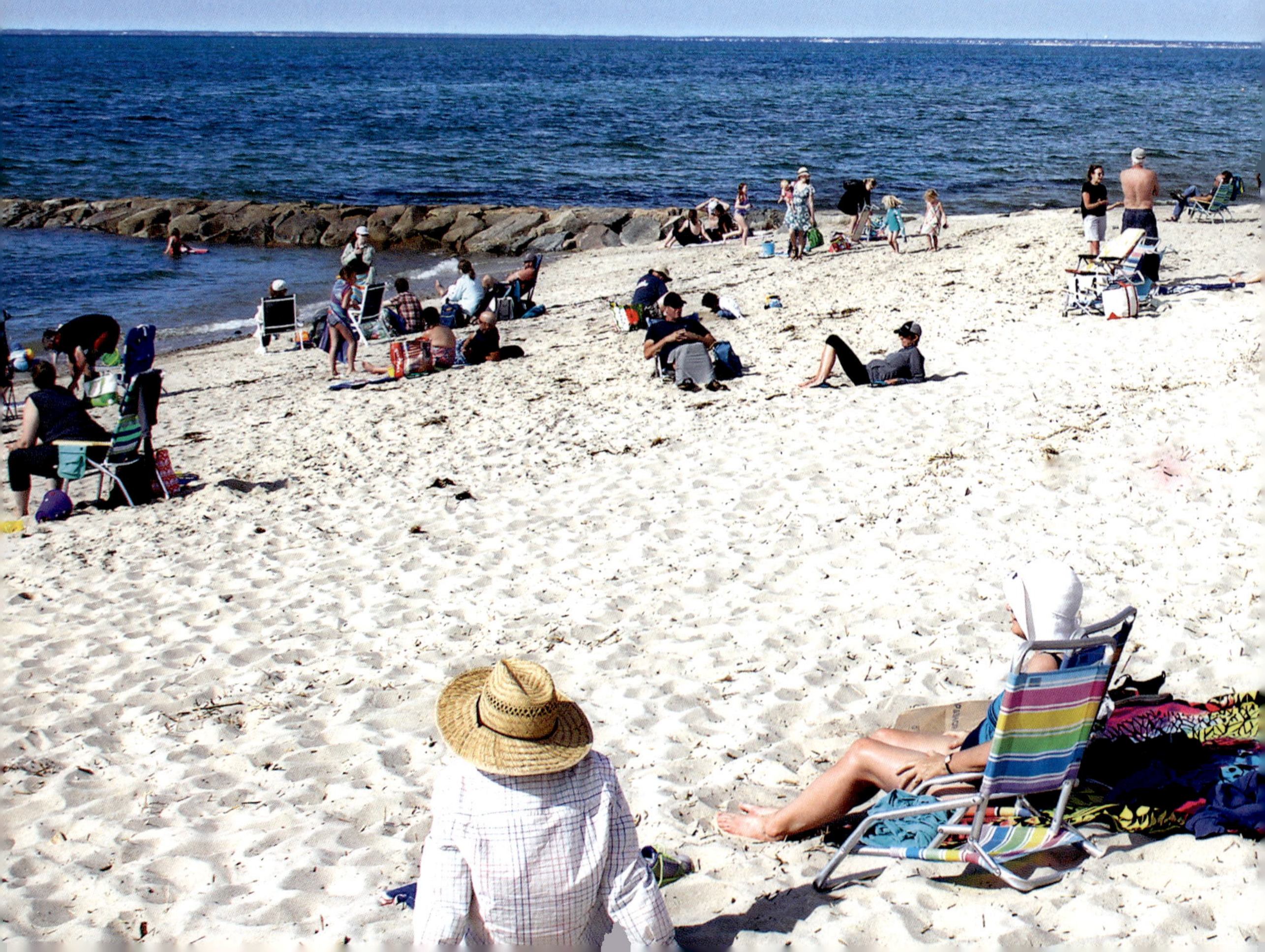

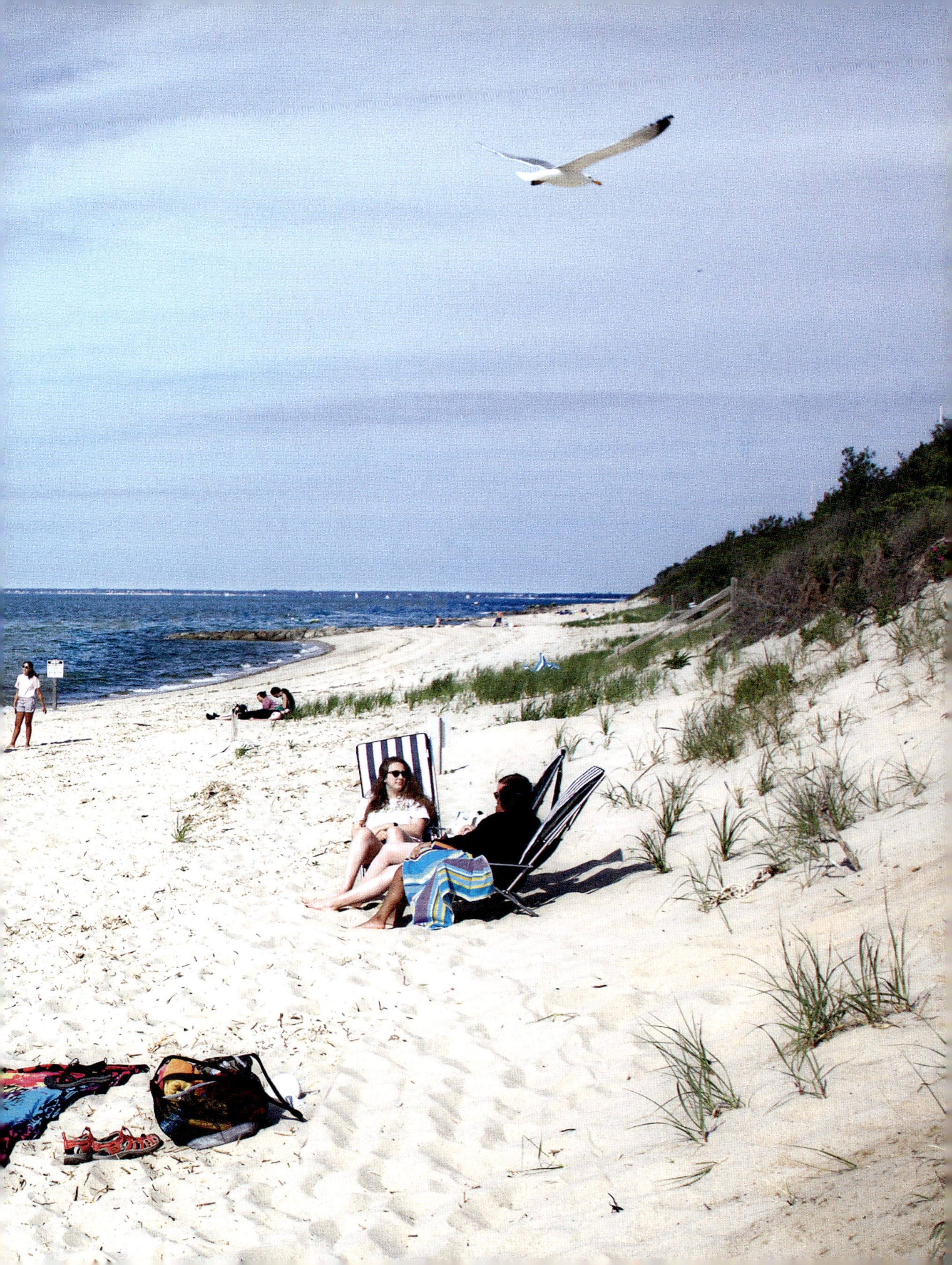

Sandwich

In the East Boat Basin at the Sandwich Marina is the *Annie Wilder*. It's a beautiful, narrow, forest green boat, and I just love her rakish angles.

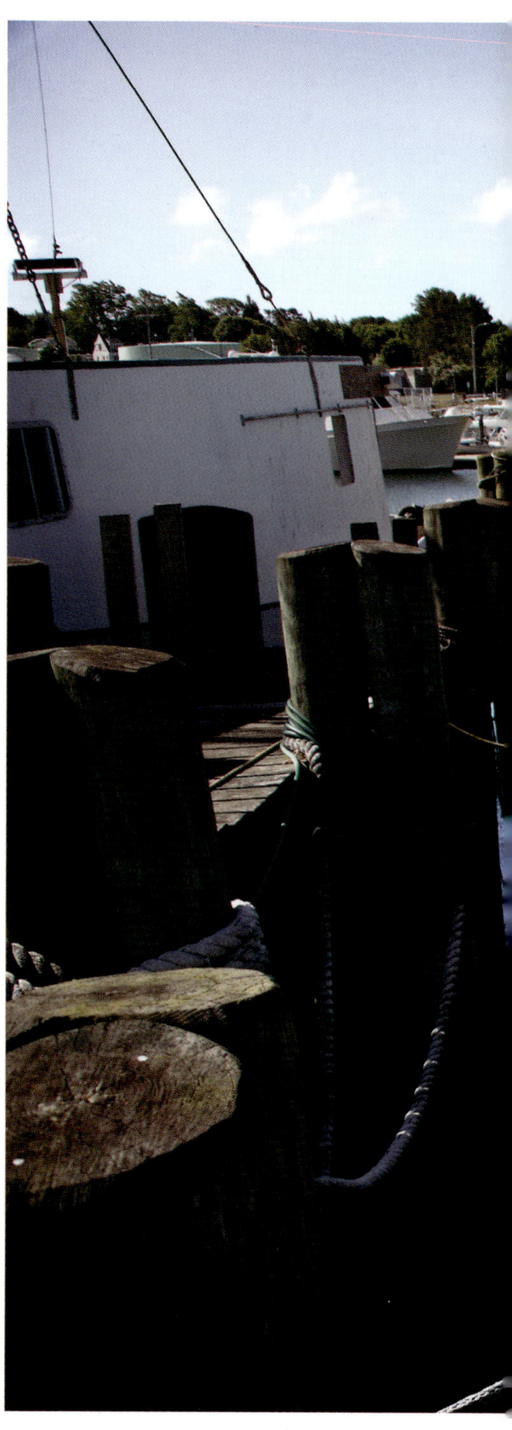

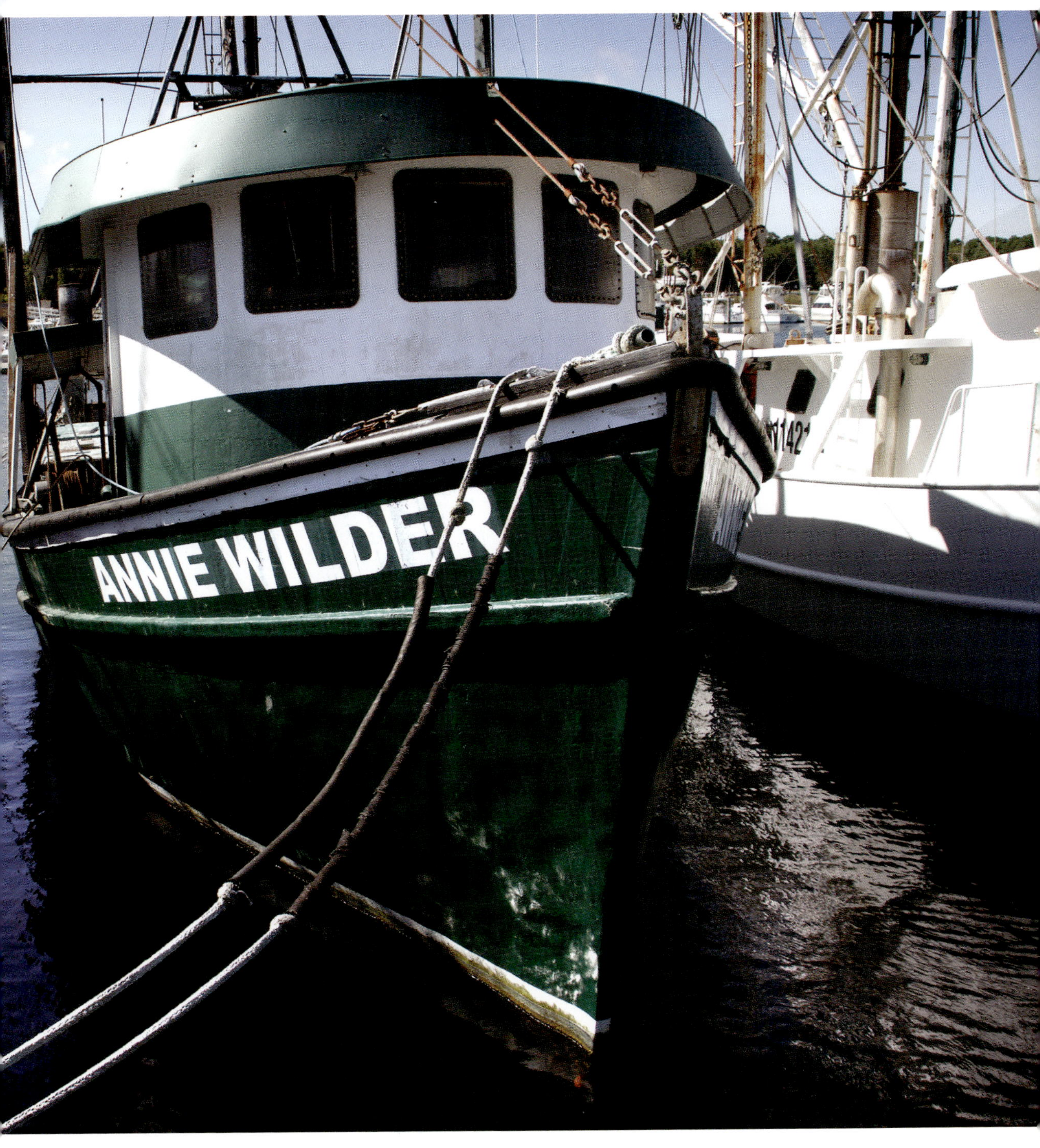

ANNIE WILDER

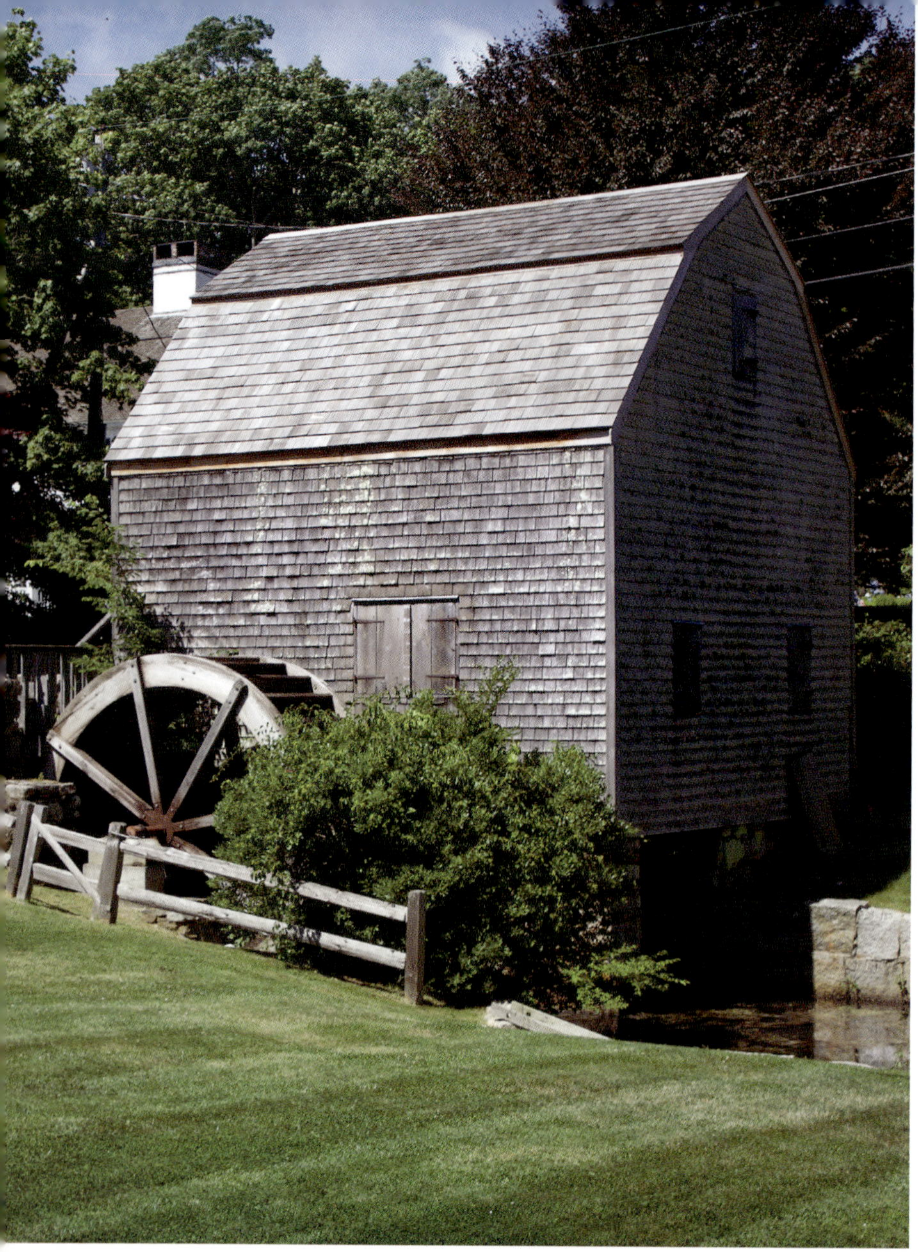

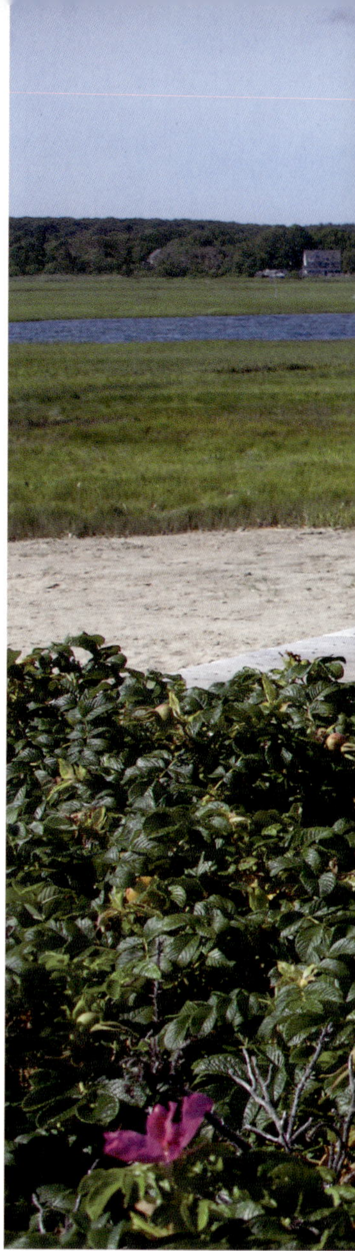

Dexter's Grist Mill has been in operation since around 1654. Early settlers here used the mill to grind corn into meal, one of their most important means of sustenance. The mill is still in operation, with freshly ground cornmeal available for purchase.

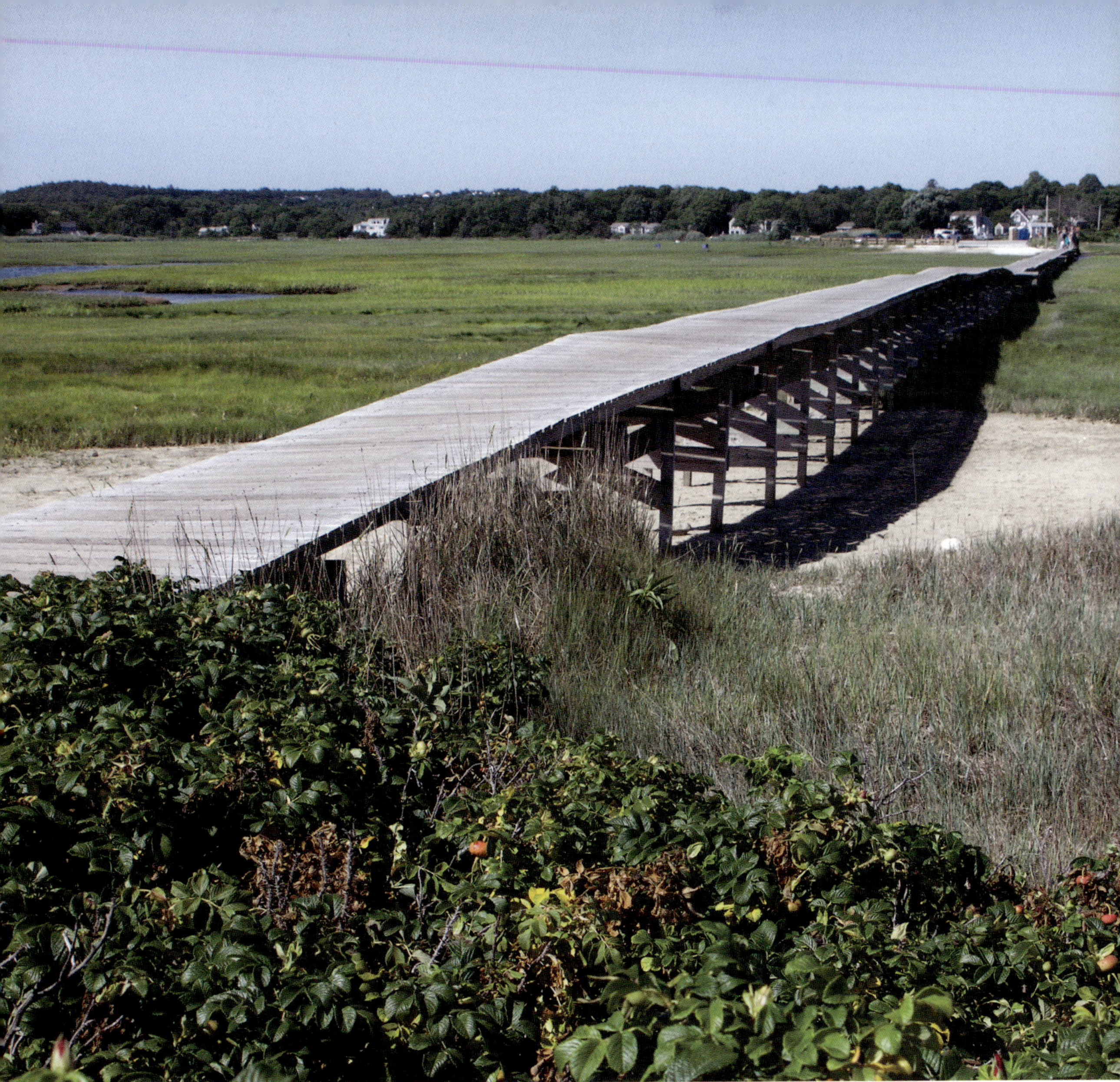

At over a thousand feet long, the Sandwich Boardwalk is a fun stroll that leads directly to the beach. It features an ideal view of Mill Creek and the marsh as you cross it. The area along the boardwalk is full of biodiversity, providing a healthy ecosystem for birds, mammals, and marine life. This includes shellfish like oysters, crabs, and periwinkles. It also includes endangered bird species, like the piping plover.

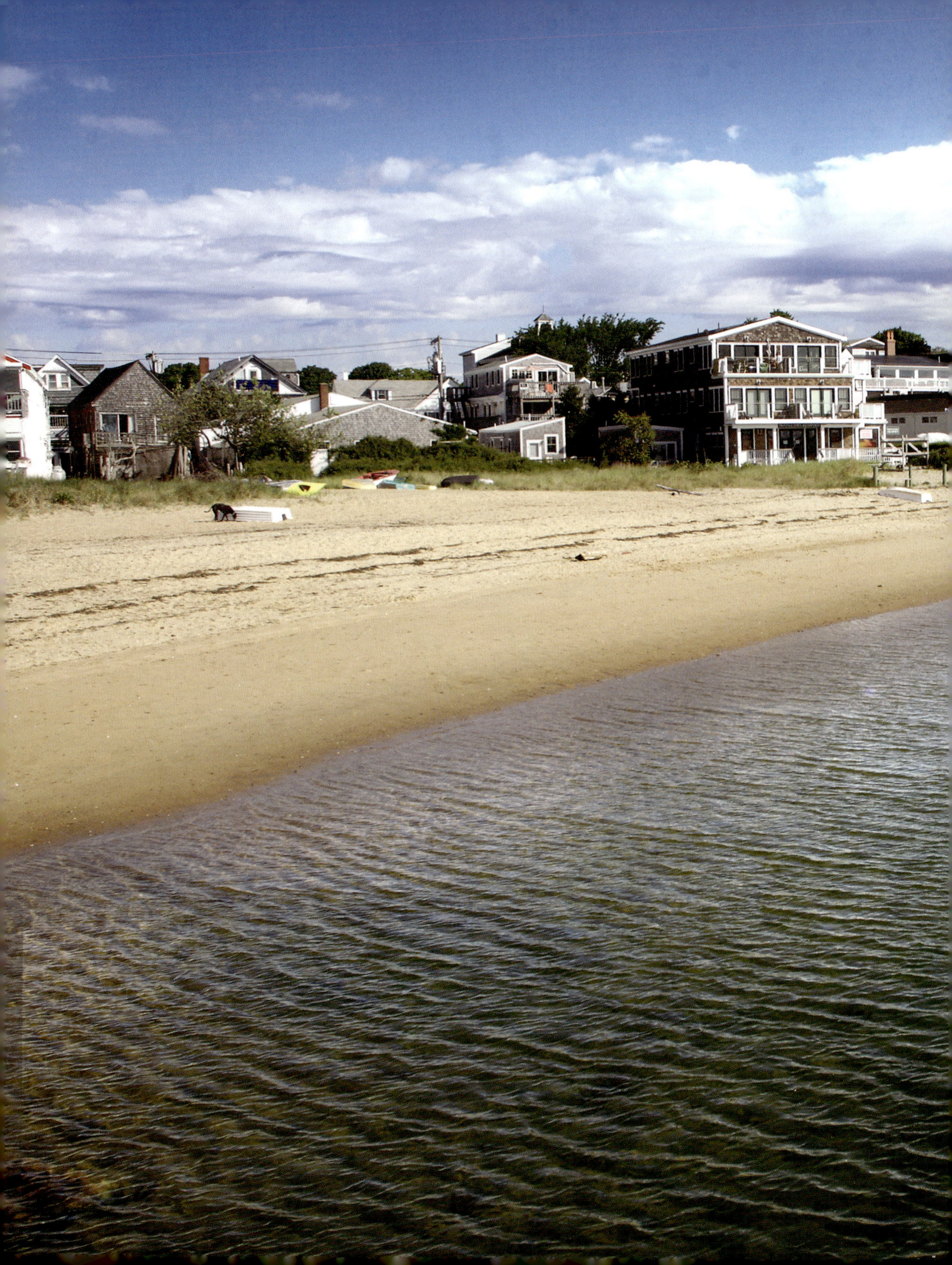

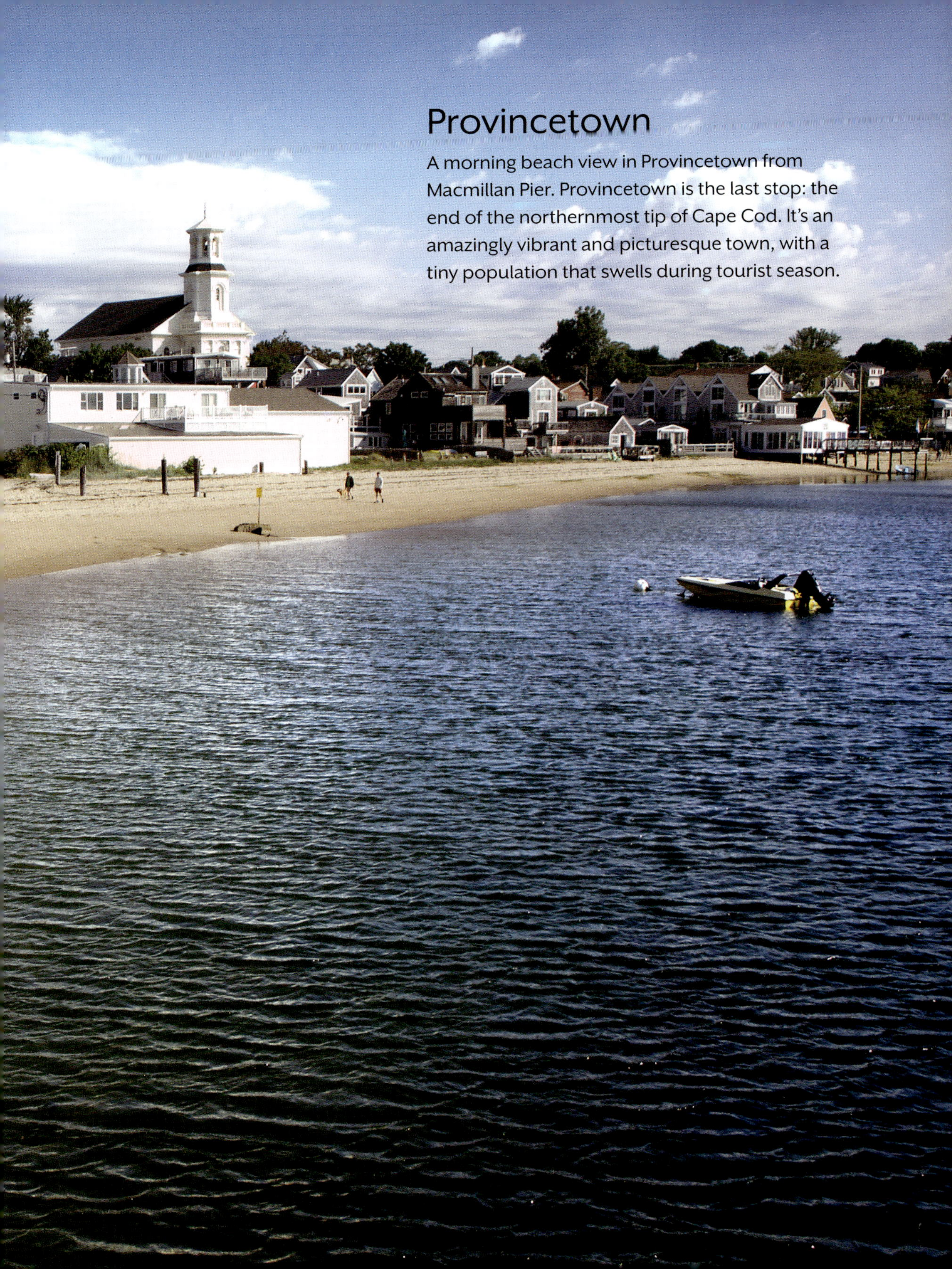

Provincetown

A morning beach view in Provincetown from Macmillan Pier. Provincetown is the last stop: the end of the northernmost tip of Cape Cod. It's an amazingly vibrant and picturesque town, with a tiny population that swells during tourist season.

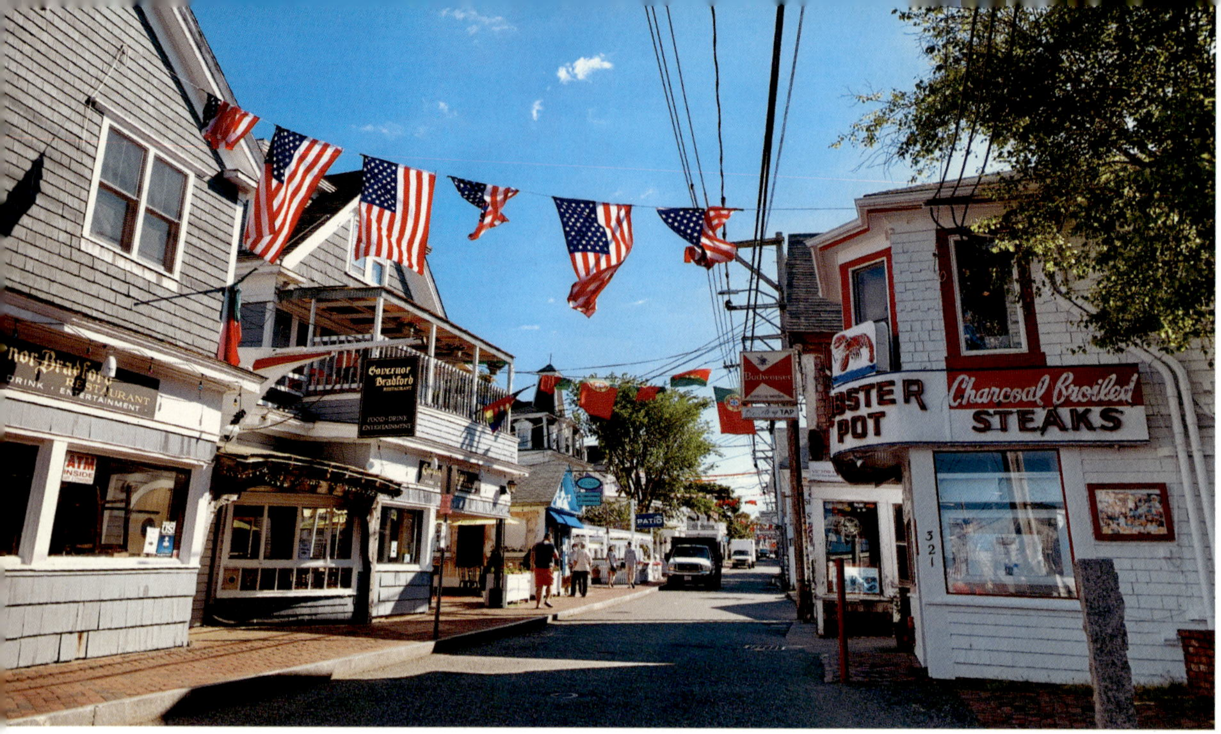

There are lots of choices for shopping and eating in town. One popular destination is the Lobster Pot. With its harbor views and classic neon signs, it's been a tradition for decades.

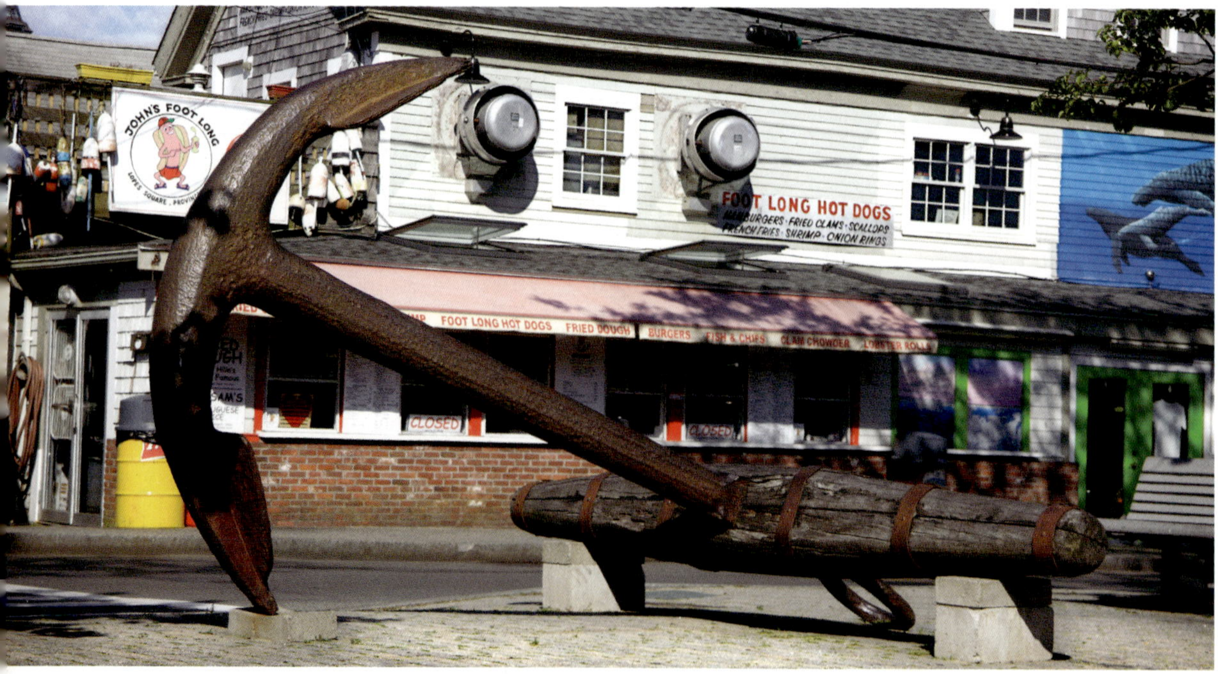

There's plenty to see in town, and everything is within walking distance. It's a concentrated area with lots of colorful characters, interesting history, and great views of Provincetown Harbor.

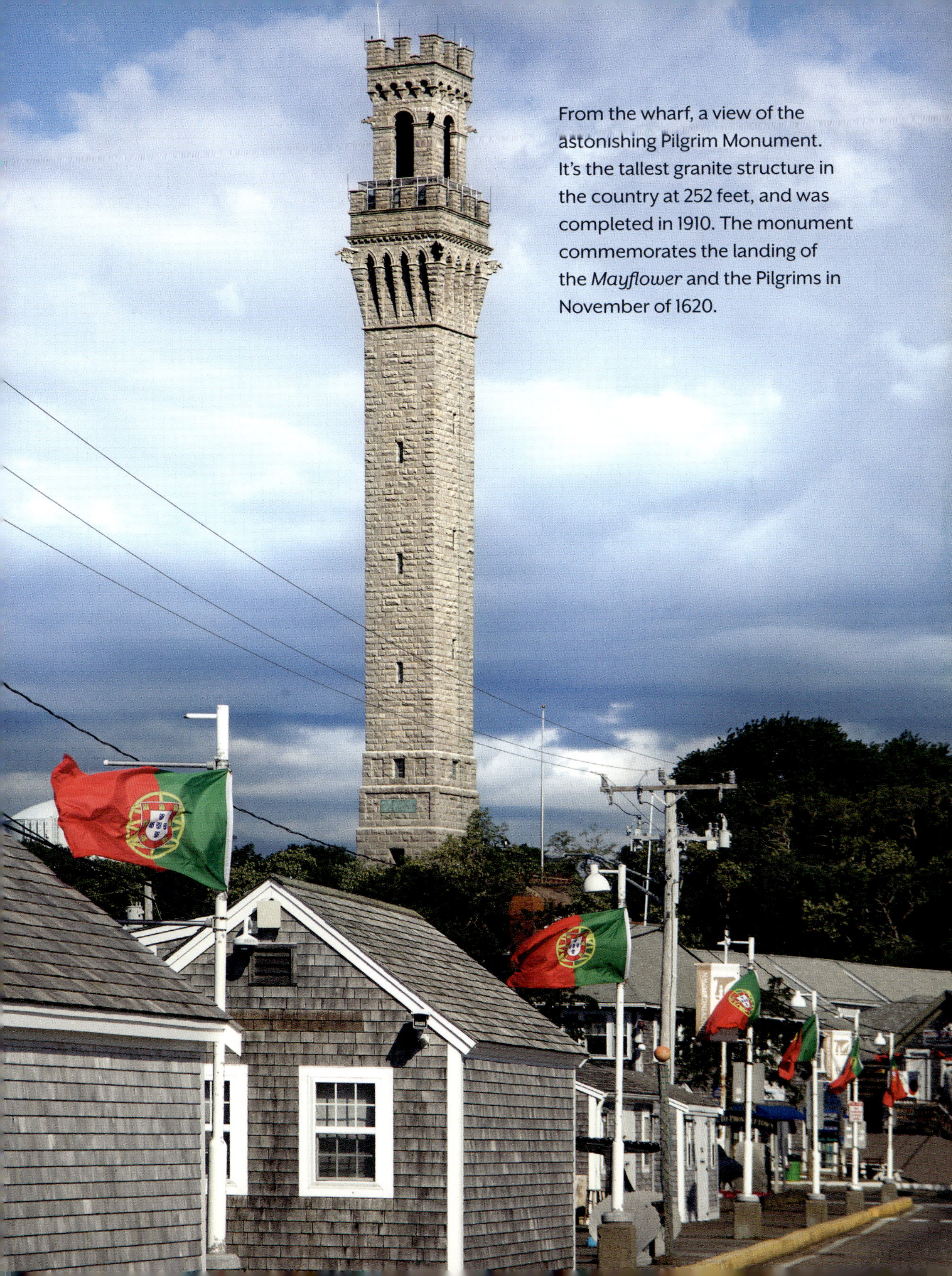

From the wharf, a view of the astonishing Pilgrim Monument. It's the tallest granite structure in the country at 252 feet, and was completed in 1910. The monument commemorates the landing of the *Mayflower* and the Pilgrims in November of 1620.

Truro

Highland Light strikes a regal pose on its perch near a cliff, on the Cape Cod National Seashore. The lighthouse is located at one of Truro's most scenic spots, Highland Links Golf Course. Truro sits on the Outer Cape, and was settled in 1700.

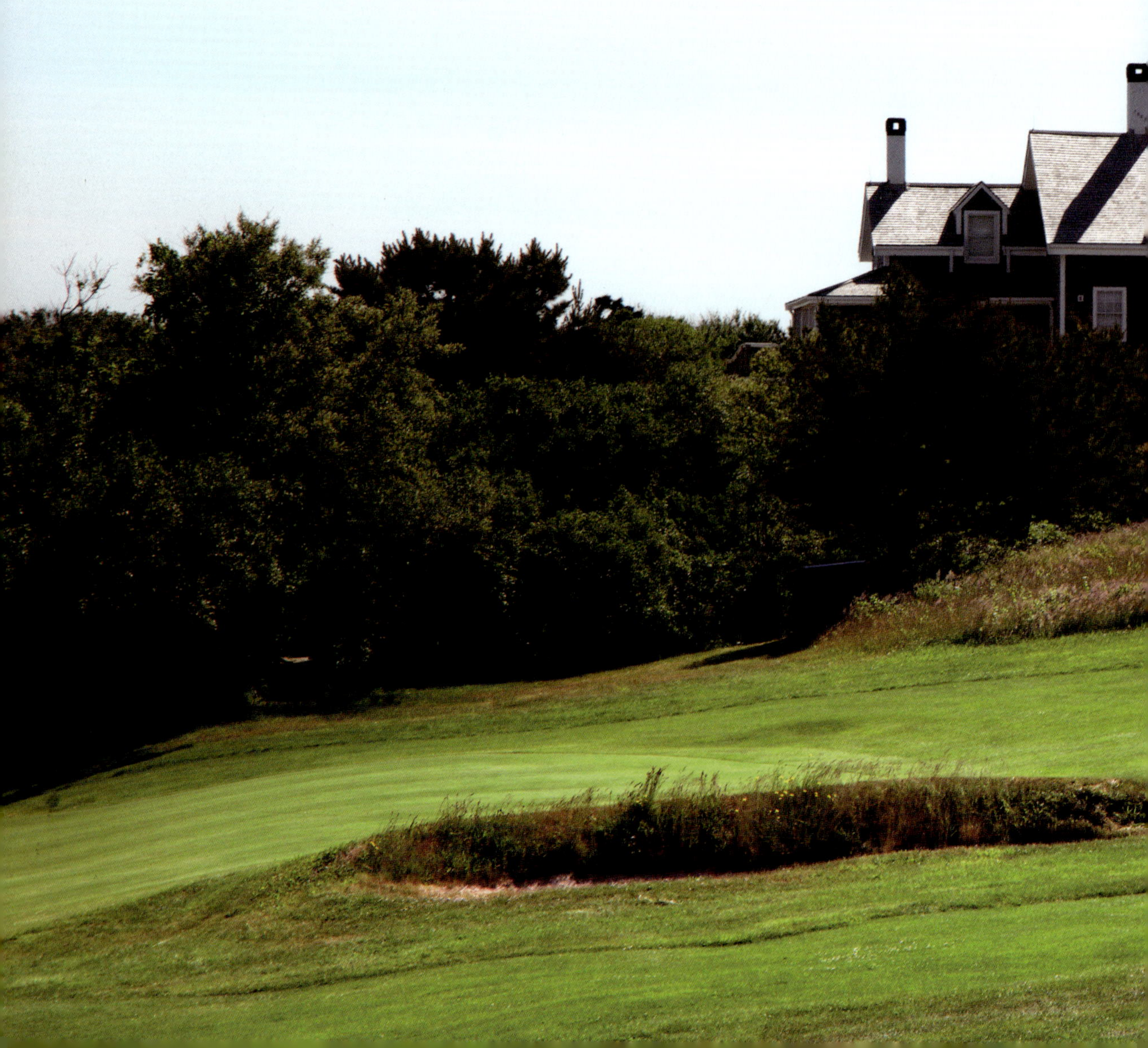

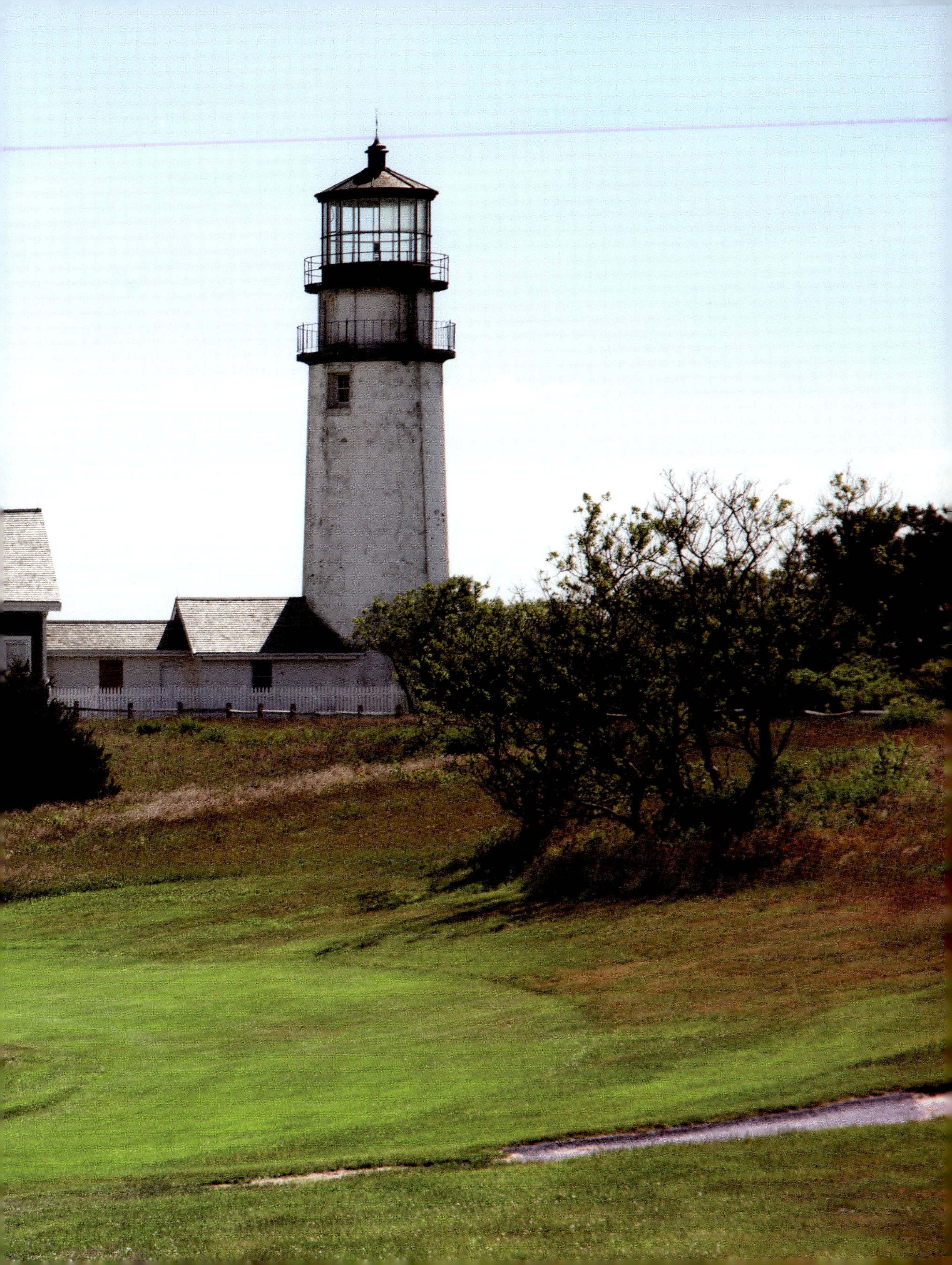

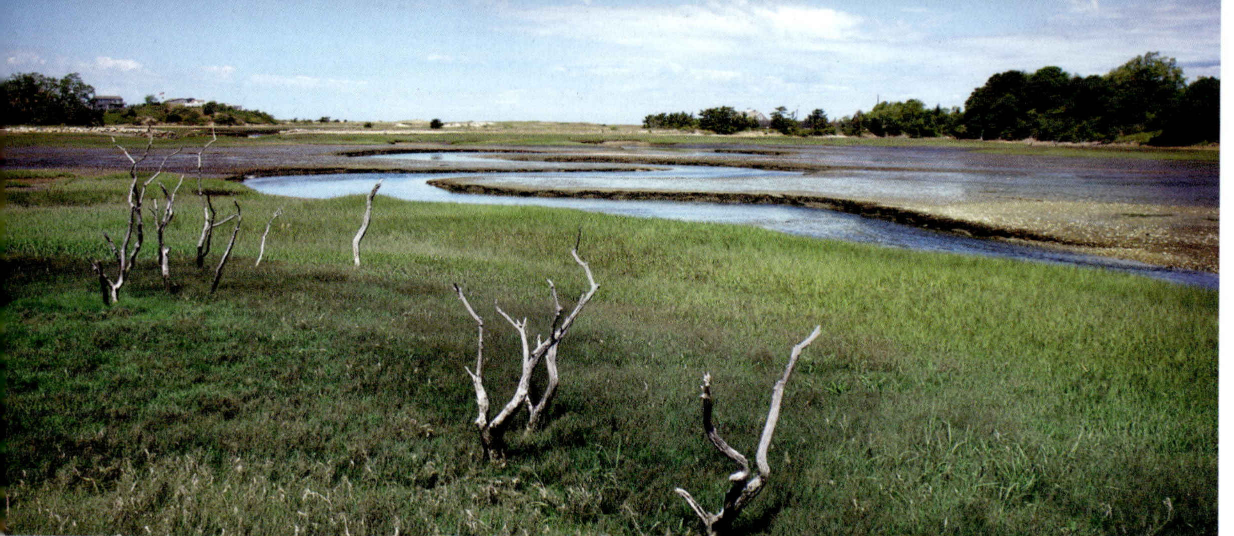

Driving along a winding road in Truro, I stopped to take in this picture-perfect scene. The contrast between the snarled white limbs of the dead trees, with the verdant marsh grass, and the meandering teal water, made it too good to pass up.

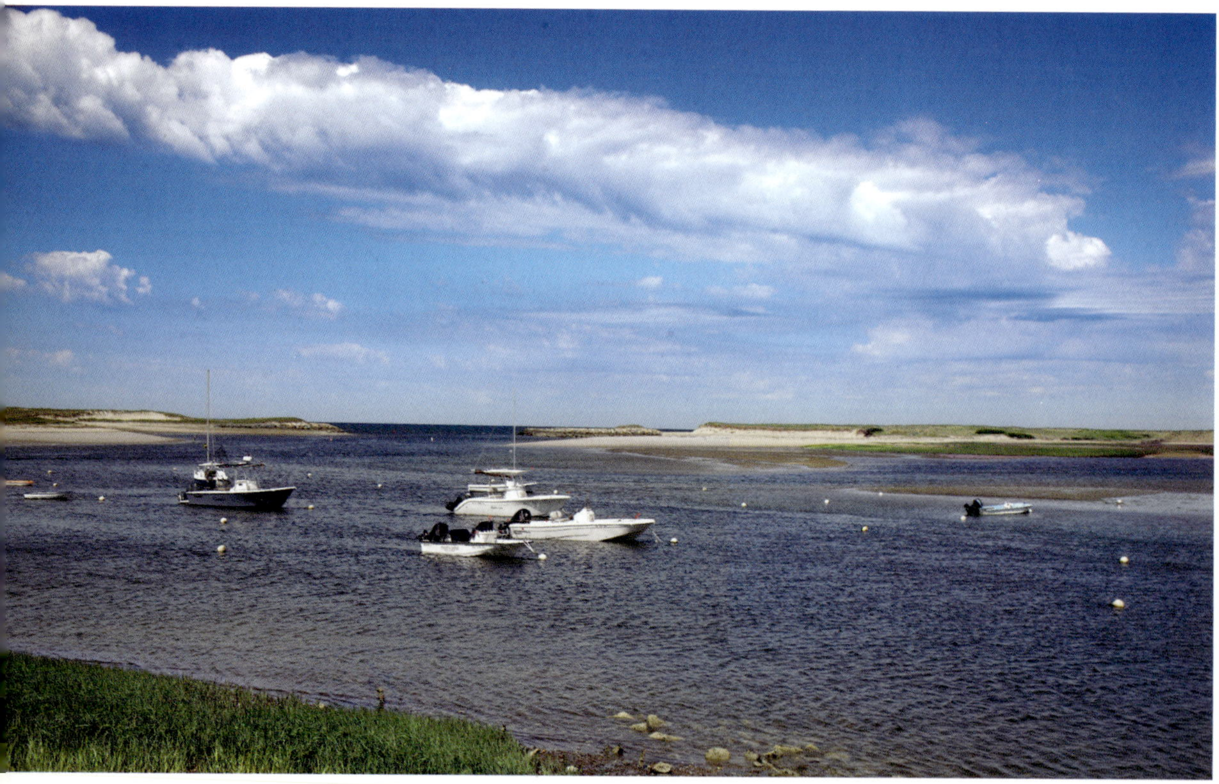

A warm, relaxing breeze was blowing in from the ocean at Pamet Harbor. It was 75 degrees, with almost no humidity, and a few puffy clouds for some occasional shade. What a nice day to sit in the sand and smell the salty air in Truro.

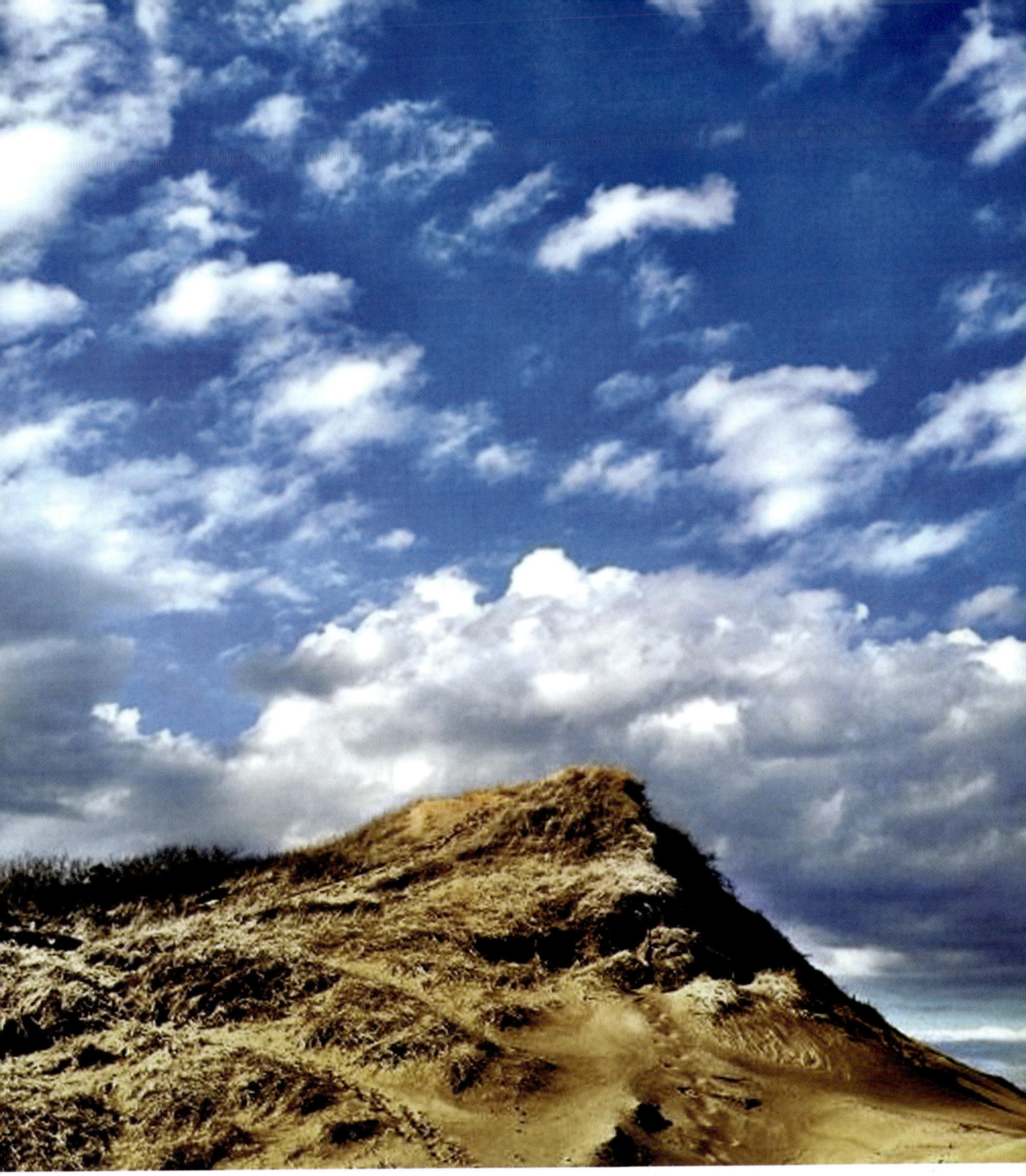

Walking down the beach late in the afternoon, I noticed this golden sand dune set against a sapphire-blue sky. A nice way to wrap up a pleasant visit to Truro.

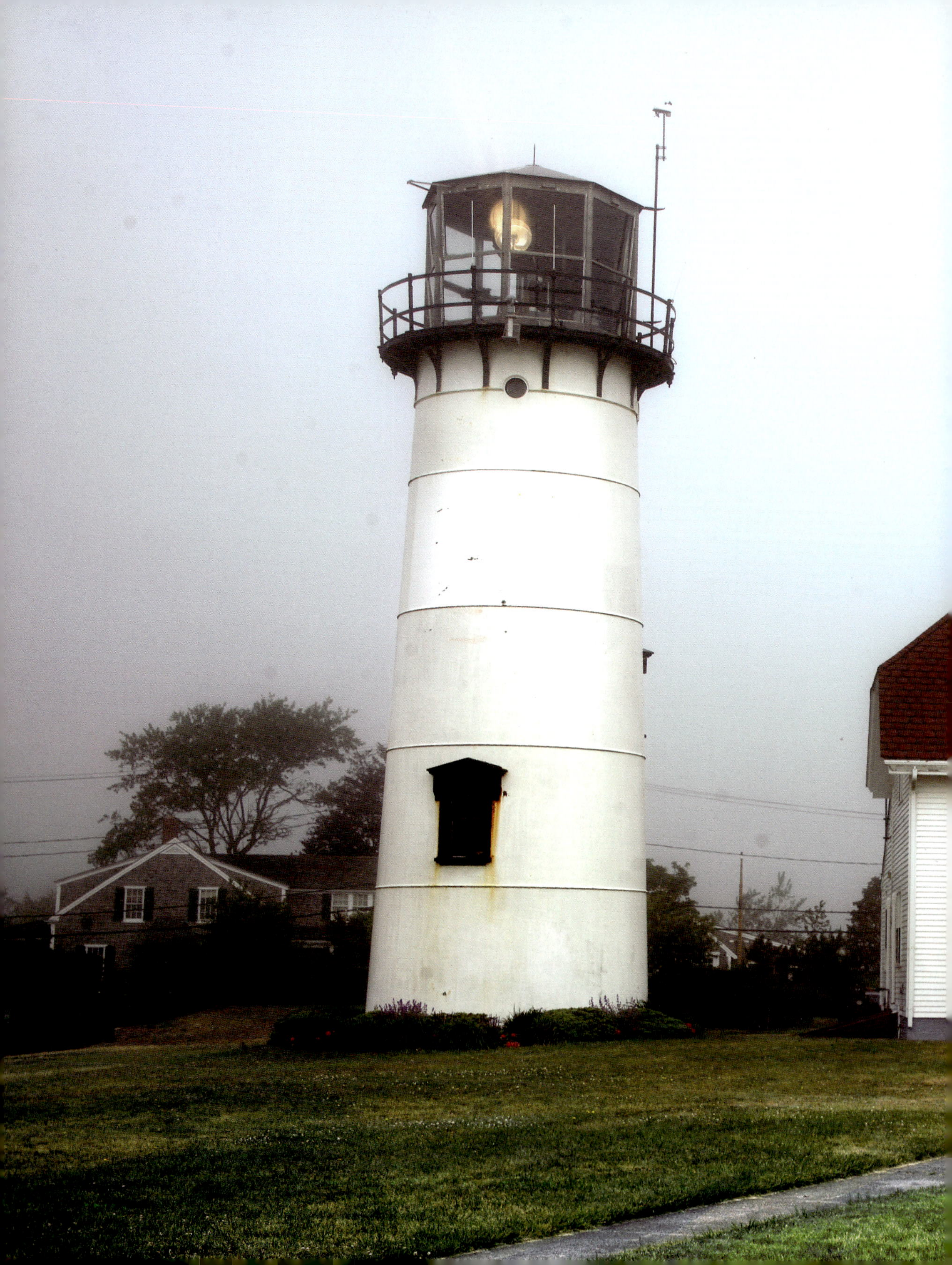

Chatham

Early morning sun tries to burn through the fog at Chatham Light. The current lighthouse here stands 48 feet tall, and was first lit in 1877. Chatham lies at the southeastern tip of Cape Cod, and was settled in 1665.

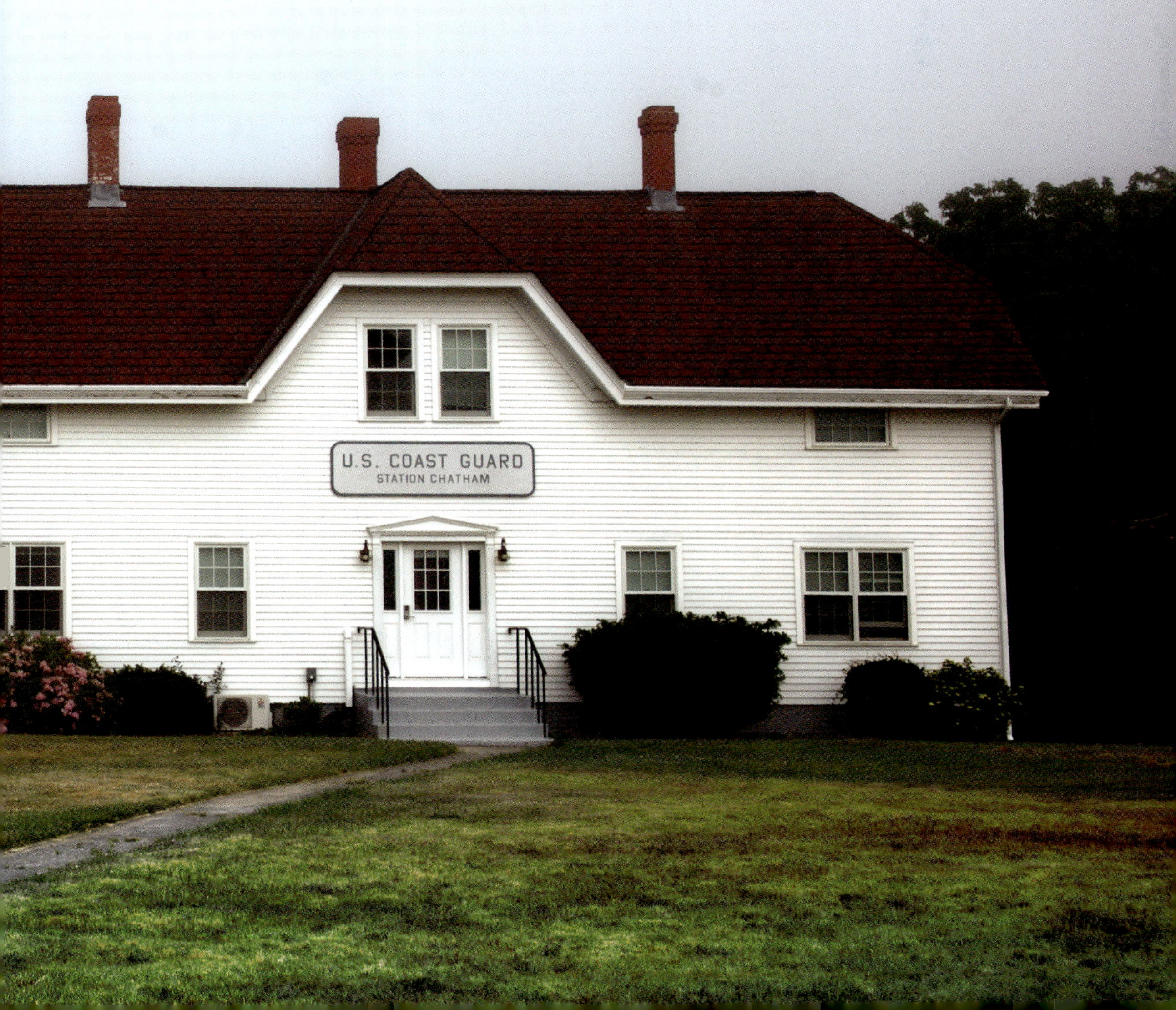

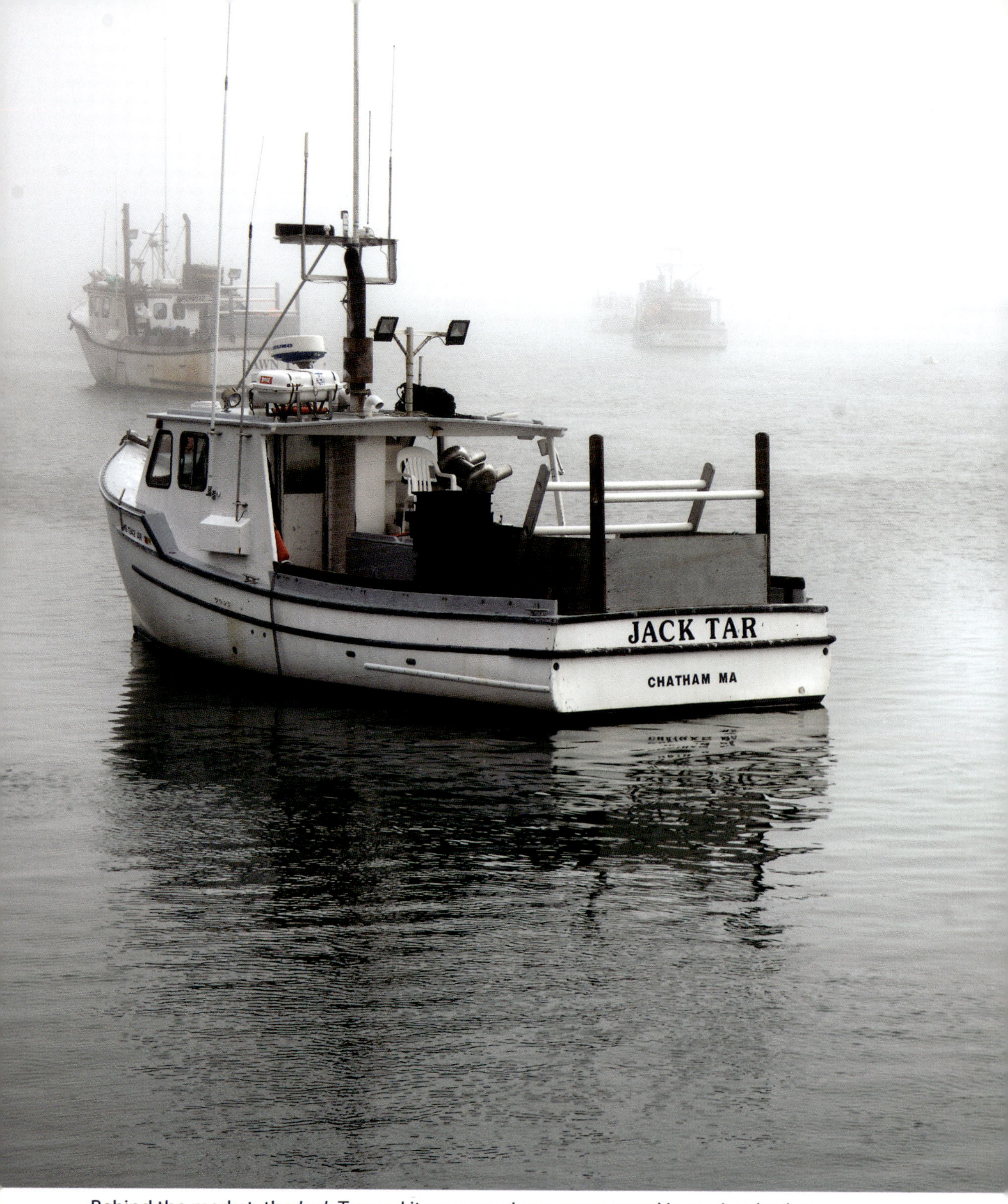

Behind the market, the *Jack Tar* and its companions are moored in a misty harbor.

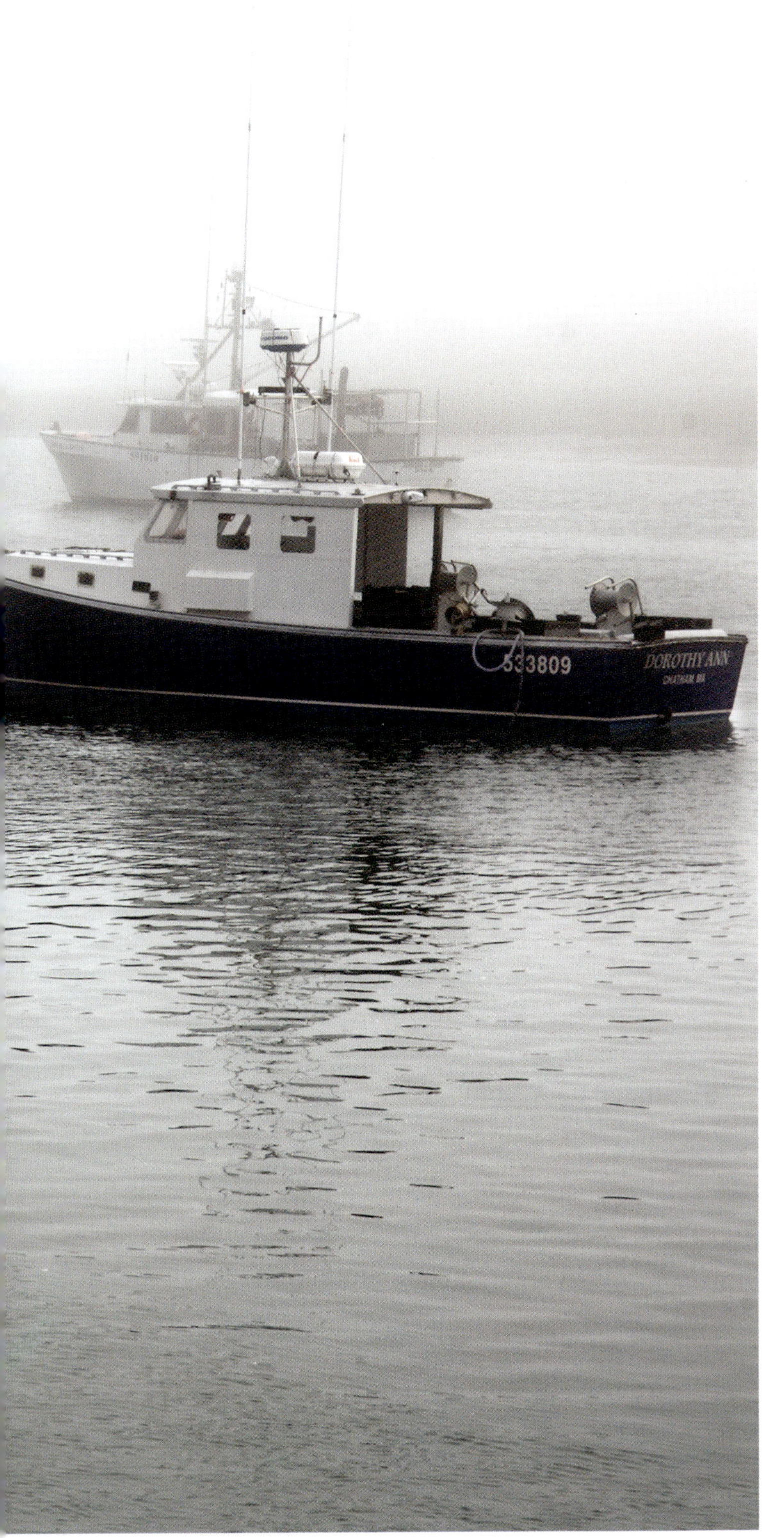

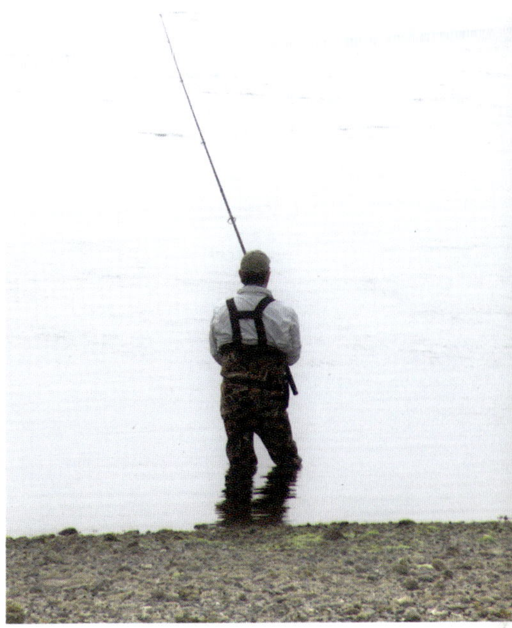

Up the road a bit at the town landing, a lone fisherman wades in knee-deep to try his luck.

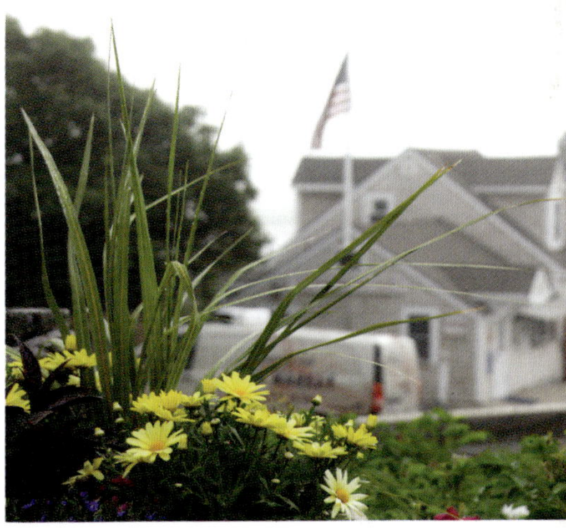

Flowers add some color to a hazy sunrise at Chatham Pier Fish Market.

Harwich

A typical cycle on Cape Cod is early morning fog, with the sun eventually winning through. When I took this photo at Red River Beach in Harwich, there were no takers yet. Within a half hour, the sun was shining, and I counted 30 people on the beach. Harwich faces Nantucket Sound, and was incorporated as a town in 1694.

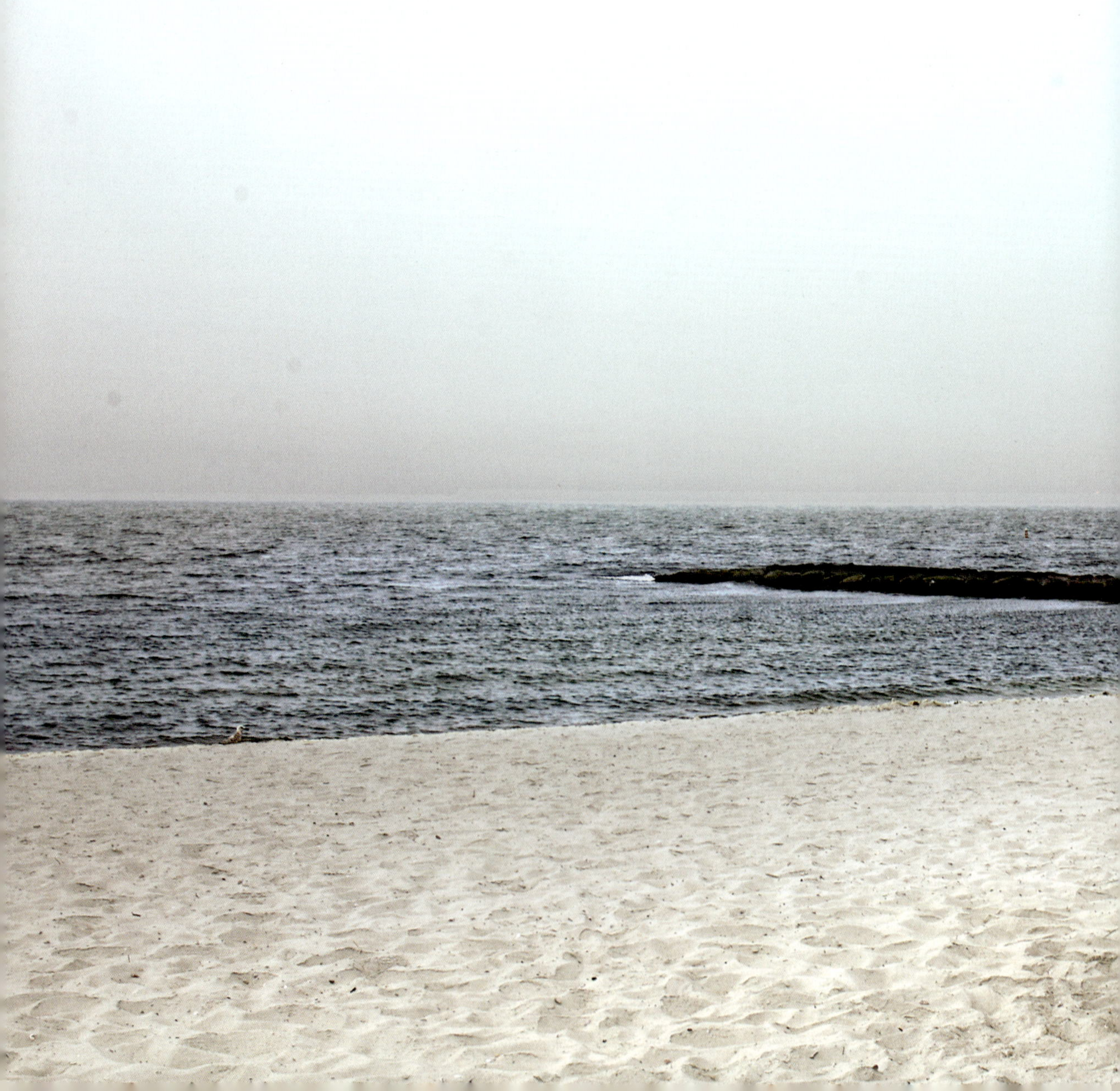

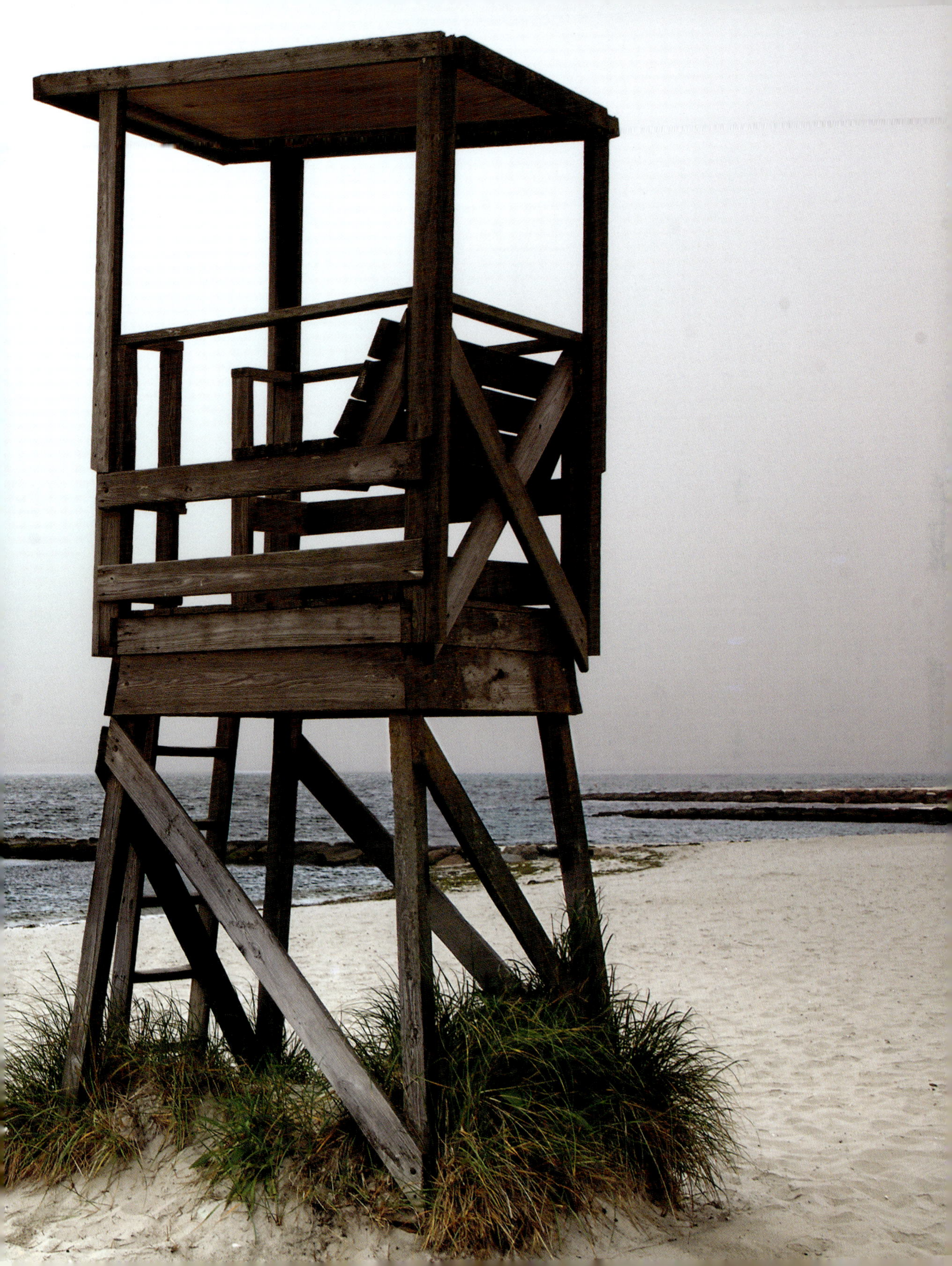

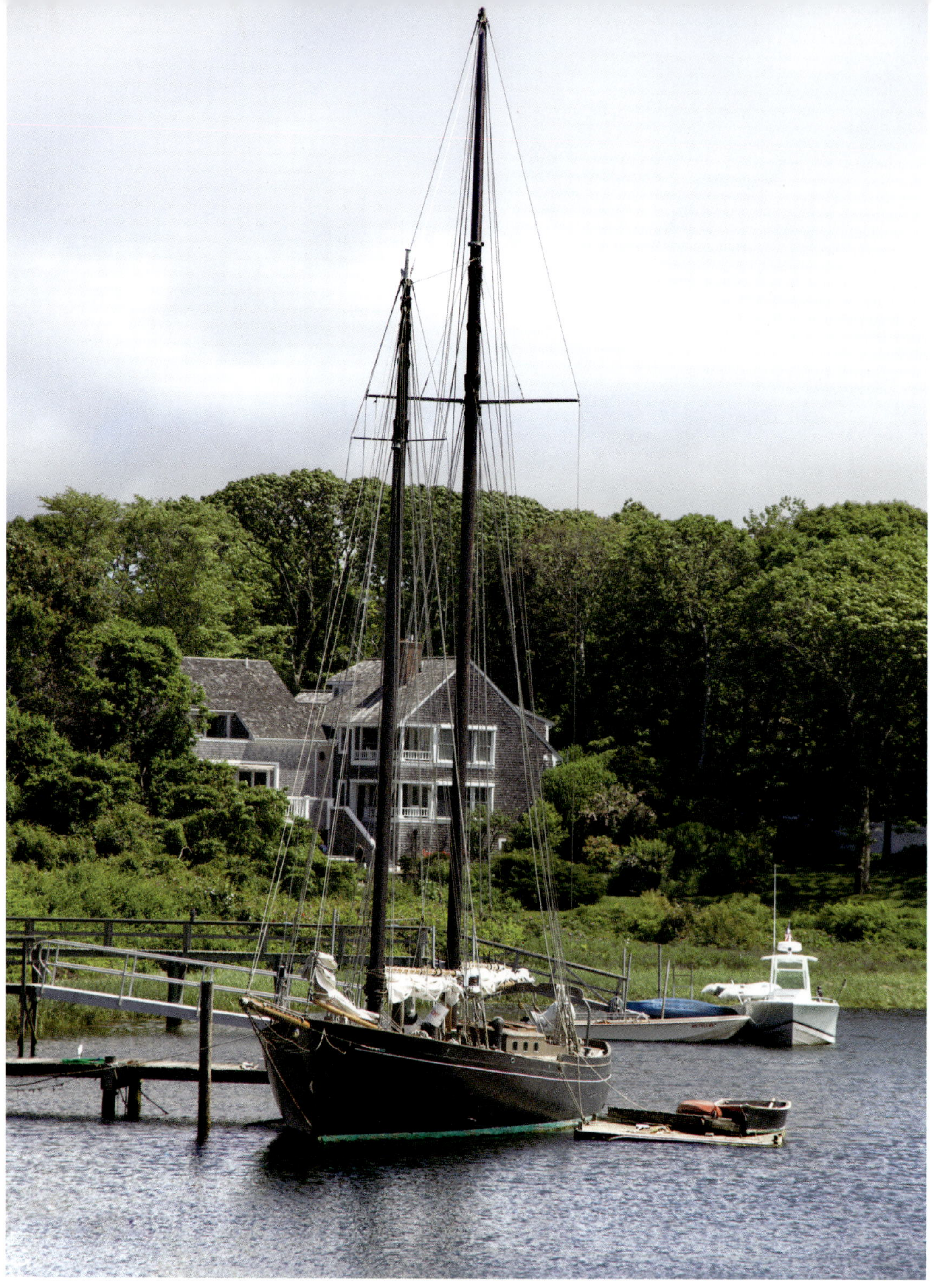

A classic wooden two-masted sailboat docked in Wychmere Harbor.

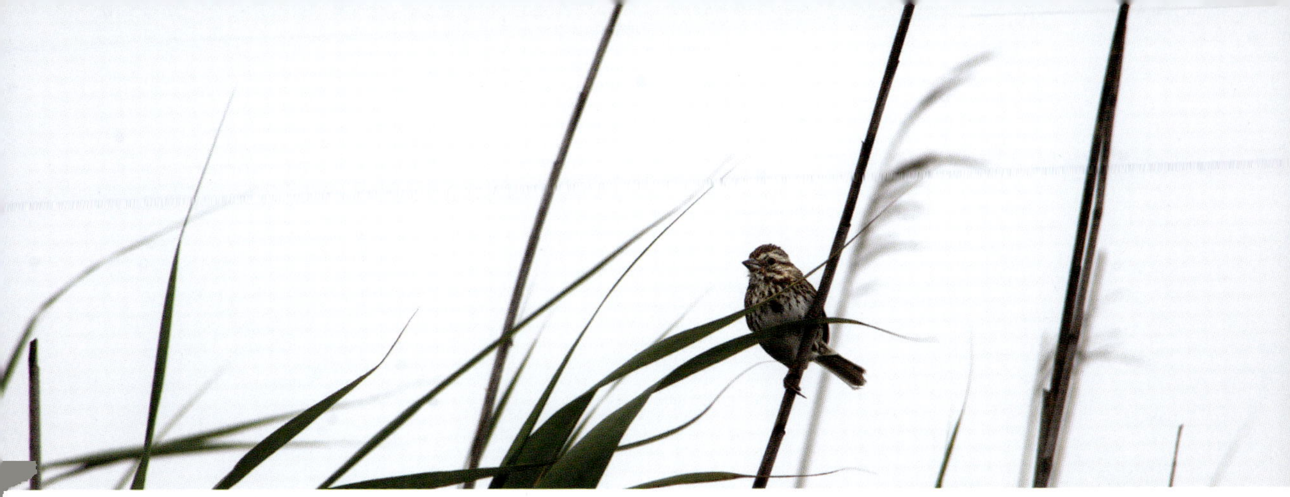

Right behind the beach is a marsh area with tall, slender reeds and beach rose. Taking a break from flying to chirp away, this swallow pleaded its case to all its nearby competitors.

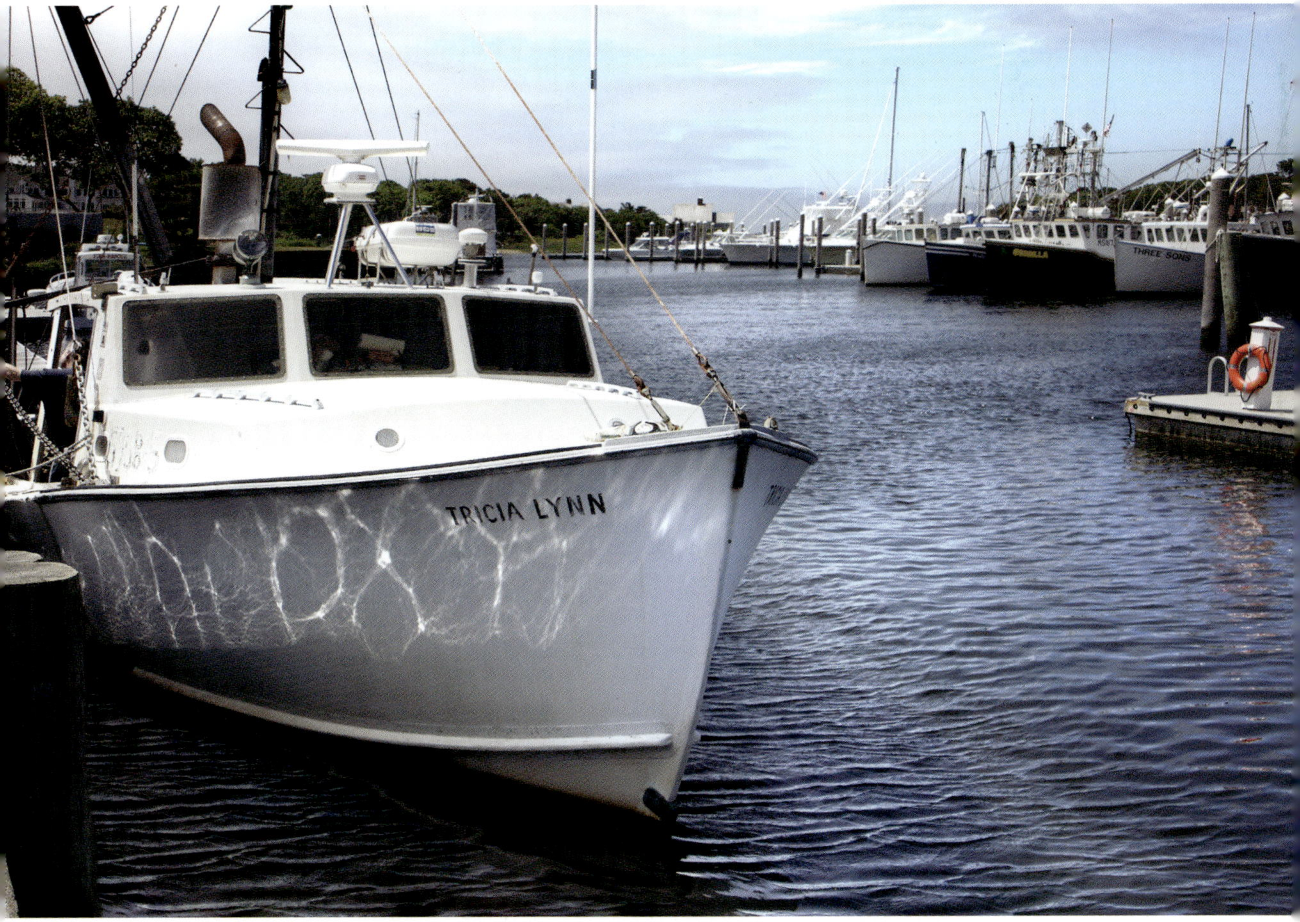

At Saquatucket Harbor, the crew of the *Tricia Lynn* prepares for a day on the water. One of the crewmen, a great guy named Danny, told me he spotted a seal in the harbor.

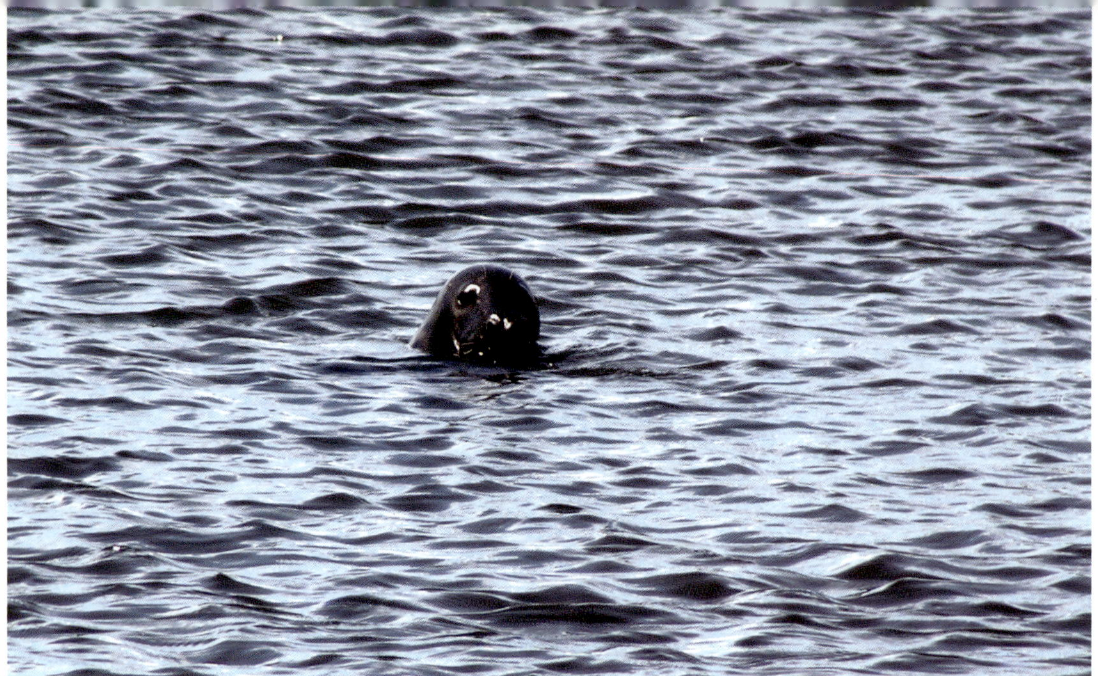

Sure enough, he was right about that seal! About 20 minutes after chatting with the guys as they got the boat ready, the seal popped his head up for a moment, and gave us a curious stare. No doubt he wondered if any fish were forthcoming.

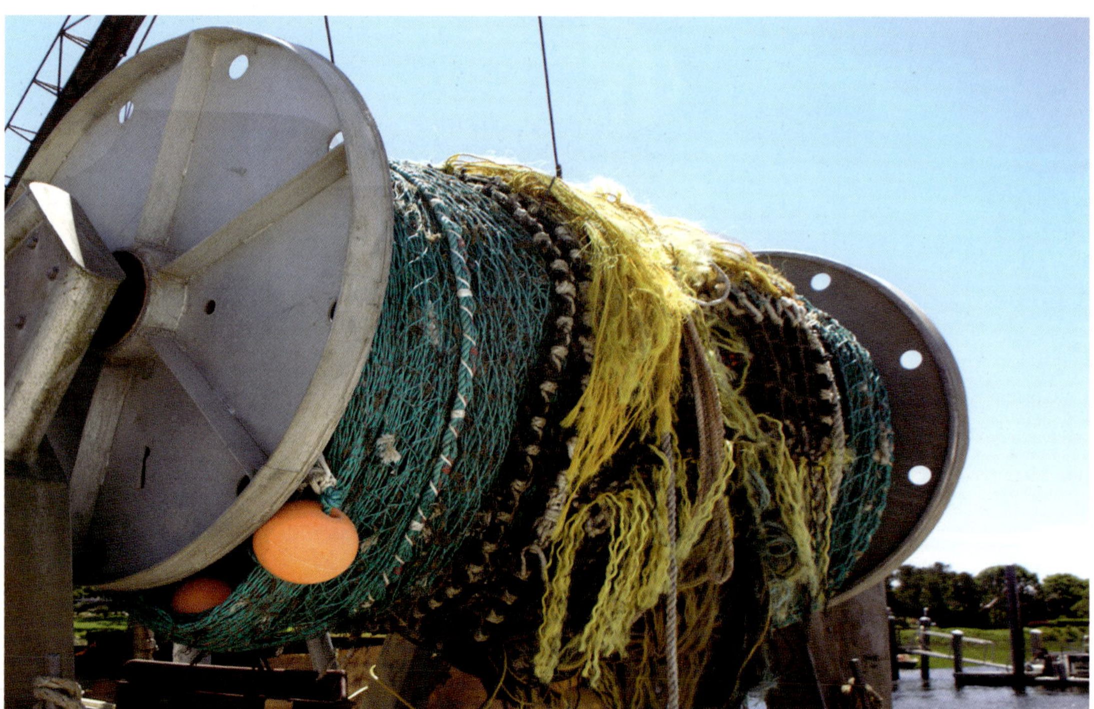

A boat across the harbor had colorful fishing nets spooled up on a drum winch.

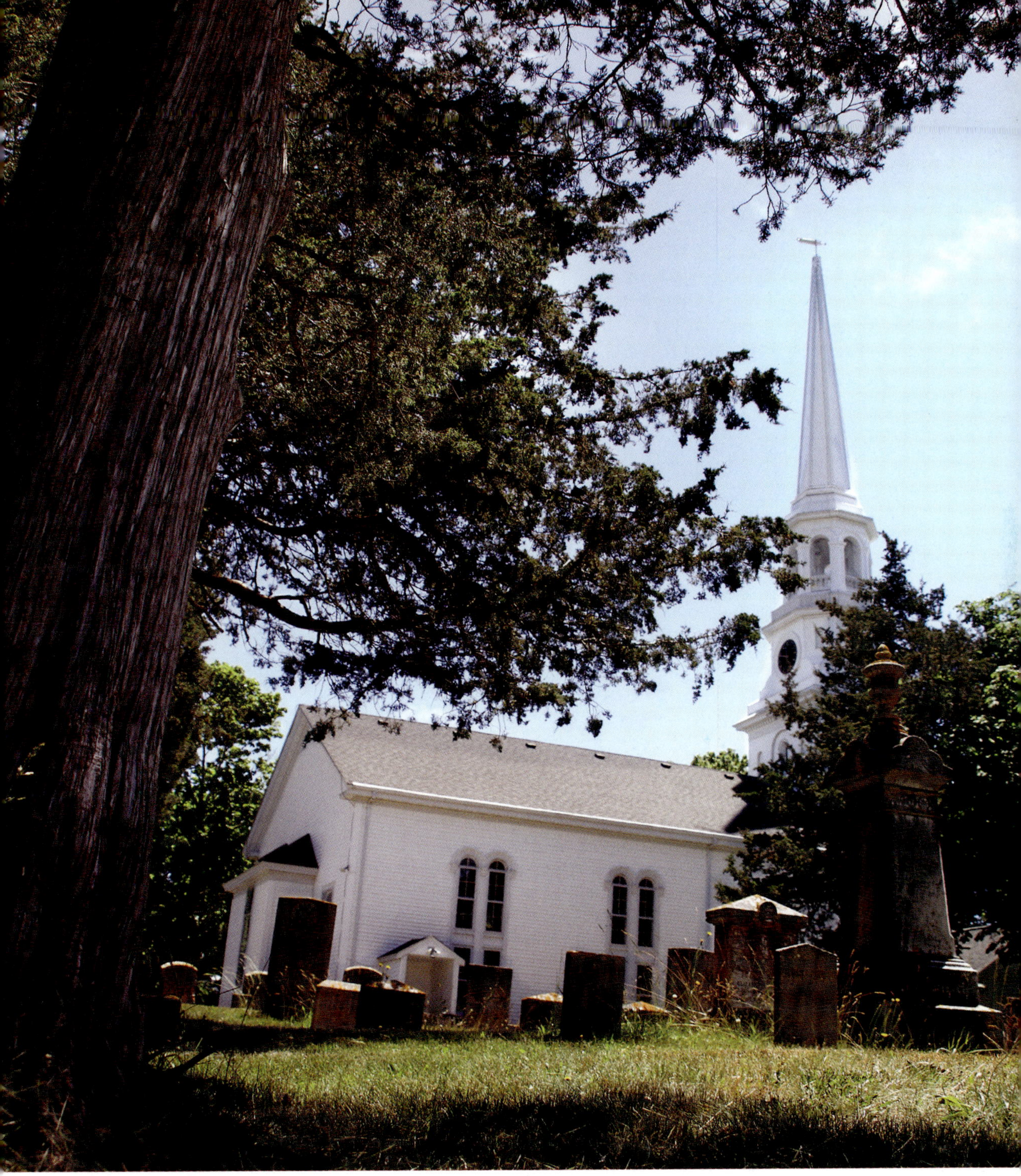

Sitting in the shade of a tree in Harwich Center. Here there's a view of old, ornate headstones next to the Congregational Church, with its tall and impressive spire.

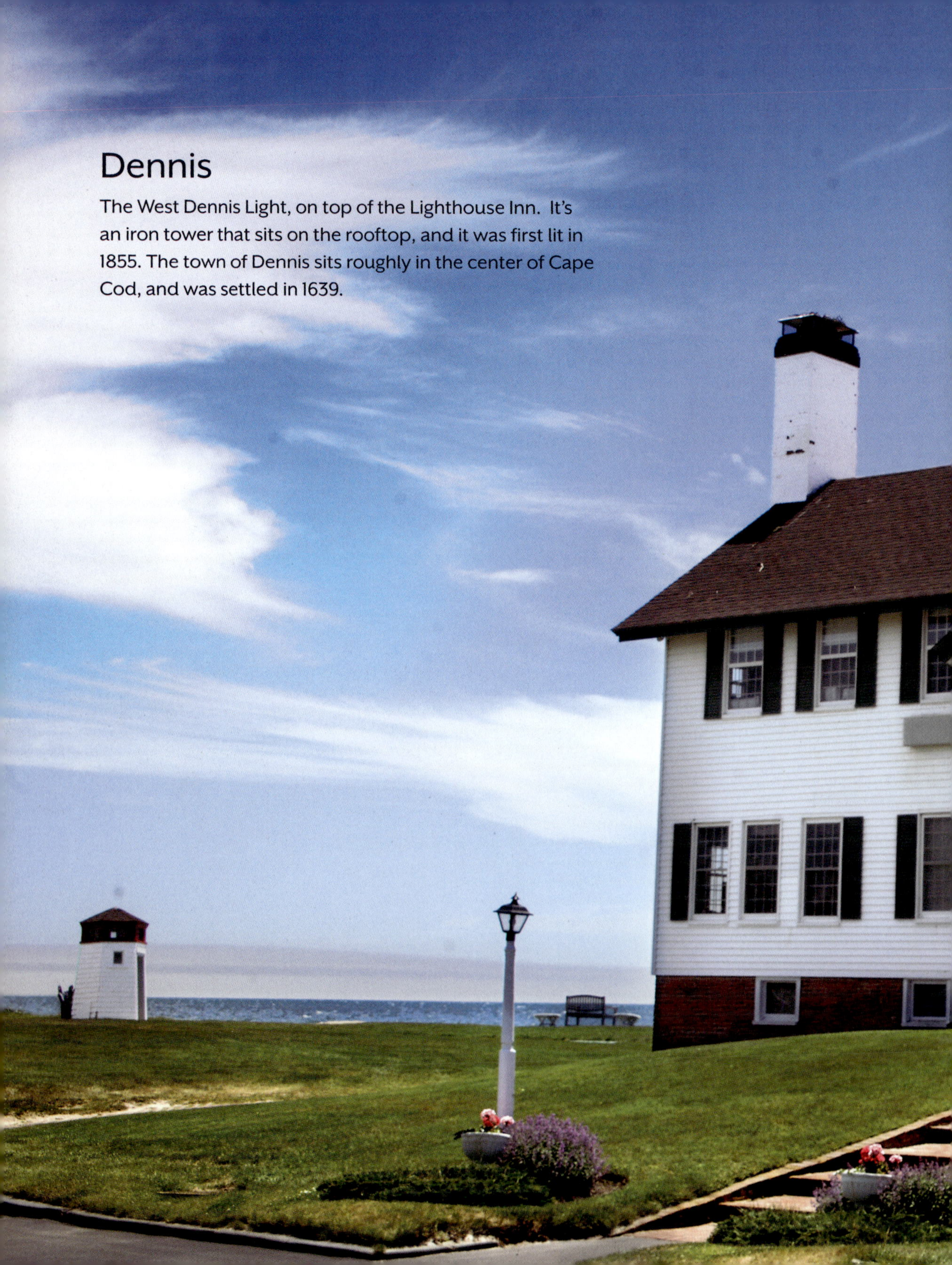

Dennis

The West Dennis Light, on top of the Lighthouse Inn. It's an iron tower that sits on the rooftop, and it was first lit in 1855. The town of Dennis sits roughly in the center of Cape Cod, and was settled in 1639.

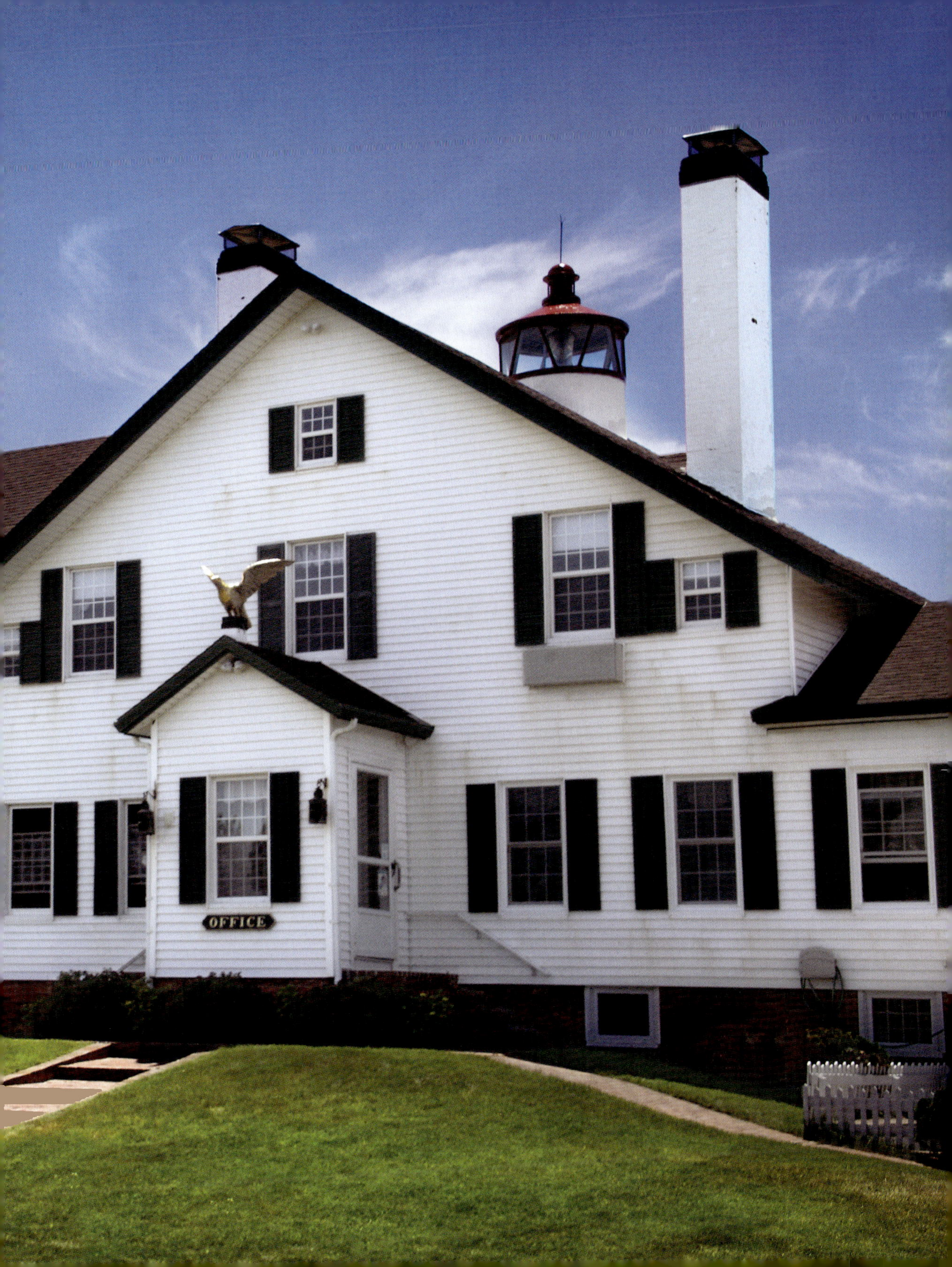

OFFICE

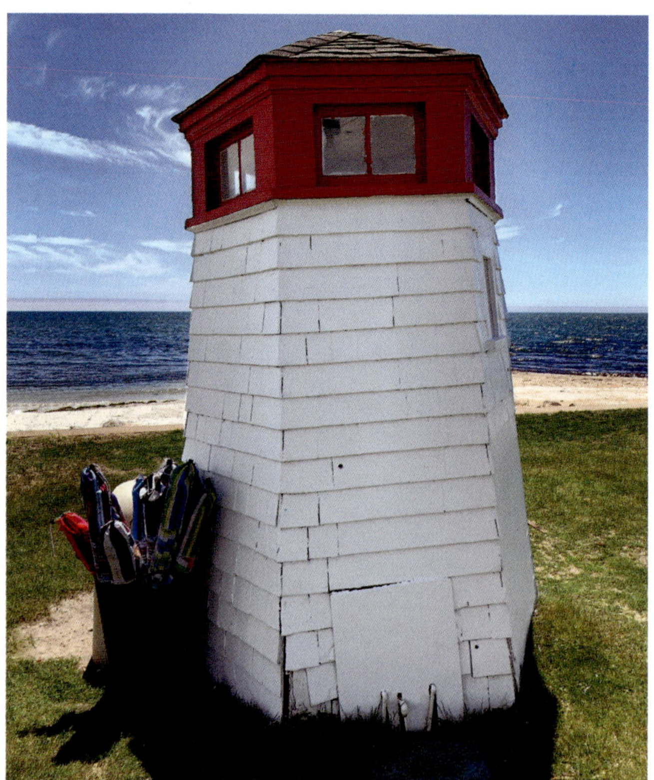

If you stay at the hotel you can enjoy using this little "lighthouse." It's right next to the beach, and inside you can shower the sand off.

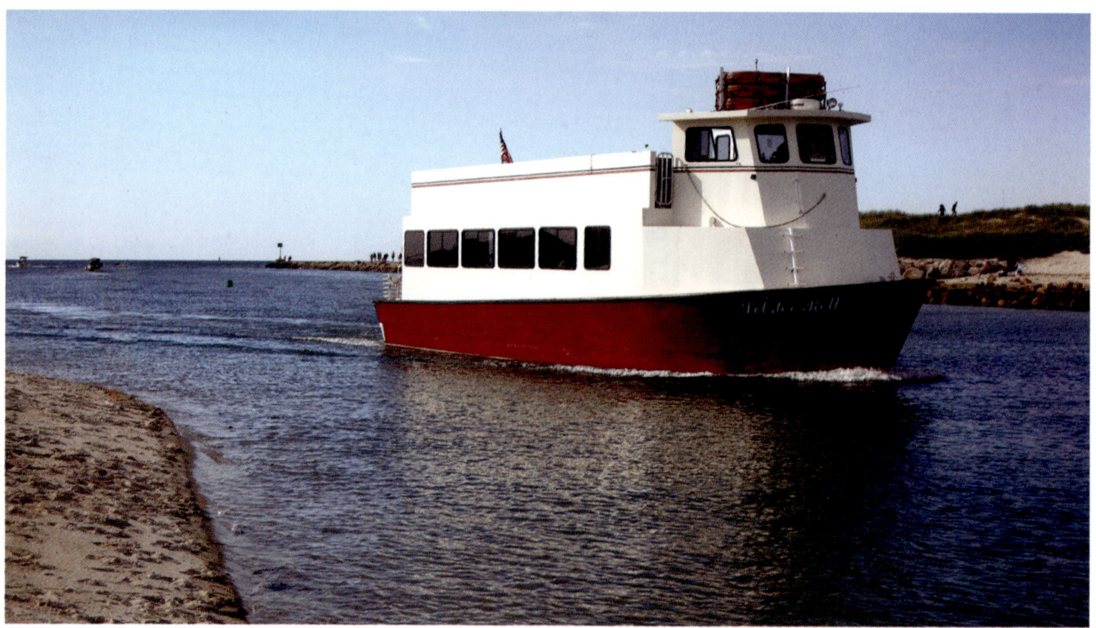

The cruise ship *Lobster Roll* makes her way into Sesuit Harbor, after taking a tour of Cape Cod Bay.

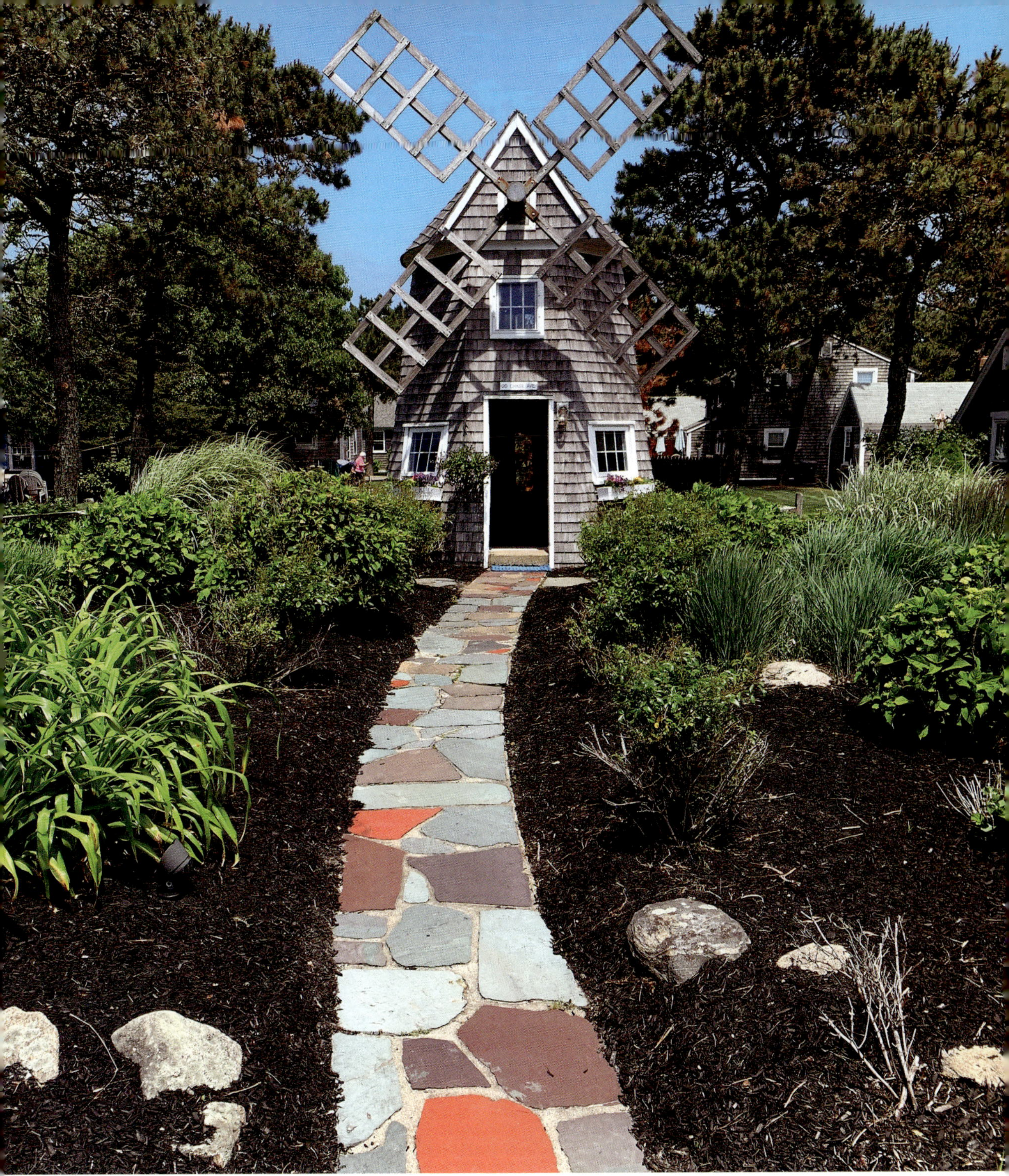

A beautiful stone path leading to a little windmill at Dennis Seashores, where you can rent a nice cottage with an ocean view.

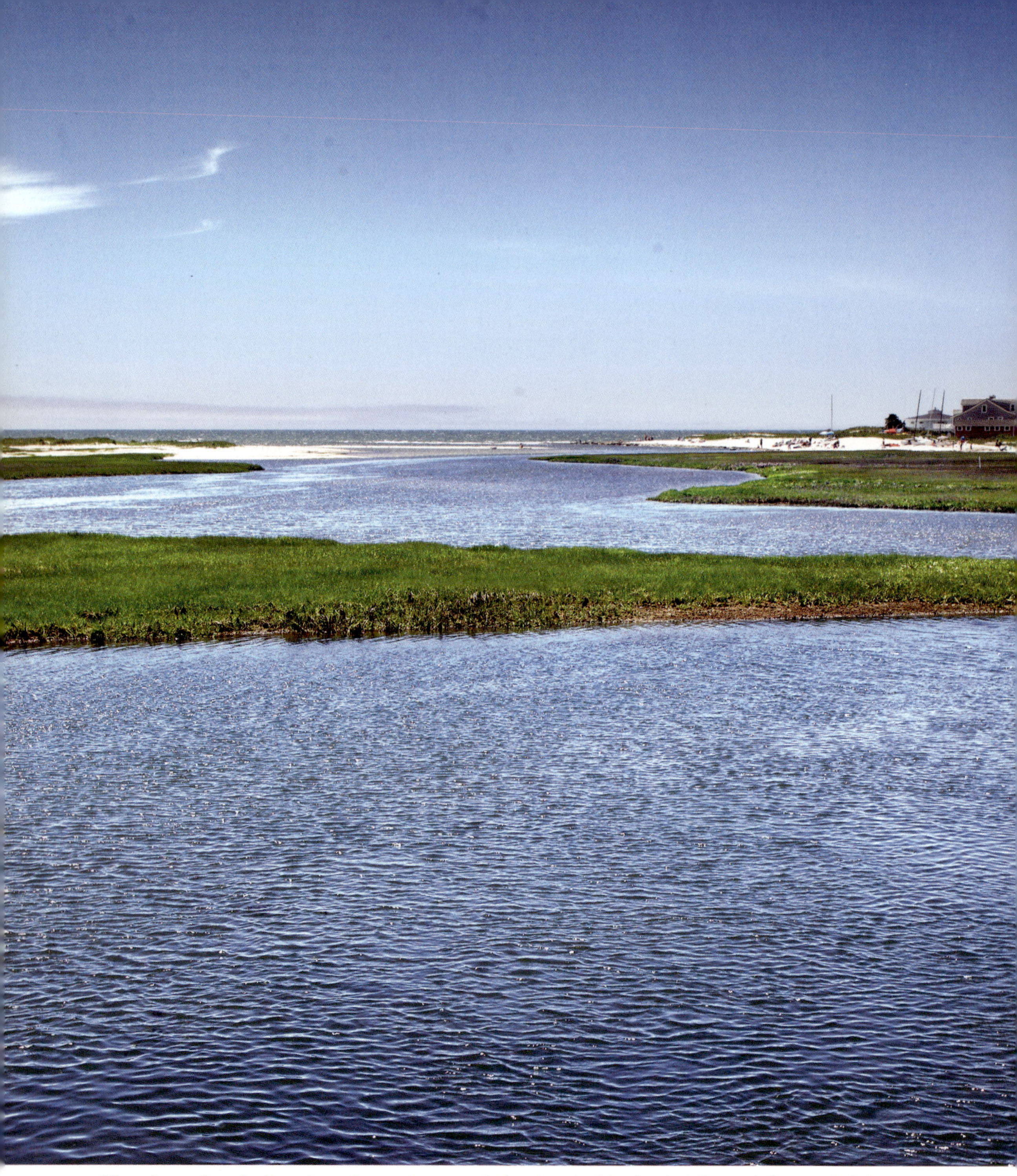

The view of a winding river through a marsh leading to Nantucket Sound, from a bridge crossing Lower County Road.

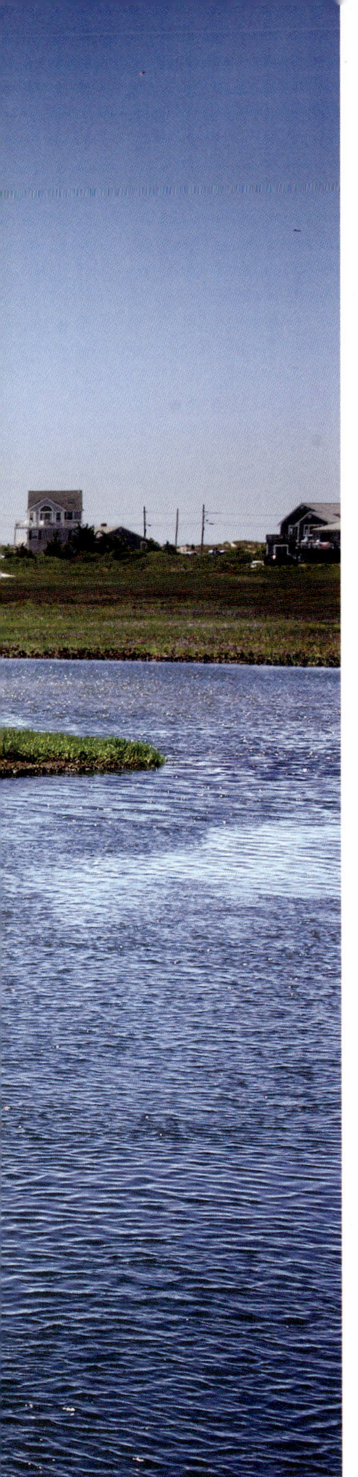

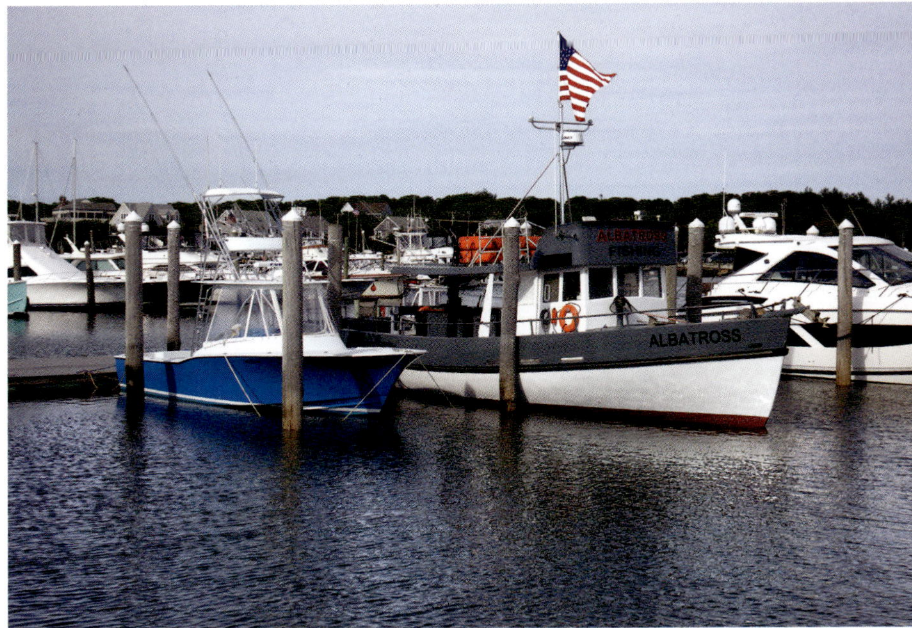

The *Albatross* docked with other boats in Sesuit Harbor. You can go fishing in Cape Cod Bay with the folks on this charter boat.

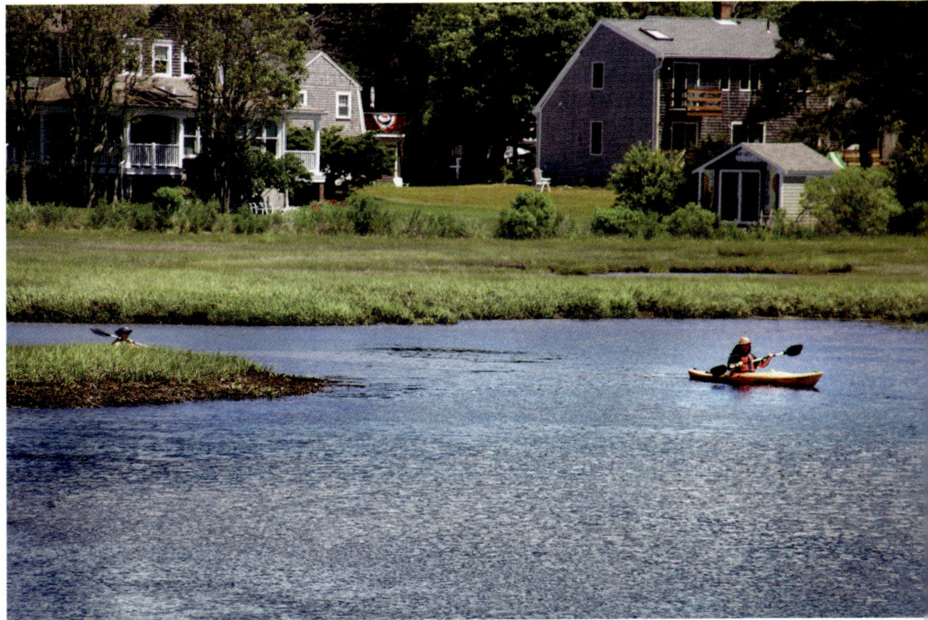

Kayakers paddling their way down a river through the marsh.

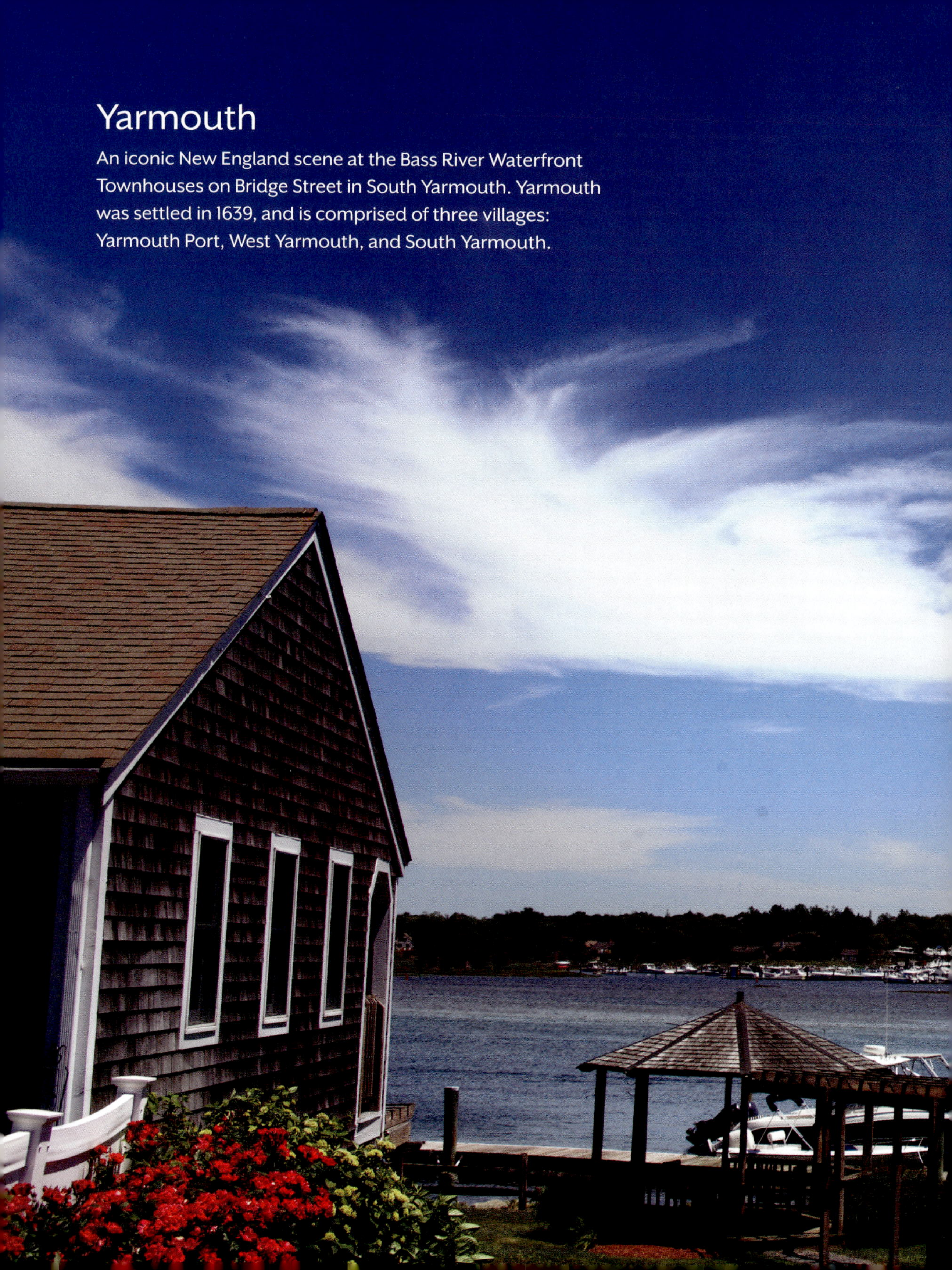

Yarmouth

An iconic New England scene at the Bass River Waterfront Townhouses on Bridge Street in South Yarmouth. Yarmouth was settled in 1639, and is comprised of three villages: Yarmouth Port, West Yarmouth, and South Yarmouth.

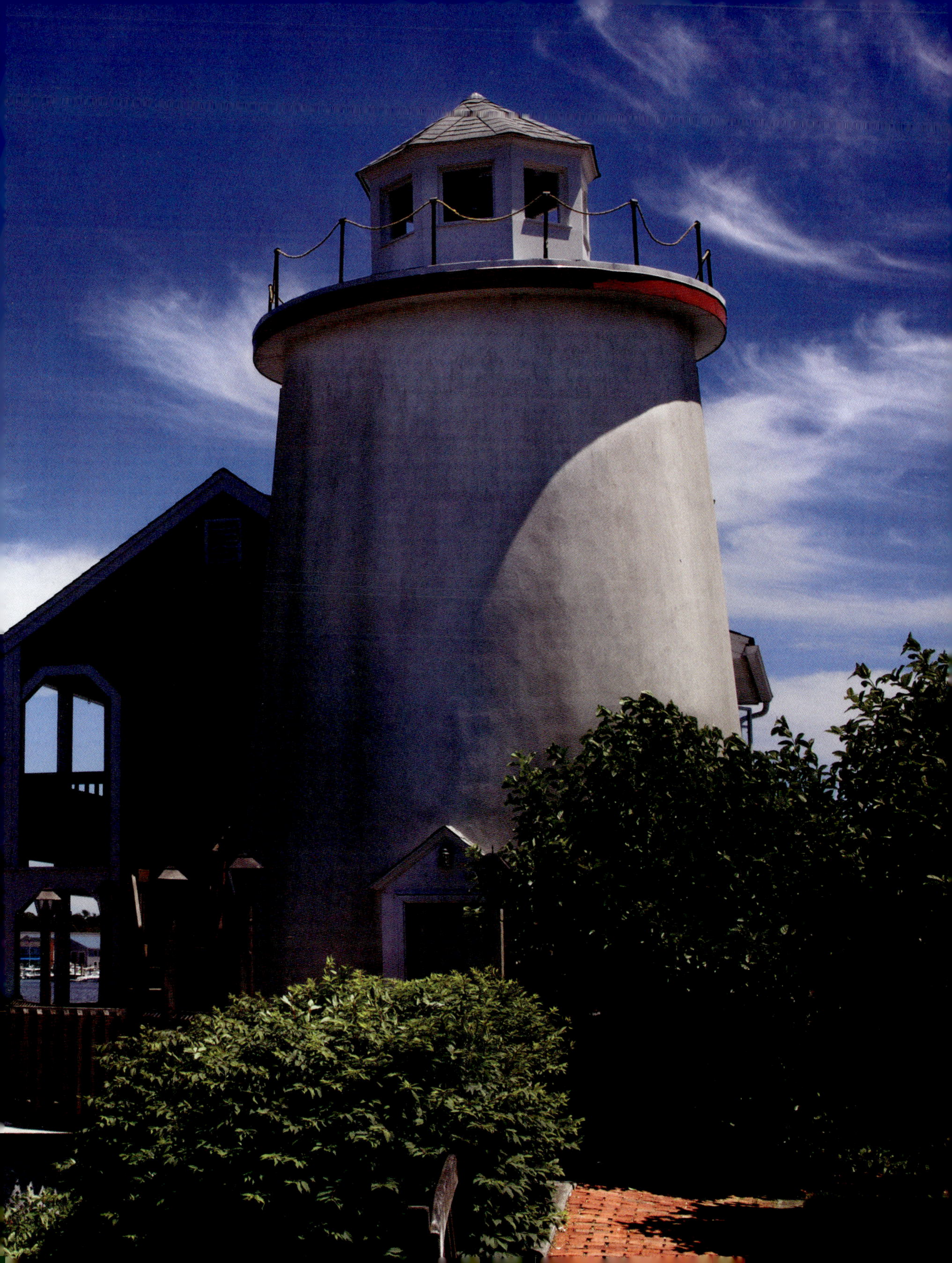

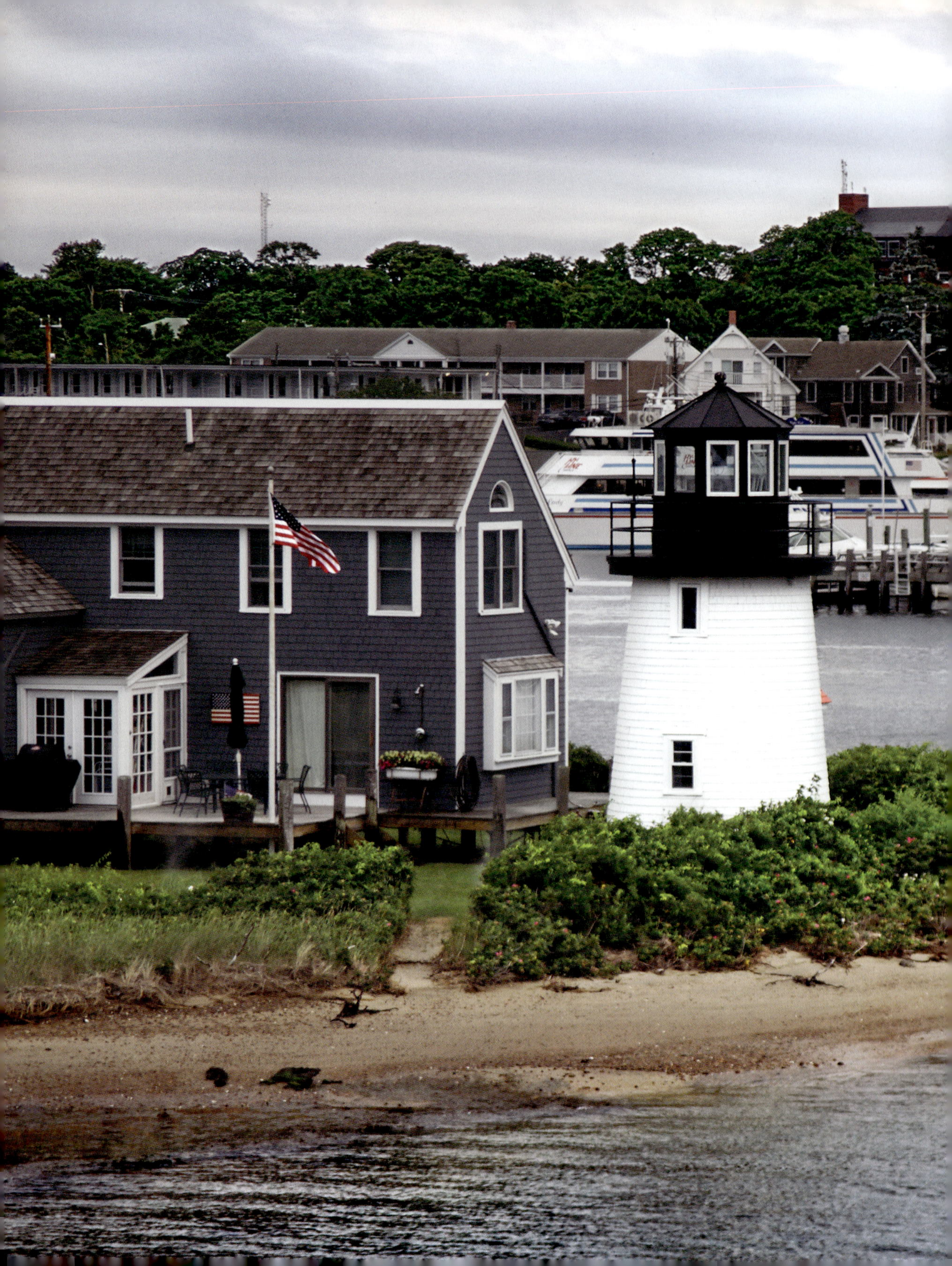

Hyannis

Ferrying into the harbor on a warm and sultry morning, we pass Hyannis Harbor Lighthouse. It's mostly cloudy at sunrise, but the forecast calls for blue skies later.

Hyannis is one of the busiest fishing and recreational ports on the Cape. It's also a major transportation hub, with an airport, and ferry service to the islands.

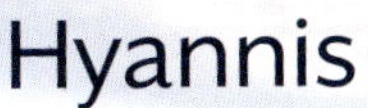

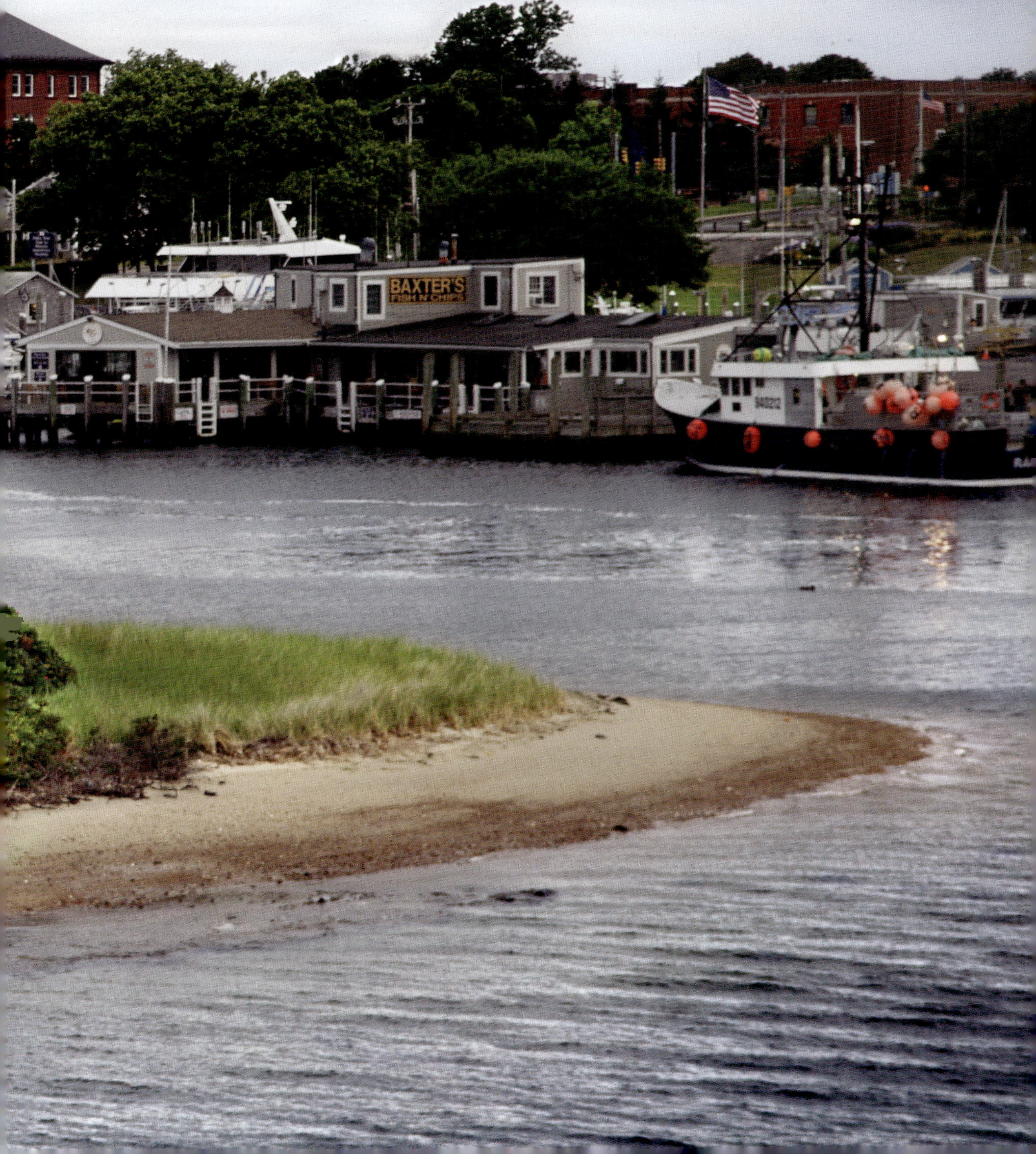

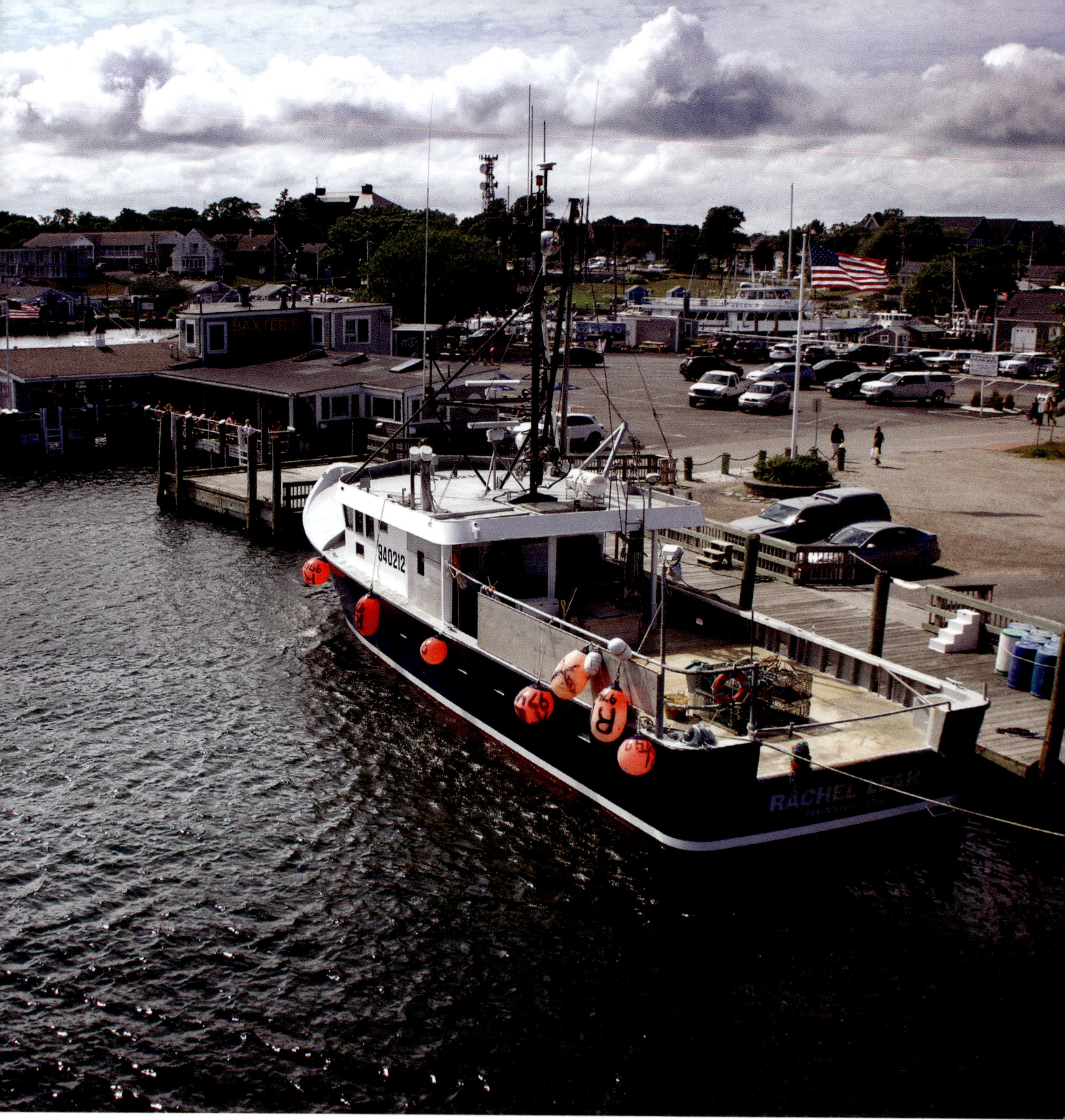

A view of Hyannis Harbor and the waterfront. The *Rachel Leah* is tied up to the dock, with a few lobster traps left on deck.

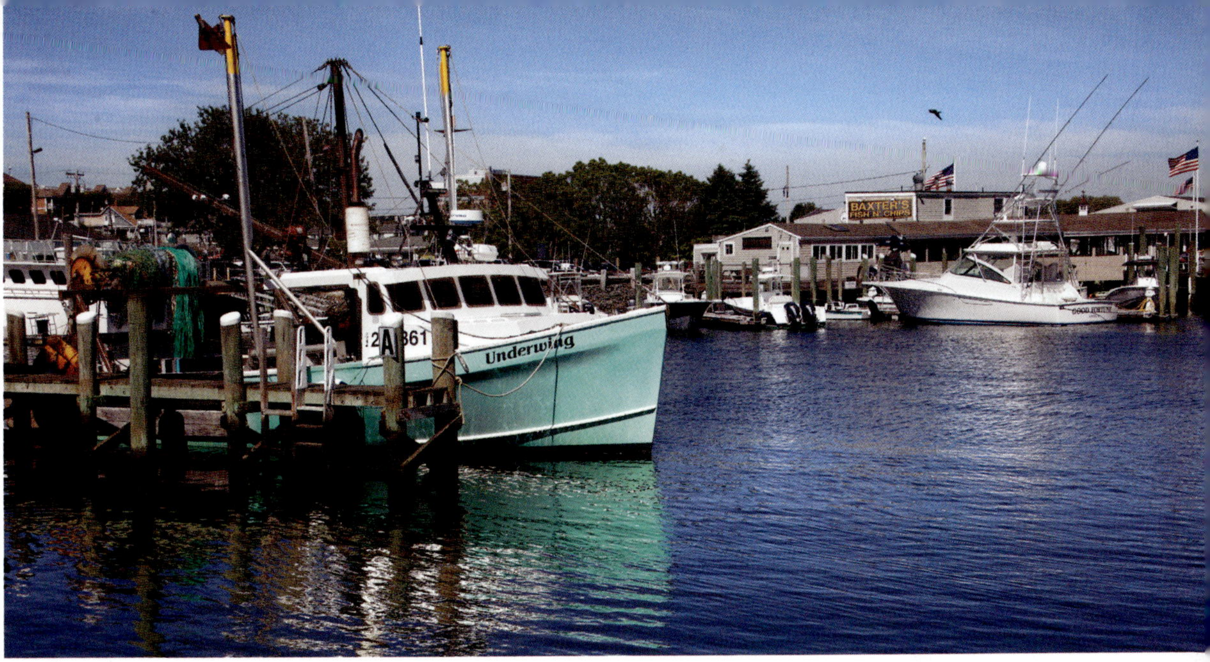

The *Underwing* docked in Hyannis Harbor. The aquamarine hull and wooden pier are reflected in the gently rippling water.

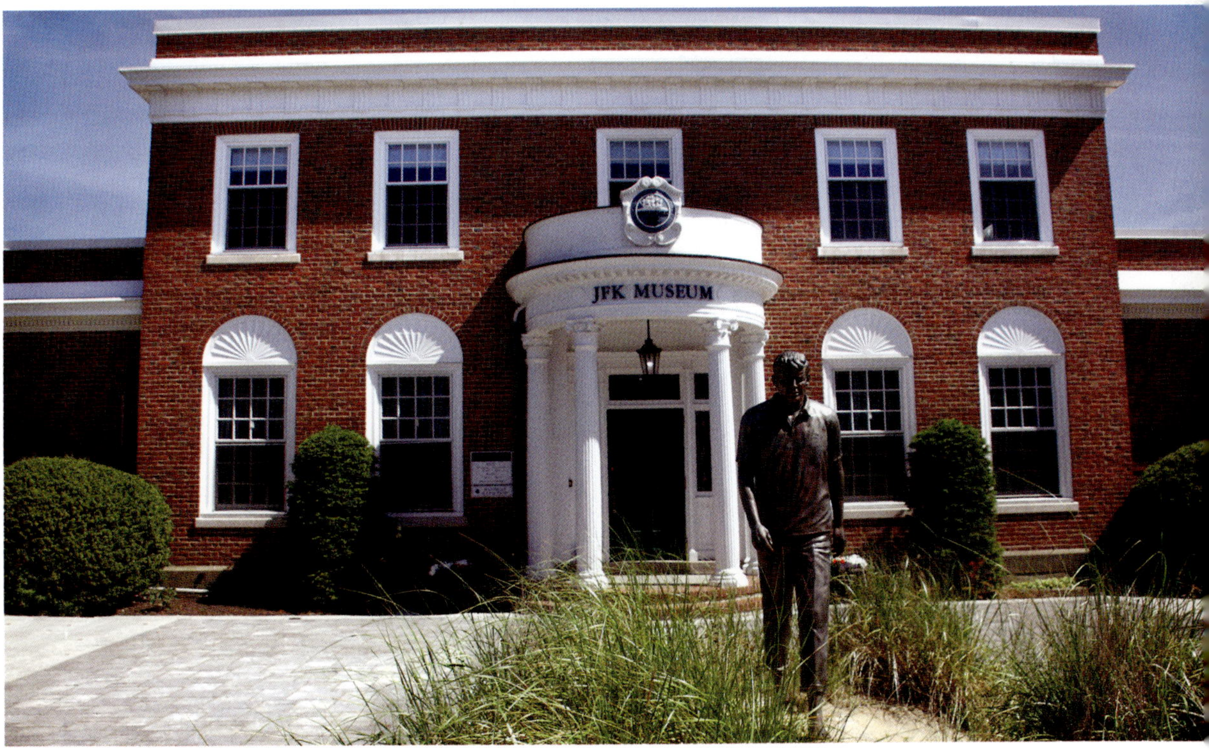

A statue of President John F. Kennedy in front of the JFK Hyannis Museum. The museum has been open since 1992.

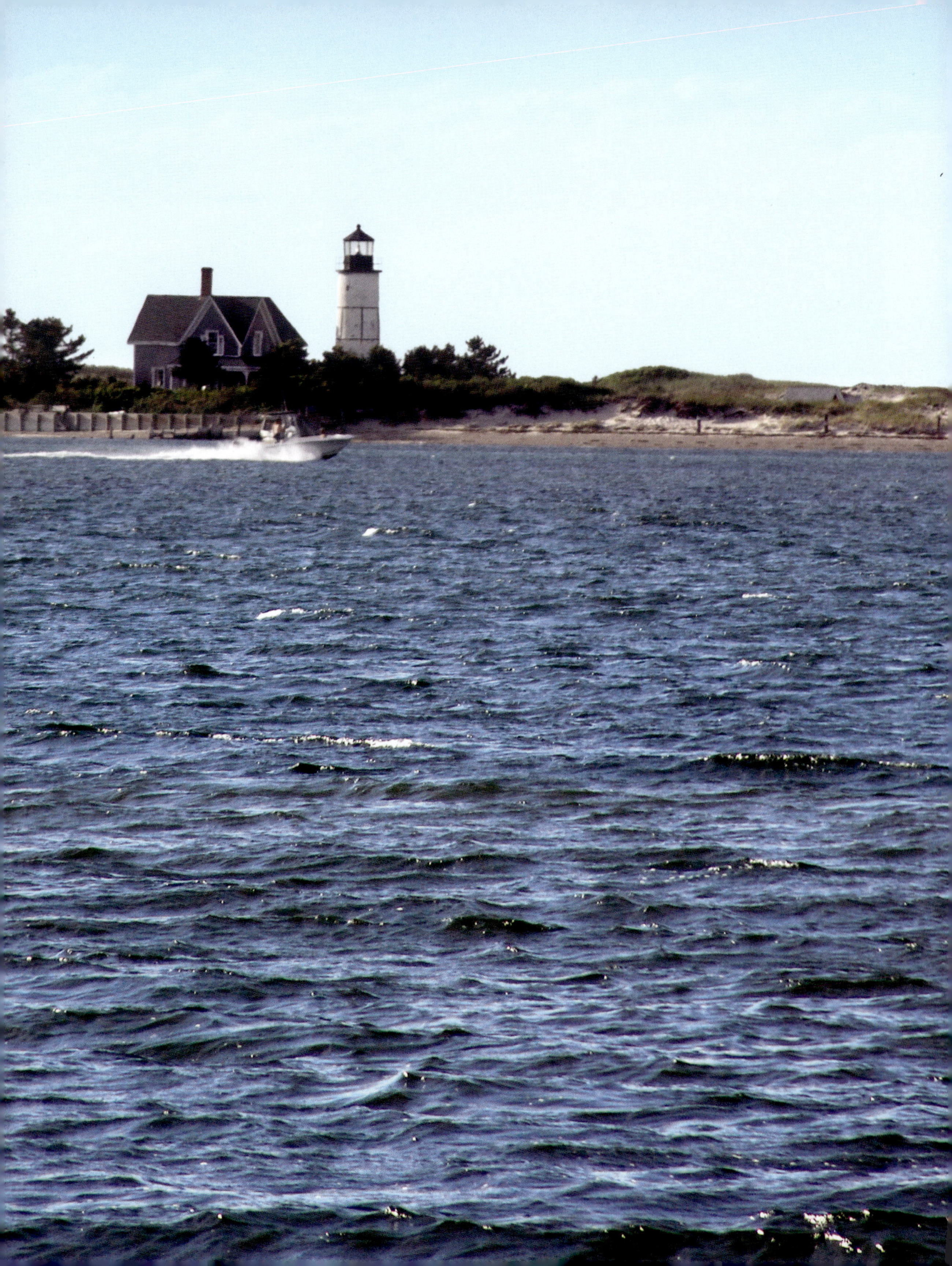

Barnstable

A view from across the bay of Sandy Neck Light, near the entrance to Barnstable Harbor. The current lighthouse tower was built in 1857. Barnstable has several villages, and the highest population on Cape Cod. It was settled in 1638.

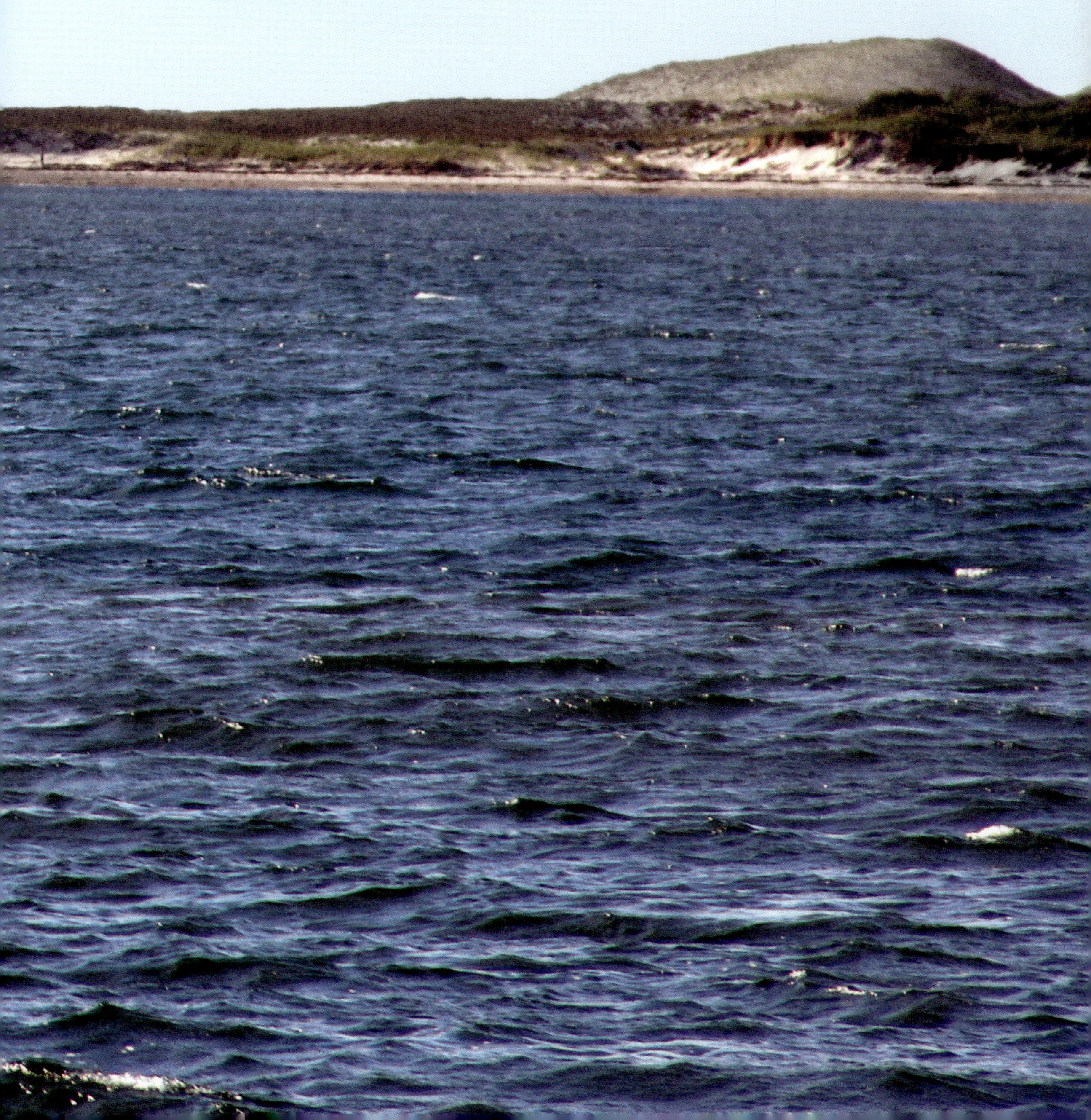

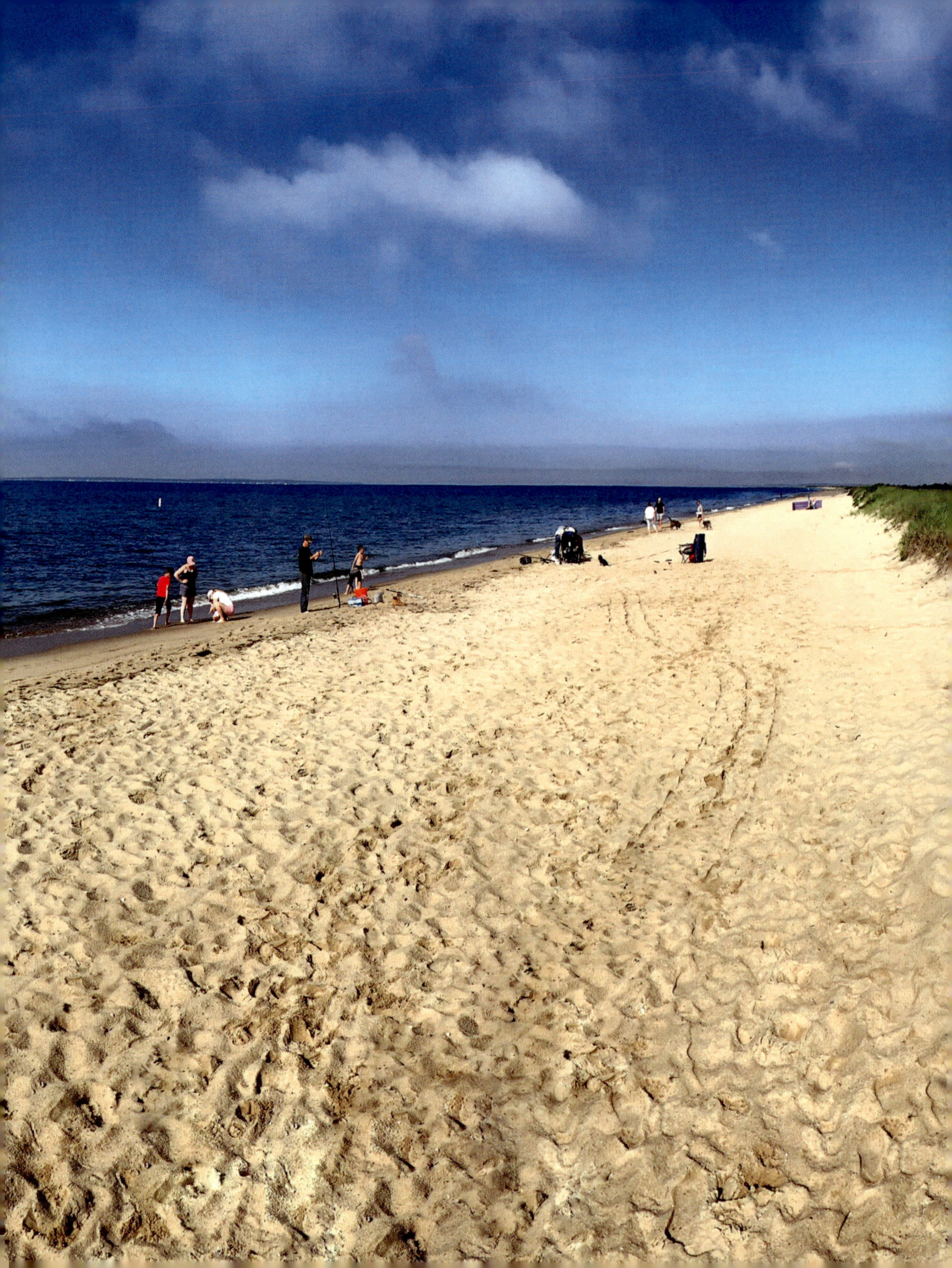

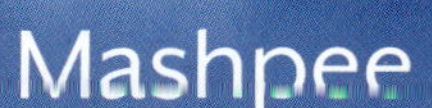

Mashpee

The inviting entrance to South Cape Beach in Mashpee. It's surrounded by beautiful marshes, has fine white sand, and a view of Nantucket Sound.

Mashpee is home to the headquarters of the Wampanoag Tribe. Indigenous Peoples pre-dated the English settlers by more than 10,000 years. The English settled Mashpee in 1660.

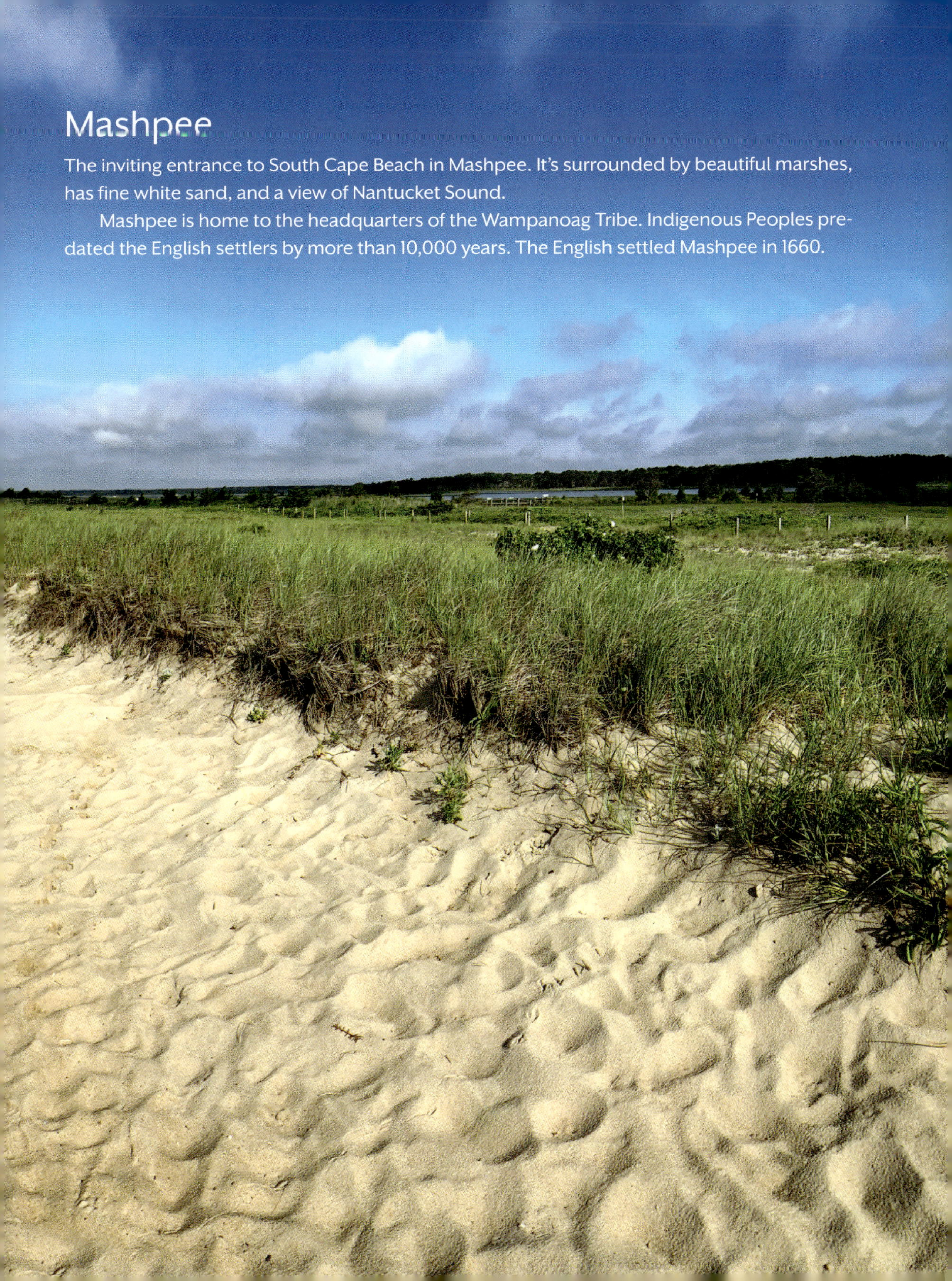

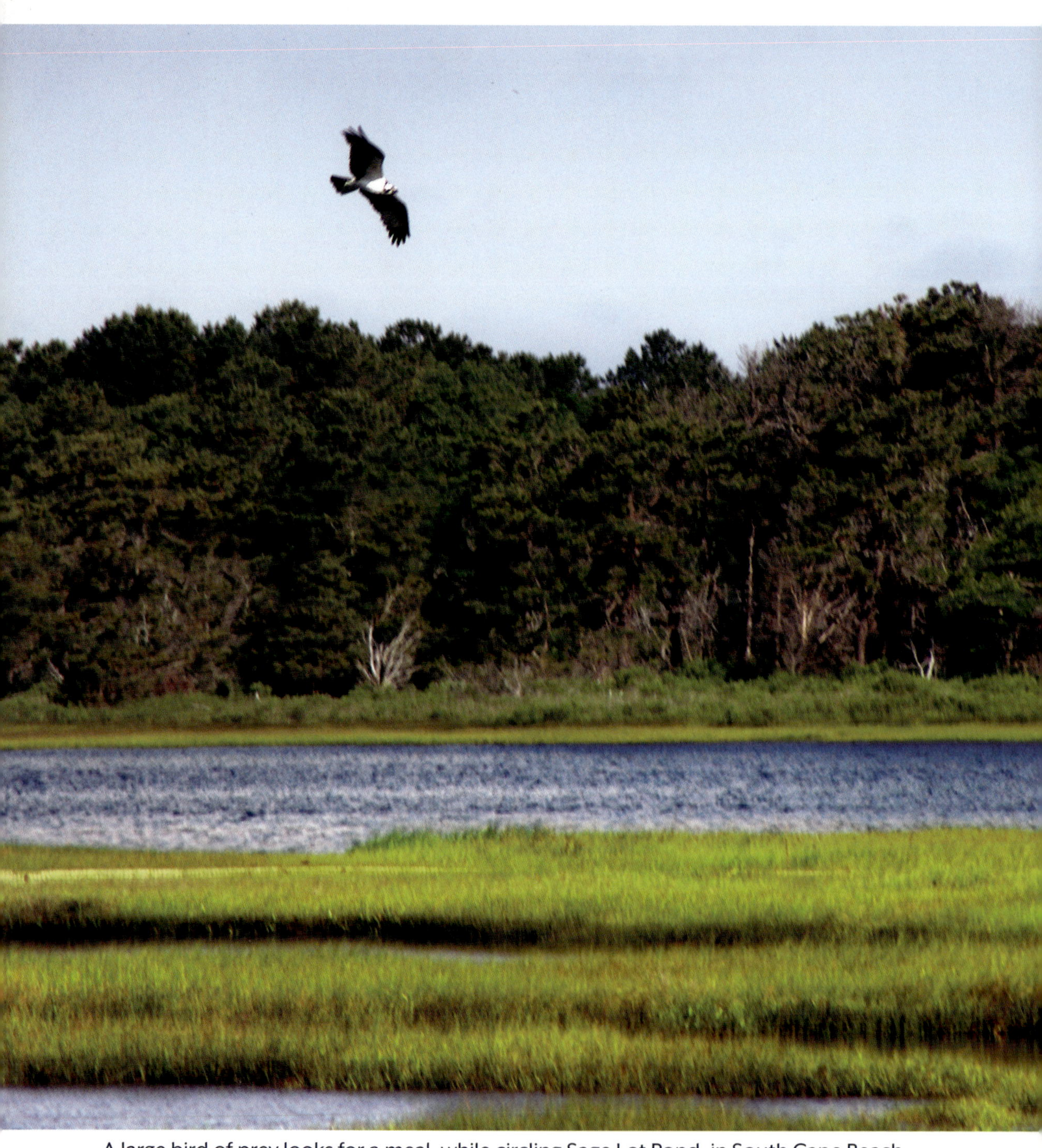

A large bird of prey looks for a meal, while circling Sage Lot Pond, in South Cape Beach State Park.

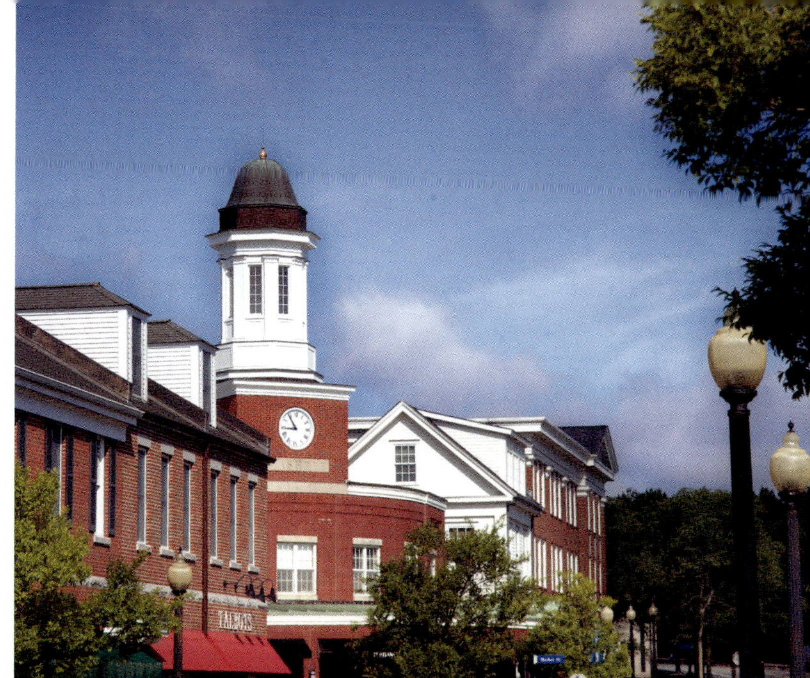

Mashpee Commons is a combination residential and business area, with over a hundred stores, and almost as many residences.

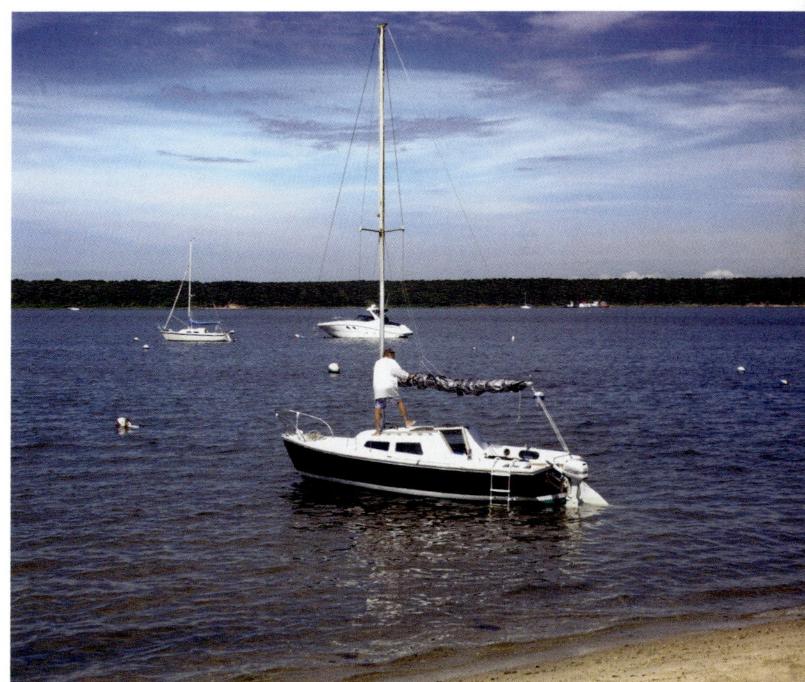

A sailor starts prepping for a day on the water at Seconsett Island in Mashpee.

Falmouth

Nobska Point Light is one of the most iconic and recognizable landmarks on Cape Cod. Its beacon beams out from high on a bluff overlooking the sea, in the village of Woods Hole in Falmouth. The current lighthouse tower was built in 1876, and stands at 40 feet tall.

The area is known for its beaches, the lighthouse, NOAA's Science Aquarium, Woods Hole Oceanographic Institution, ferry service to Martha's Vineyard, and a charming village with restaurants and shops. Falmouth was settled in 1660.

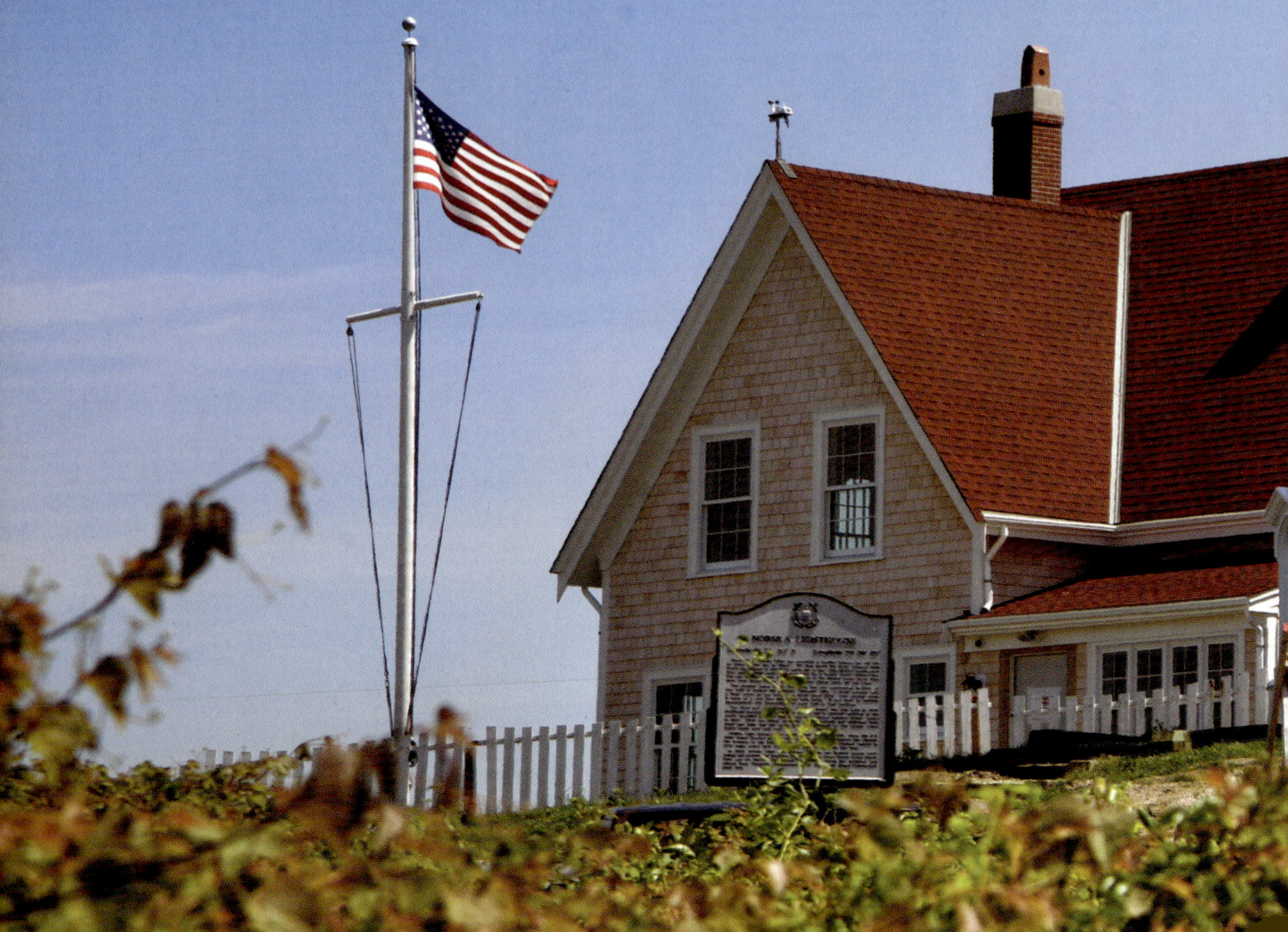

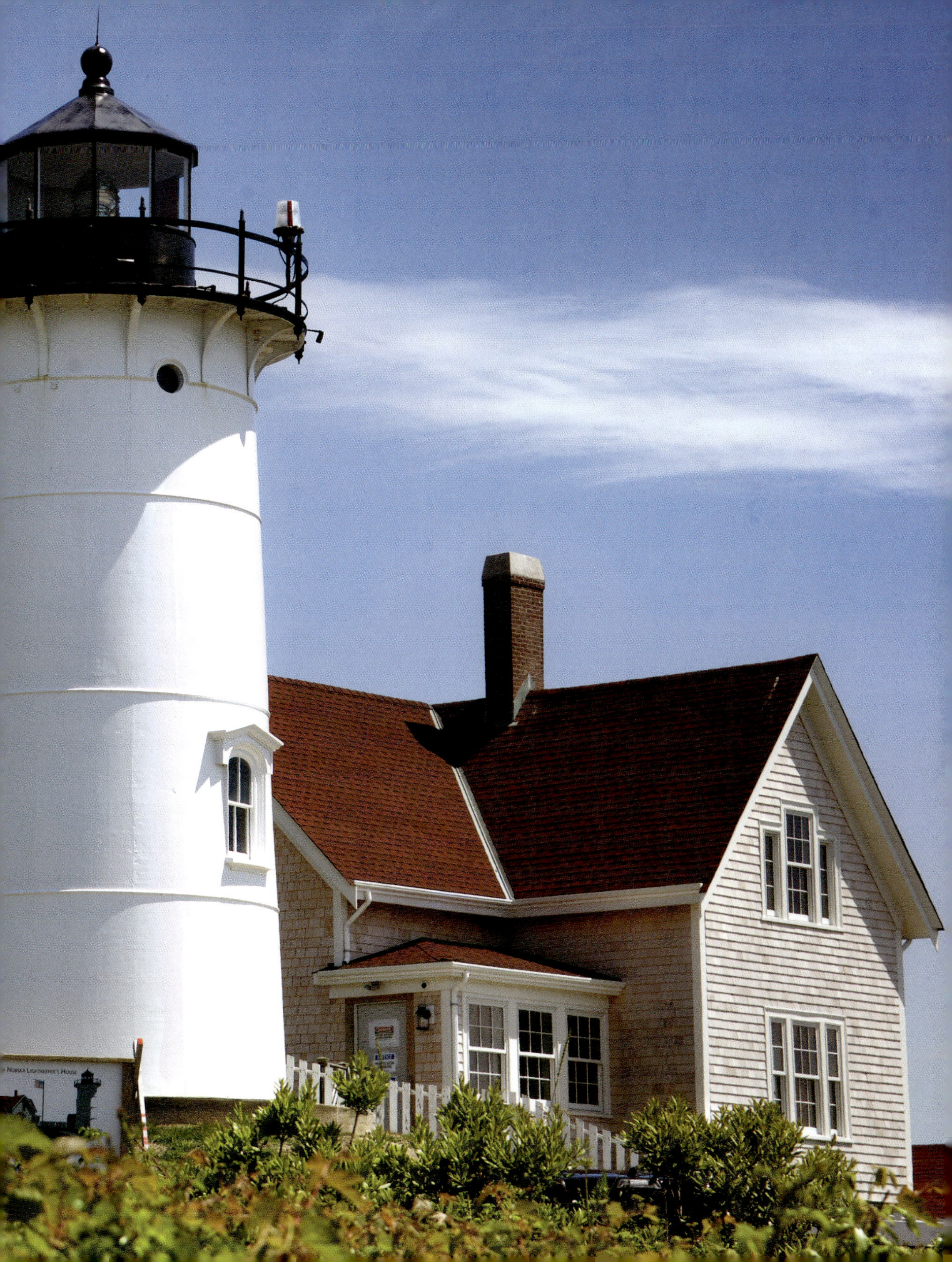
NOBSKA LIGHTKEEPER'S HOUSE

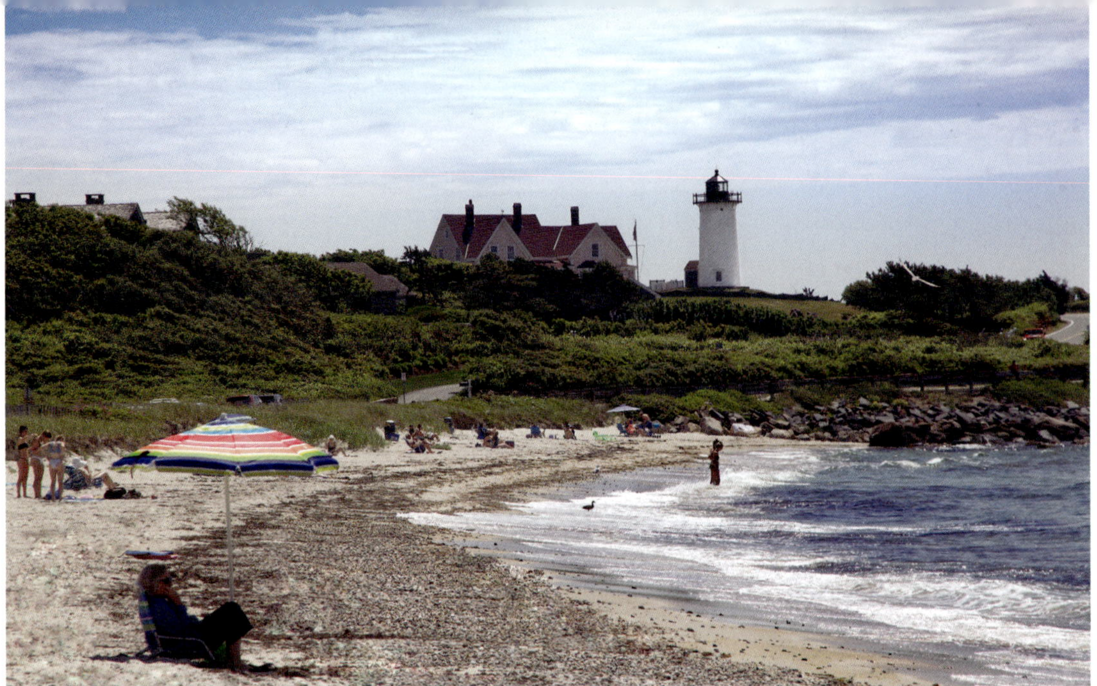

Folks enjoying Nobska Beach, which lies on the waters of Vineyard Sound, and has a stellar view of Nobska Point Light.

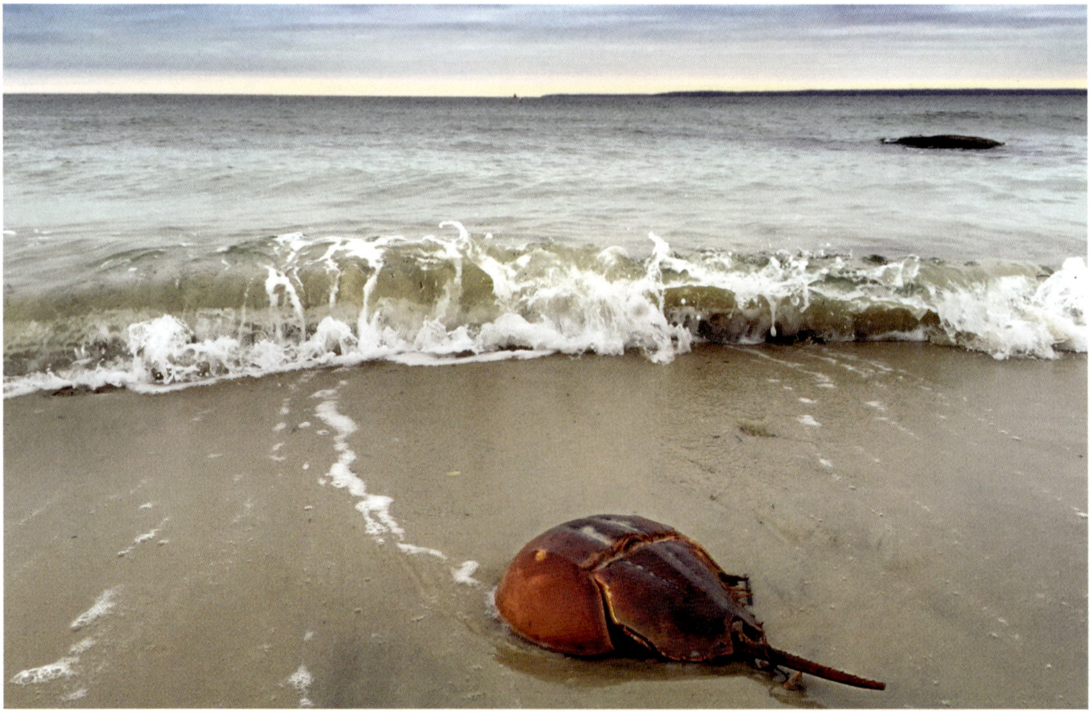

Surf's up for this horseshoe crab who's about to re-enter the sea. I've seen two of them in the wild, and been fortunate to have a camera handy both times.

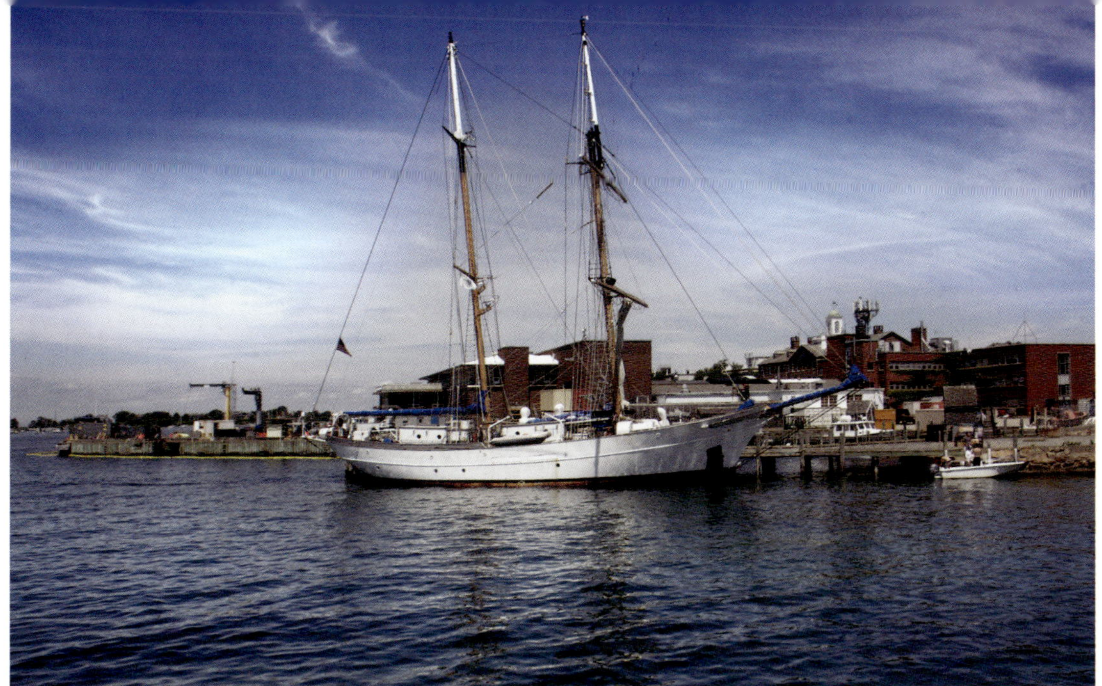

The SSV *Corwith Cramer* tied to a pier at Great Harbor in Woods Hole. She's a tall ship operated by the Sea Education Association, Woods Hole, Massachusetts.

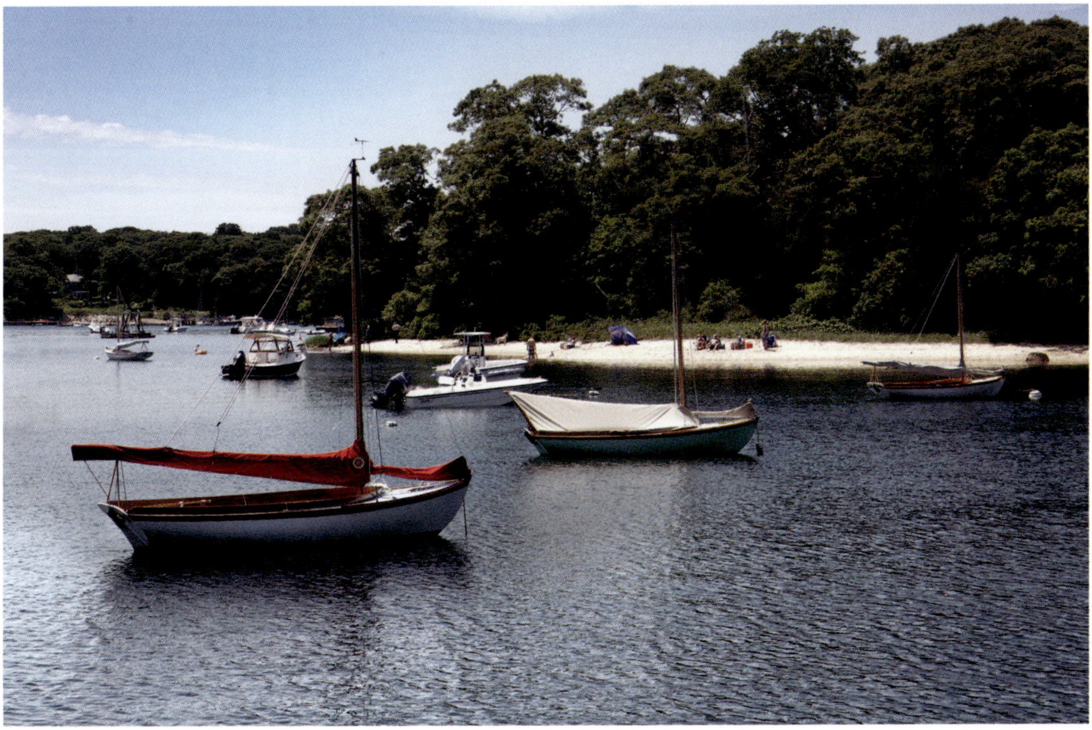

Boats tied up in Quissett Harbor, with the Knob in the background.

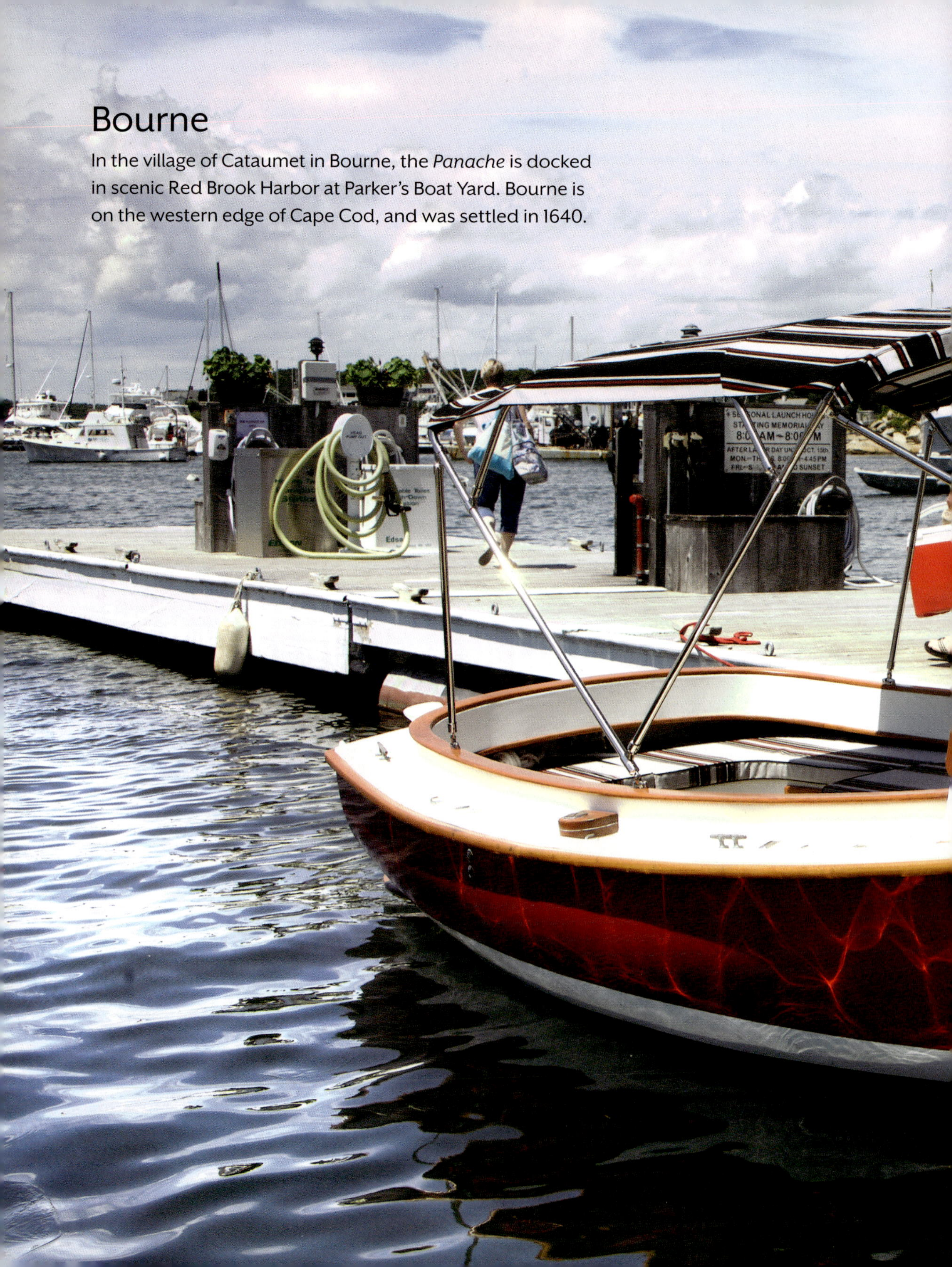

Bourne

In the village of Cataumet in Bourne, the *Panache* is docked in scenic Red Brook Harbor at Parker's Boat Yard. Bourne is on the western edge of Cape Cod, and was settled in 1640.

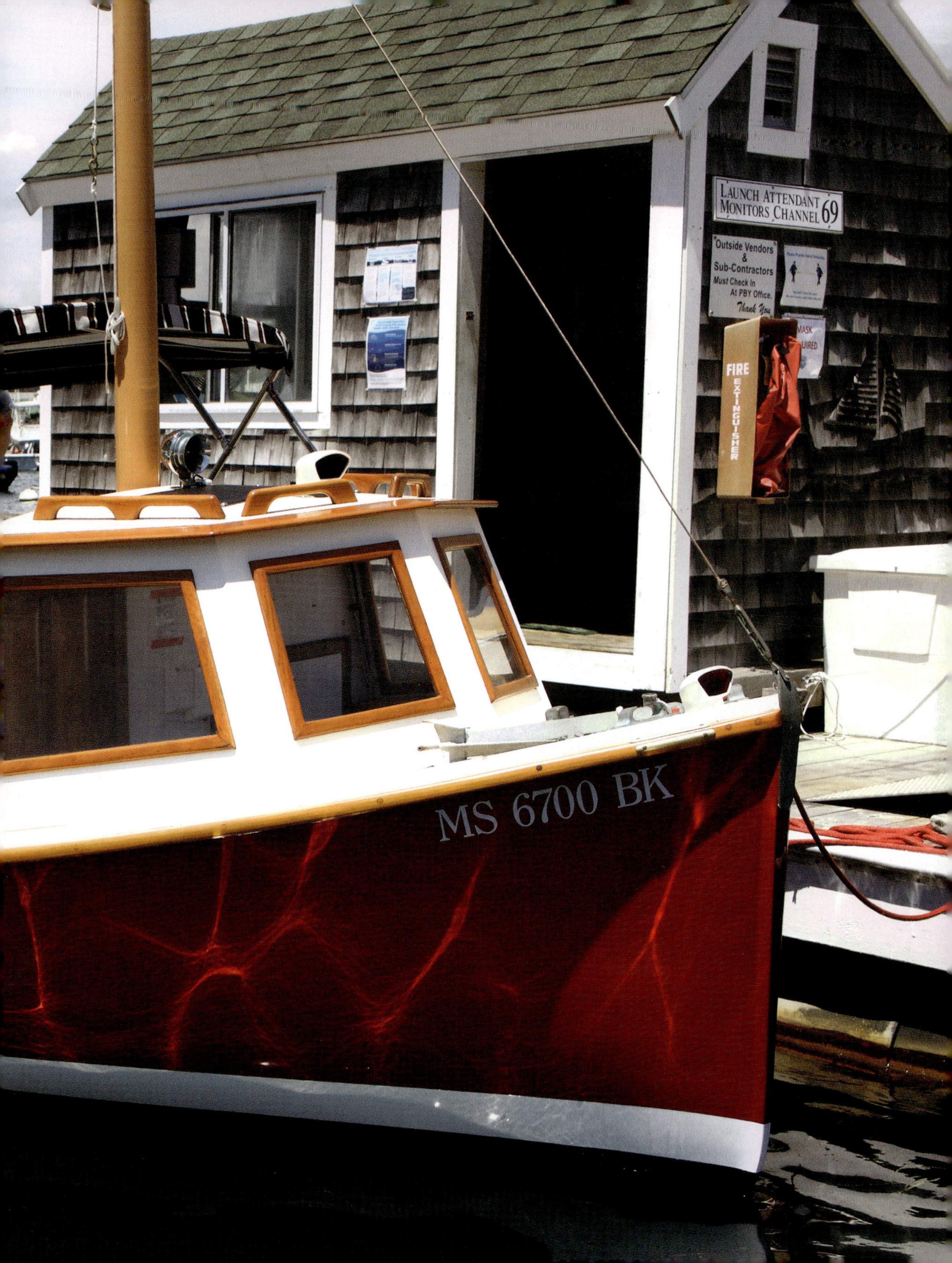

LAUNCH ATTENDANT
MONITORS CHANNEL 69
Outside Vendors
&
Sub-Contractors
Must Check In
At PBY Office.
Thank You
FIRE EXTINGUISHER
MS 6700 BK

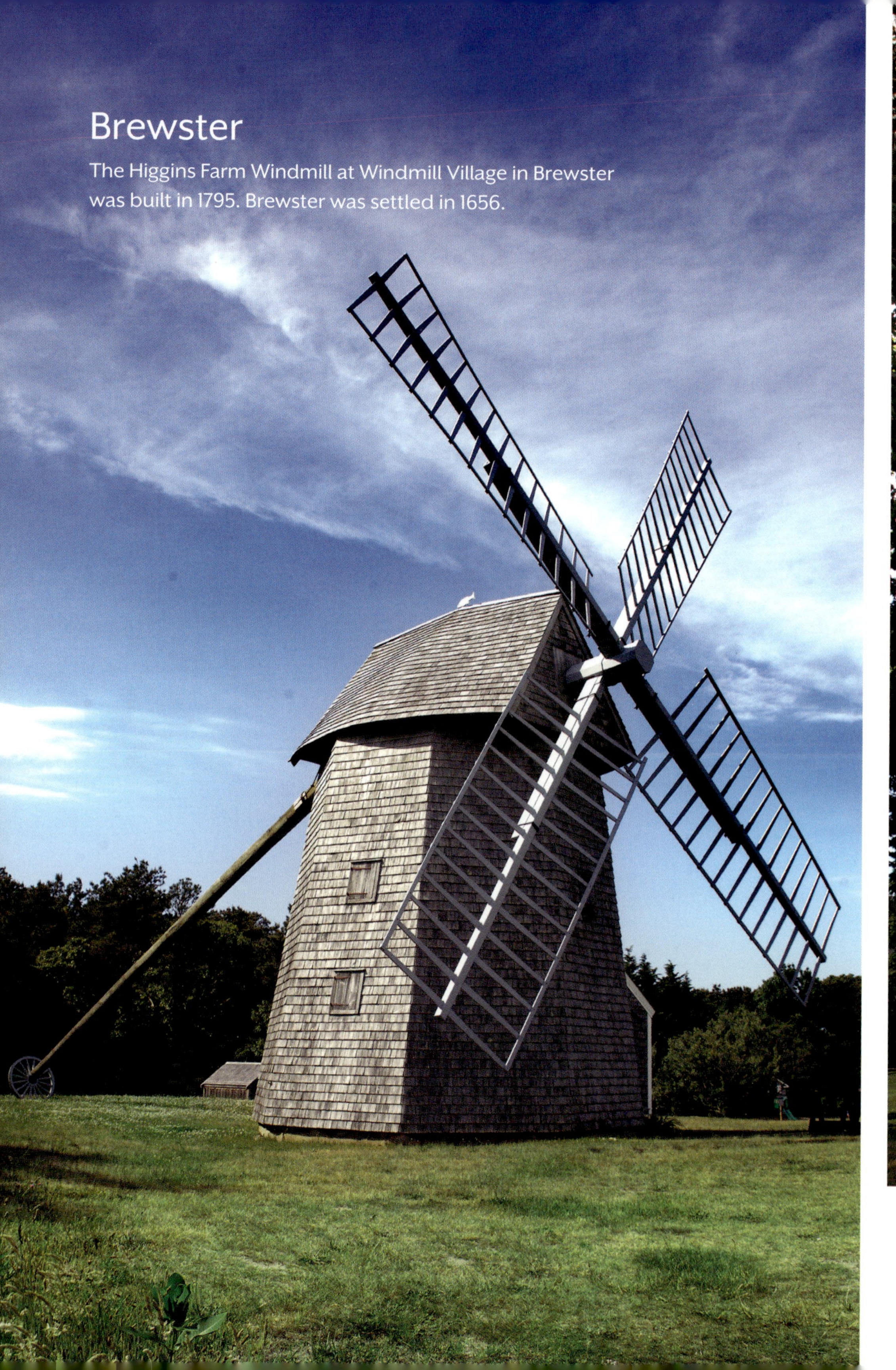

Brewster

The Higgins Farm Windmill at Windmill Village in Brewster was built in 1795. Brewster was settled in 1656.

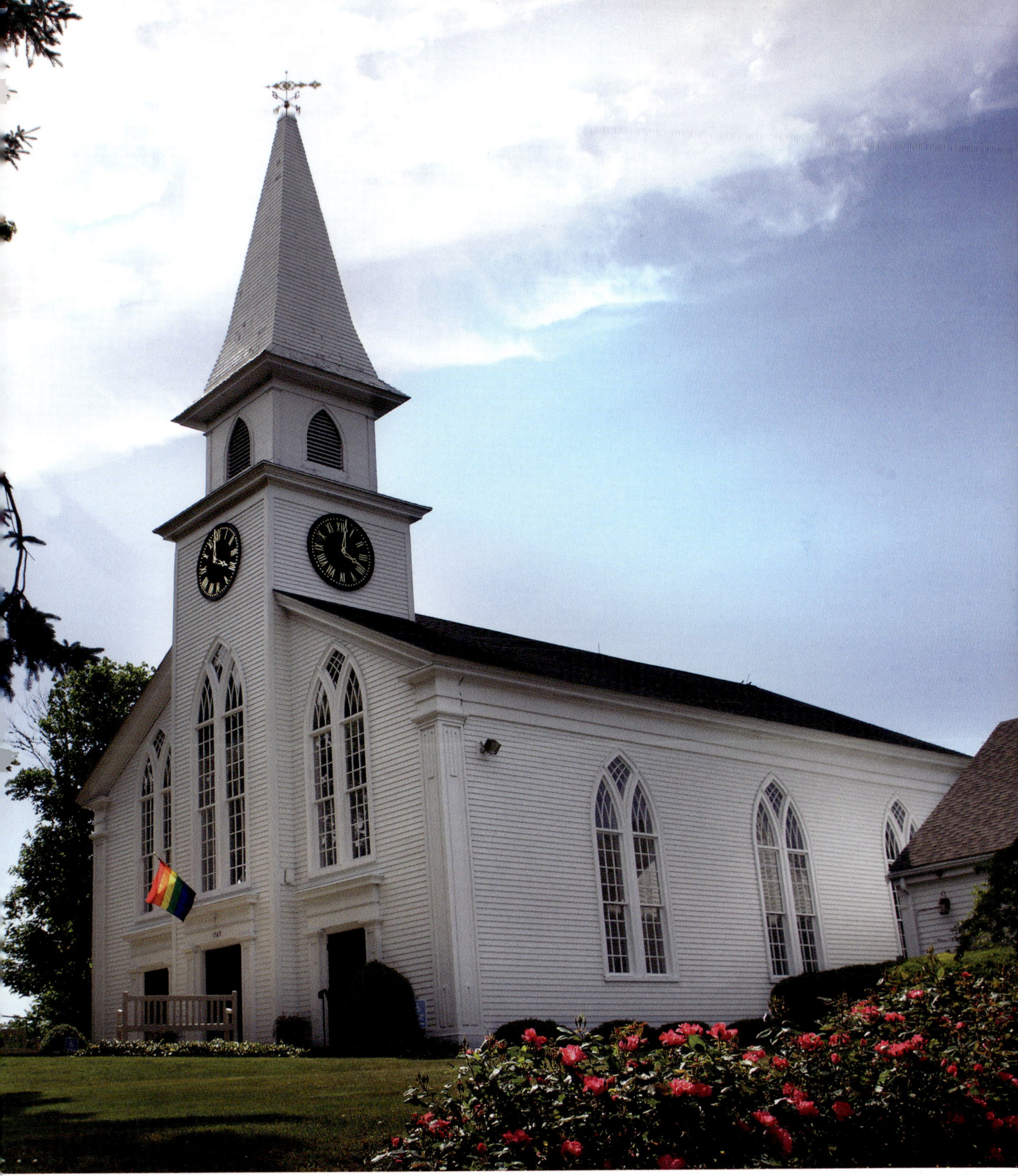

Early summer flowers blooming on a hedge in front of the First Parish, on Main Street in Brewster. The building was constructed in 1834.

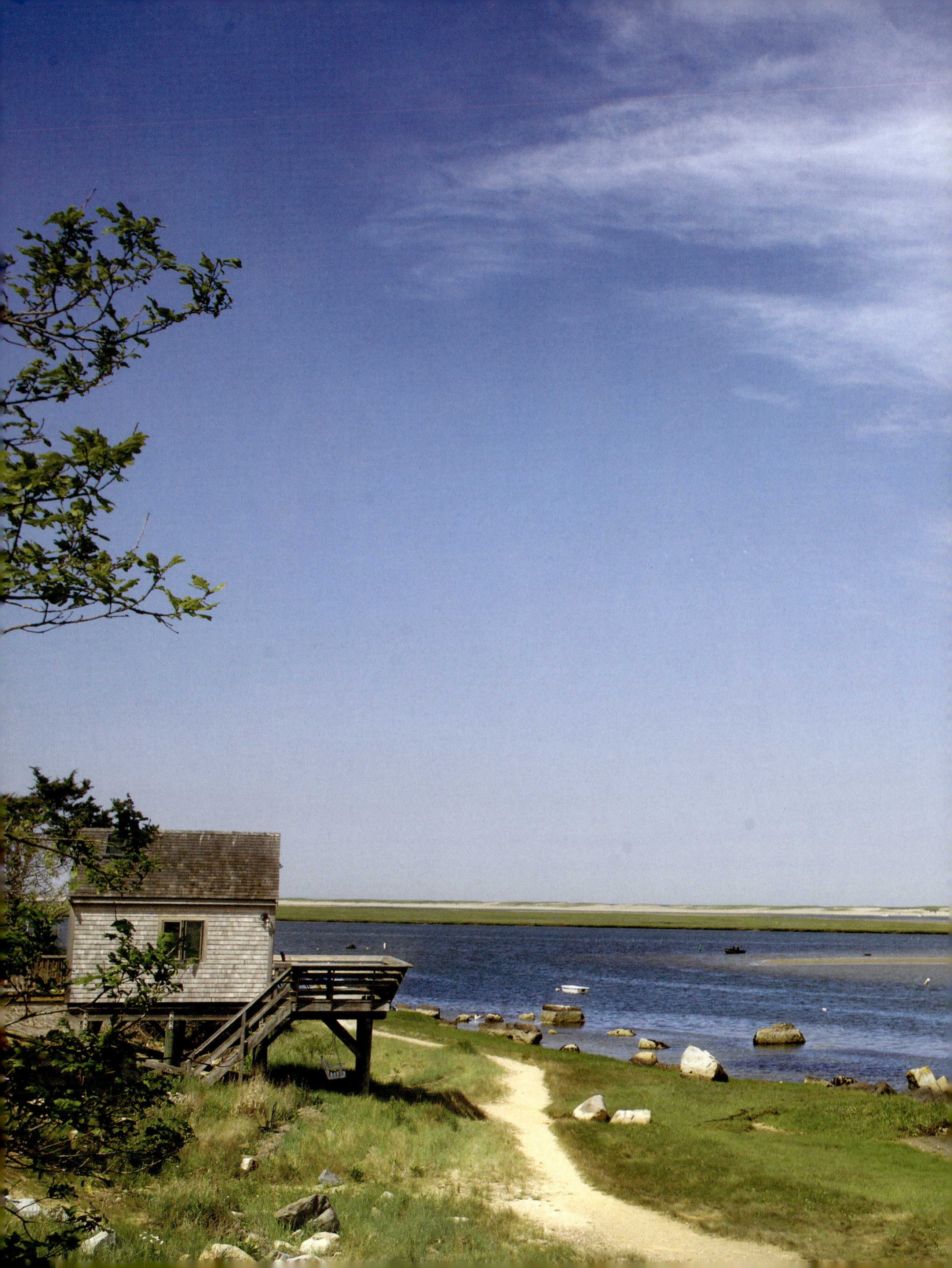

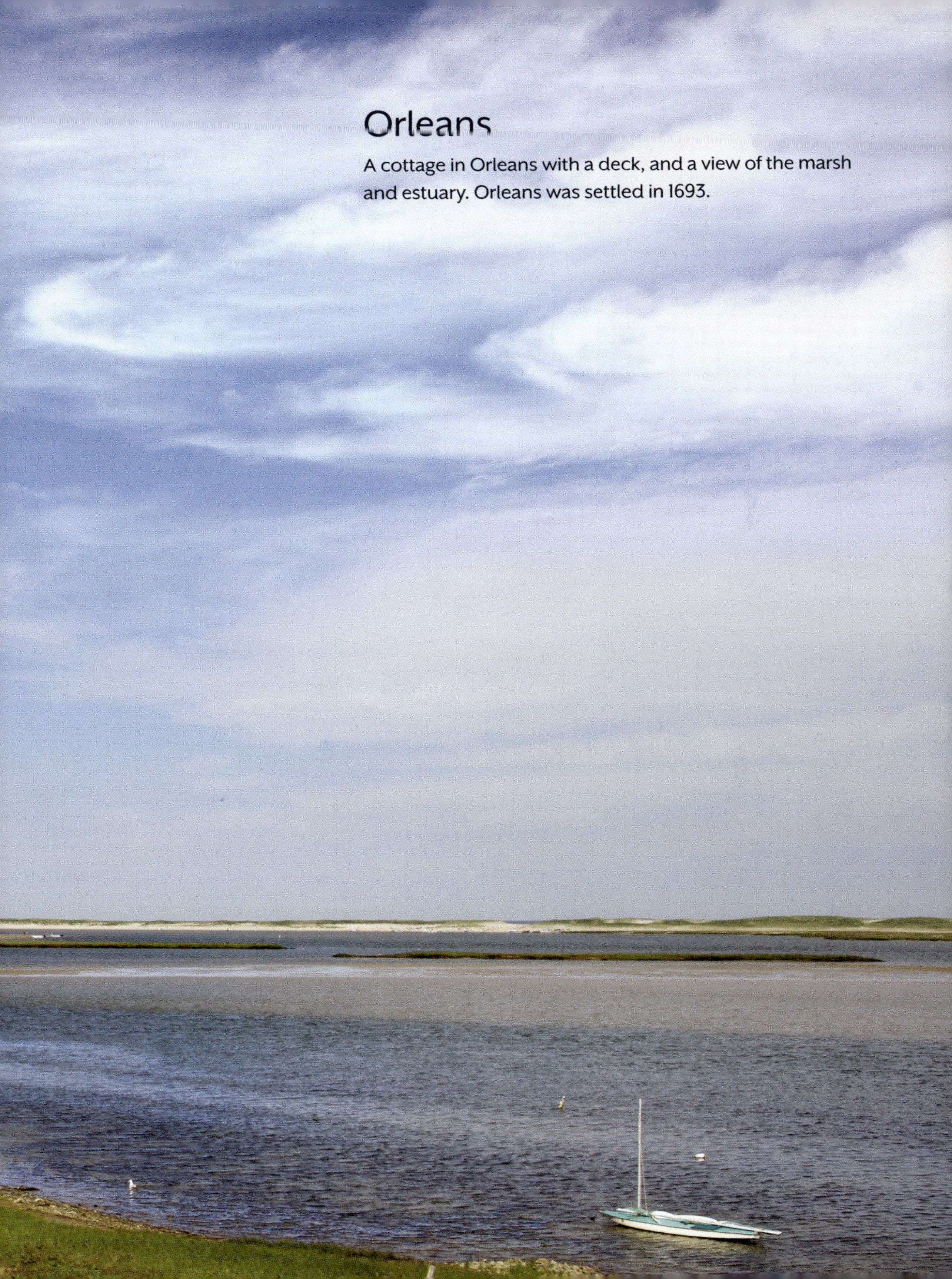

Orleans

A cottage in Orleans with a deck, and a view of the marsh and estuary. Orleans was settled in 1693.

Eastham

Nauset Beach Light, built in 1877, is a New England classic listed on the National Register of Historic Places. Eastham was settled in 1644 and played an important role amongst the Pilgrims and indigenous Nauset people.

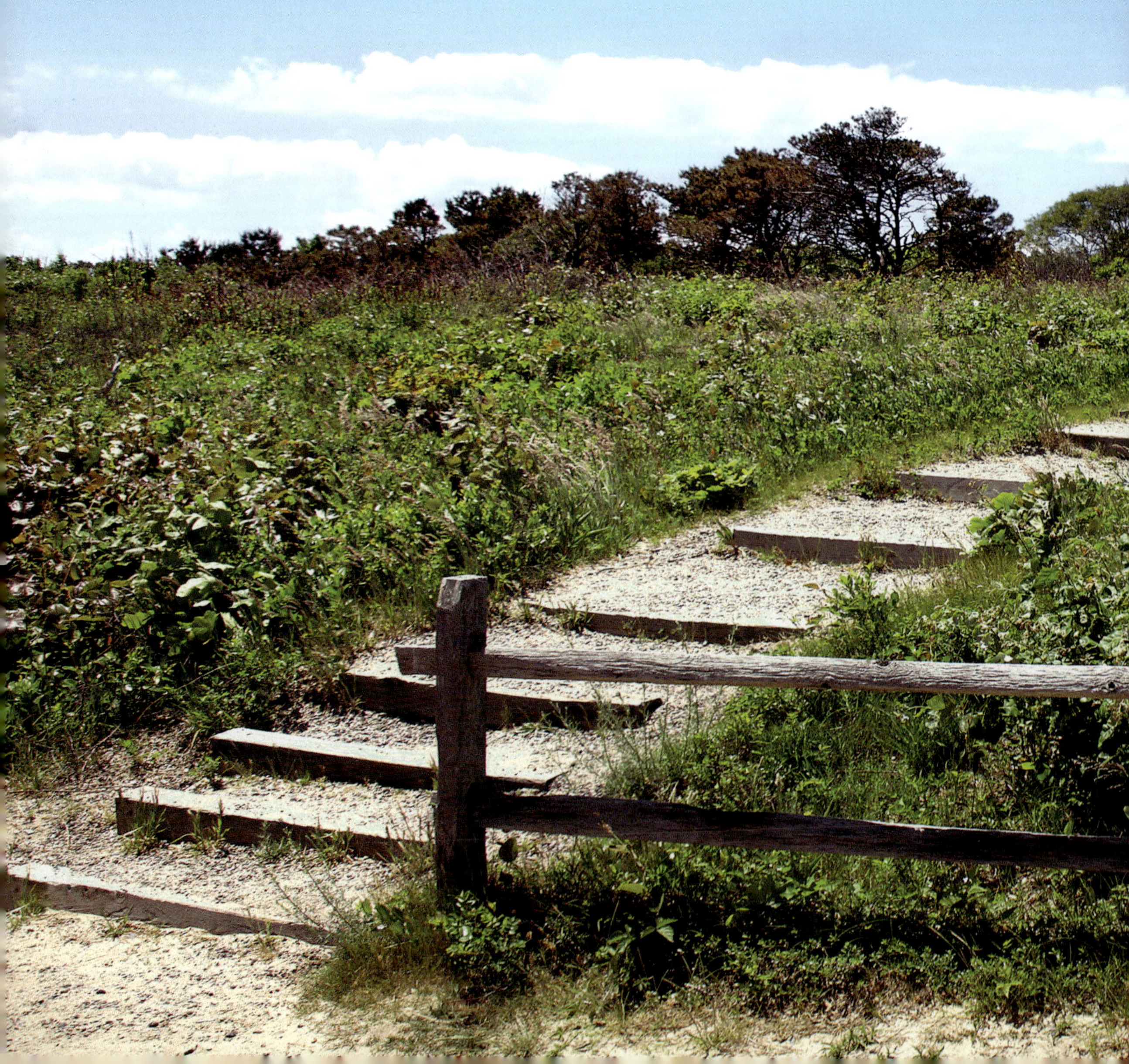

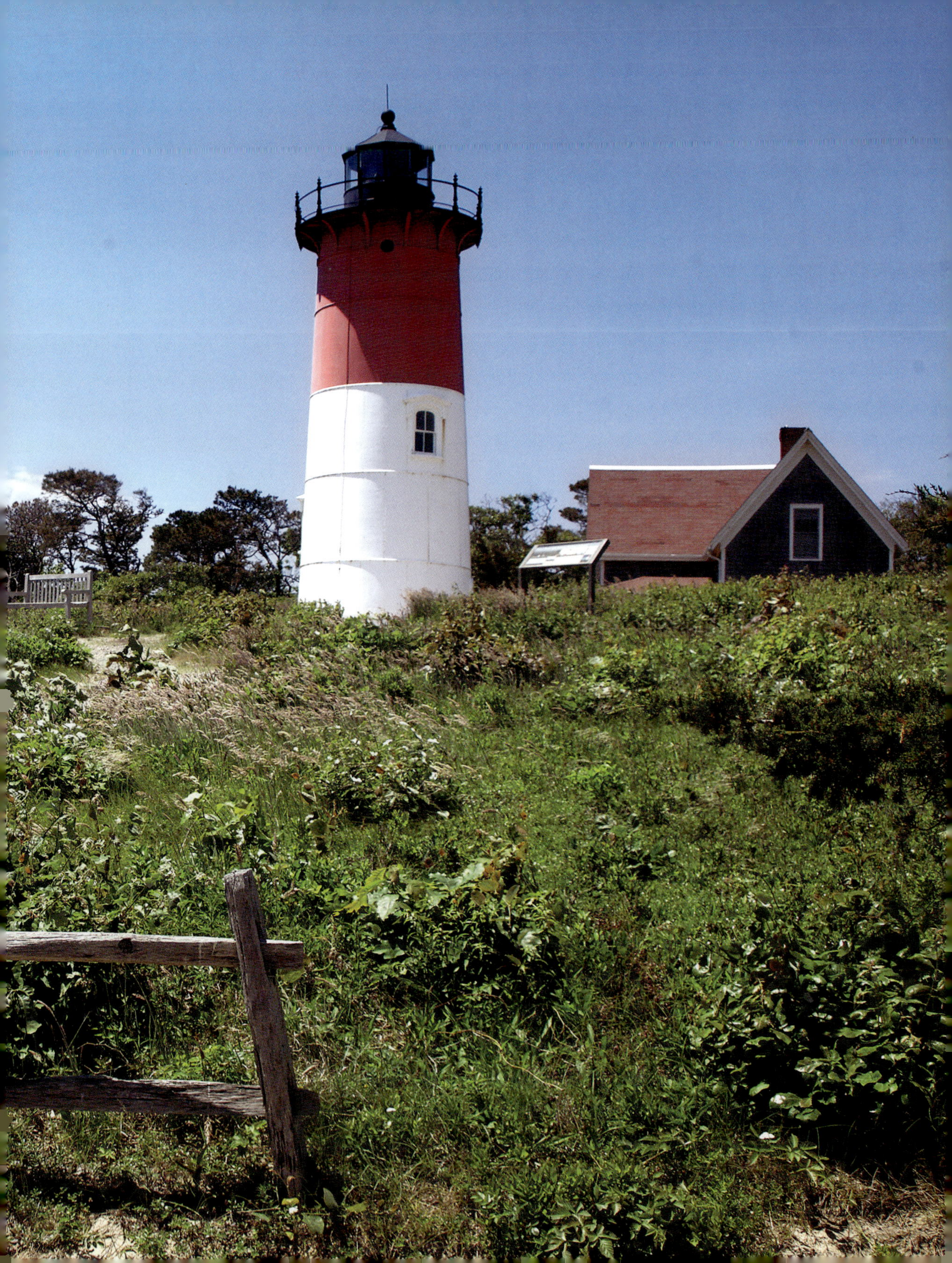

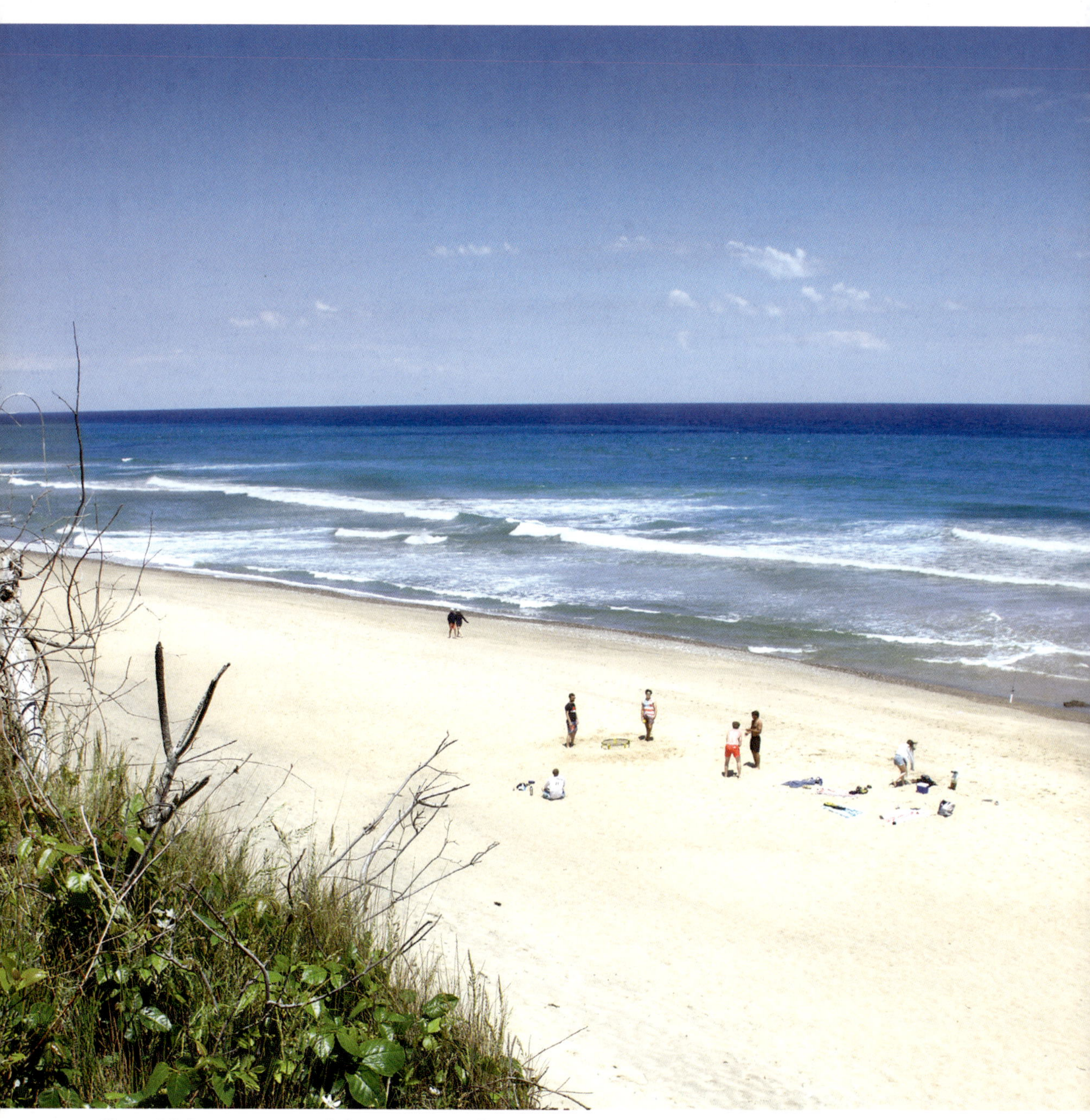

From high up on a sand dune, a view of pristine Nauset Beach, and a two-tone blue sea.

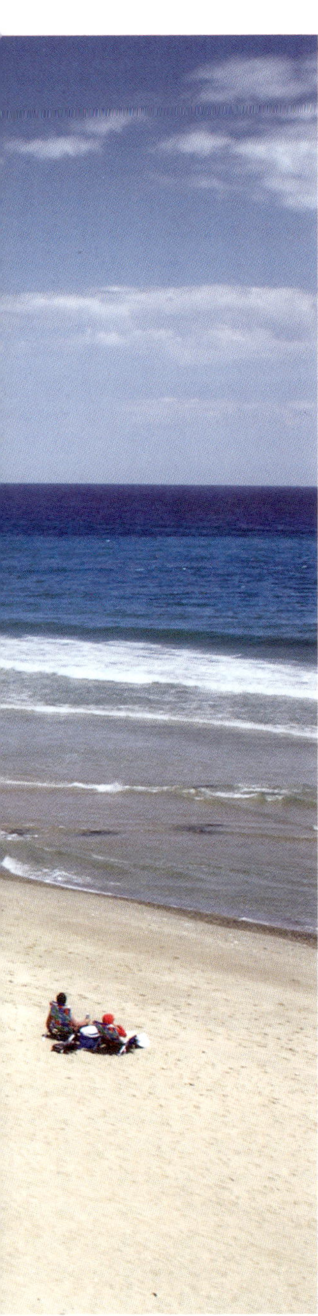

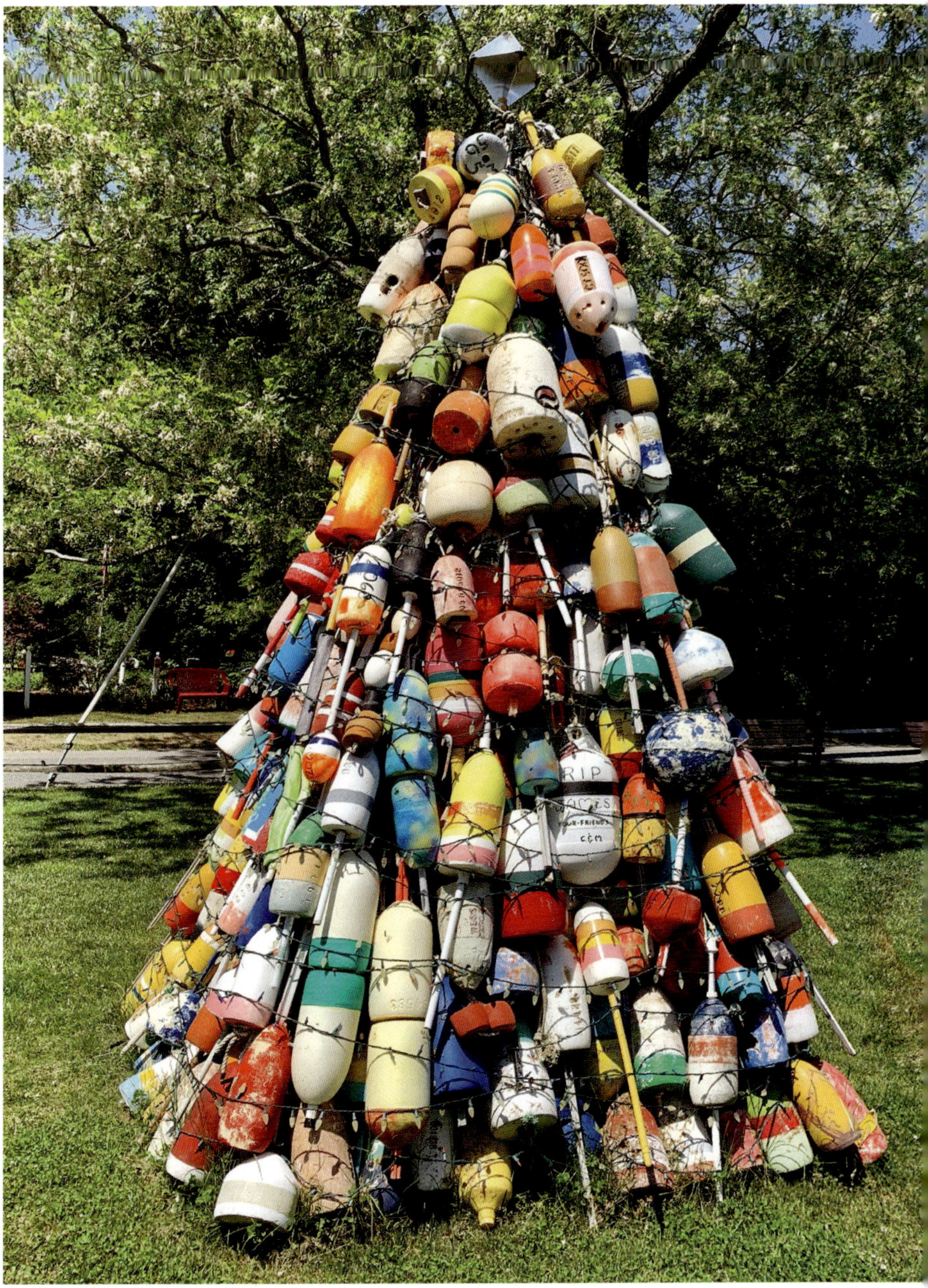

This memorial buoy tree pays tribute to James Filliman, a popular young local man who passed away. It's located in Windmill Park, right next to the Eastham Windmill.

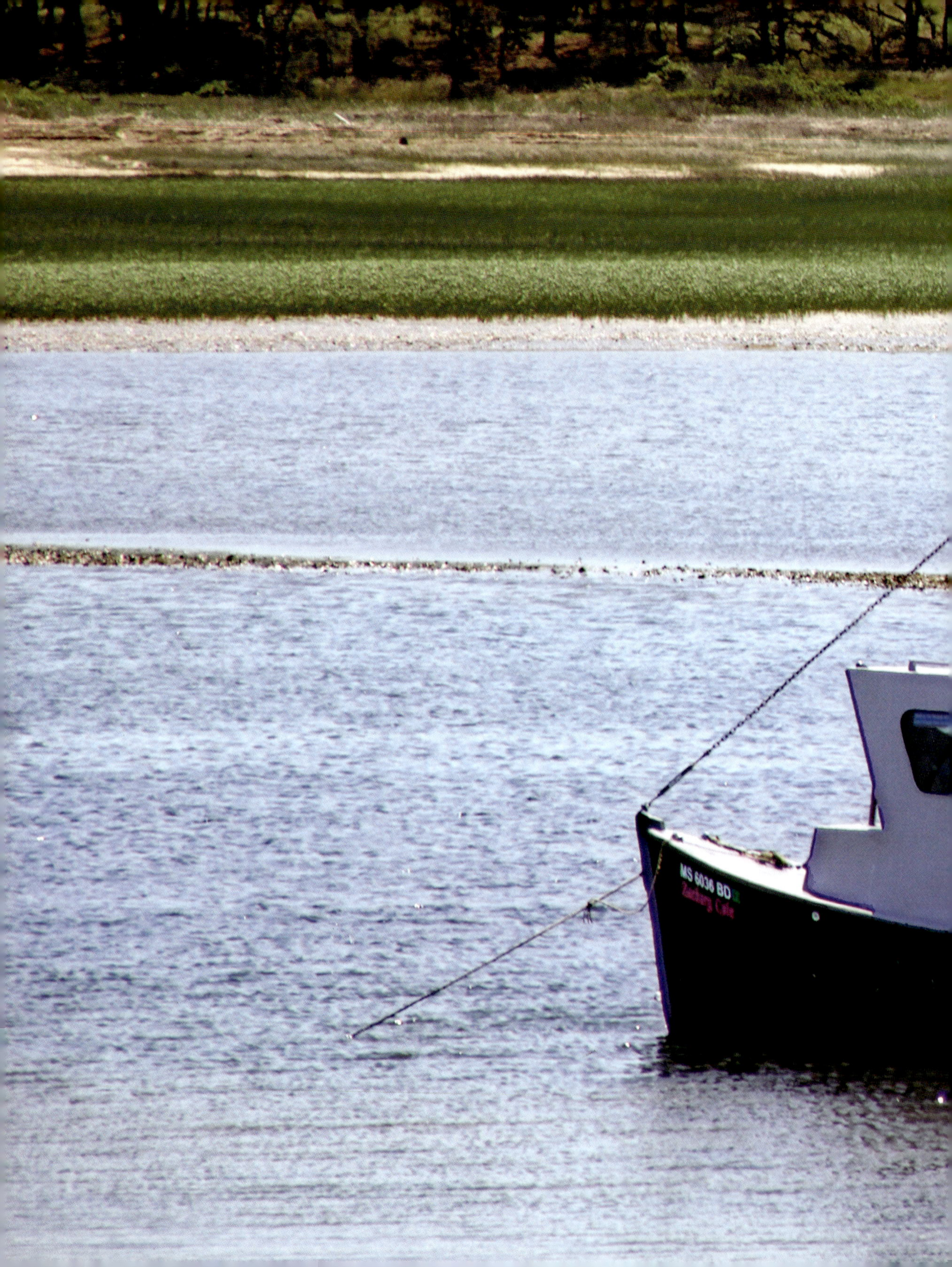

MS 6036 BD
Zachary Cole

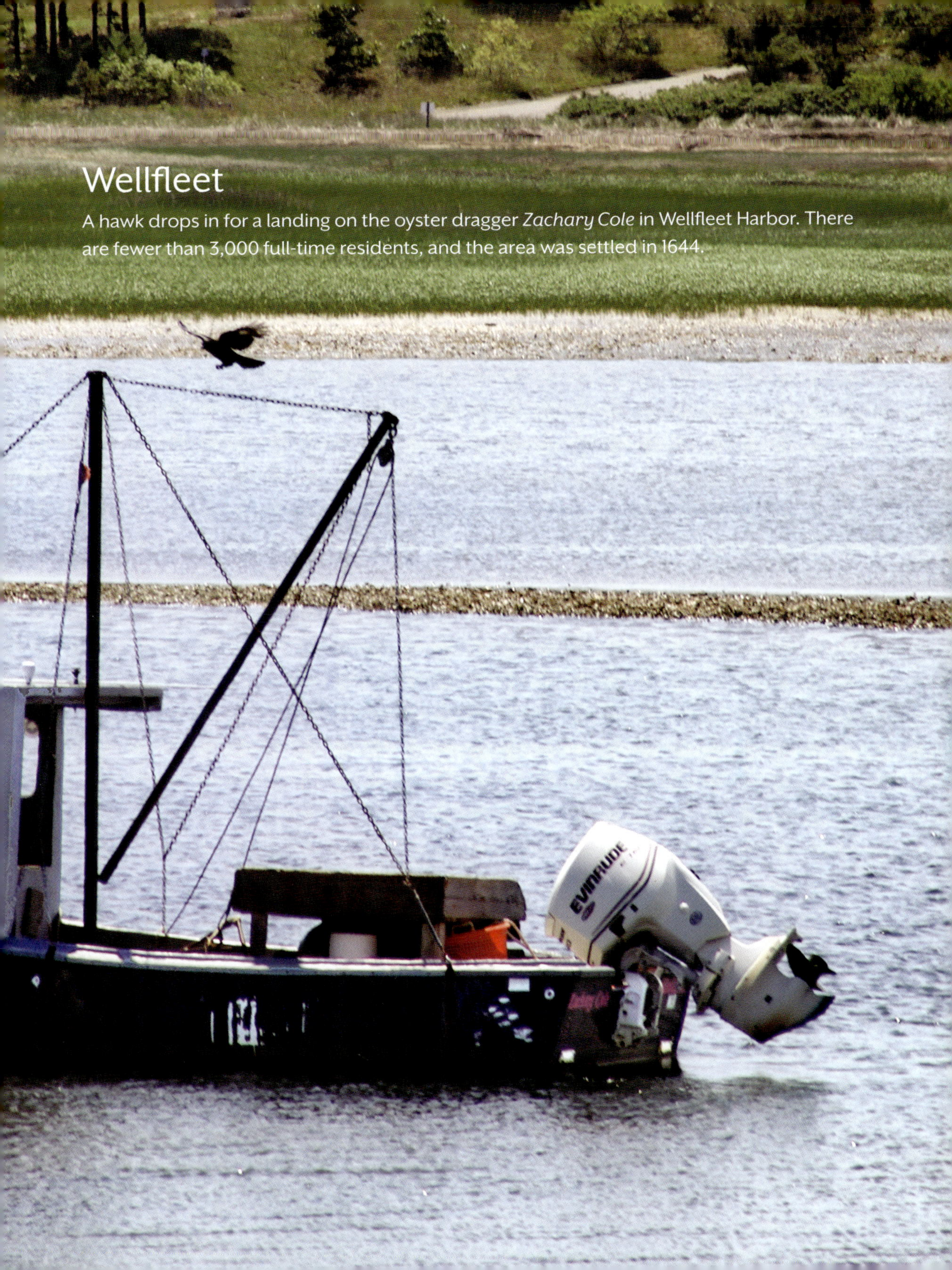

Wellfleet

A hawk drops in for a landing on the oyster dragger *Zachary Cole* in Wellfleet Harbor. There are fewer than 3,000 full-time residents, and the area was settled in 1644.

Boston

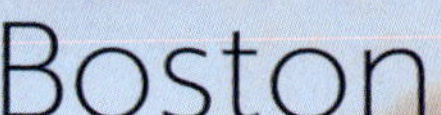

Boston's Back Bay and skyline at sunset. Boston is the capital city of Massachusetts, with a population of almost 700,000. If you include the Greater Boston area, the number swells to almost 5 million. Boston was settled in 1630.

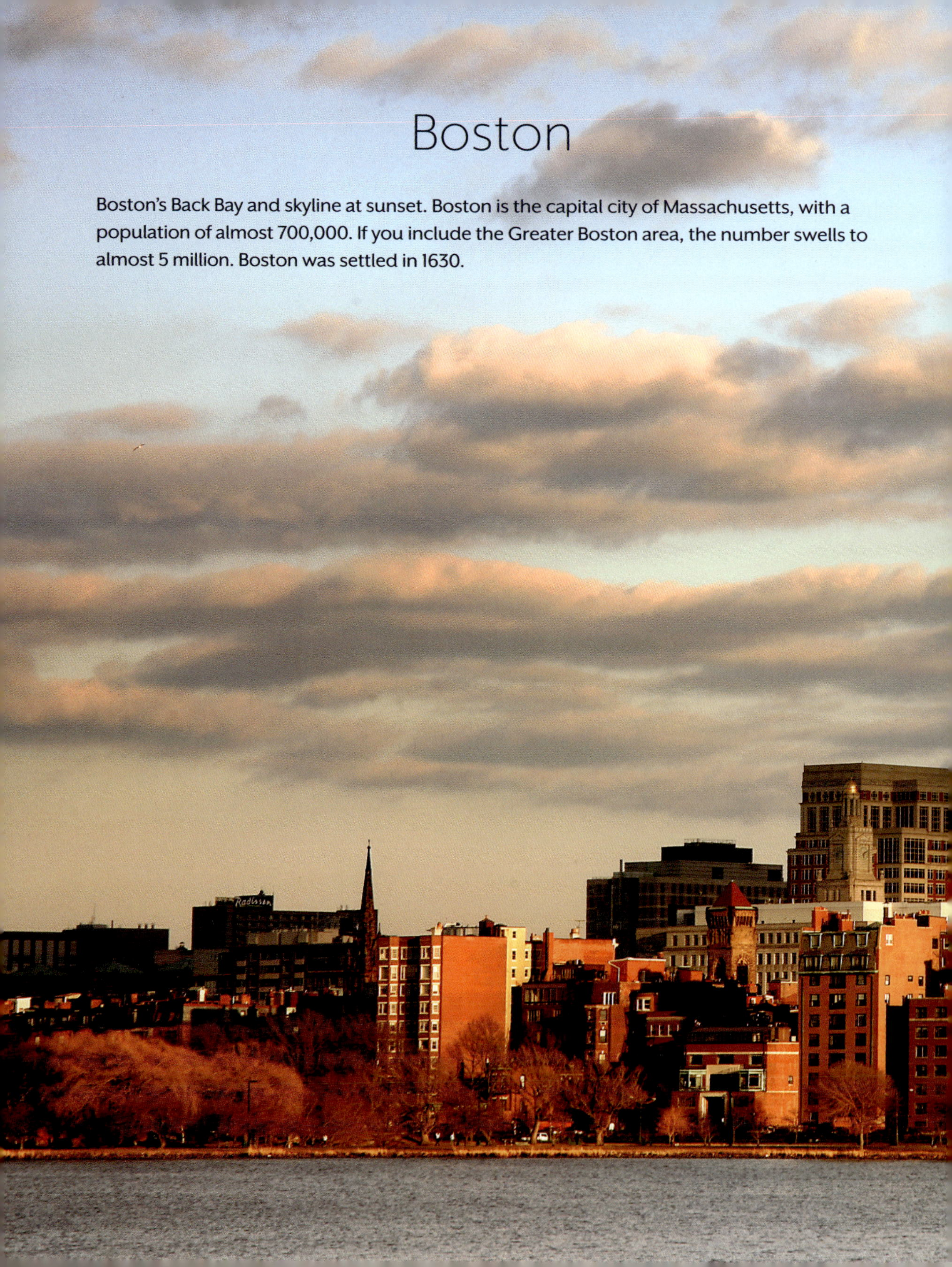

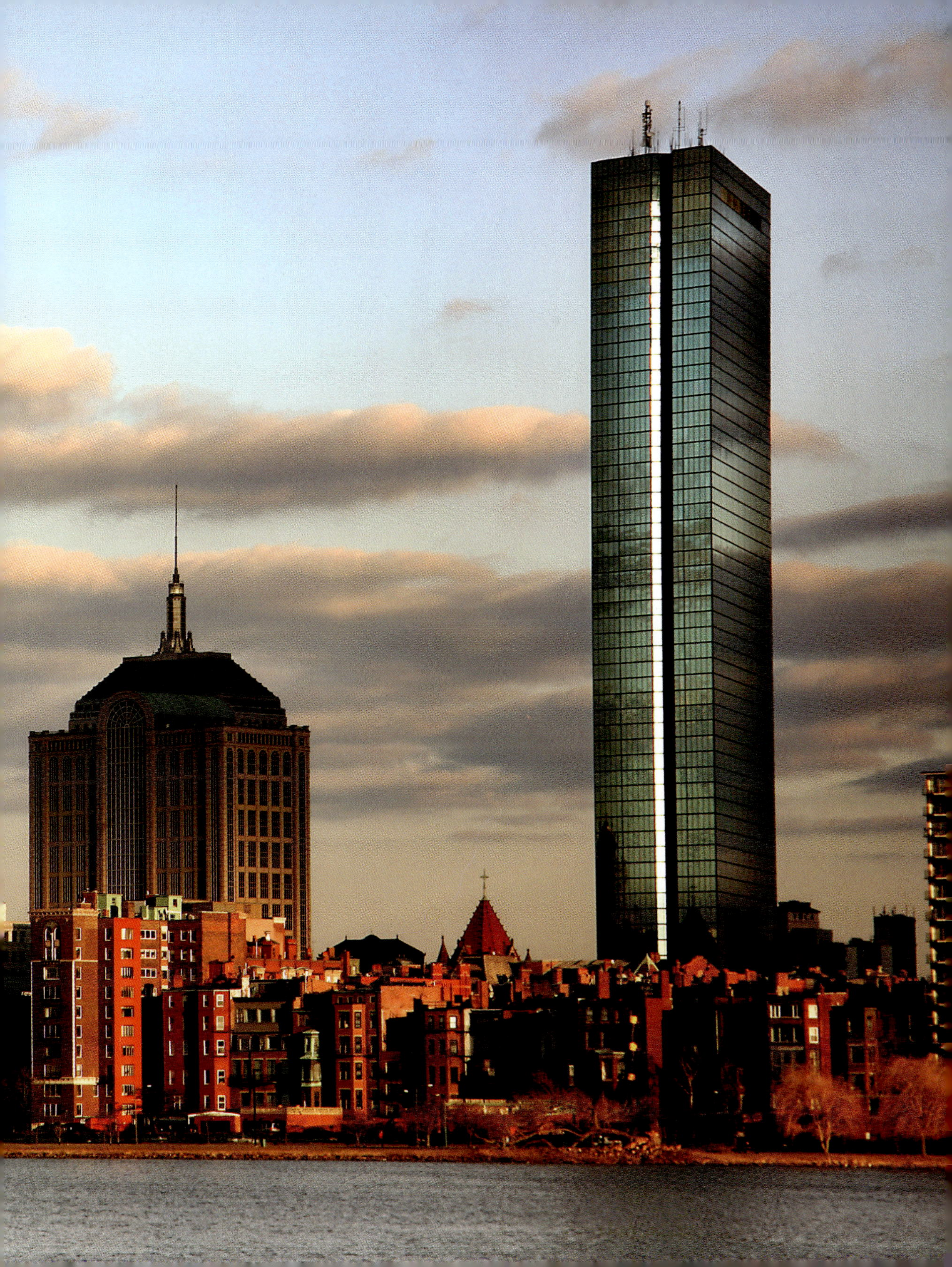

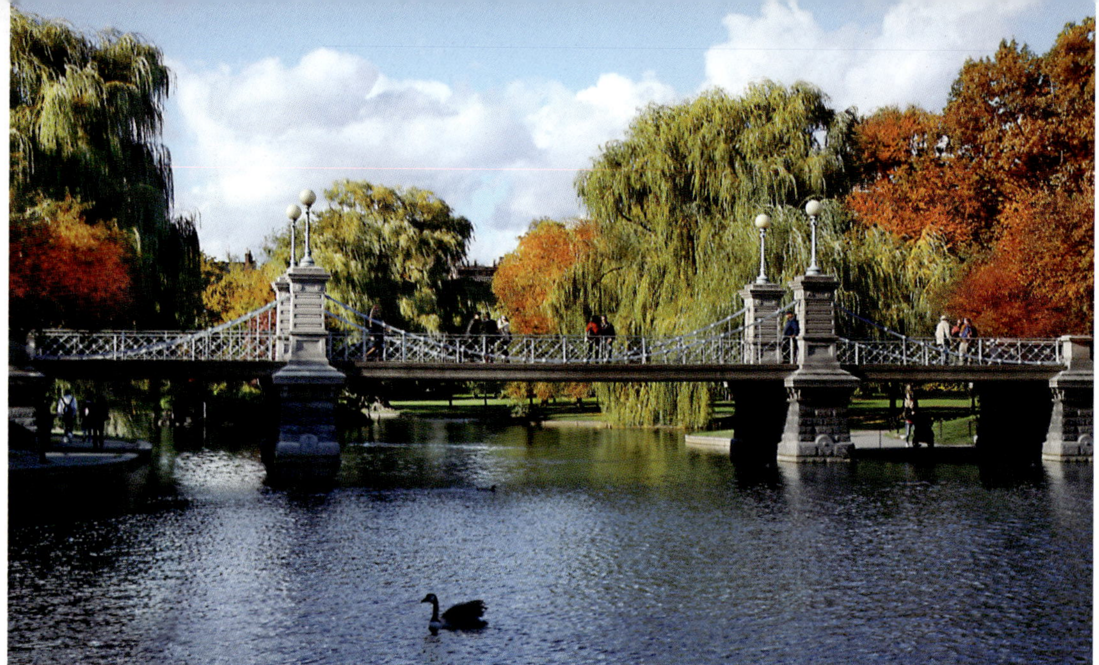

To some, Boston is known as "The Cradle of Liberty." Others simply call it "The Hub." But if you're a visitor, don't call it "Beantown." We don't call it that! At any rate, it's a beautiful city to visit any time of year. Fall is an especially great time to experience a broad spectrum of changing colors in the trees.

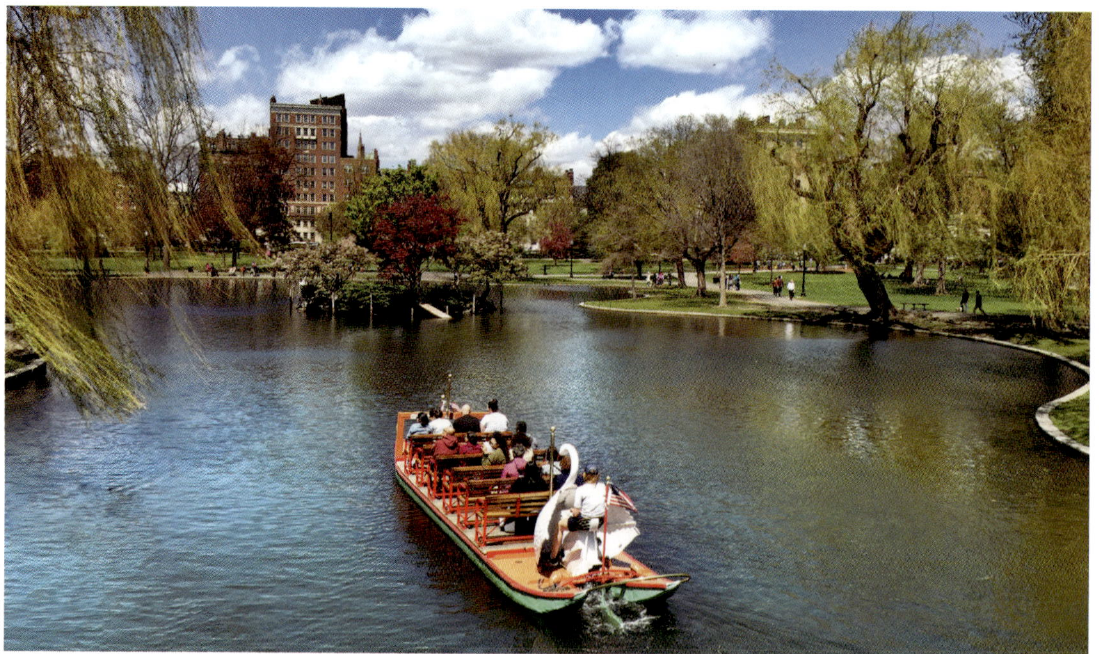

From mid-April through mid-September you can catch a ride on the Swan Boats in the pond at the Public Garden. They're a local icon, and have been operating since the 1870s.

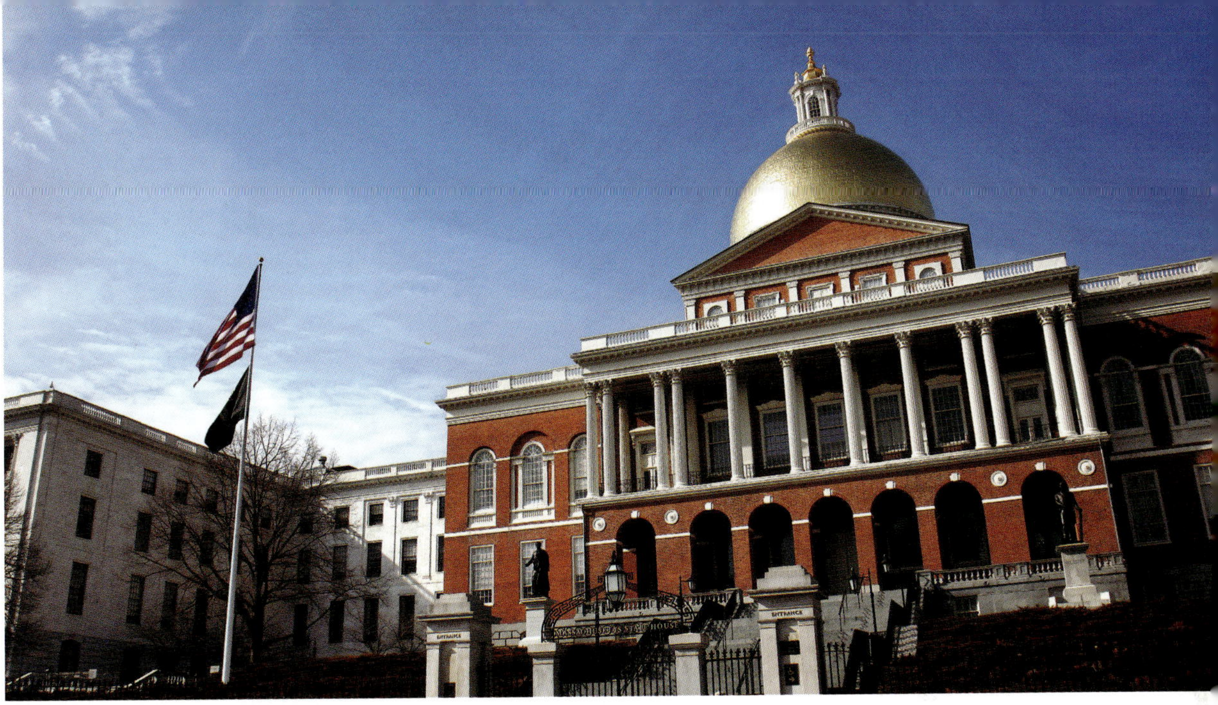

Next to the Public Garden is Beacon Hill, home to the Massachusetts State House. Built in 1798, the dome was gilded in real gold leaf in 1874.

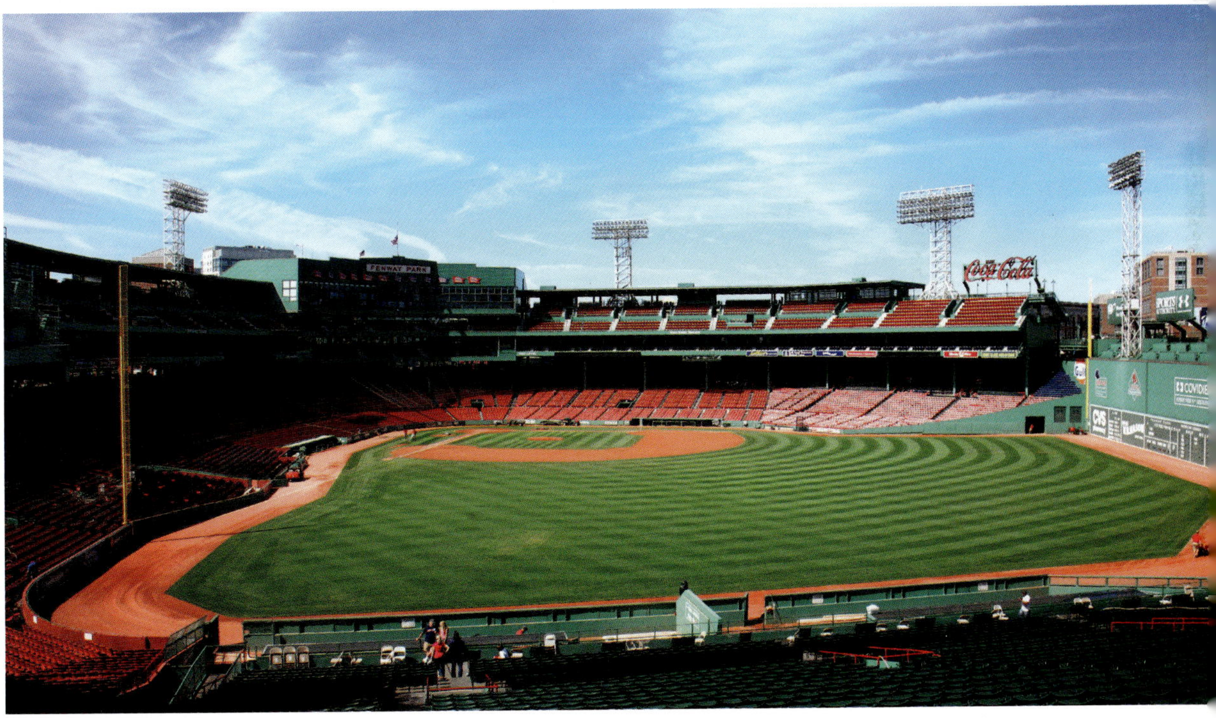

On a sky-blue day in June, this unusual photo of an empty Fenway Park shows an early morning view of the stadium.

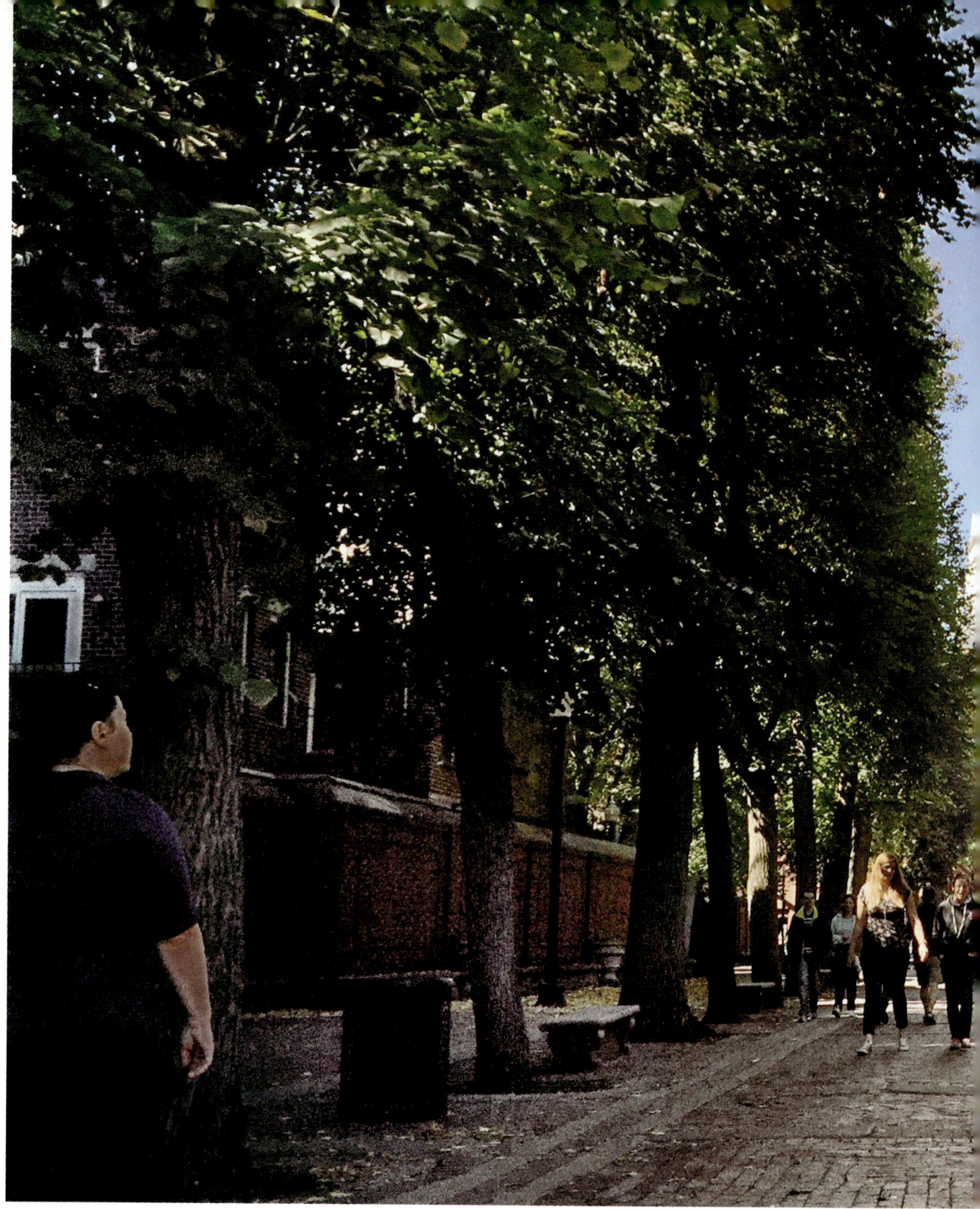

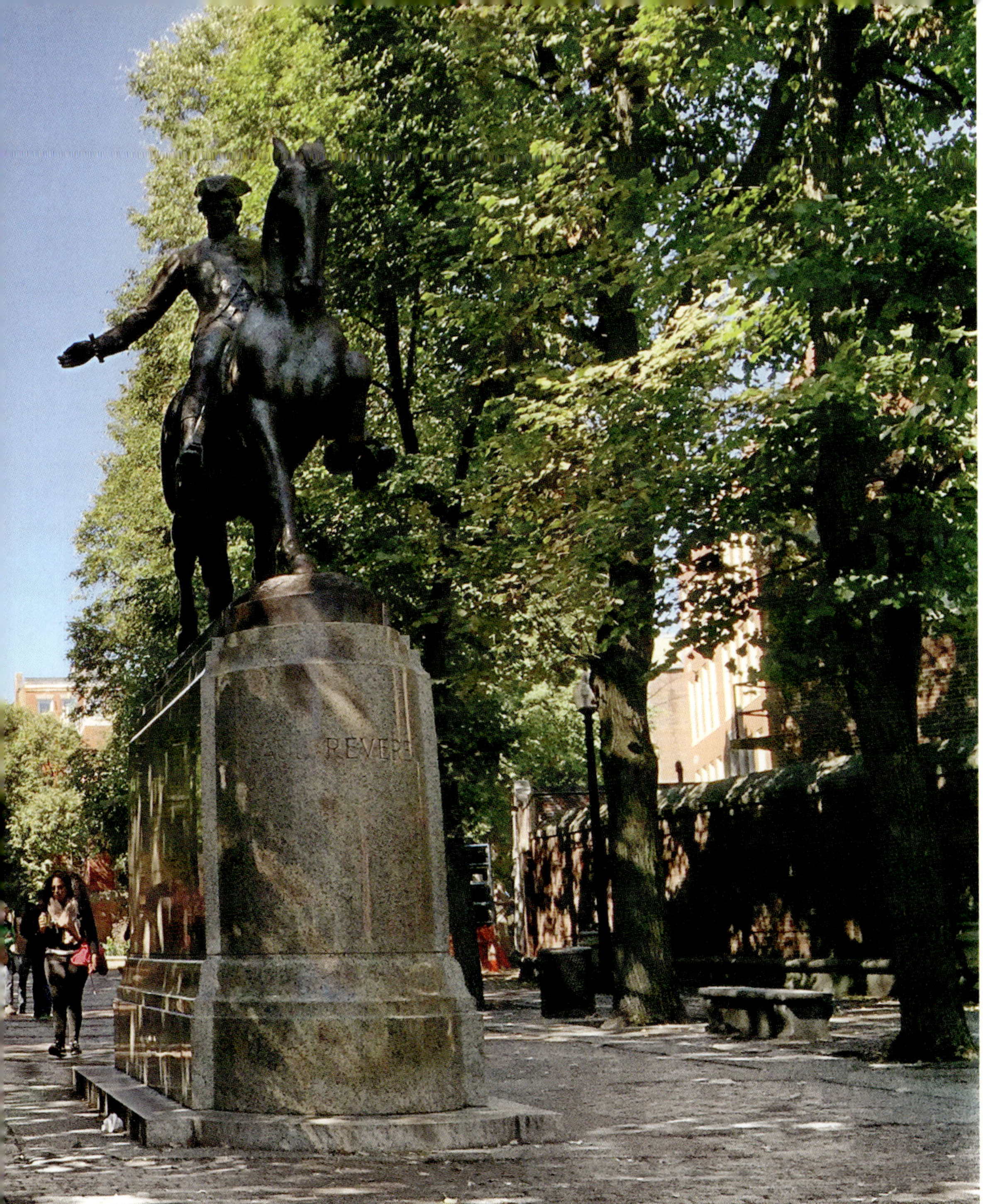

In the foreground is a statue of Paul Revere in the Paul Revere Mall. In the background is the Old North Church, famous for signaling how the British were arriving, "one if by land, two if by sea."

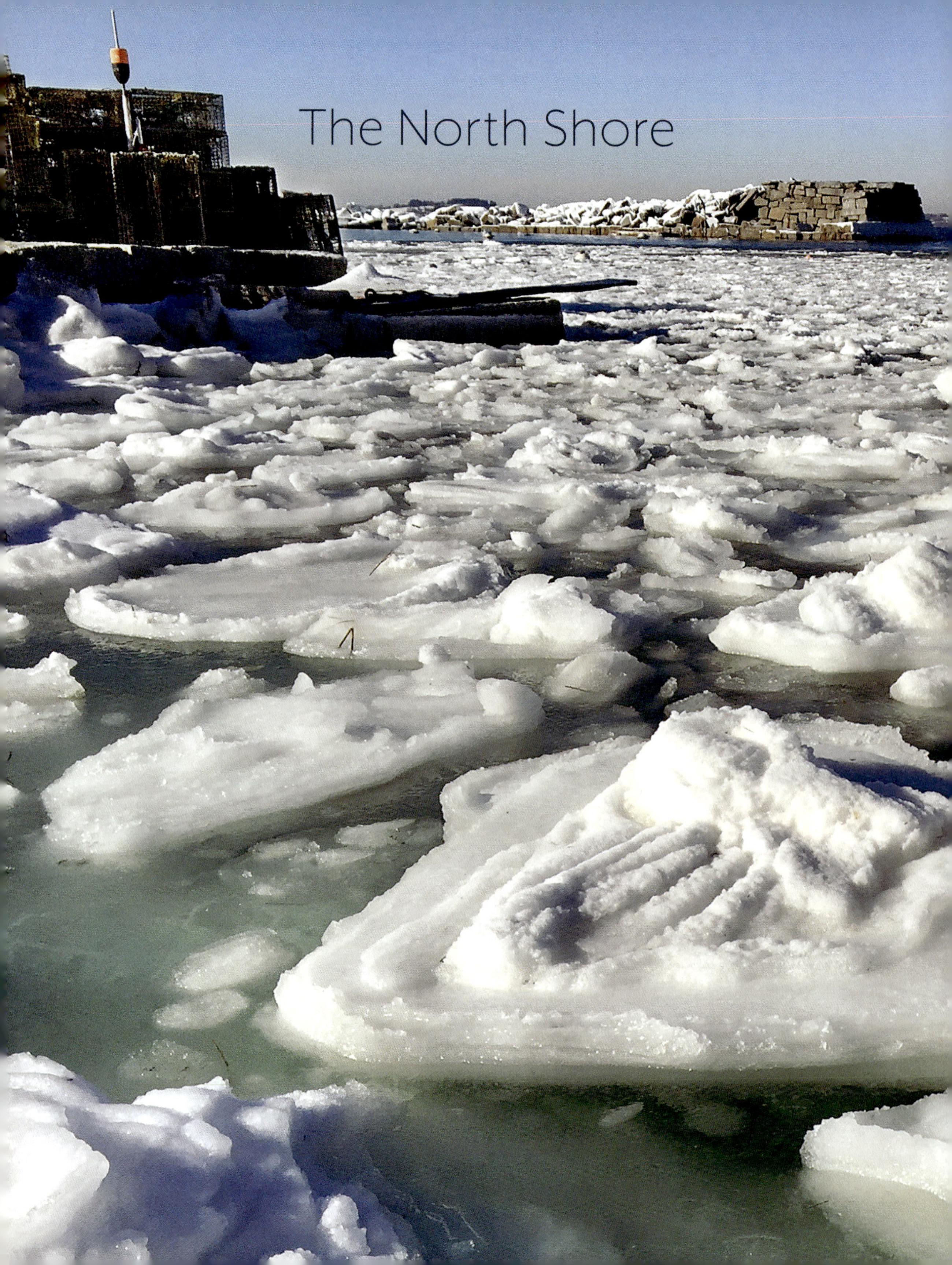
The North Shore

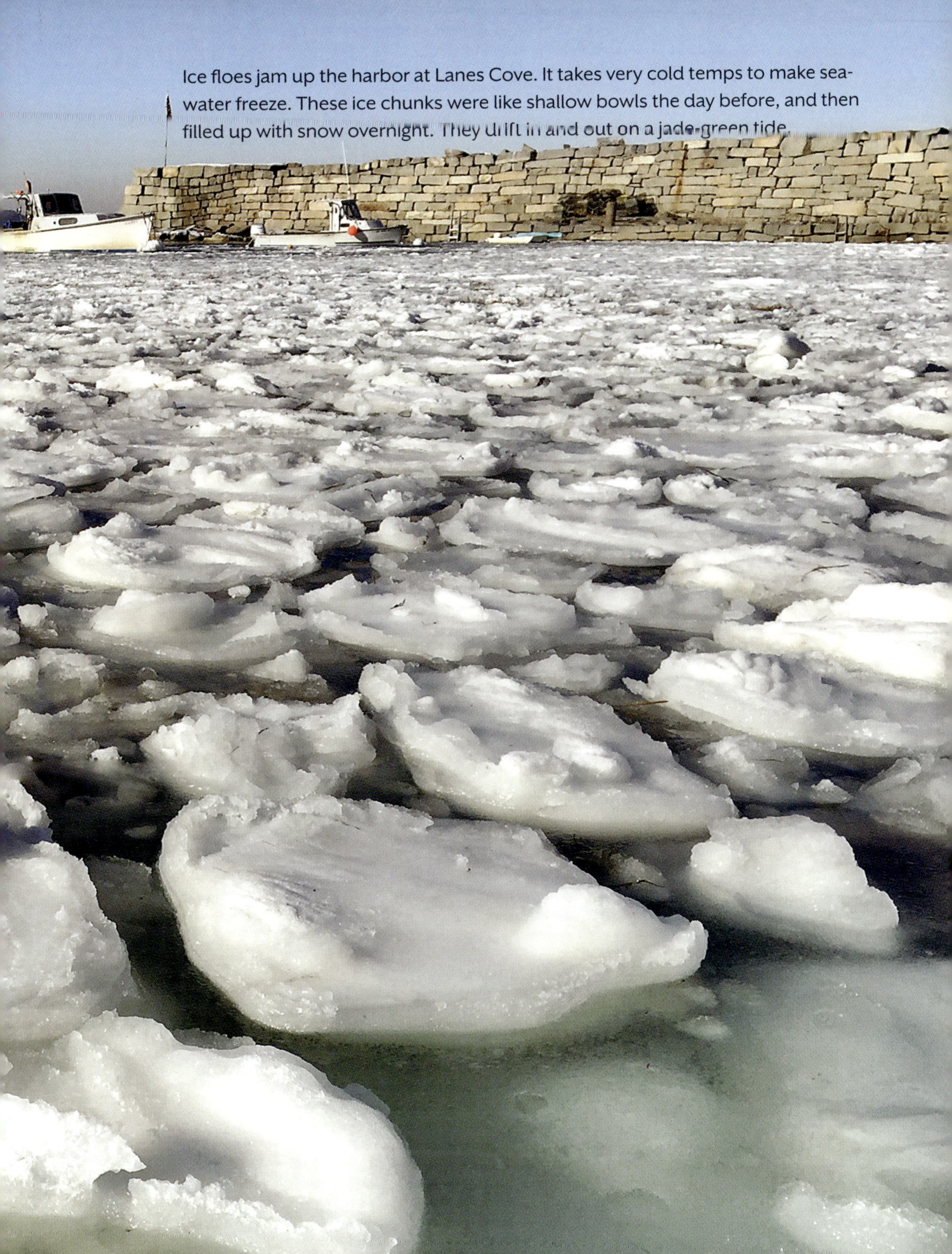

Ice floes jam up the harbor at Lanes Cove. It takes very cold temps to make seawater freeze. These ice chunks were like shallow bowls the day before, and then filled up with snow overnight. They drift in and out on a jade-green tide.

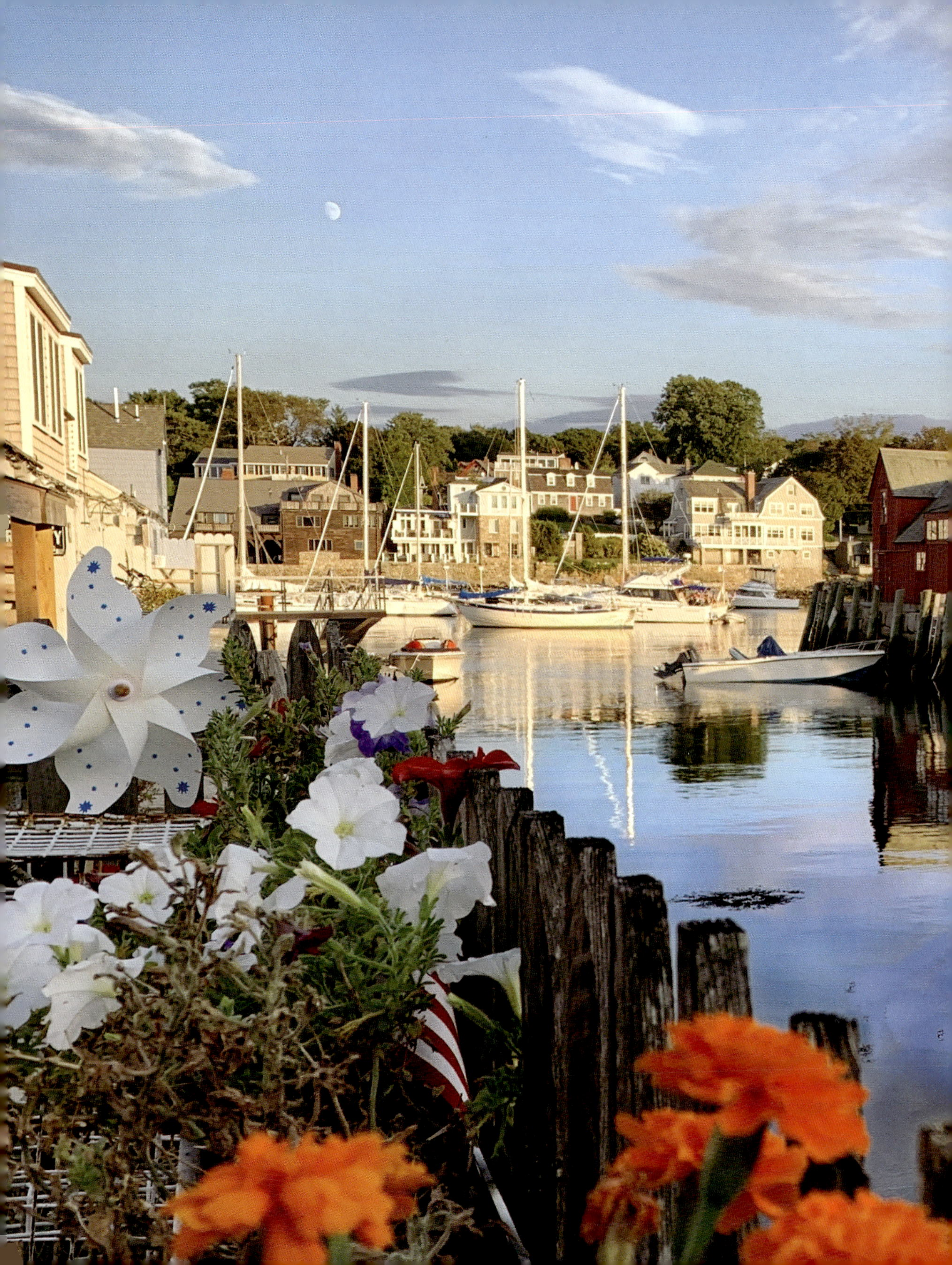

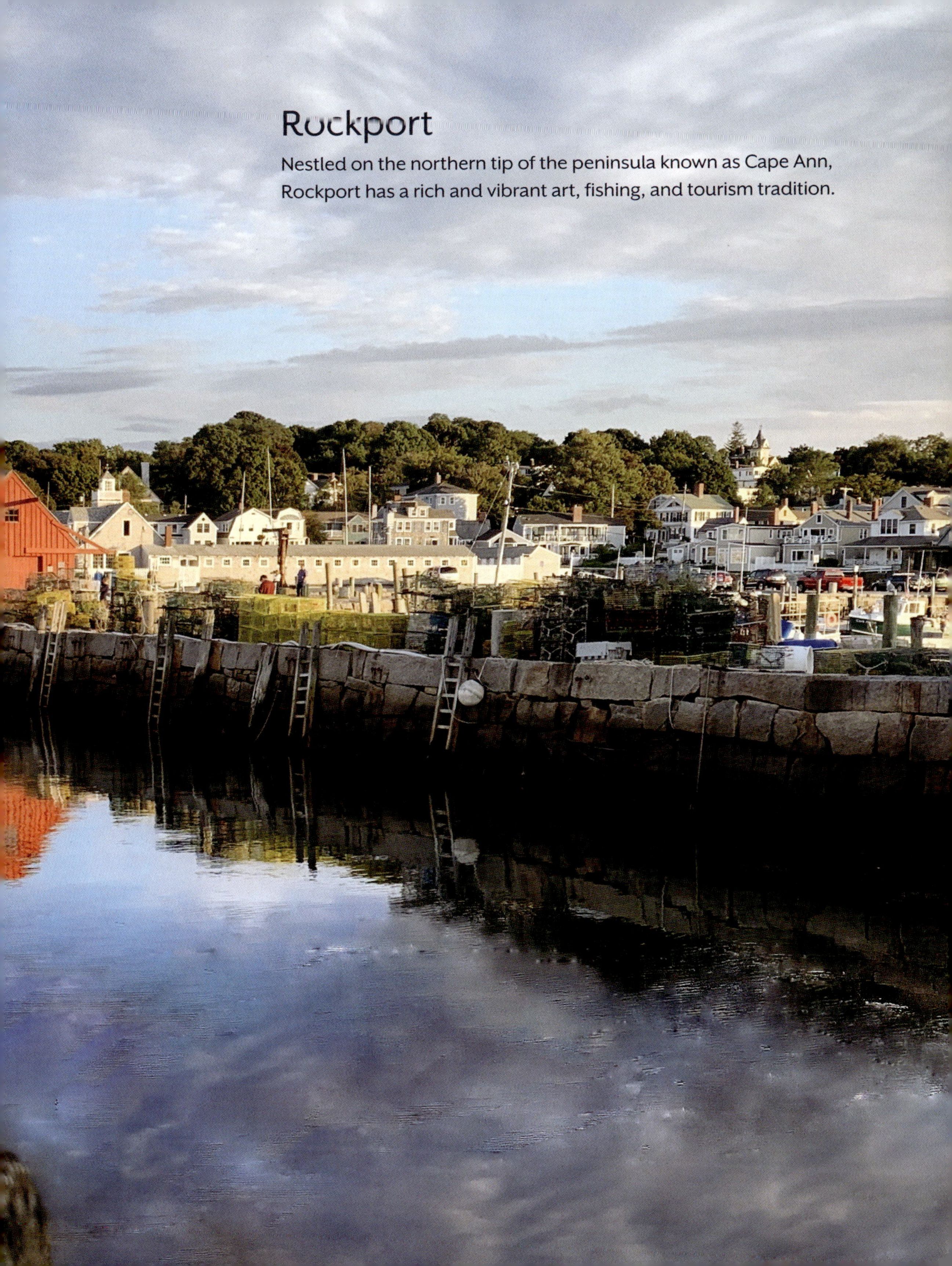

Rockport

Nestled on the northern tip of the peninsula known as Cape Ann, Rockport has a rich and vibrant art, fishing, and tourism tradition.

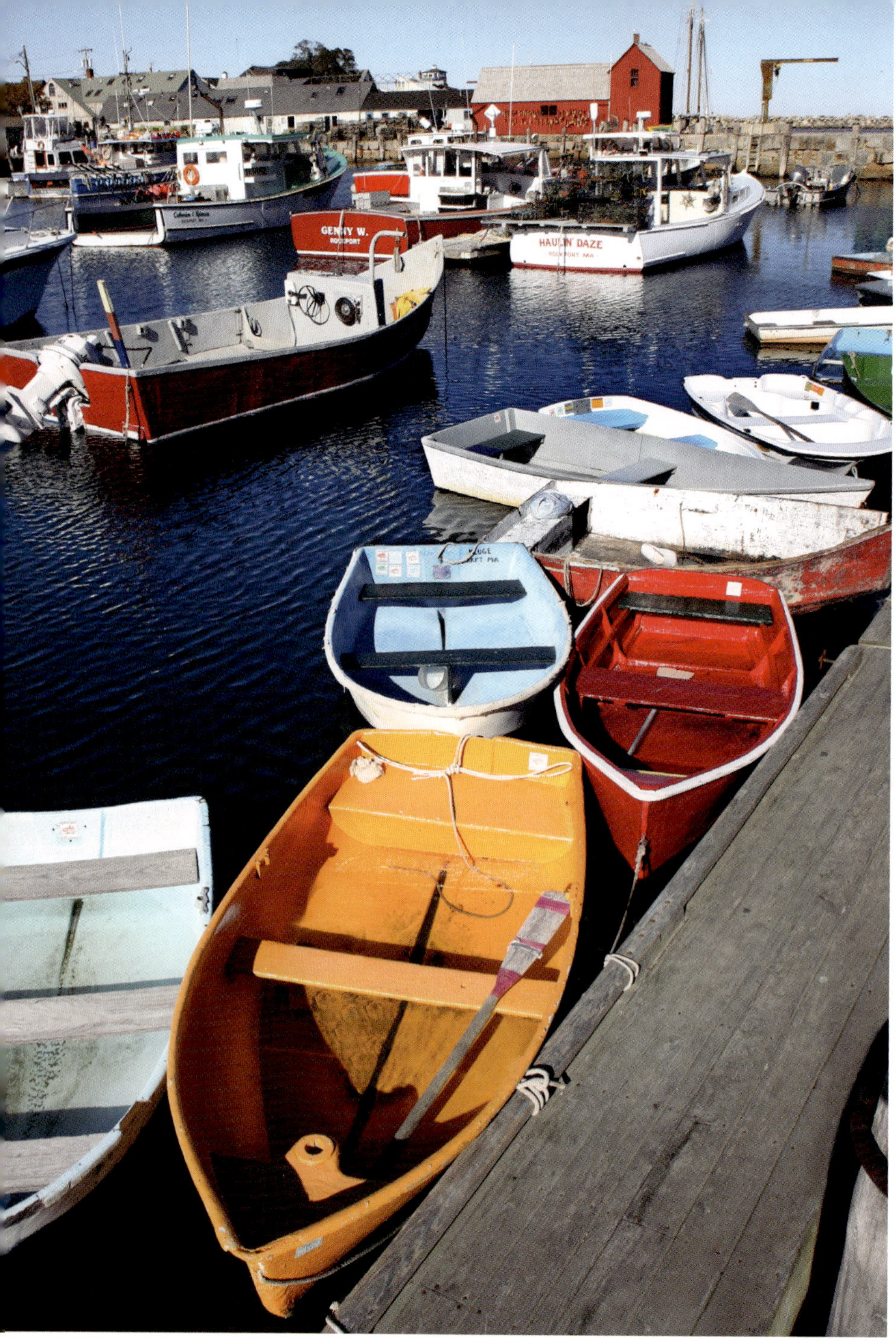

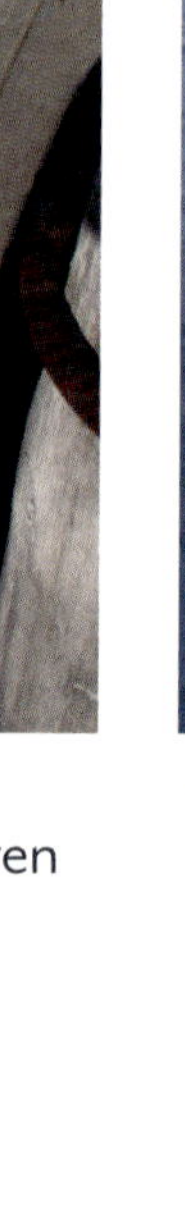

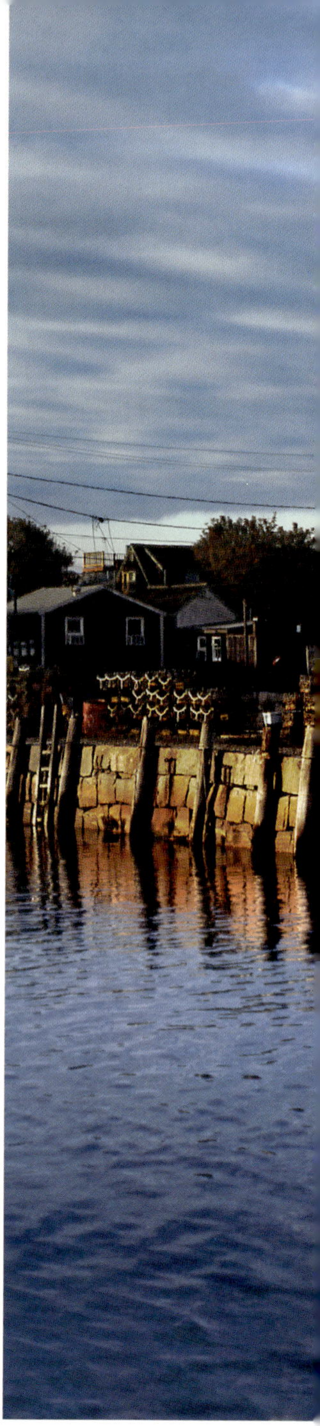

Skiffs, used by lobstermen and other seagoers, are rowboats with unique style and variety. They can remain in service for decades, even with "questionable" seaworthiness.

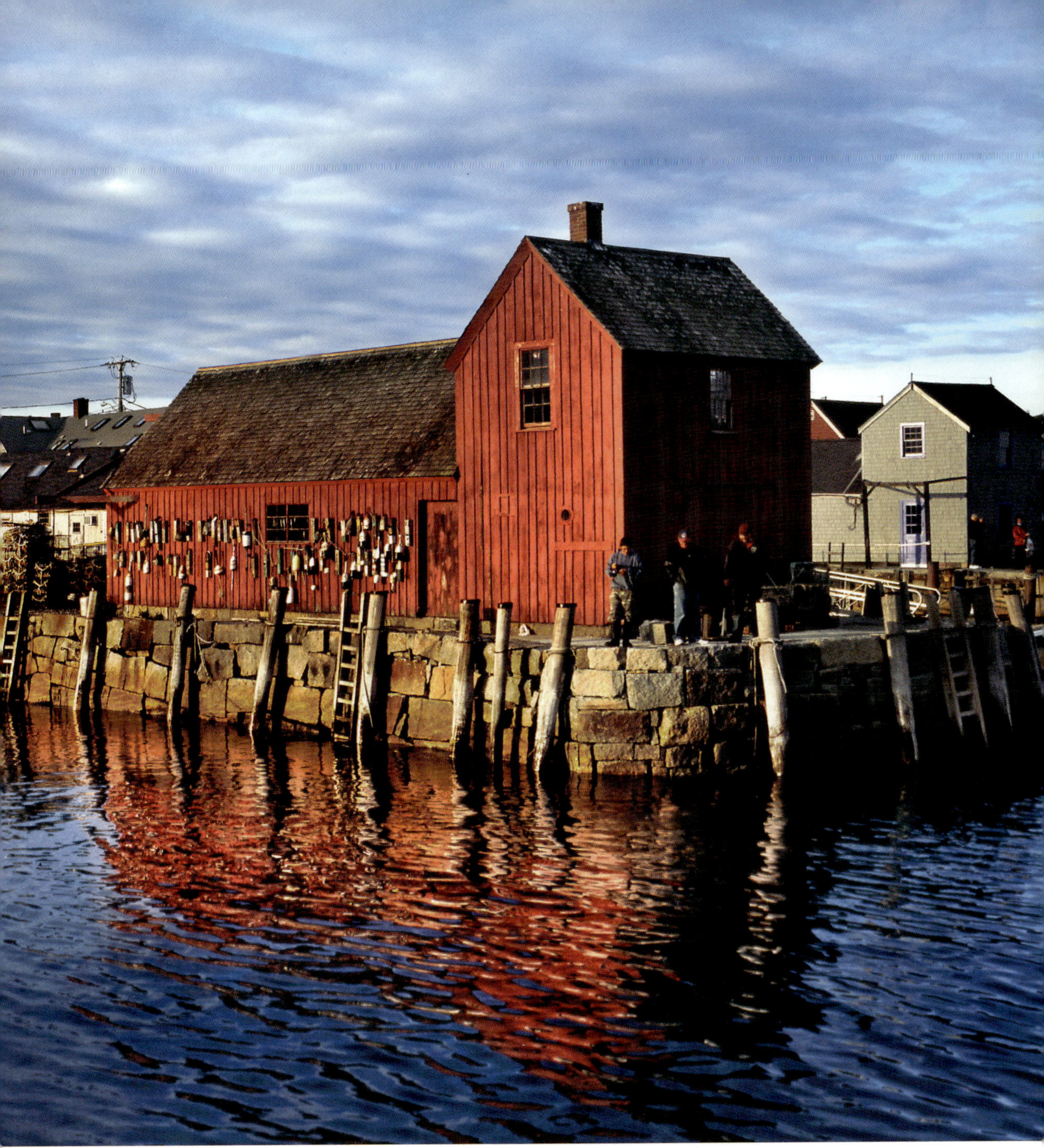

The harbor is home to one of the most iconic landmarks in New England, the red shack, known as Motif #1. The original was destroyed by what's known as "The Blizzard of '78."

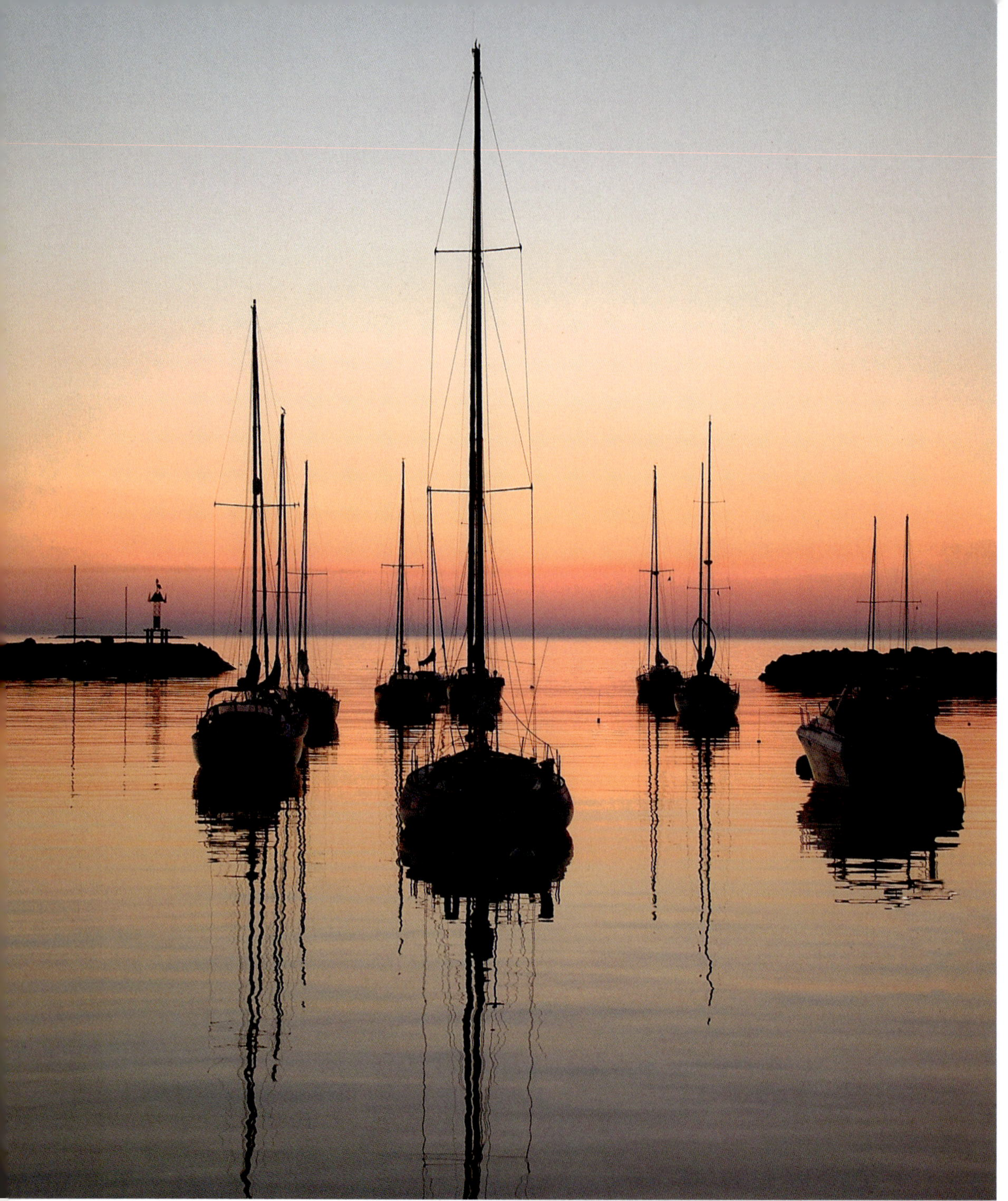

Being a lobsterman or fisherman requires early mornings and long days of hard work. Captured here is first light, playing a symphony of mirrored peach colors rippling between the sailboats, just after 4:30 a.m.

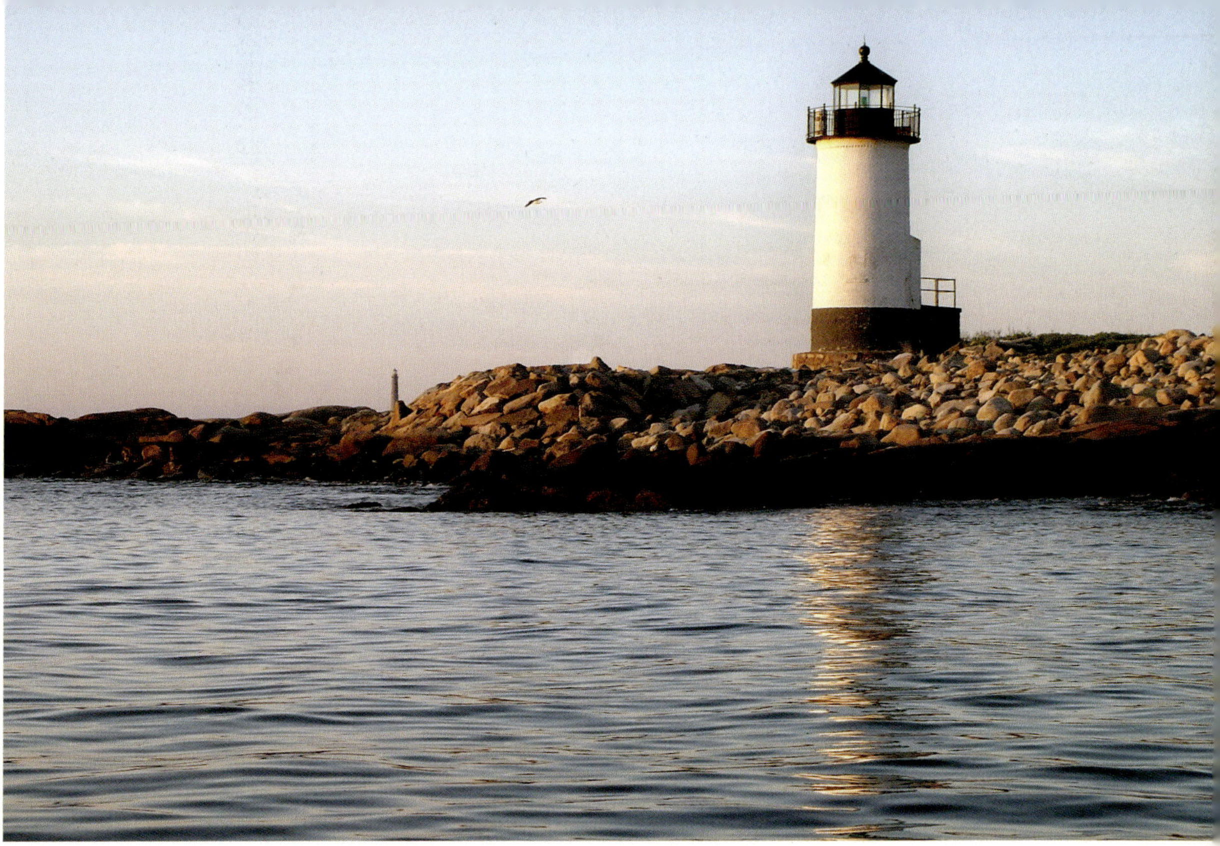

Built in 1896, Straitsmouth Lighthouse embraces the warm morning glow, flashing its green light every six seconds when dark as a warning for those at sea.

Out on the water life can be full of surprises. This lobster hitched a ride on the outside of the trap. "First time I've seen that!" says Captain Gus. The red boat he skippers is called *Gussy's Girls,* named for his family.

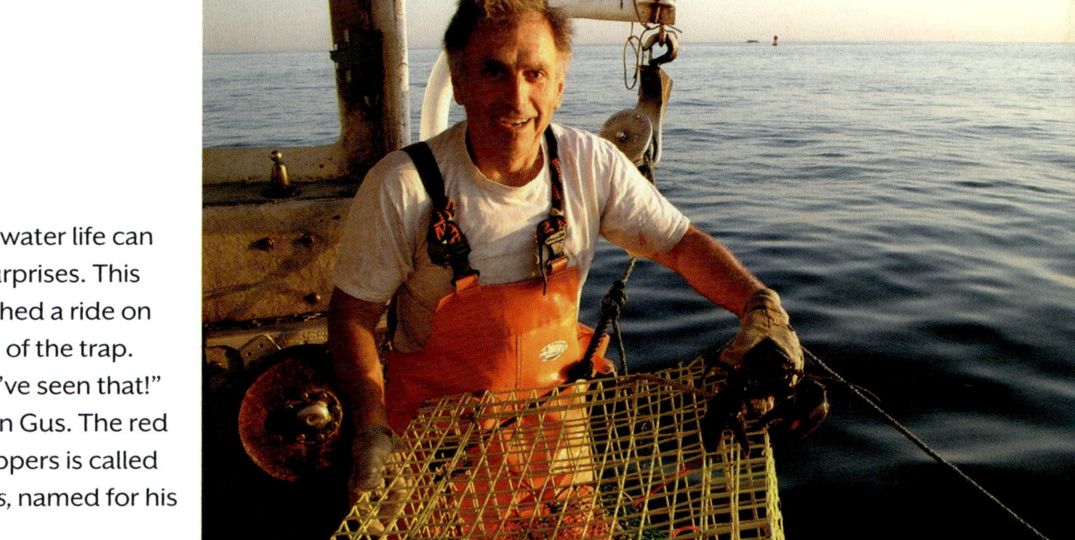

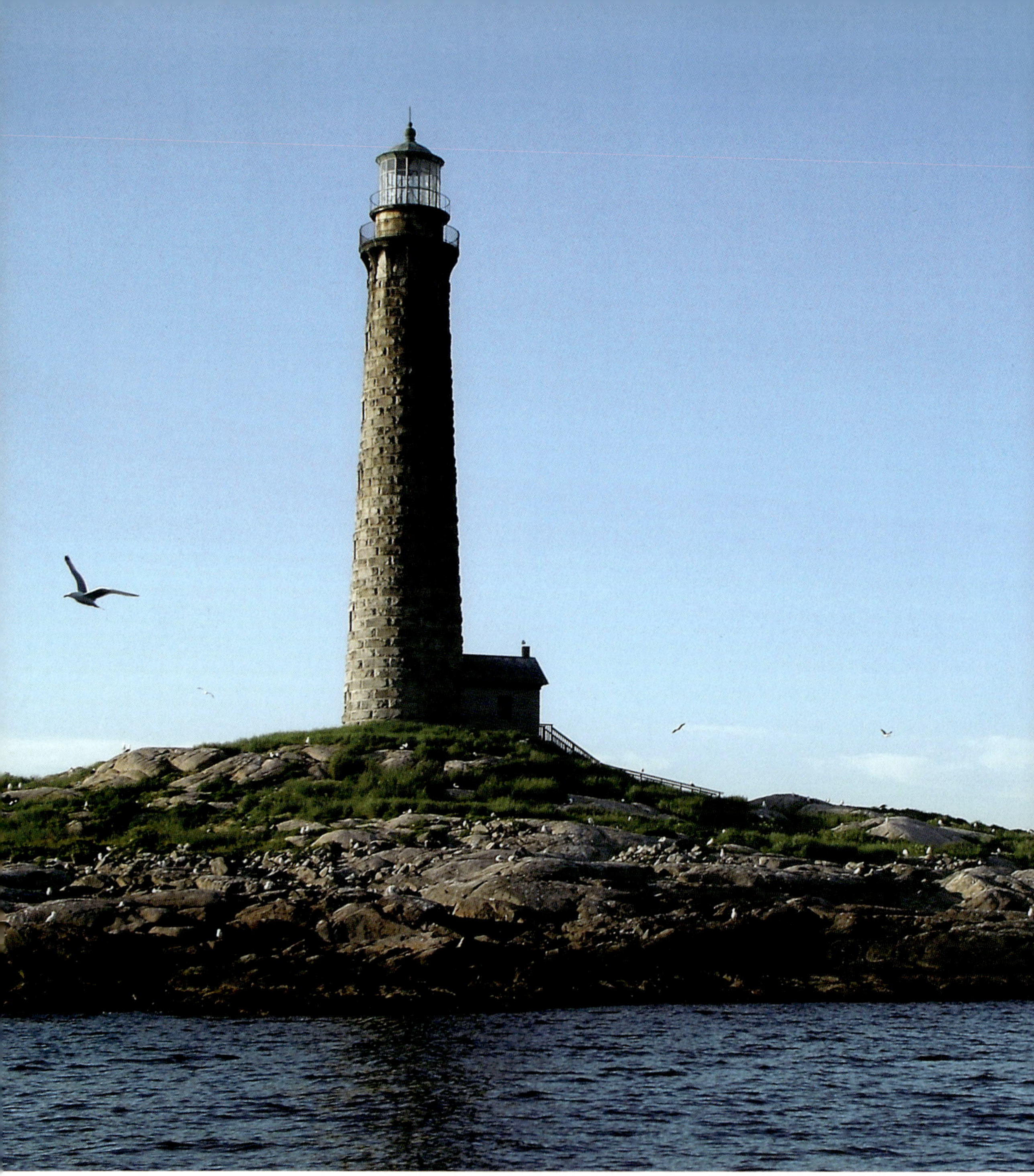

The Twin Lights on Thacher Island, originally built in 1771 and rebuilt for height in 1861, serve as a crucial guide for captains searching for a north heading, as the lights were constructed on a north to south axis.

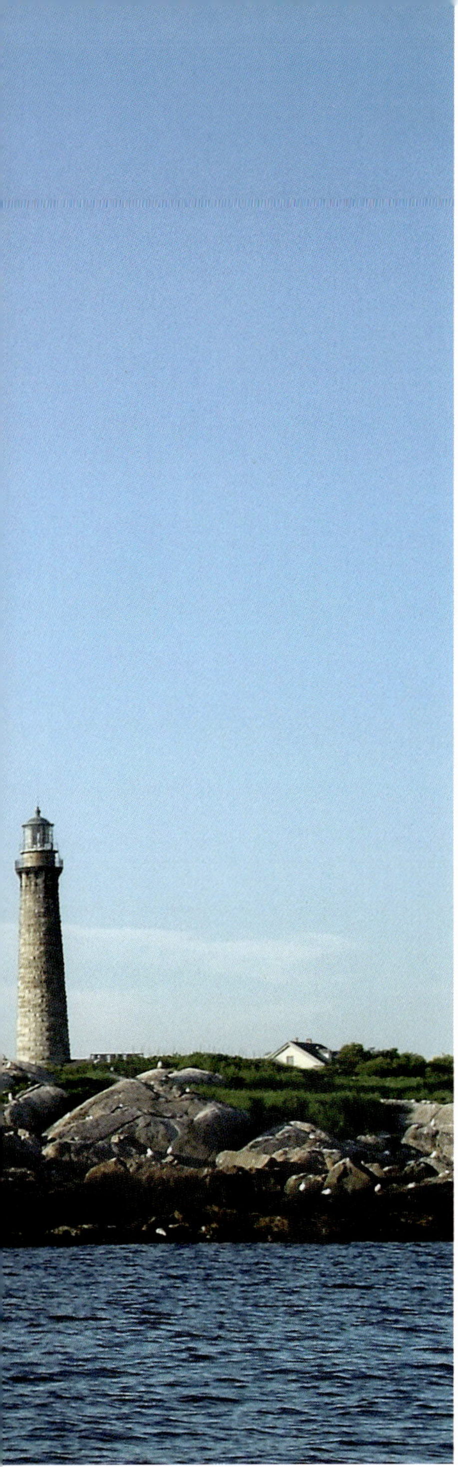

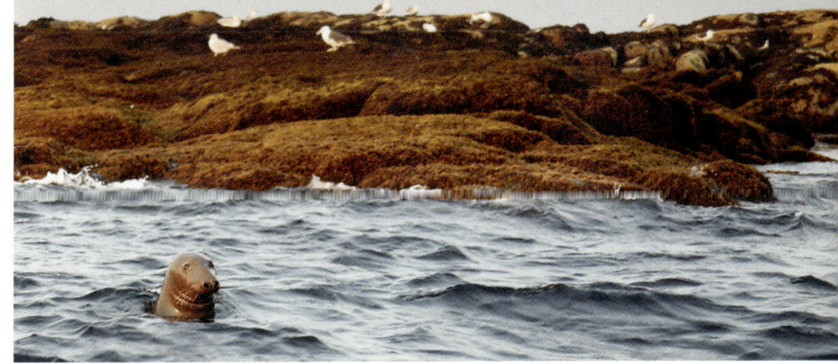

As we head back in towards the harbor, we're passing a reef called Salvages. It's good to keep your eyes on the water . . . you never know who might pop up! Here a young seal takes an interest in our voyage. After a brief moment of reflection, he gets back to fishing.

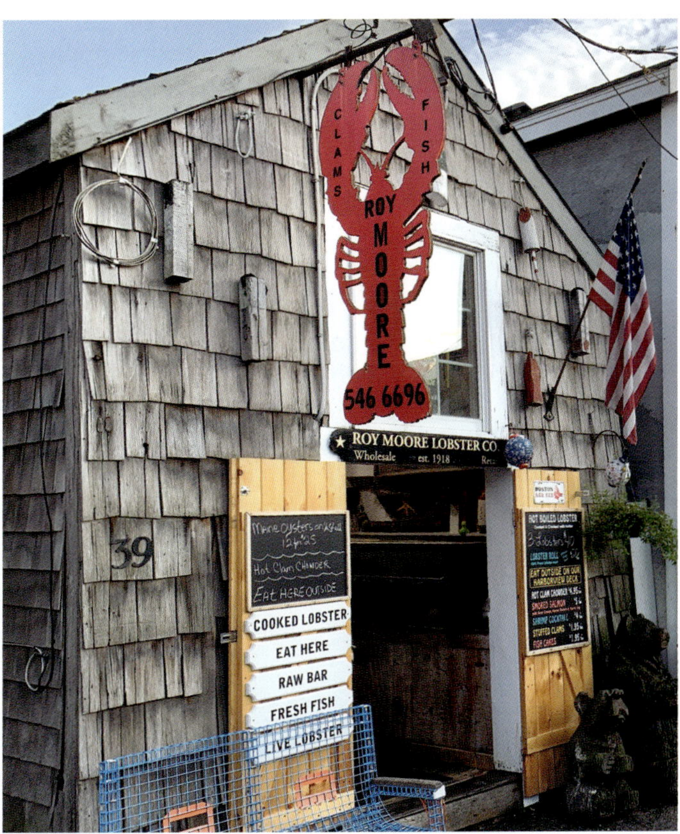

Roy Moore Lobster Company, established in 1918, is a family-run business owned and operated by Rockporters. They have pools filled with live lobster and crab. They'll cook your lunch on the spot. Then you can enjoy it on their deck, with a harbor view.

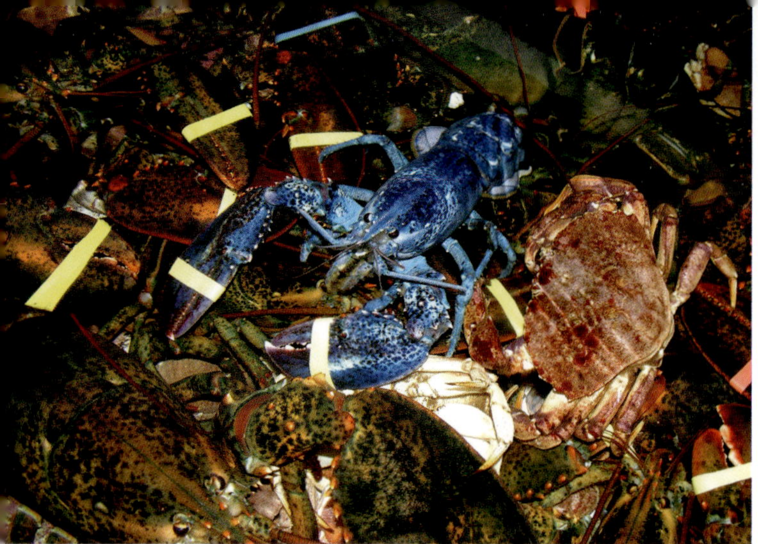

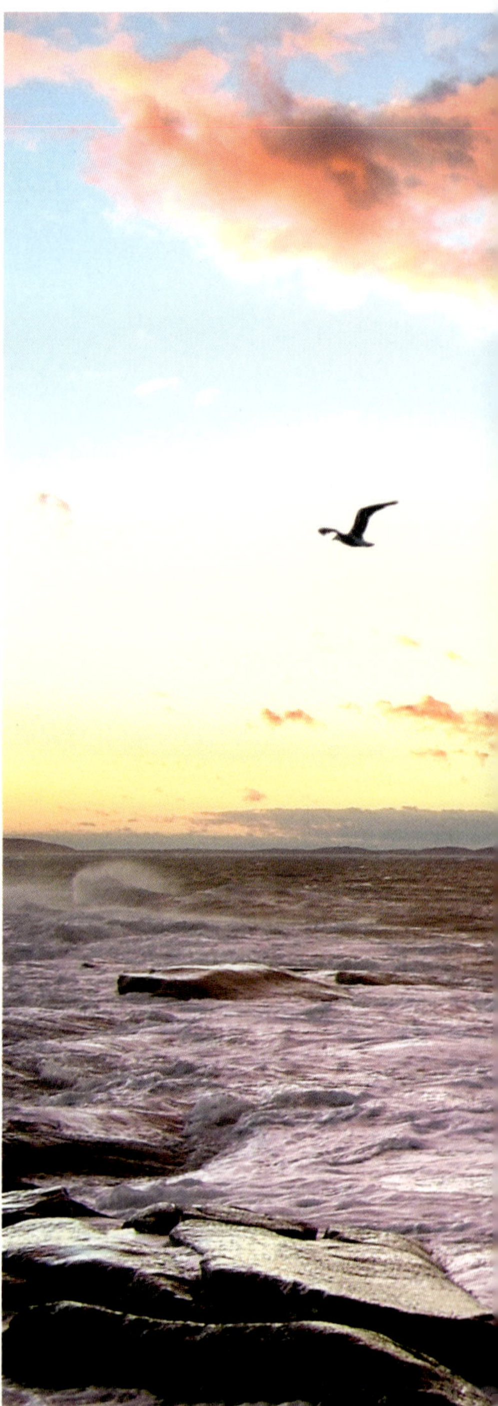

Typically, lobsters are a mix of greens and browns, a perfect camouflage in the rocks and seaweed where they dwell. Occasionally, a genetic mutation occurs adding more of a specific type of protein, causing the dramatic sapphire color. No dinner plate for this crustacean, he's sent off to the safety of an aquarium where he can be studied and returned to the ocean.

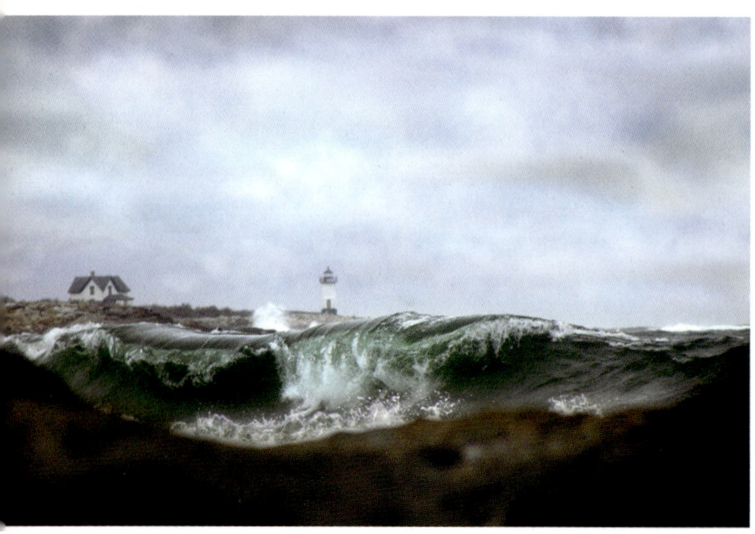

For those who live in or visit Rockport in the winter, there are some rewards. This time of season can bring wild weather, with stunning atmospherics, invigorating wind, and colossal green waves. Straitsmouth Lighthouse is in the background, stoically enduring the storm.

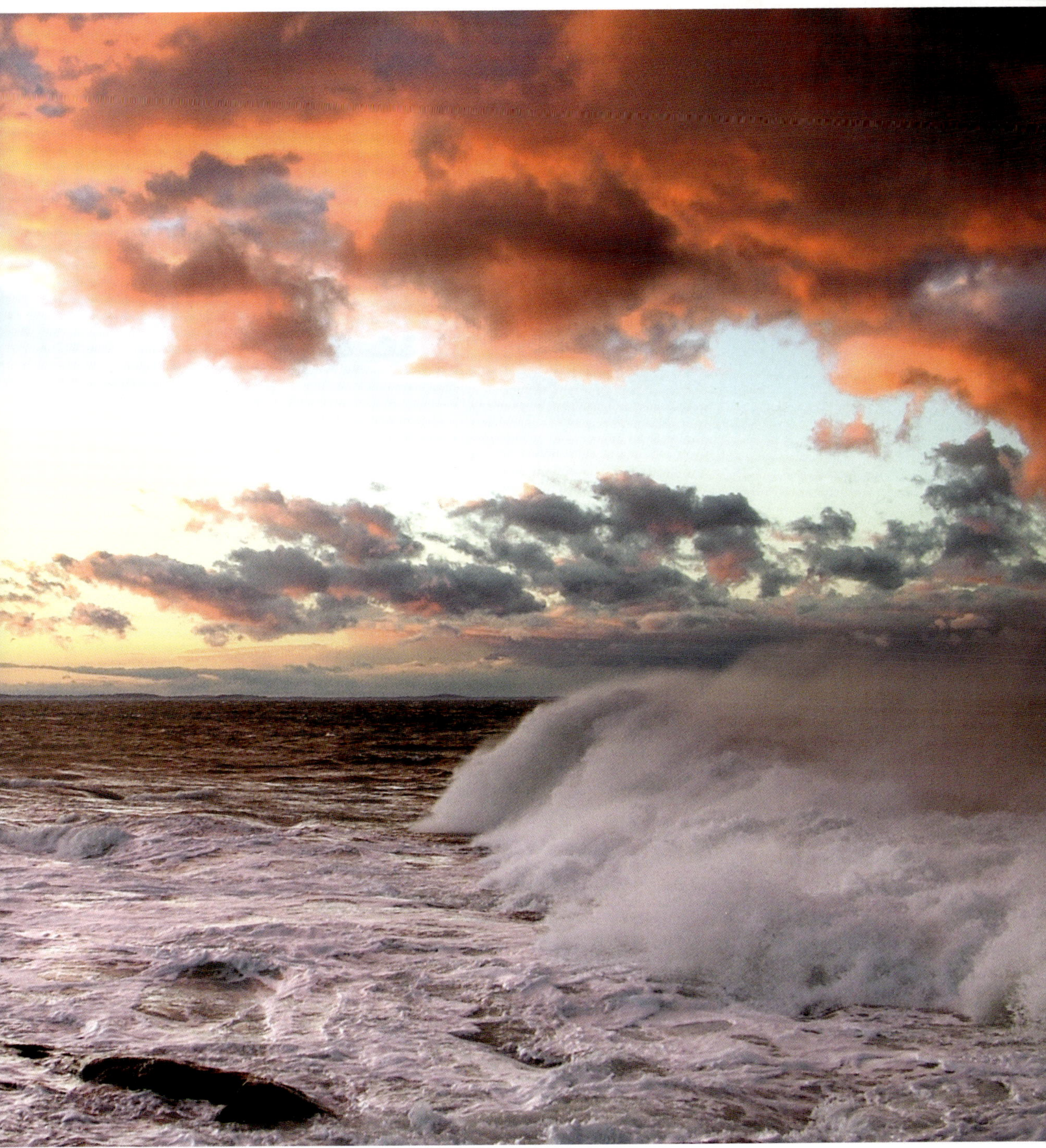

A gull makes its way through a ripping gale under pink sunset clouds. Storm waves crash on the windswept coast at Halibut Point State Park. Winter often means turbulent weather, and menacing conditions at sea.

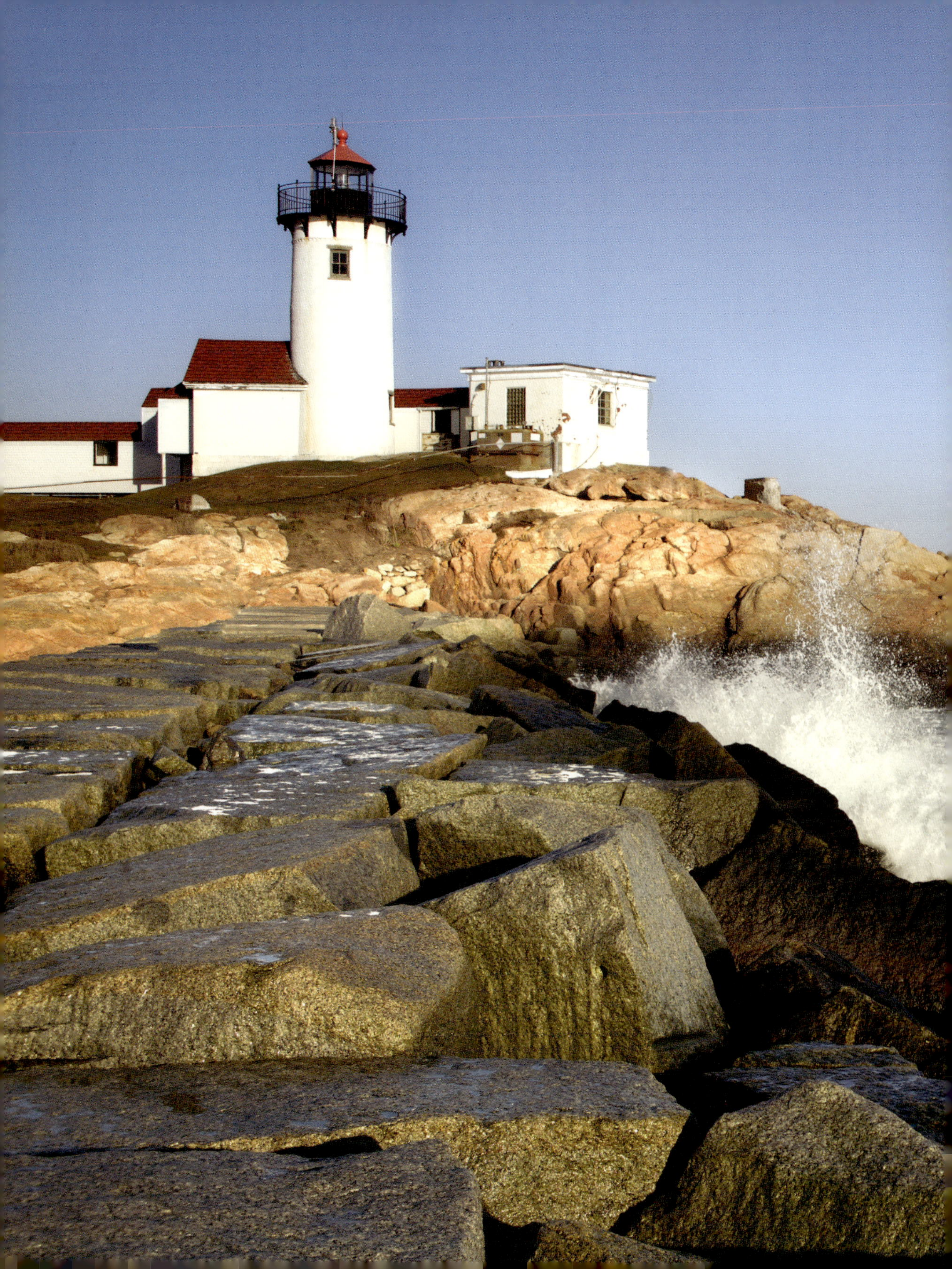

Gloucester

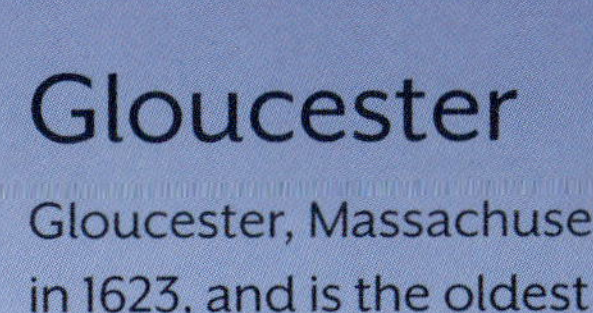

Gloucester, Massachusetts, was settled by voyagers from England in 1623, and is the oldest seaport in America. It occupies the larger portion of the peninsula called Cape Ann. When founded, the area was originally known as the Massachusetts Bay Colony.

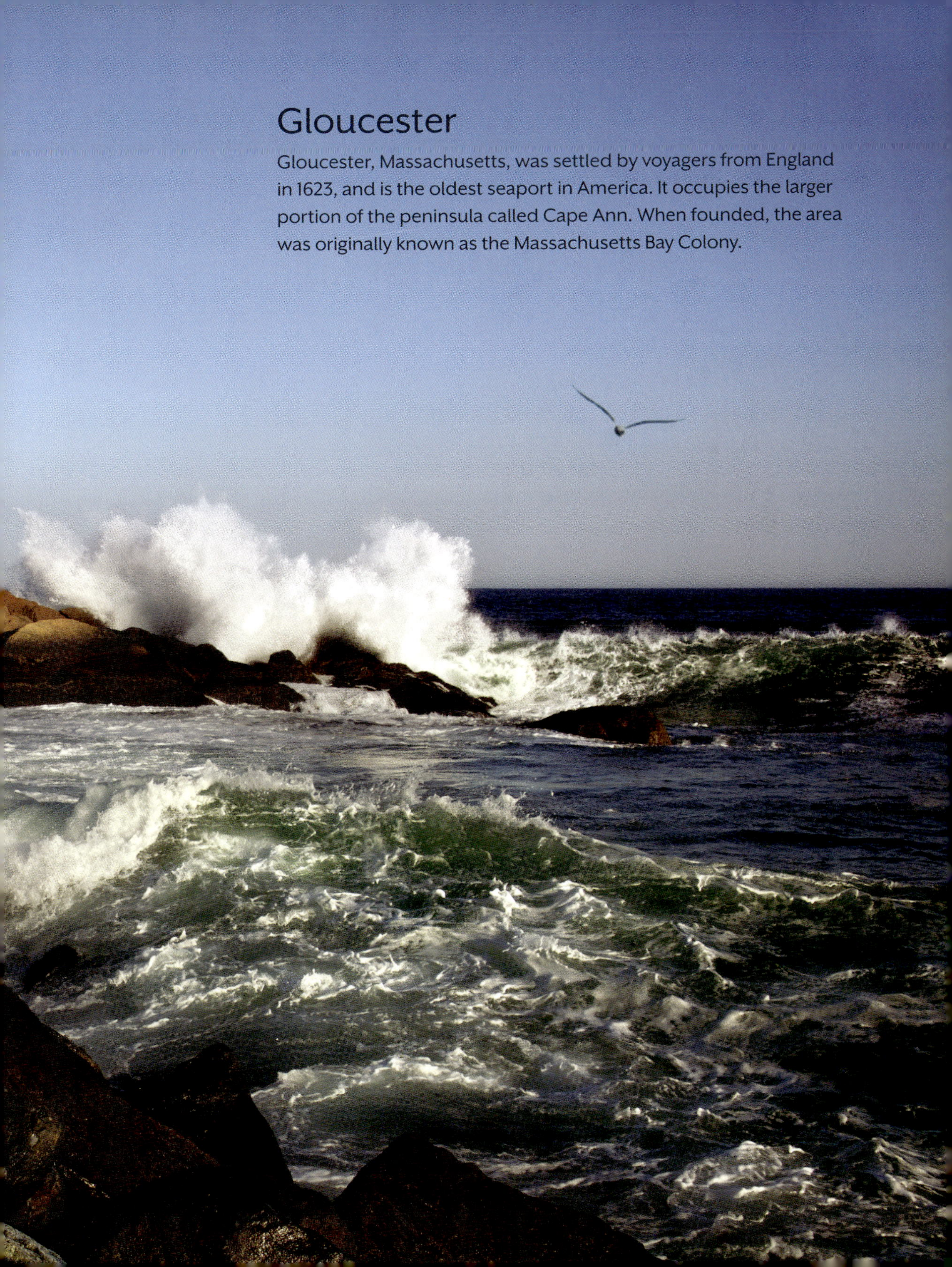

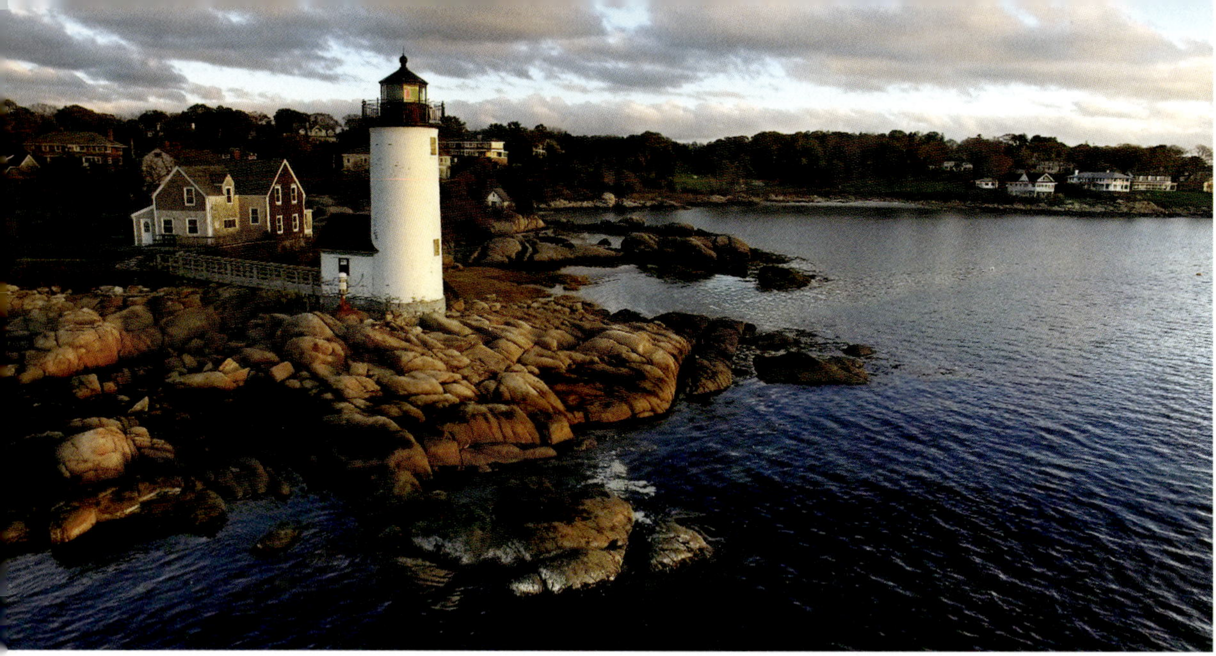

Annisquam Harbor Lighthouse stands at a pugnacious 41 feet tall. Originally built in 1801, this lighthouse has been featured in a movie, advertisements, paintings, and calendars.

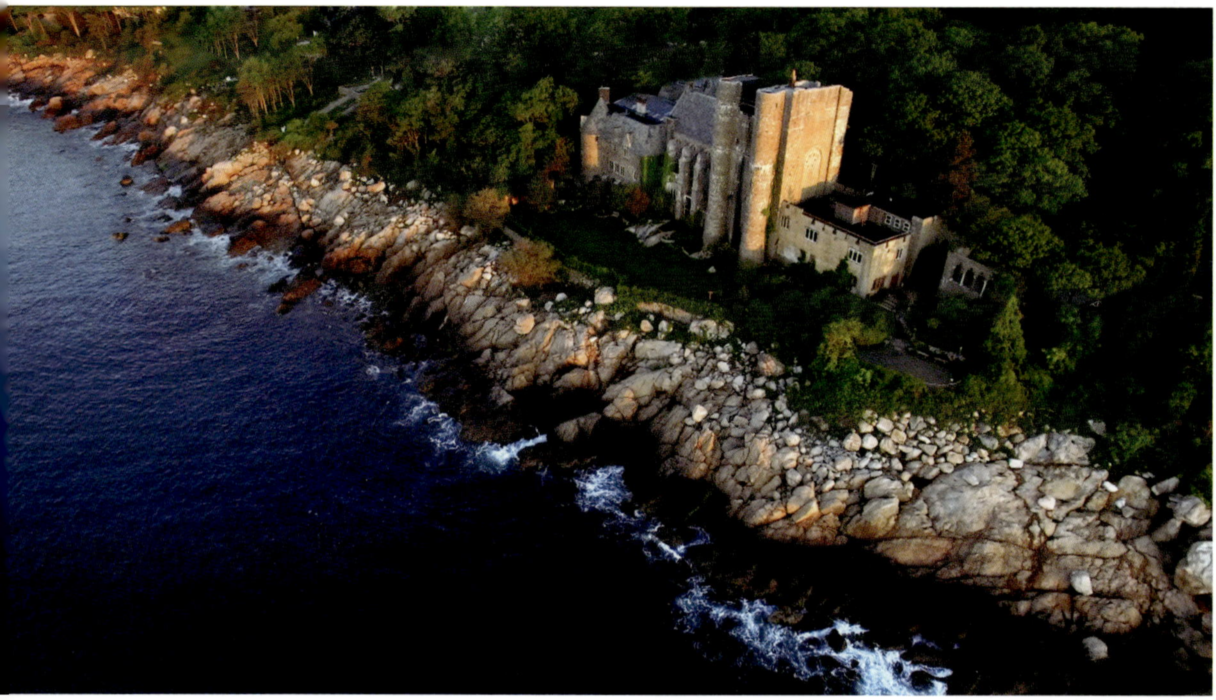

Hammond Castle, constructed from 1926 to 1929, was the brainchild and home of inventor John Hays Hammond, Jr. Today it is home to the Hammond Castle Museum.

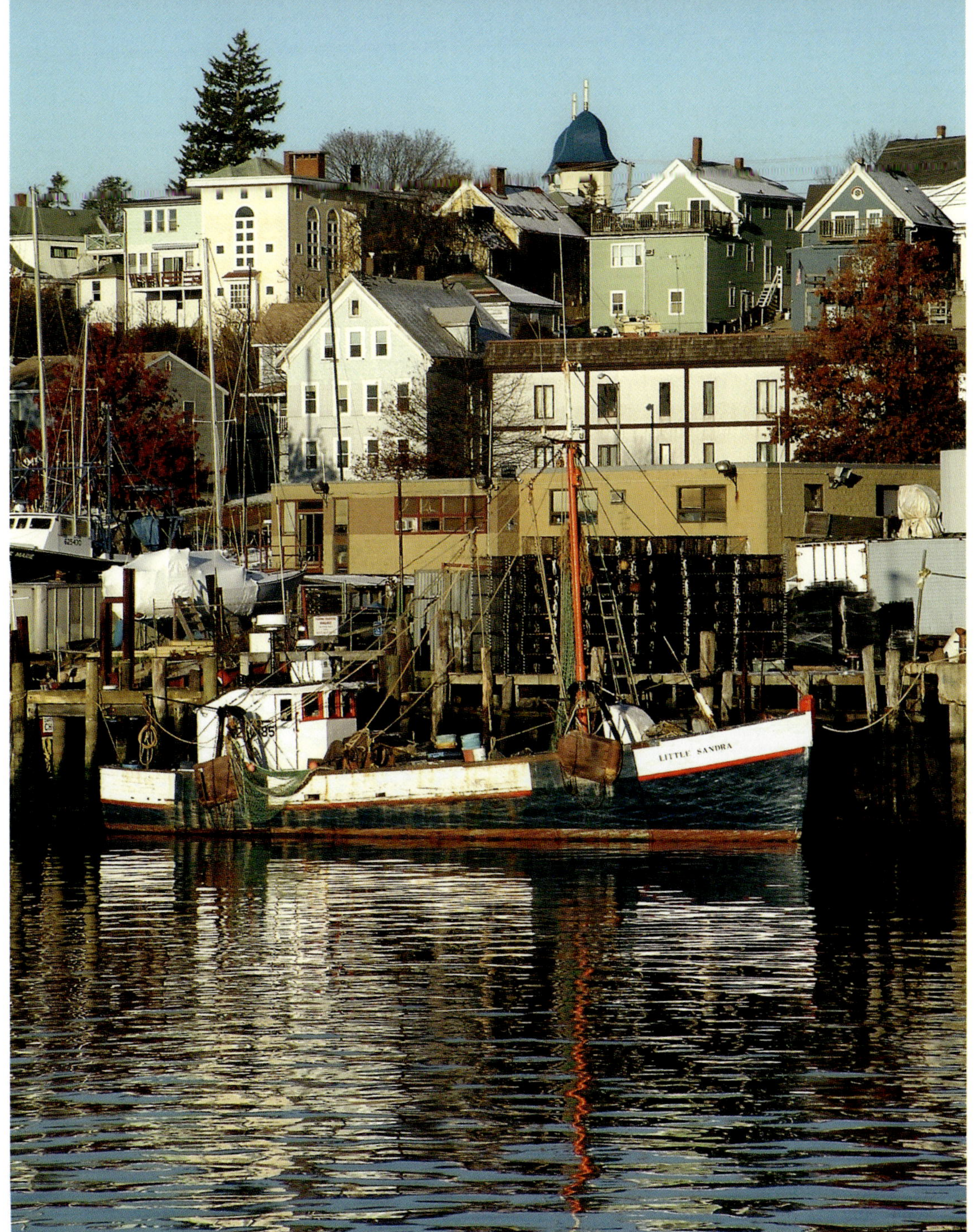

This iconic photo has tons of history. In the foreground is the fishing vessel *Little Sandra,* docked near Rose's Marine. Before sinking, she was the very last example of Gloucester's historic eastern-rig trawlers. Just past the dock is a three-story building that's home to the Crow's Nest bar, which played a starring role in *The Perfect Storm* movie.

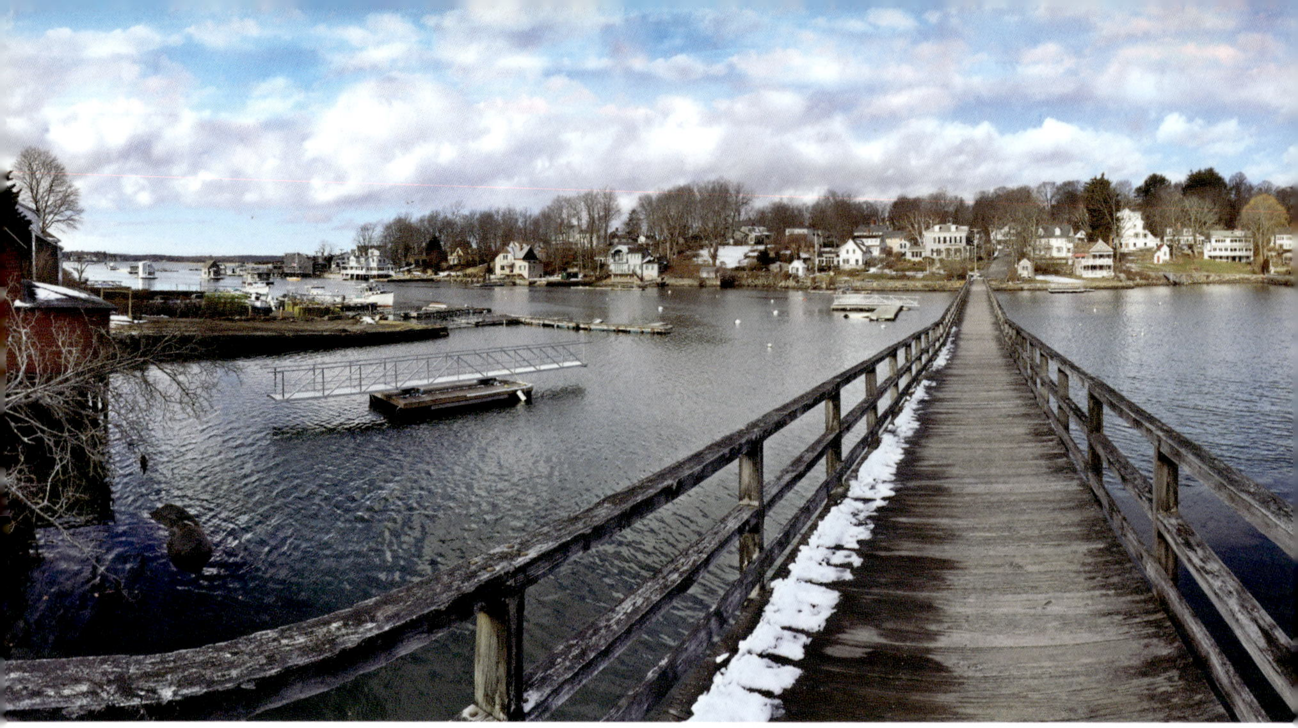

An inviting old bridge, with the last remnants of winter snow. This historic wooden pile bridge crosses Lobster Cove and provides foot-traffic to the village of Annisquam. It is 440 feet long and used to be wide enough for automobiles. It was closed to cars in 1968 and is now open to pedestrians only. It was listed on the National Register of Historic Places in 1983.

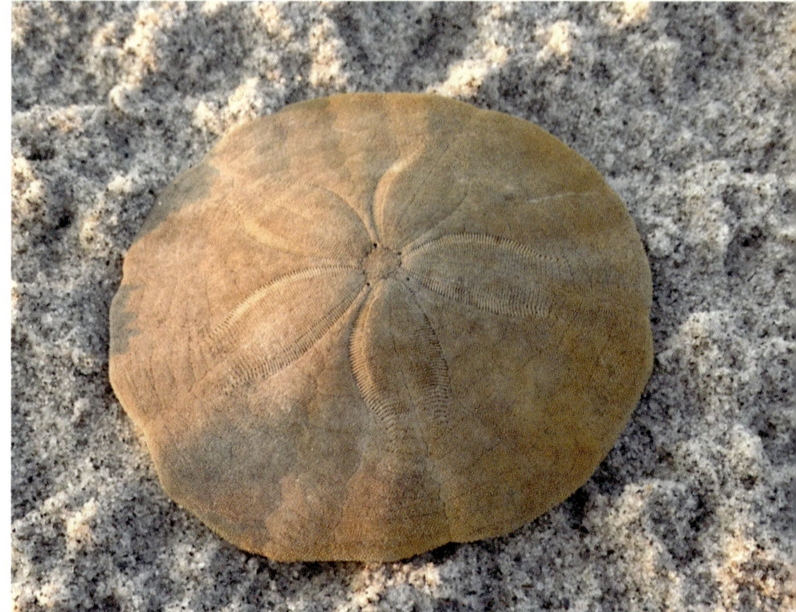

A sand dollar basks in afternoon sunlight on a rain-dappled beach. They are actually a species of sea urchin that has become extremely flat, which helps them burrow in the sand. You can occasionally see them at low tide in Gloucester.

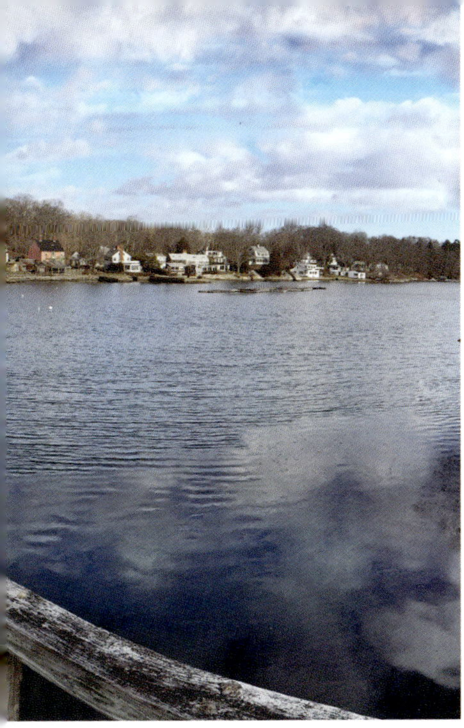

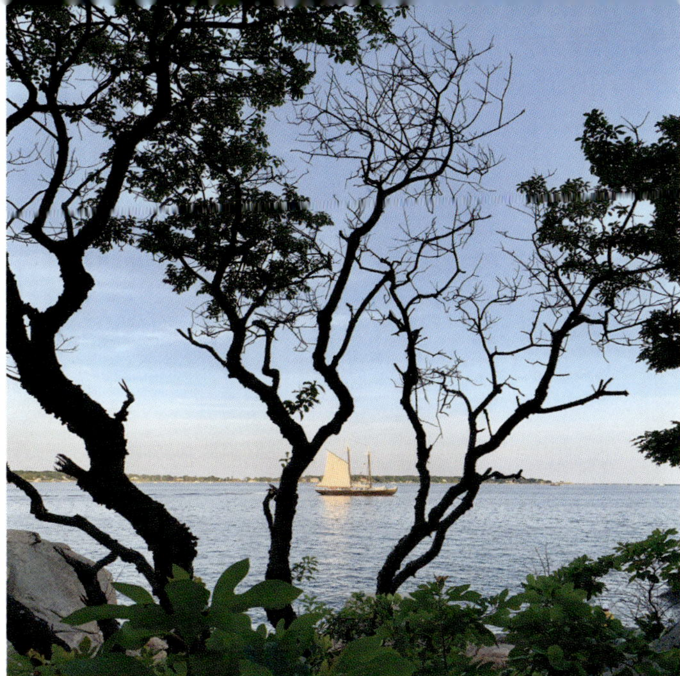

A two-masted schooner under sail. It is believed that the first American schooner was built in Gloucester around 1713.

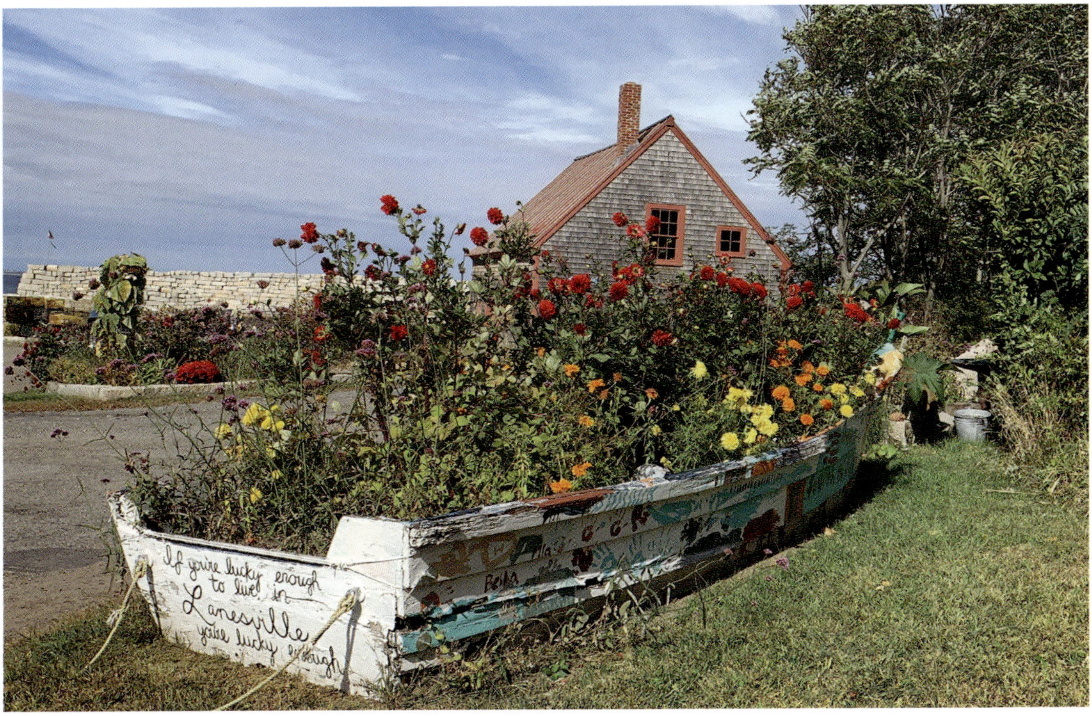

This beautiful display of wildflowers rests on the grass in Lanes Cove. The caption on the back of the boat reads, "If you're lucky enough to live in Lanesville, you're lucky enough."

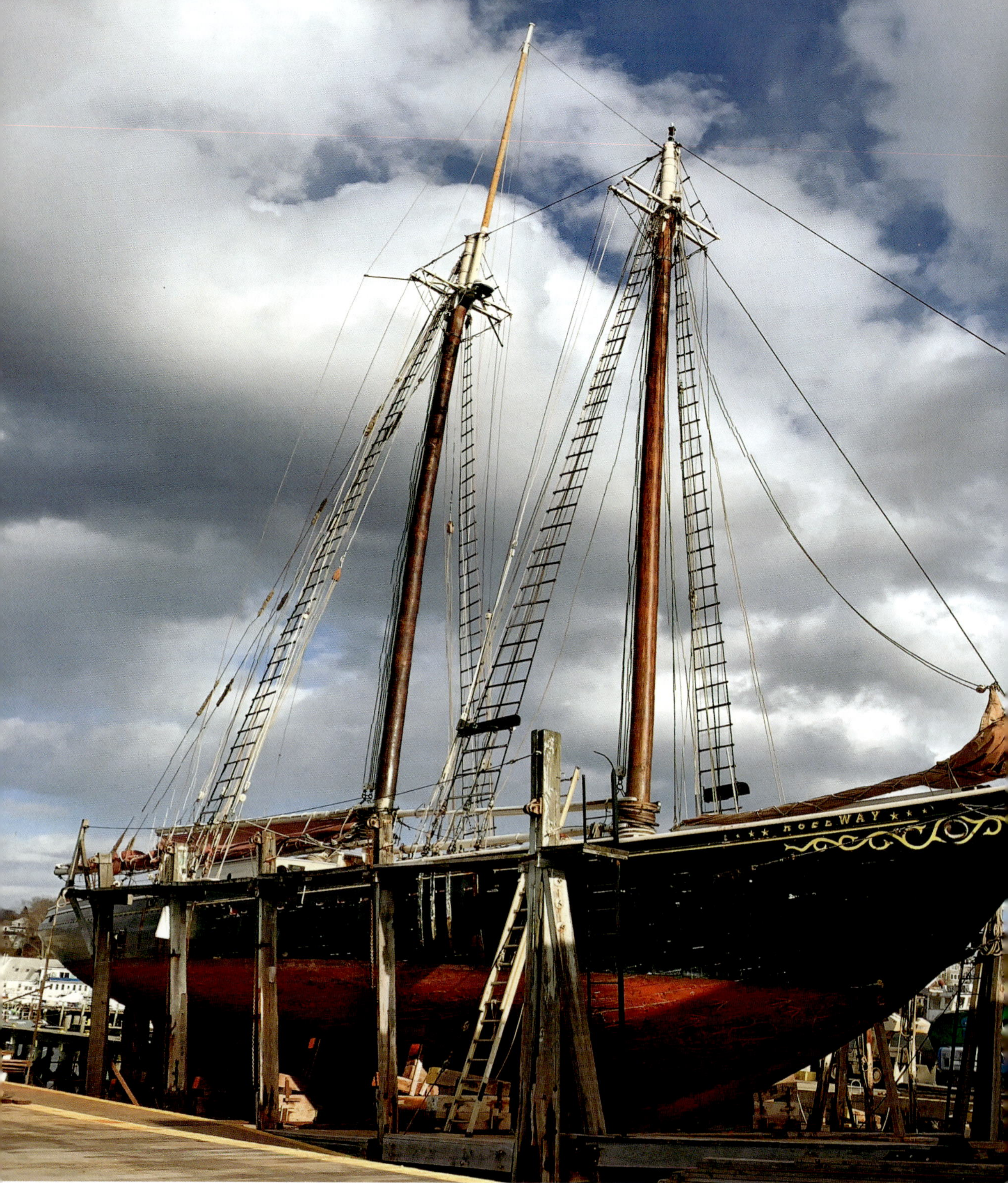

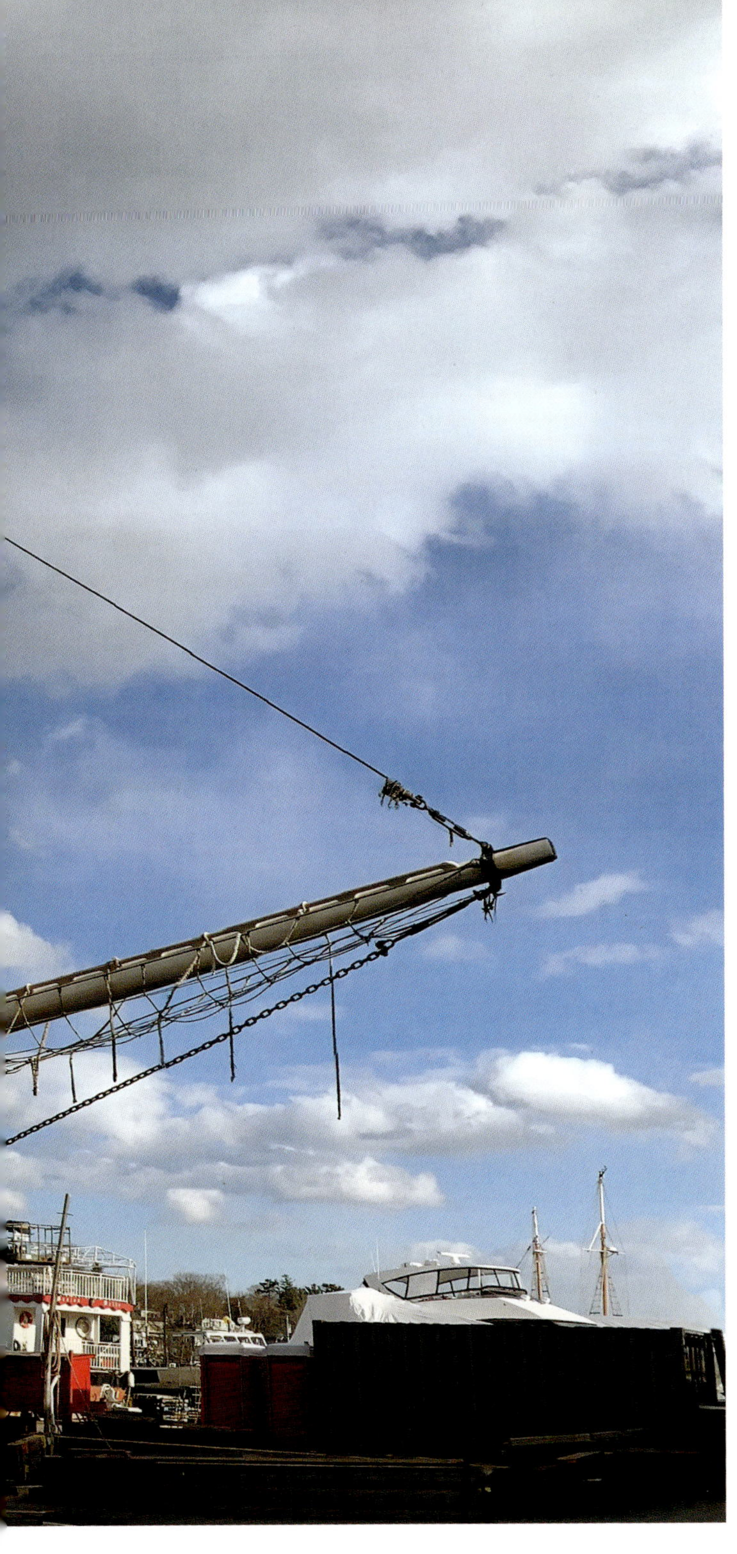

Nearby on scenic Rocky Neck, the schooner *Roseway* is being restored at a shipyard. Designed in 1925 as a fishing and racing yacht, she was pressed into service during World War II, patrolling the New England coast. In 1997, she was listed as a National Historic Landmark.

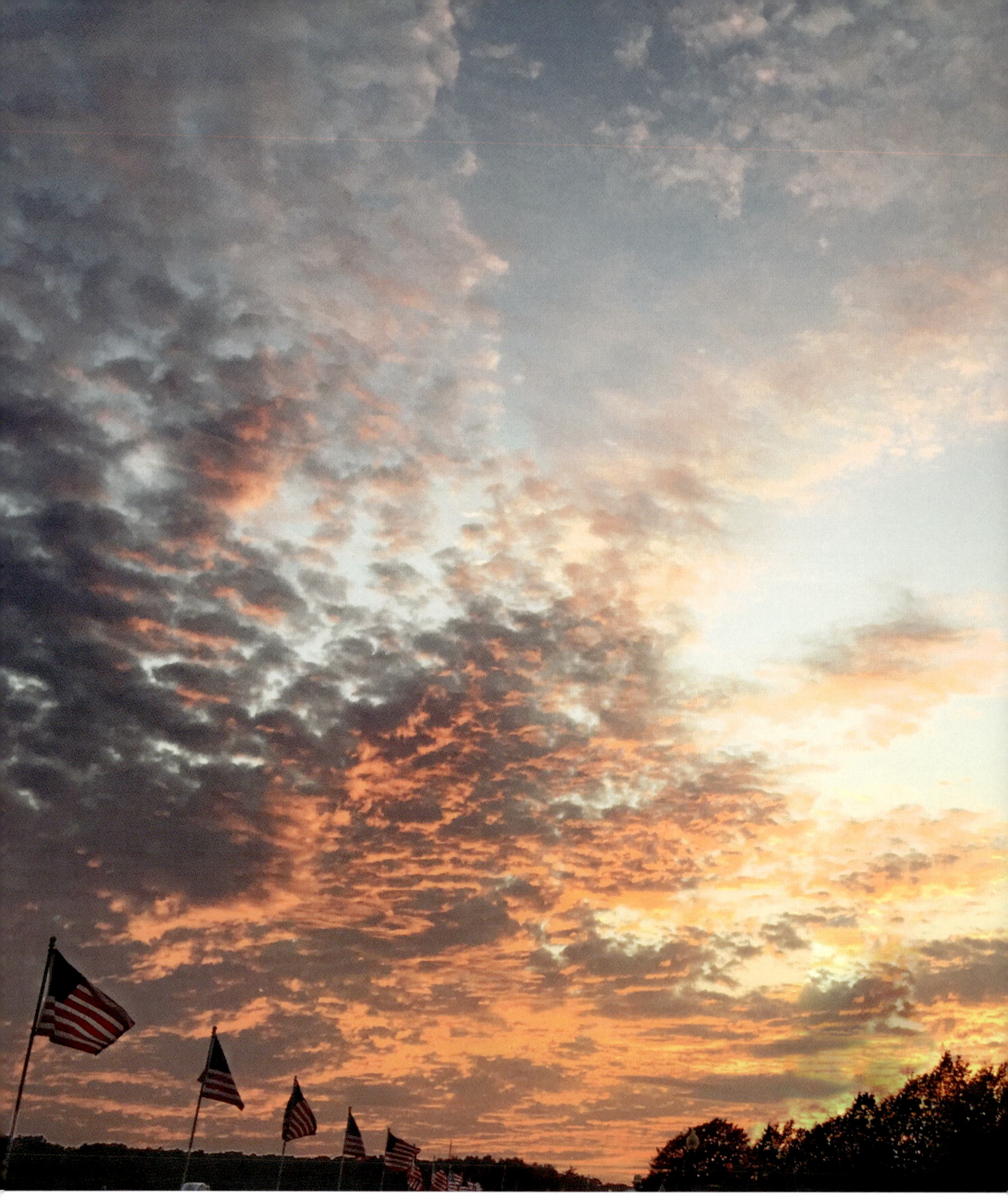

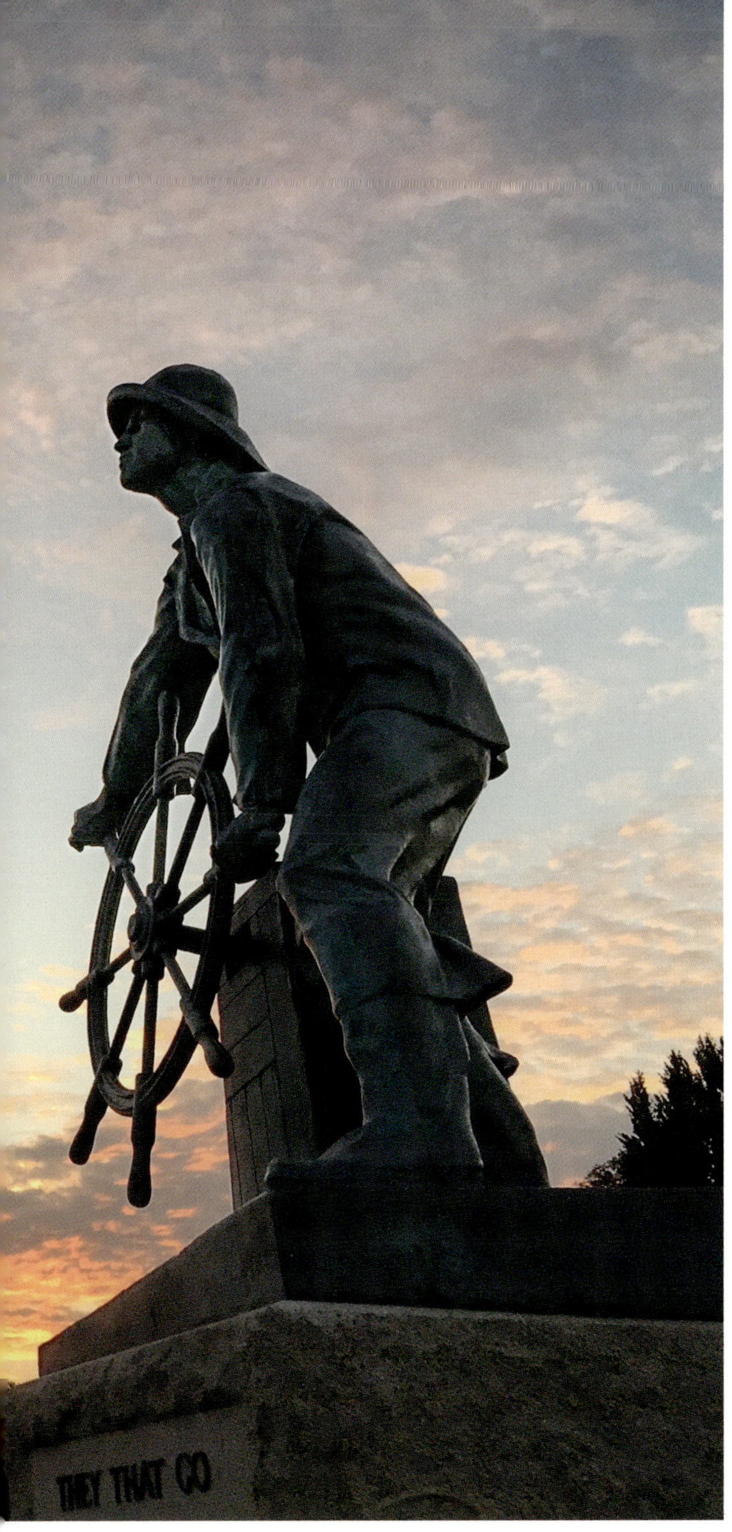

A seagull flies over the Fisherman's Memorial at twilight. Though a nuisance to some, seagulls play an important role in the ecosystems of coastal communities. They eat insects, disperse pollen, and clean up discarded food. But yes, they'll also be happy to steal your food if you're not paying attention.

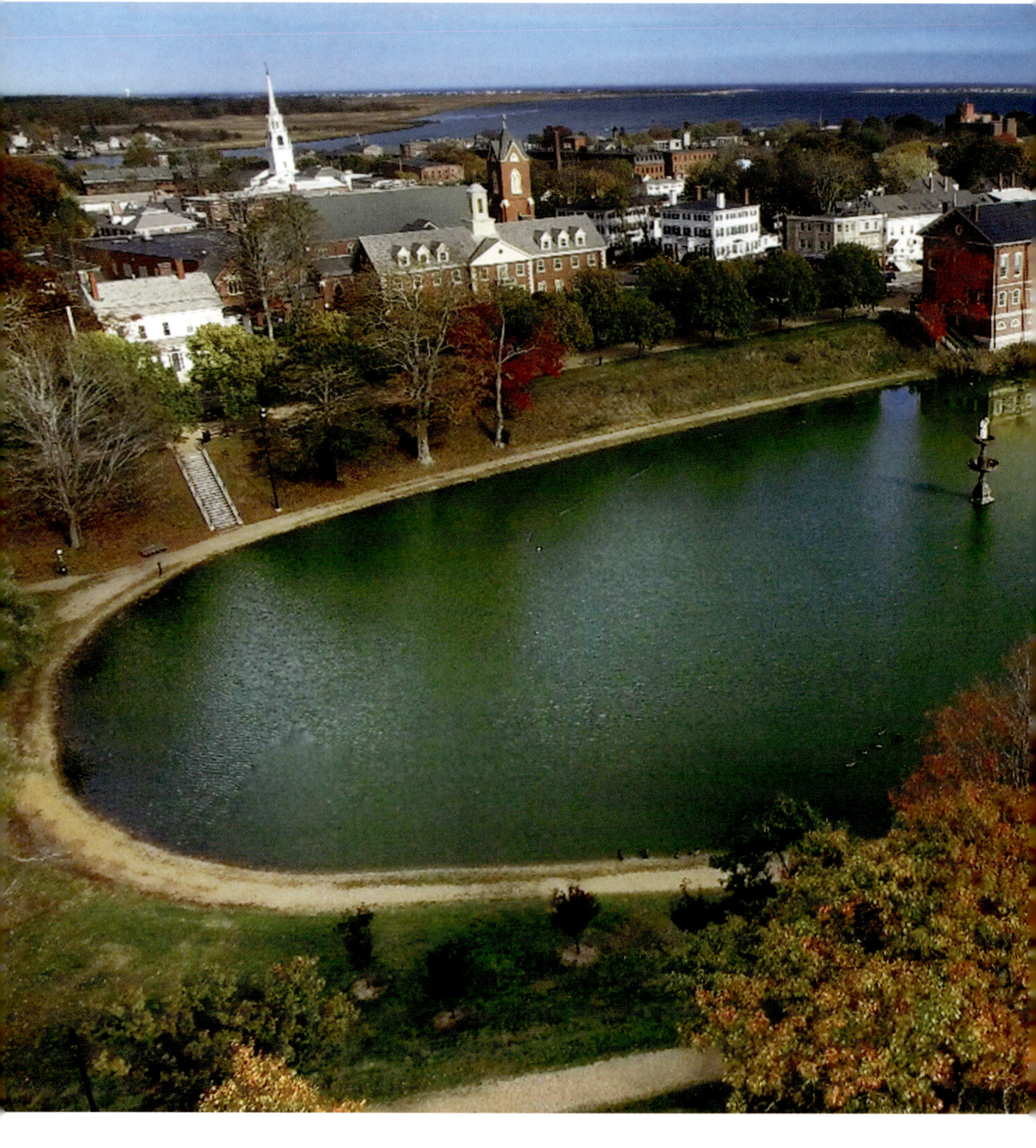

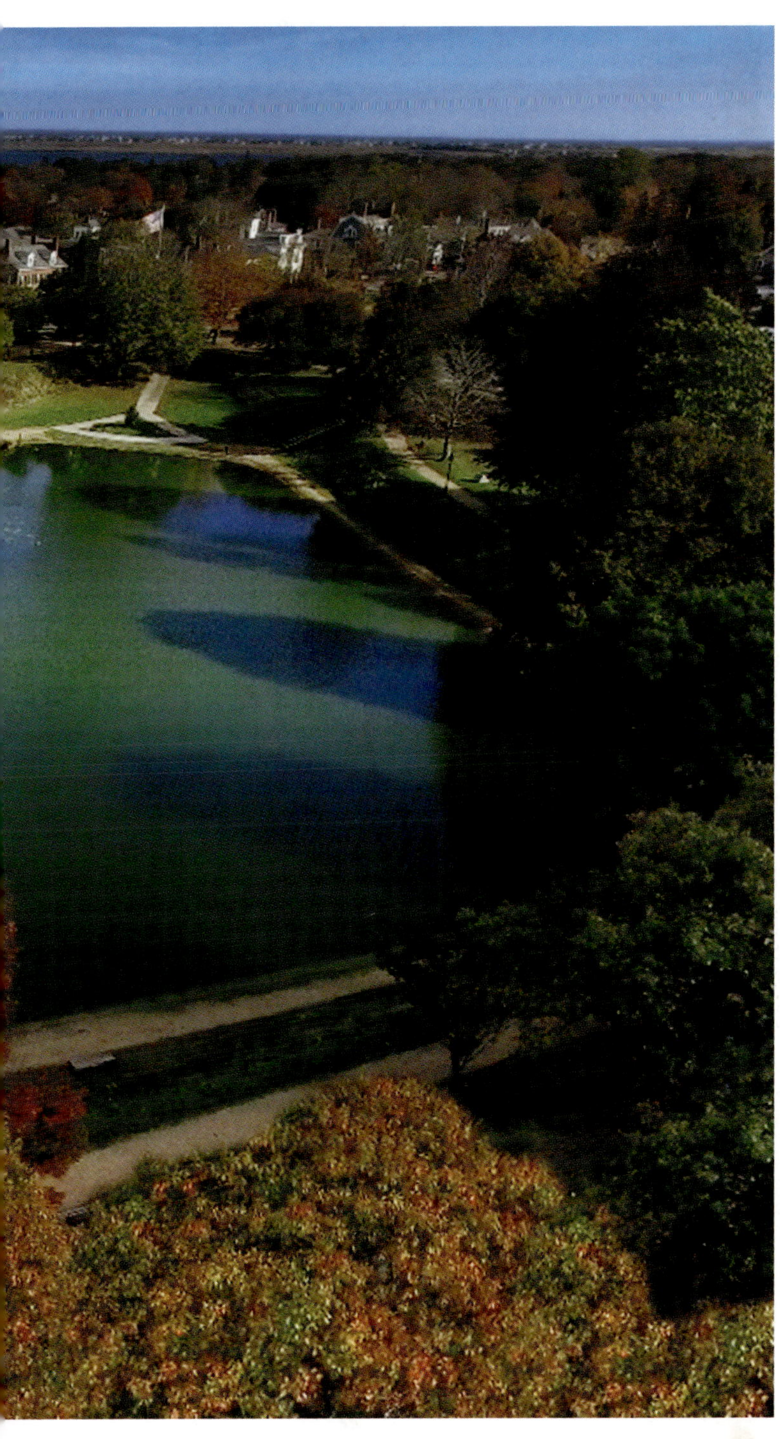

Newburyport

Newburyport is perched on the southern side of the Merrimack River, near where it spills into the Atlantic Ocean. It's a city with a rich maritime heritage, including shipping, and shipbuilding. There are impressive examples of early American architecture here, along with cultural landmarks, and vast scenic parks. Settled in 1635, Newburyport continues to be a popular destination for sightseeing along the river, hiking, restaurants, and shopping.

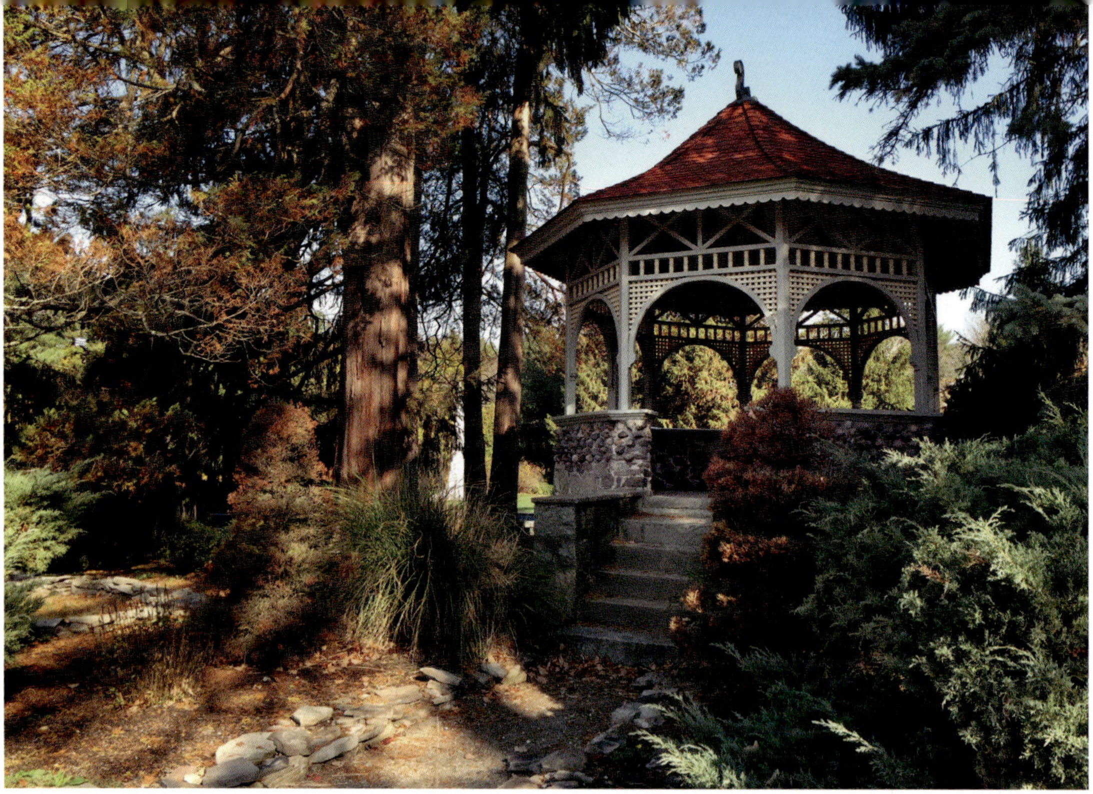

Atkinson Common, a stunning 21-acre park on High Street, features this beautiful gazebo, gardens, tennis courts, monuments, and more.

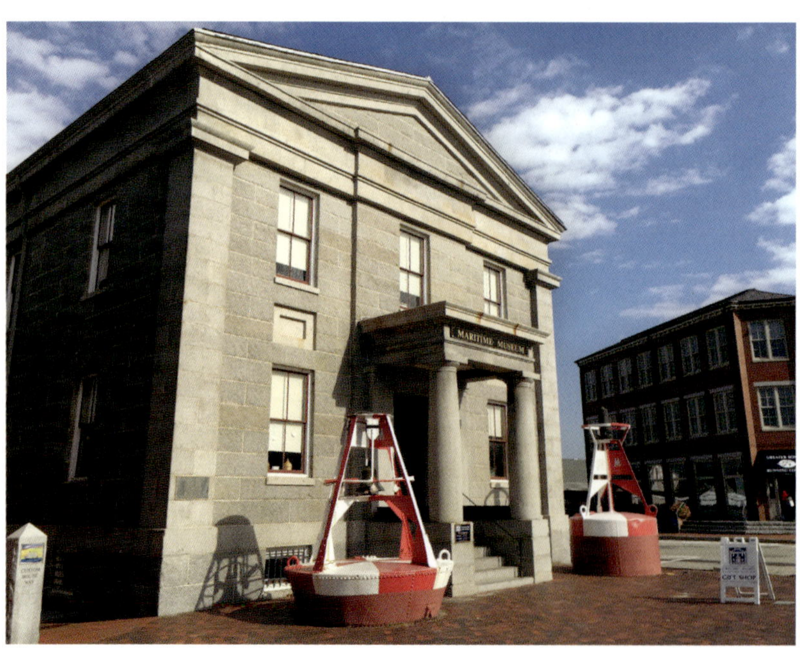

The Custom House Maritime Museum is downtown by the waterfront. The solid granite structure was built in 1835 and was originally used for tax collection on trade. It now features maritime artifacts including art, model ships, and historical info about the Coast Guard.

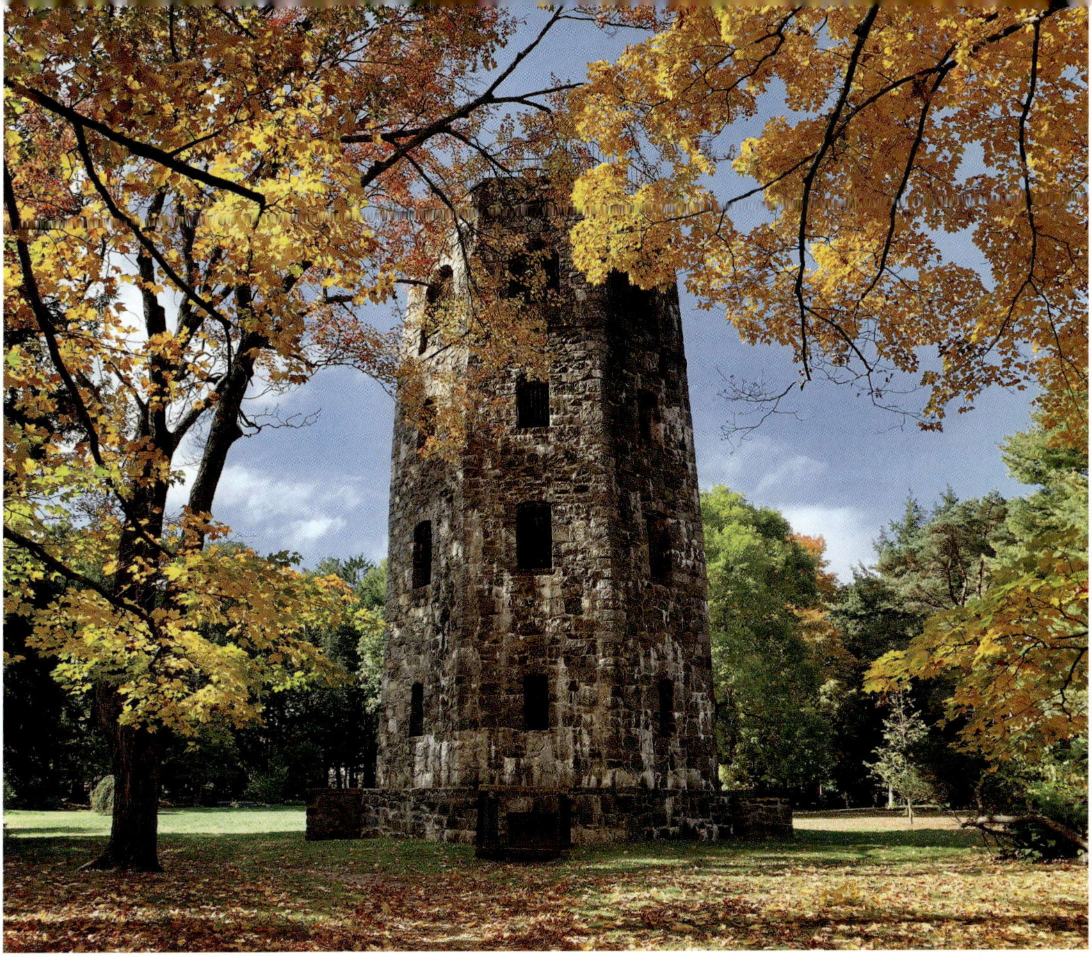

One of the most interesting features of the park is the stone observation tower. It was built in 1936, to offer visitors a panoramic view of the Merrimack River.

The museum collection also features a mesmerizing 4th Order Fresnel lens, circa 1865. It was created with dazzling lead-crystal prisms, to refract and increase light power. It came from a deactivated lighthouse in the Providence River, and is on loan from the Coast Guard. It stands 29 inches tall, and weighs over 400 pounds!

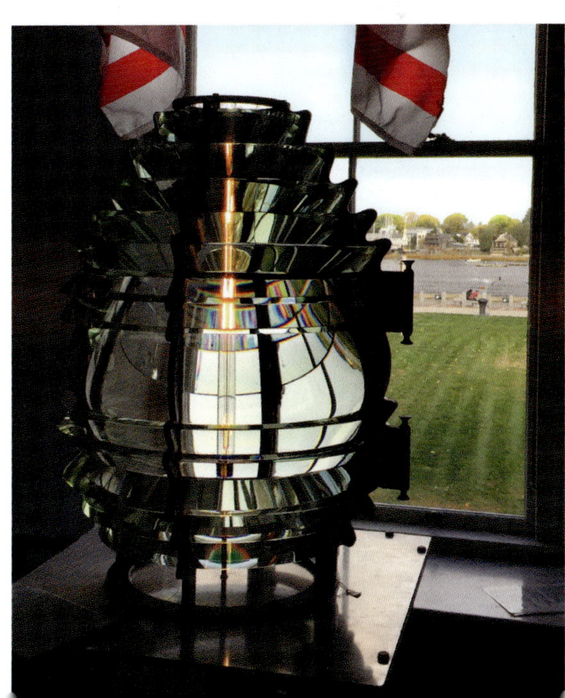

Plum Island

A blue-and-white 1966 Cessna is tethered down for winter weather at snow-covered Plum Island Airport. Handling mostly local traffic and smaller planes, the airport averages about 50 flights per week, and has two runways.

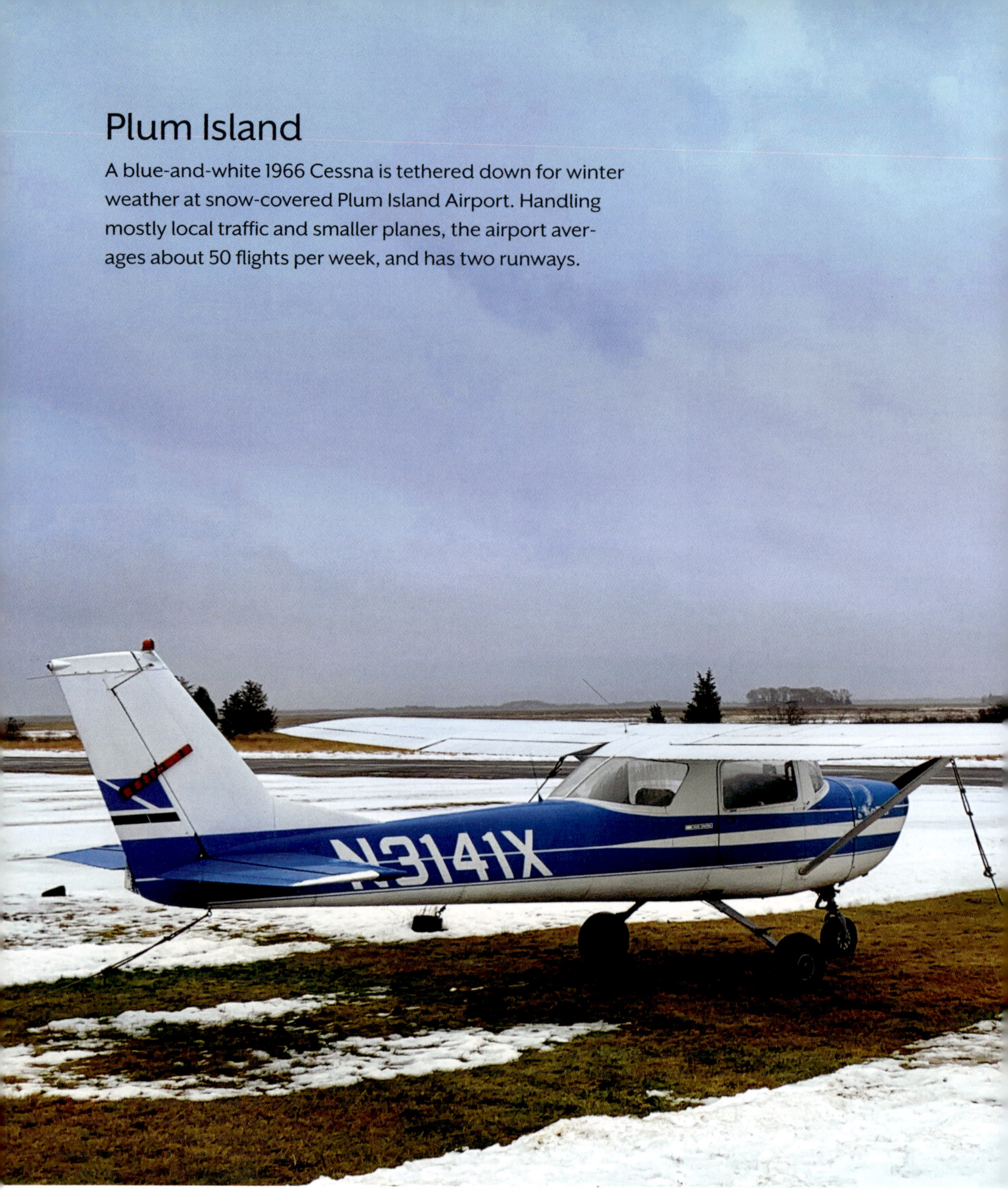

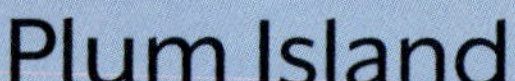

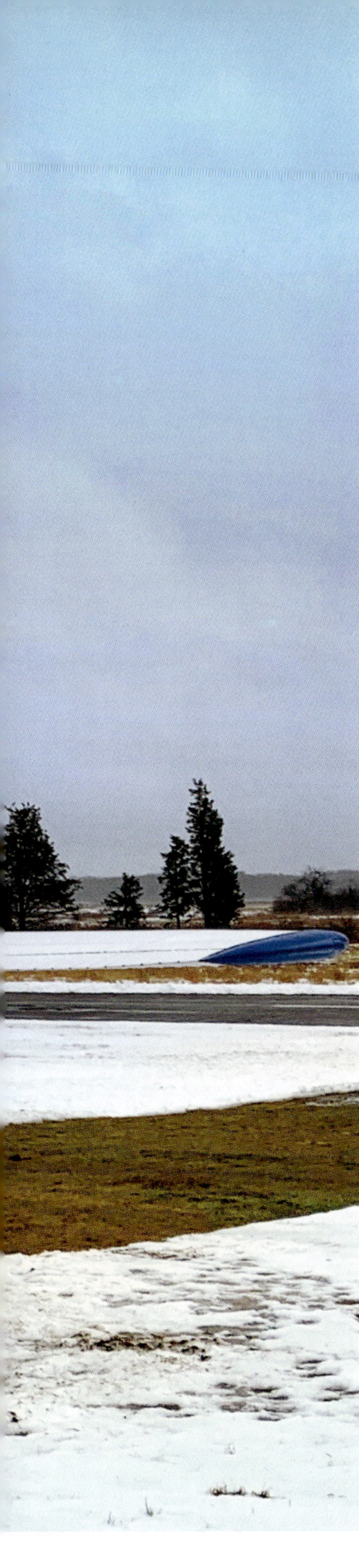

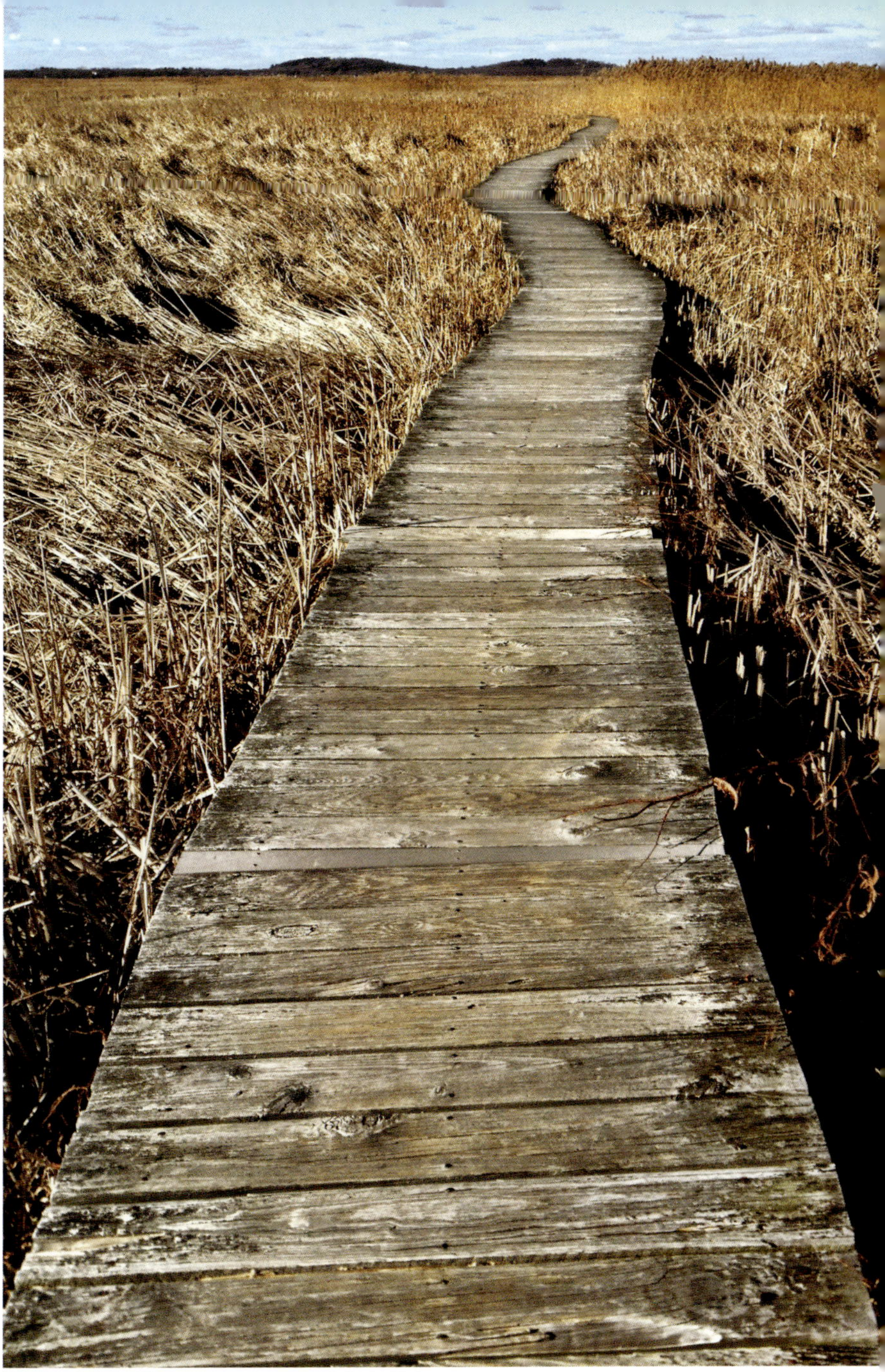

A boardwalk winds its way through a marsh in Plum
Island. At over 4,600 acres, this is the Parker River National
Wildlife Refuge, an area brimming with migratory birds
and other wildlife.

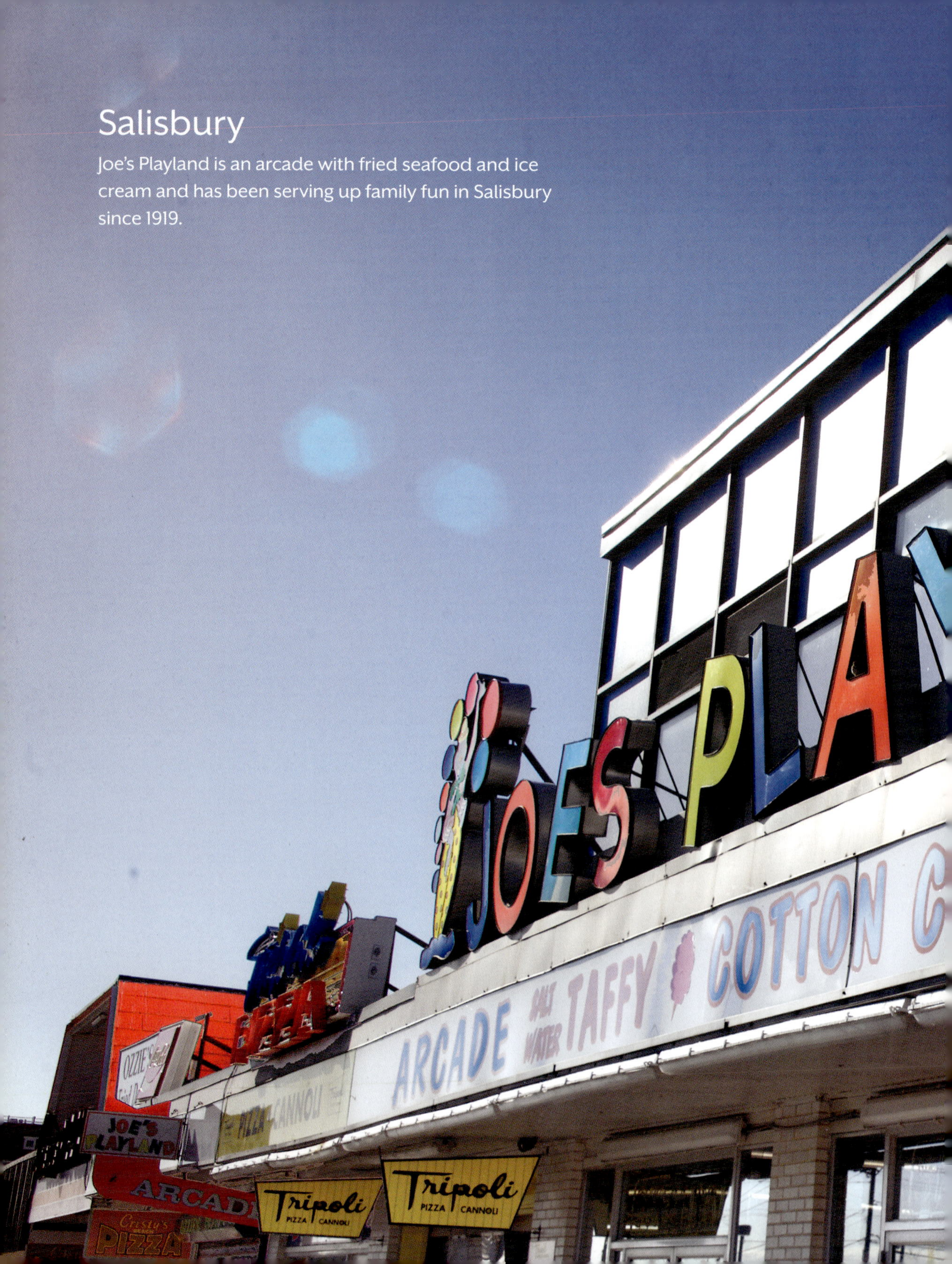

Salisbury

Joe's Playland is an arcade with fried seafood and ice cream and has been serving up family fun in Salisbury since 1919.

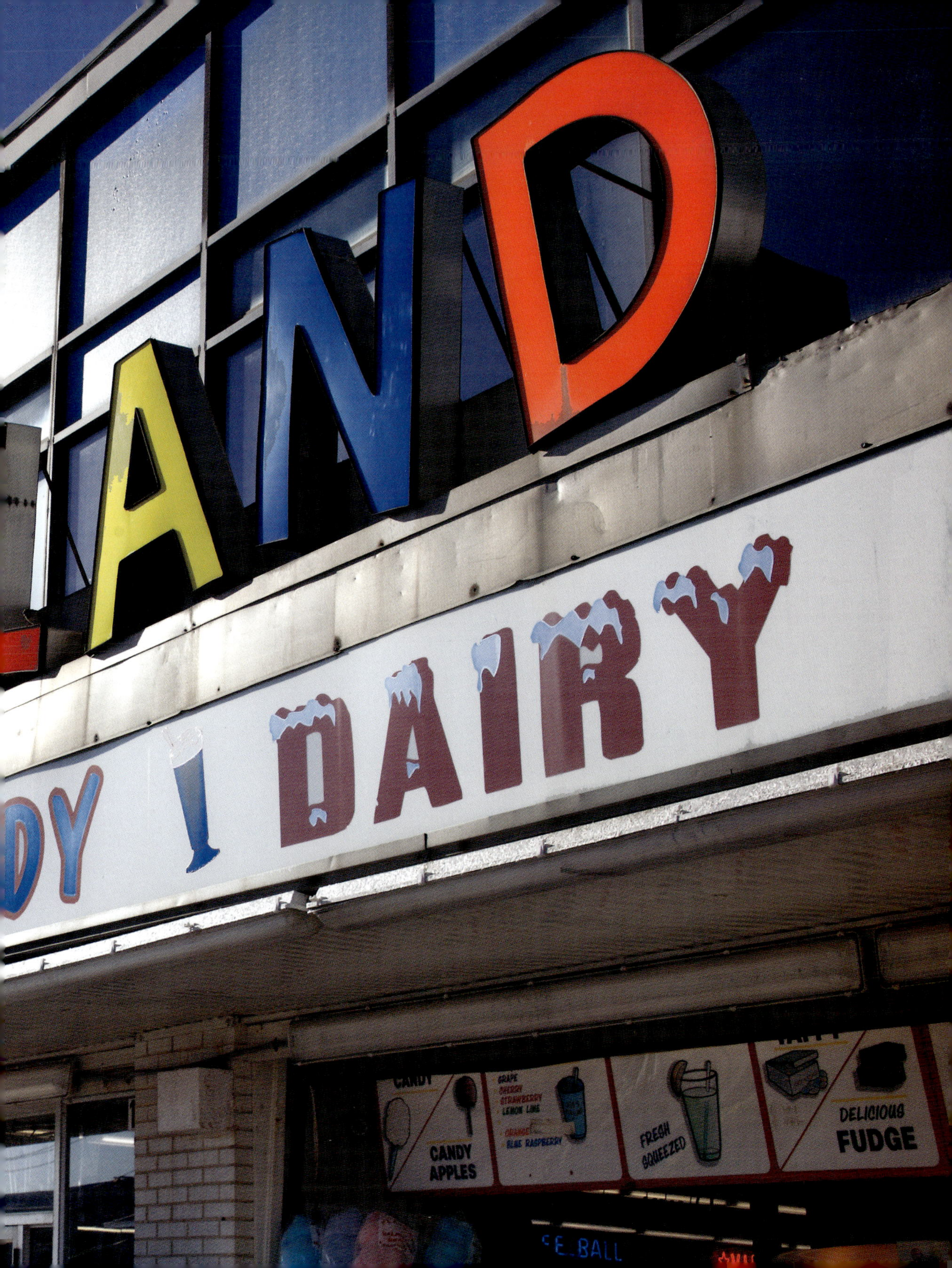
IAND
DY DAIRY
CANDY
CANDY APPLES
GRAPE
CHERRY
STRAWBERRY
LEMON LIME
ORANGE
BLUE RASPBERRY
FRESH SQUEEZED
DELICIOUS FUDGE
E BALL

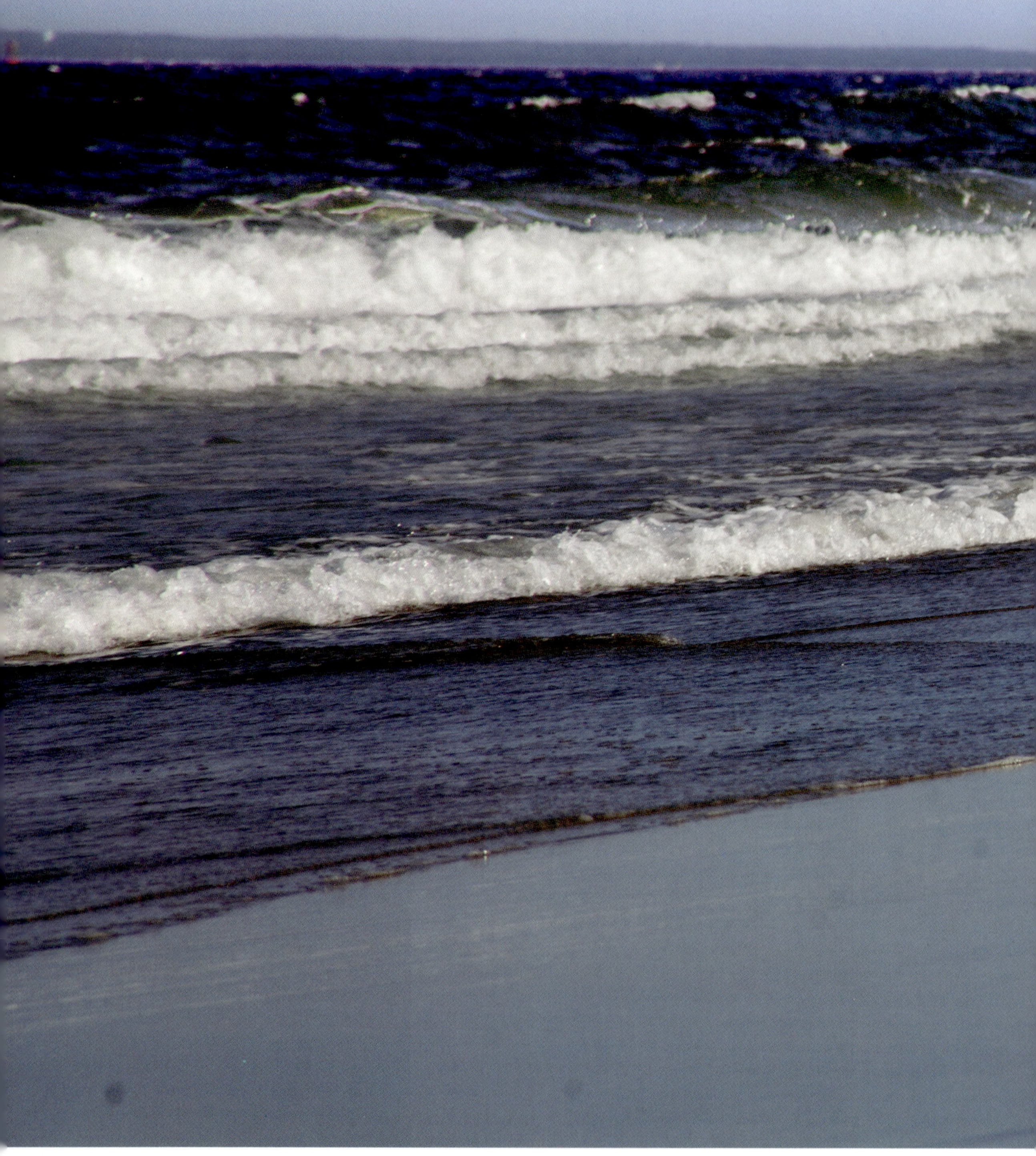

Salisbury Beach goes on for miles, and at times can get very good surf. This gull pays little interest, as three swimmers enjoy the waves in the background.

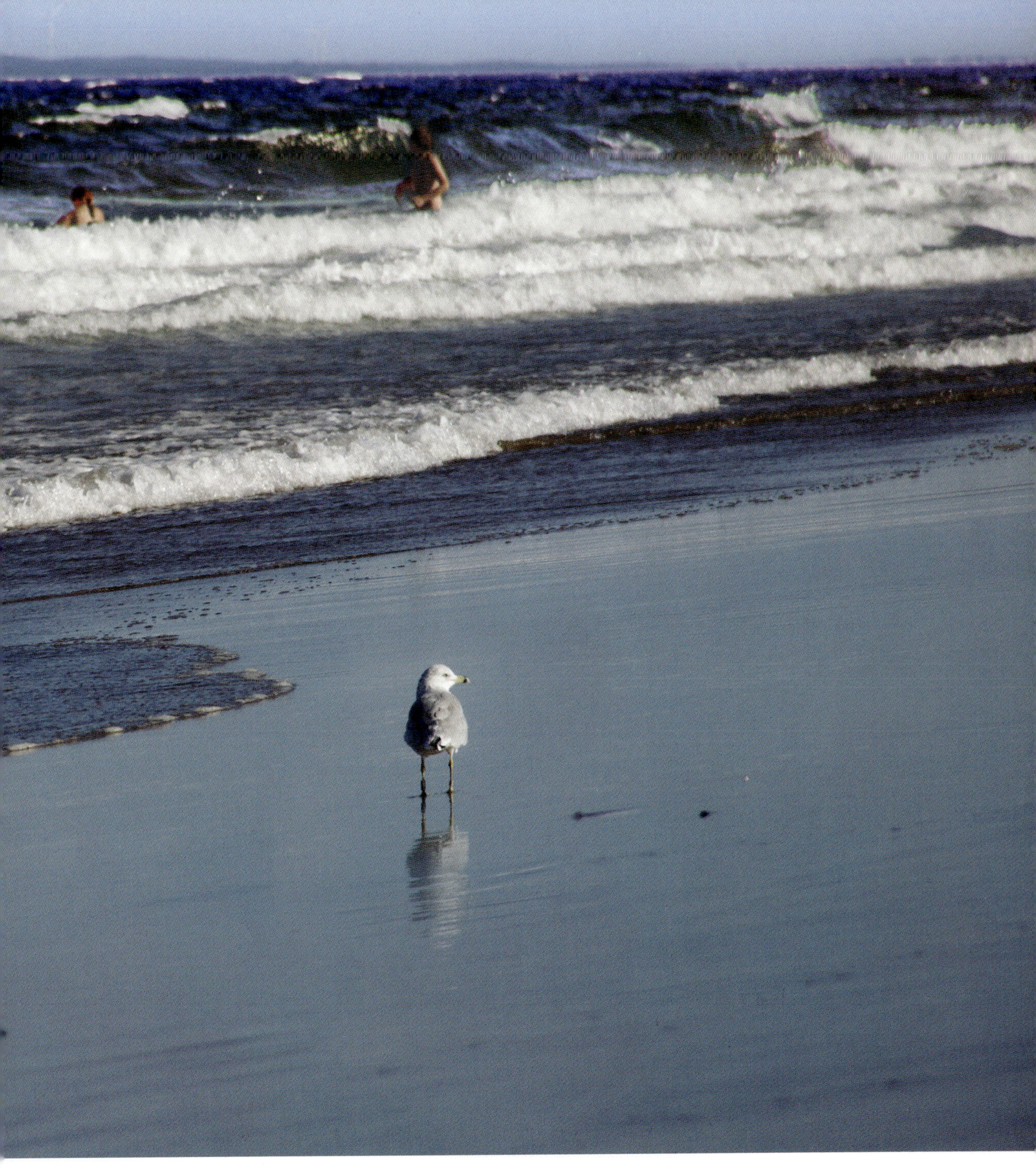

Ipswich

At over 1,200 acres, Crane Beach is a conservation area that includes a 4-mile barrier beach, covered in white sand, and bordered by sand dunes. Occasionally you'll even see folks riding horseback.

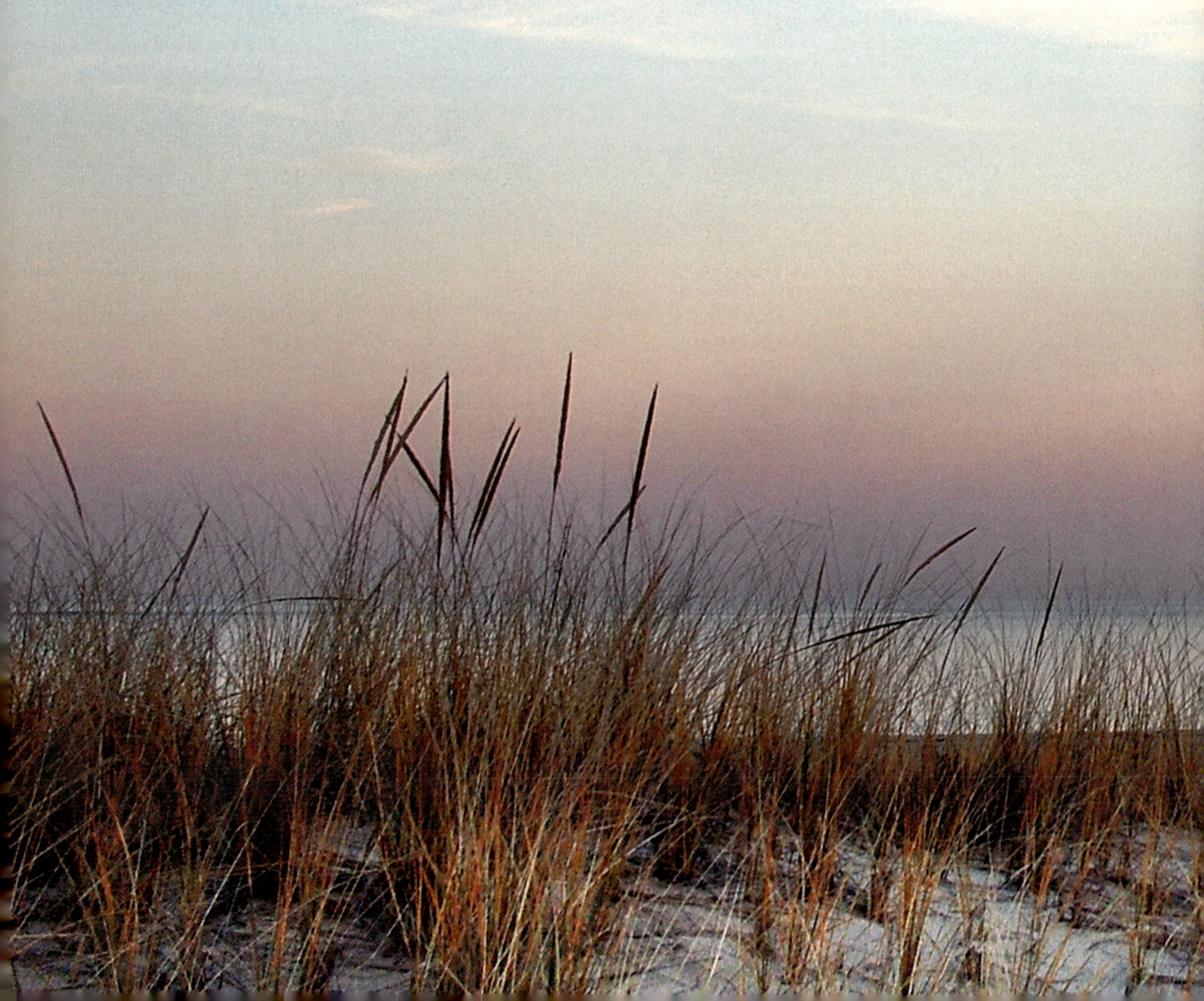

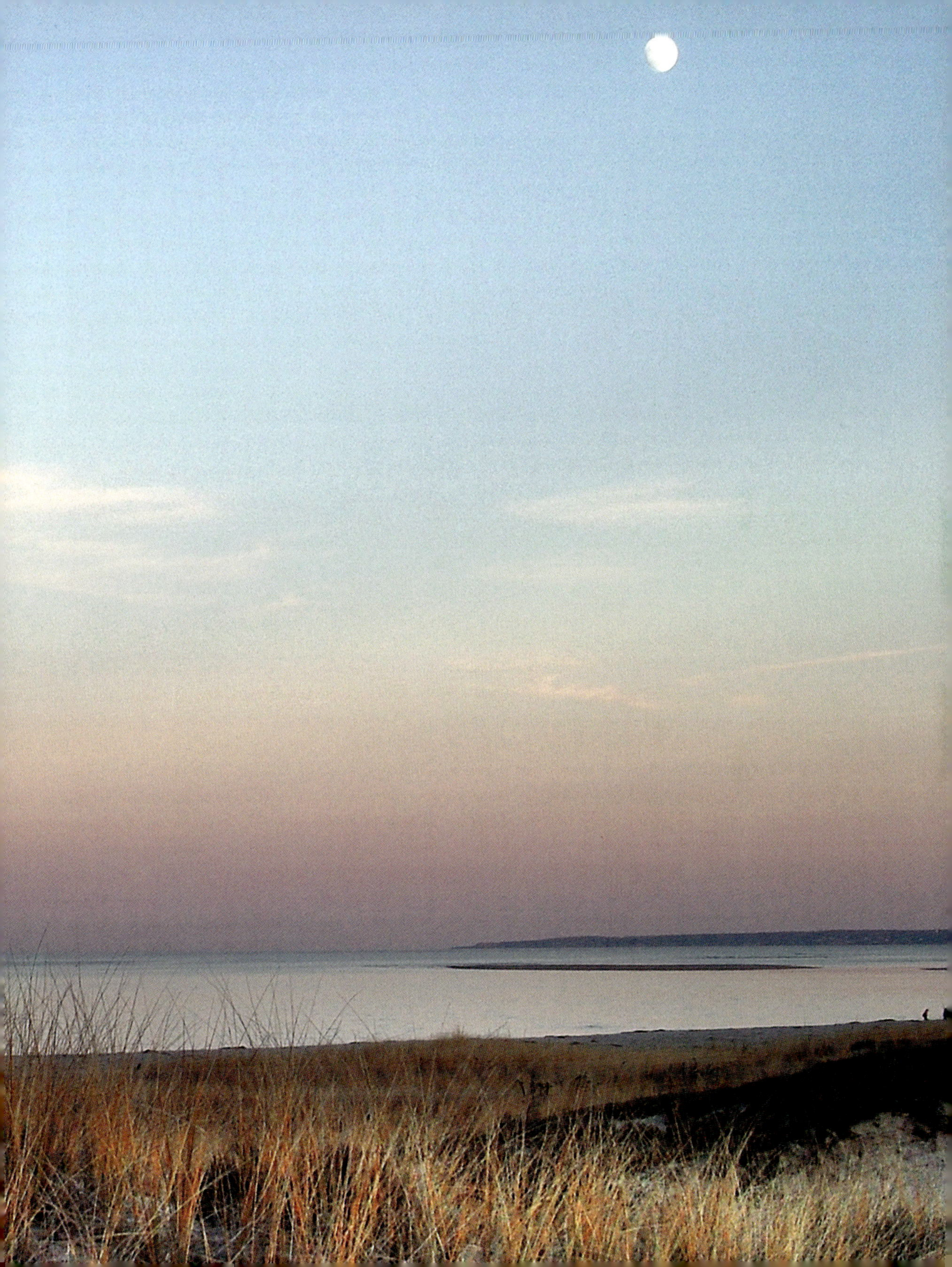

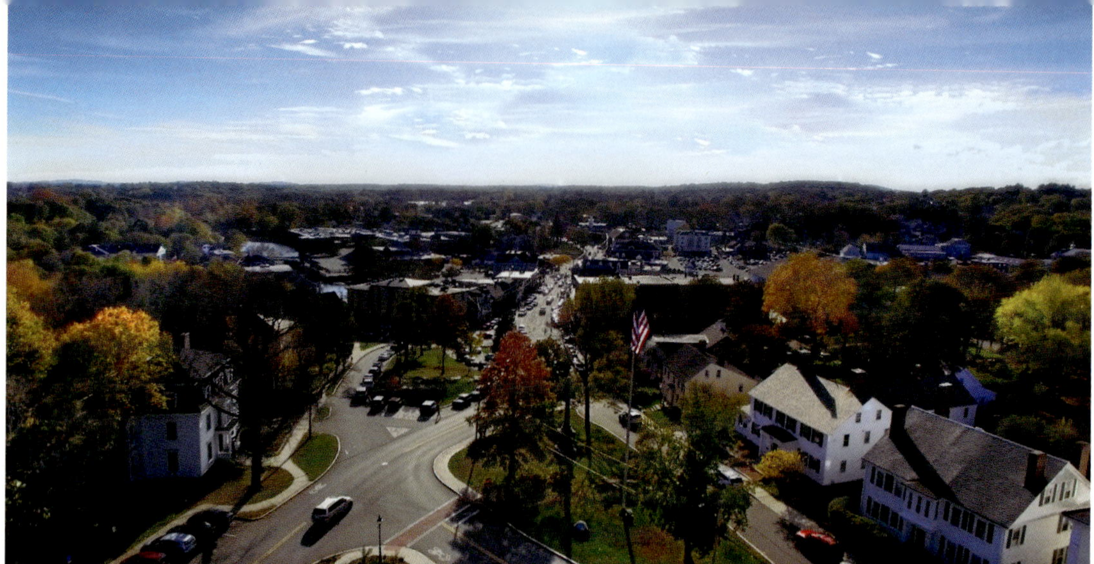

Ipswich was settled in 1633, known for its seafood, especially clams, farms, marshes, sand dune beaches, and historic architecture.

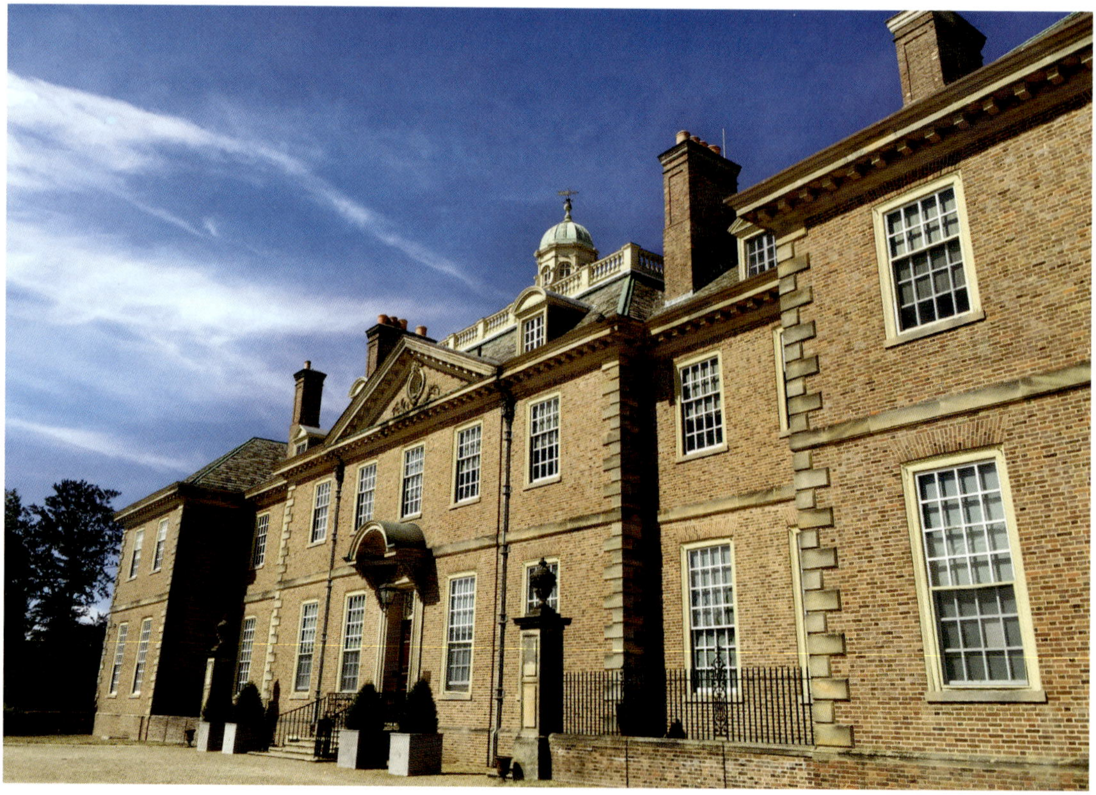

Crane Estate features a Stuart-style mansion on Castle Hill built from 1926 to 1928, with 2,100 acres filled with dramatic architecture, elegant terraced gardens, and gently rolling lawns overlooking the ocean.

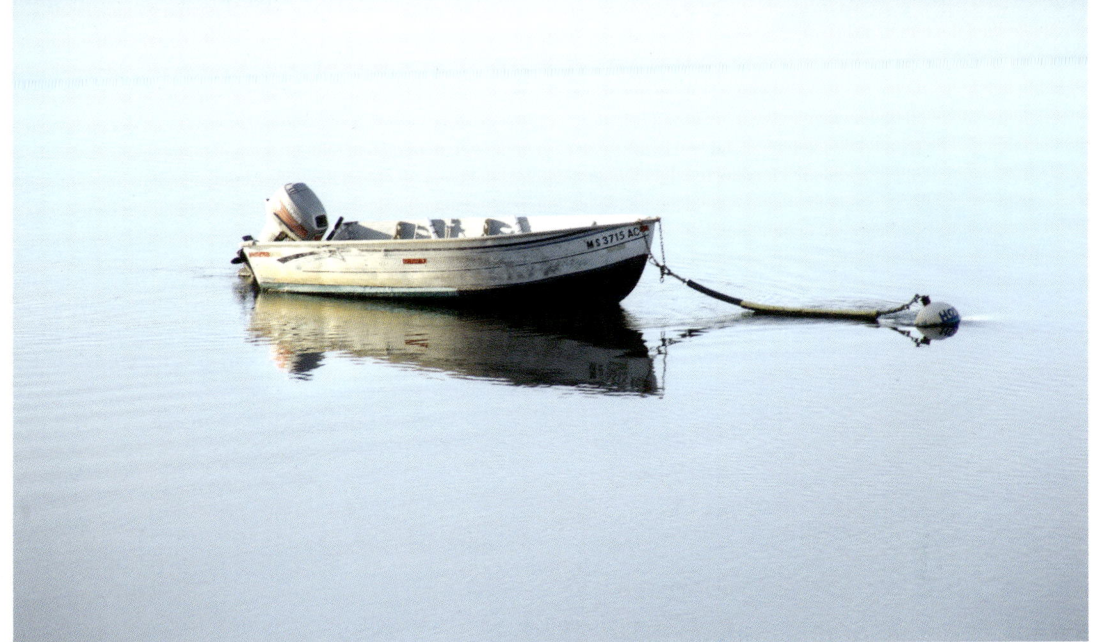

A lonely motorboat, tethered to its mooring buoy, is floating on a gentle current.

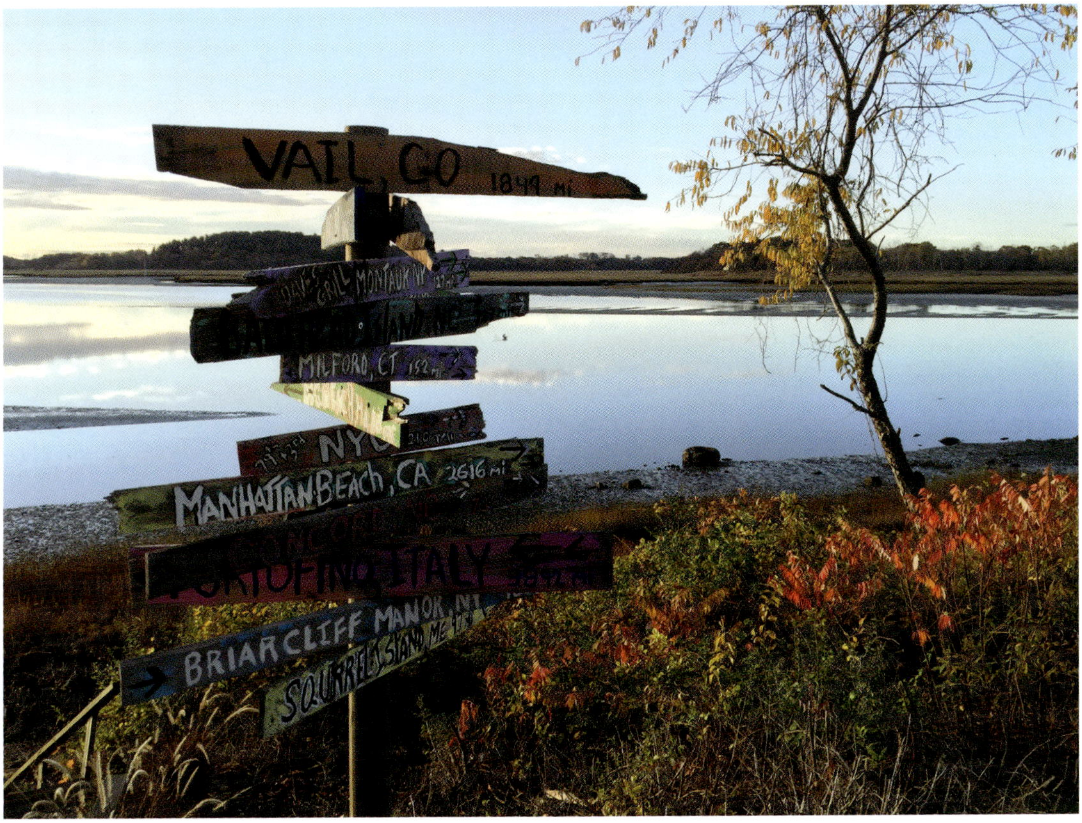

If you're looking for captivating water views, just follow the sign.

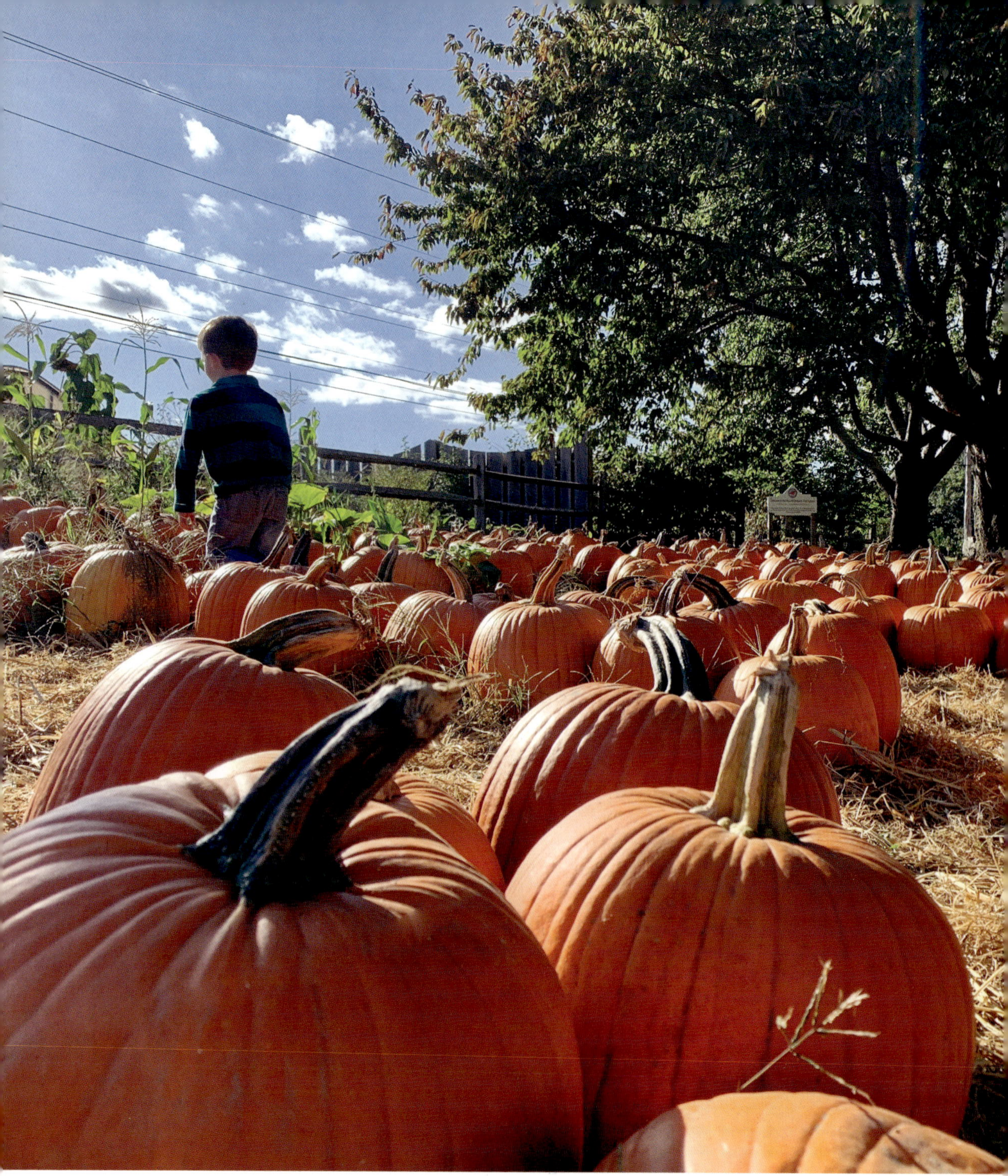

Another fall staple is the pumpkin patch. The ubiquitous orange fruit (yes it's a fruit, not a veggie) is seen almost everywhere this time of year.

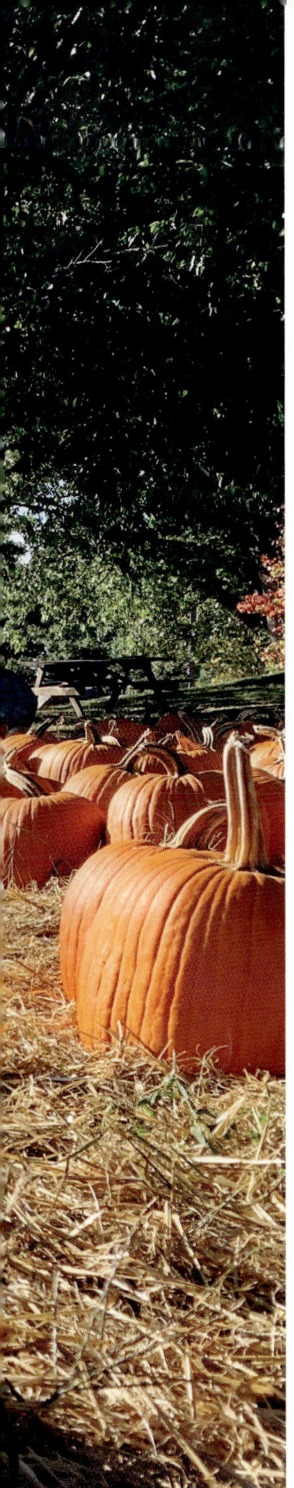

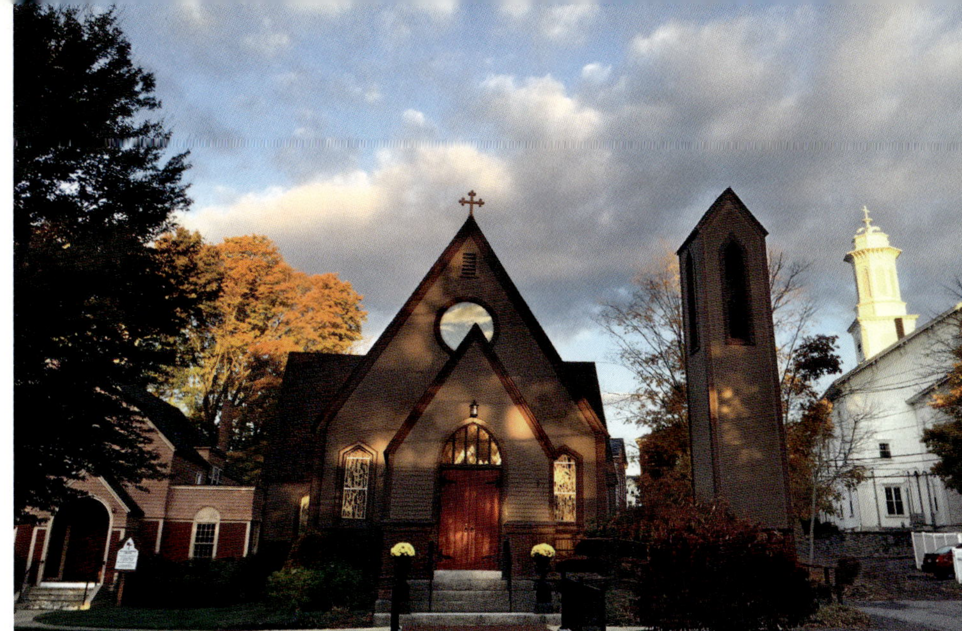

The Ascension Memorial Church is dappled by early morning light in November.

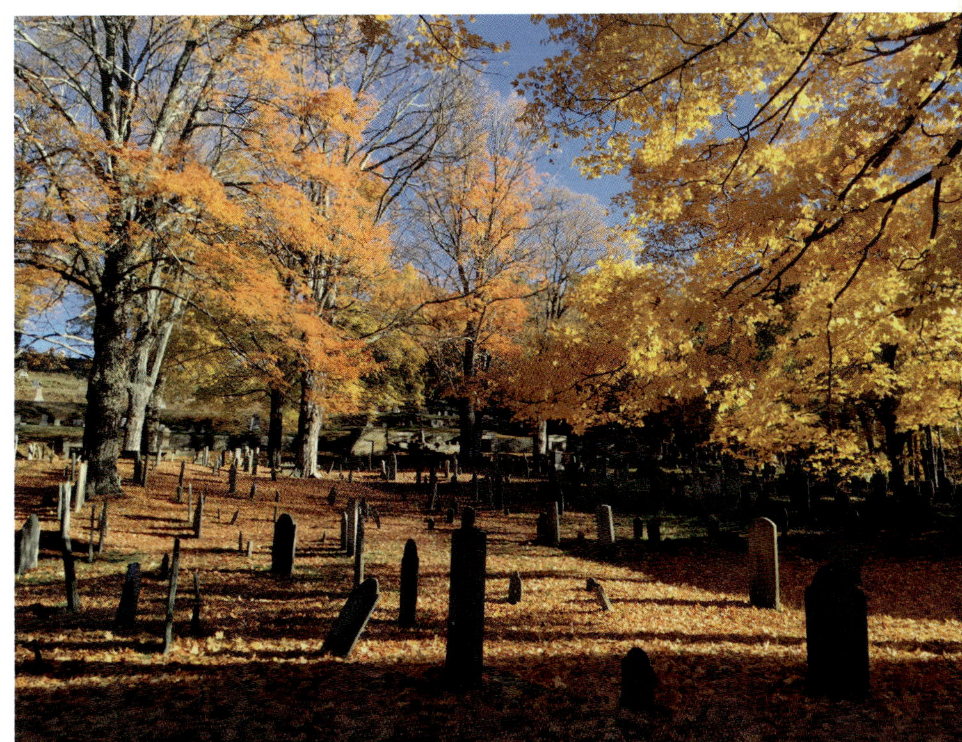

Yellow leaves rustle in the breeze at the Old North Burying Ground, established in 1634. It's one of the country's oldest cemeteries.

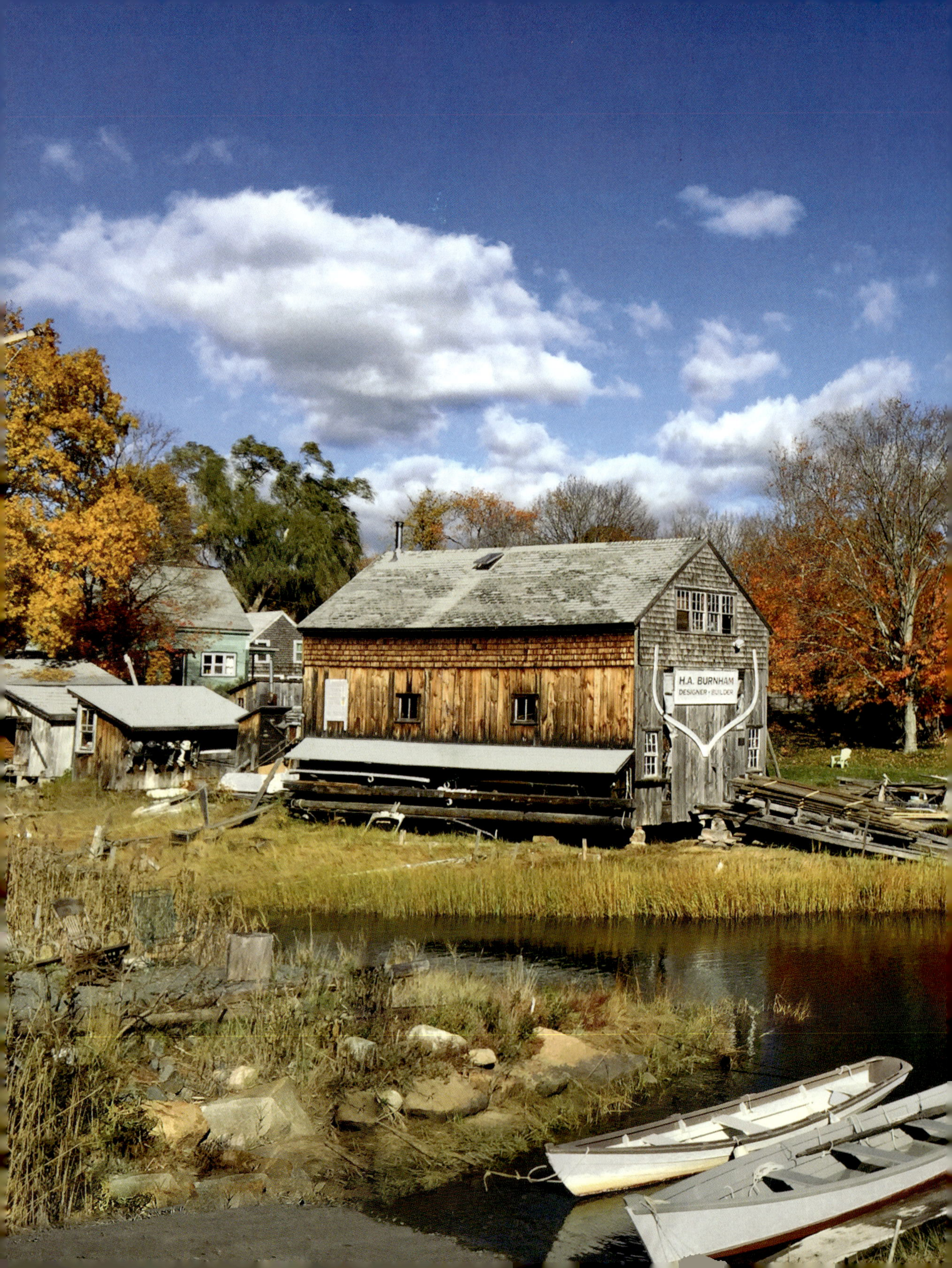

H.A. BURNHAM
DESIGNER · BUILDER

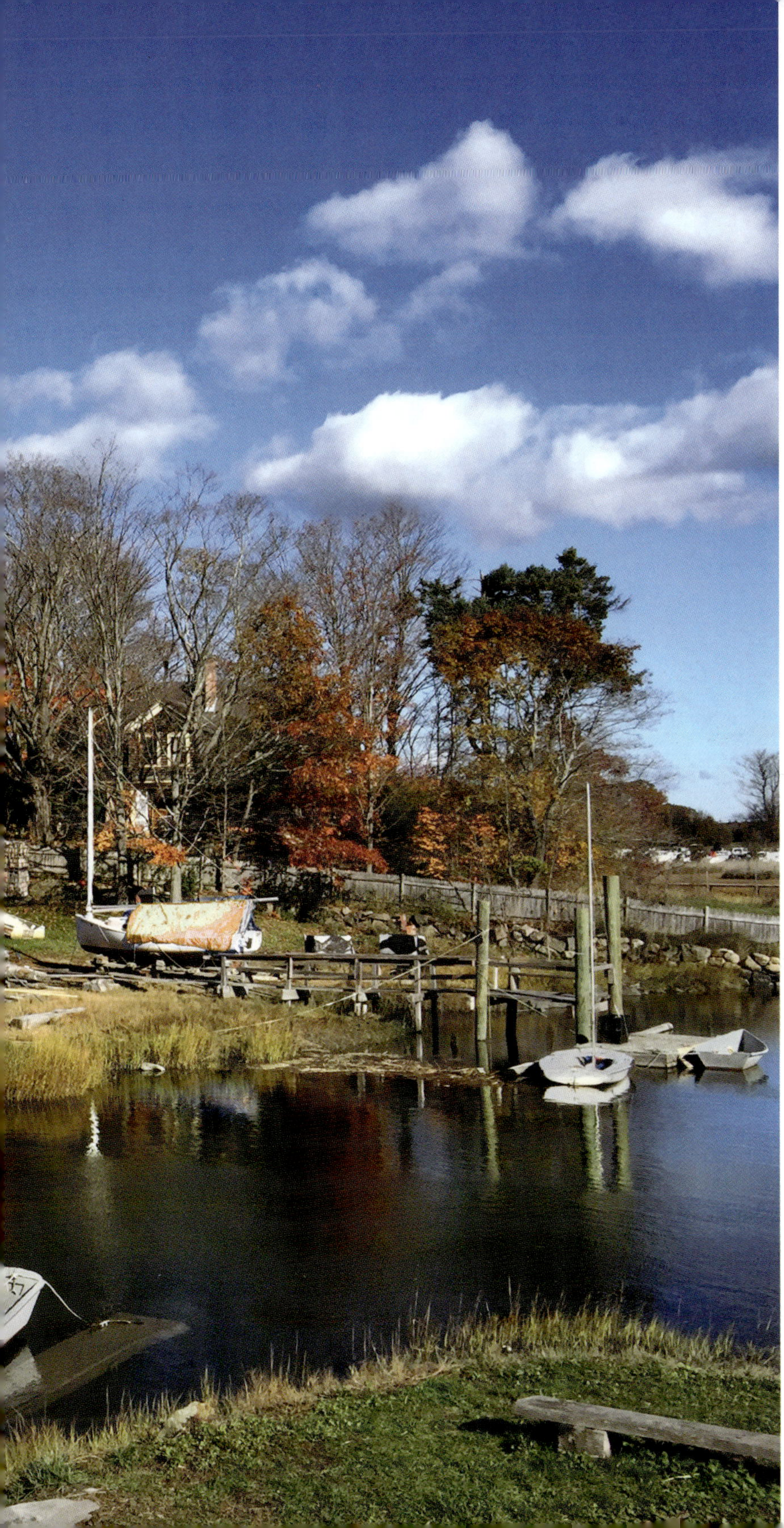

Essex

The first settlers arrived in Essex in 1634, soon starting a boat crafting legacy that carries on to this day.

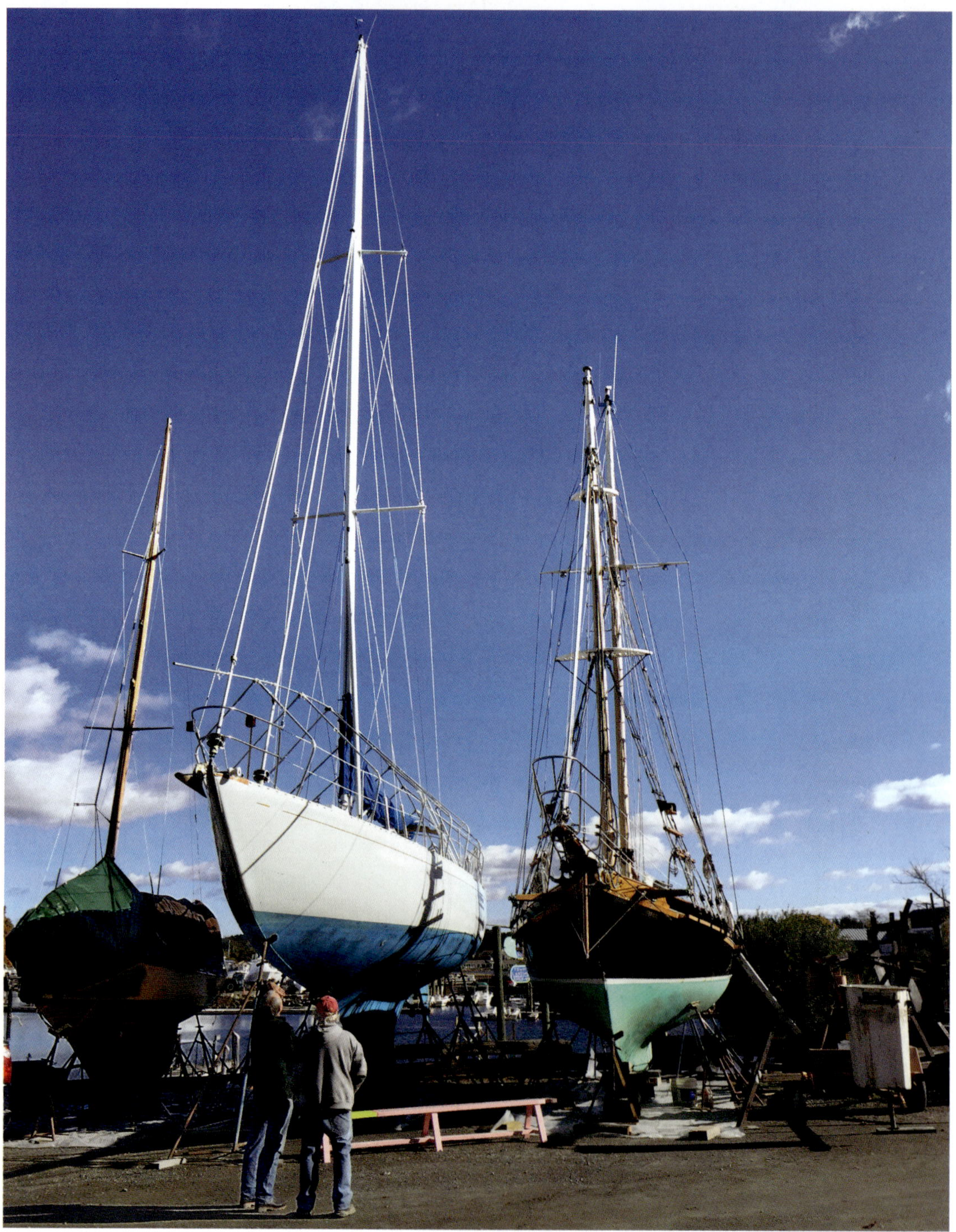

At the boatyard, a plaque indicates that in 1668 the land here was granted "for a yard to build vessels and to employ workmen for that end." Since the 1600s, approximately 4,000 wooden vessels have been fashioned here.

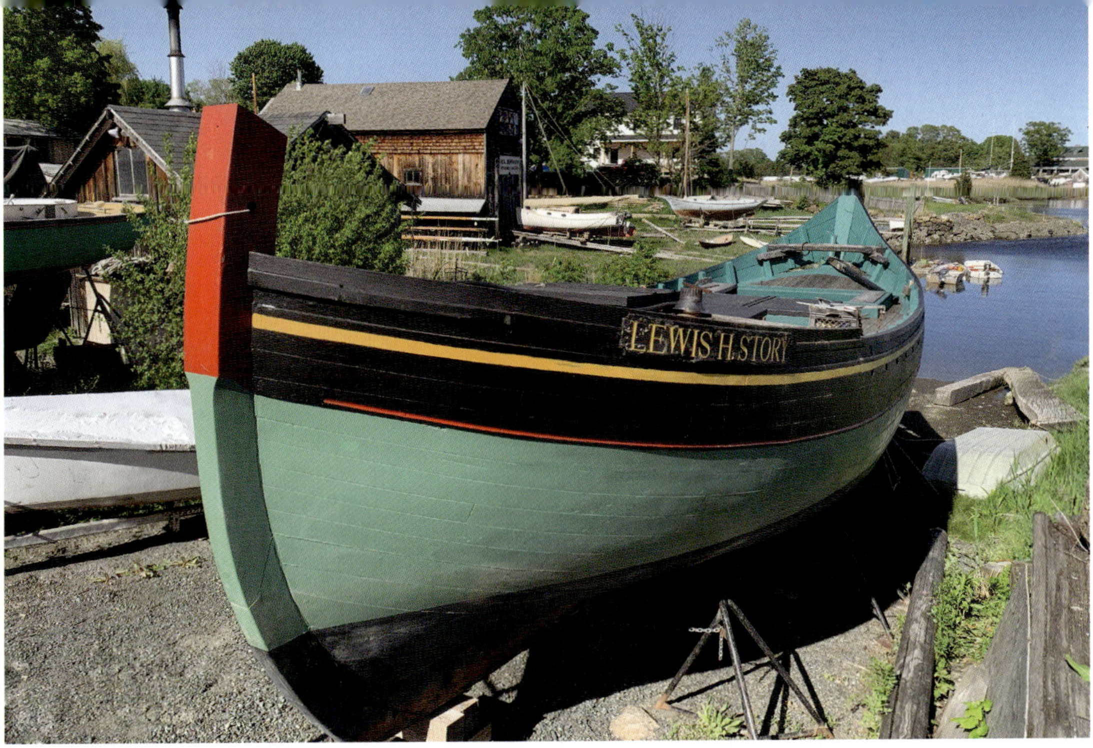

The Essex Shipbuilding Museum and the Essex Historical Society appointed local shipwright Harold Burnham to build a flagship "Chebacco"-style boat for the Museum.

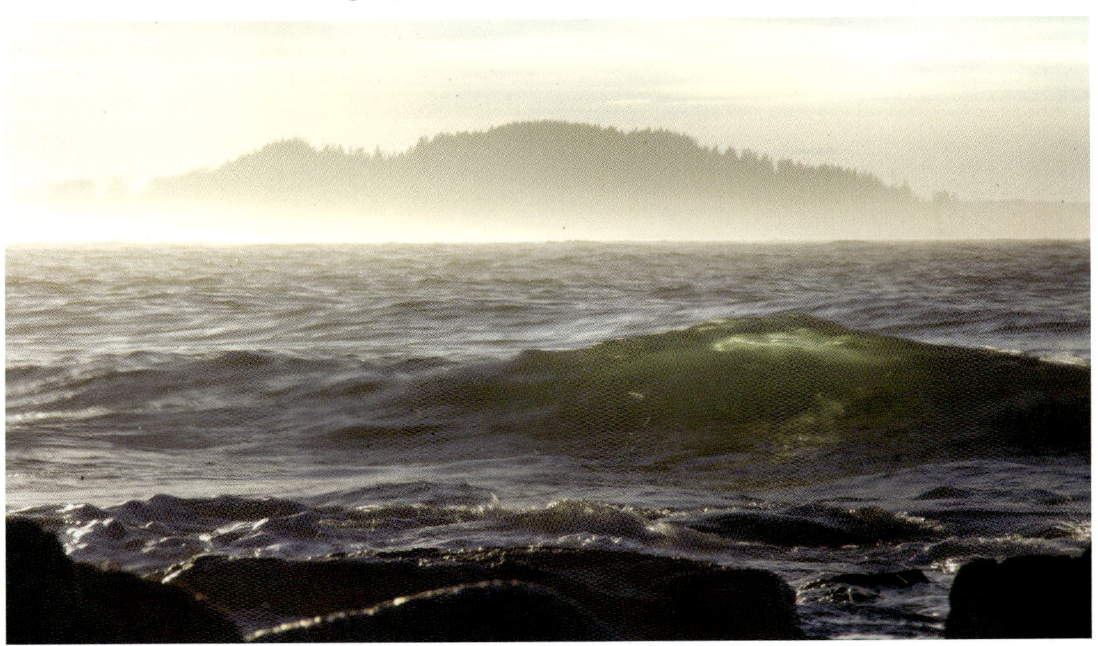

Looking across the bay we see Choate Island floating on a sea of golden mist. Also known as Hog Island, it sits in the middle of the Essex River Estuary. It's part of the Crane Wildlife Refuge, and kayak tours are available to visit the island.

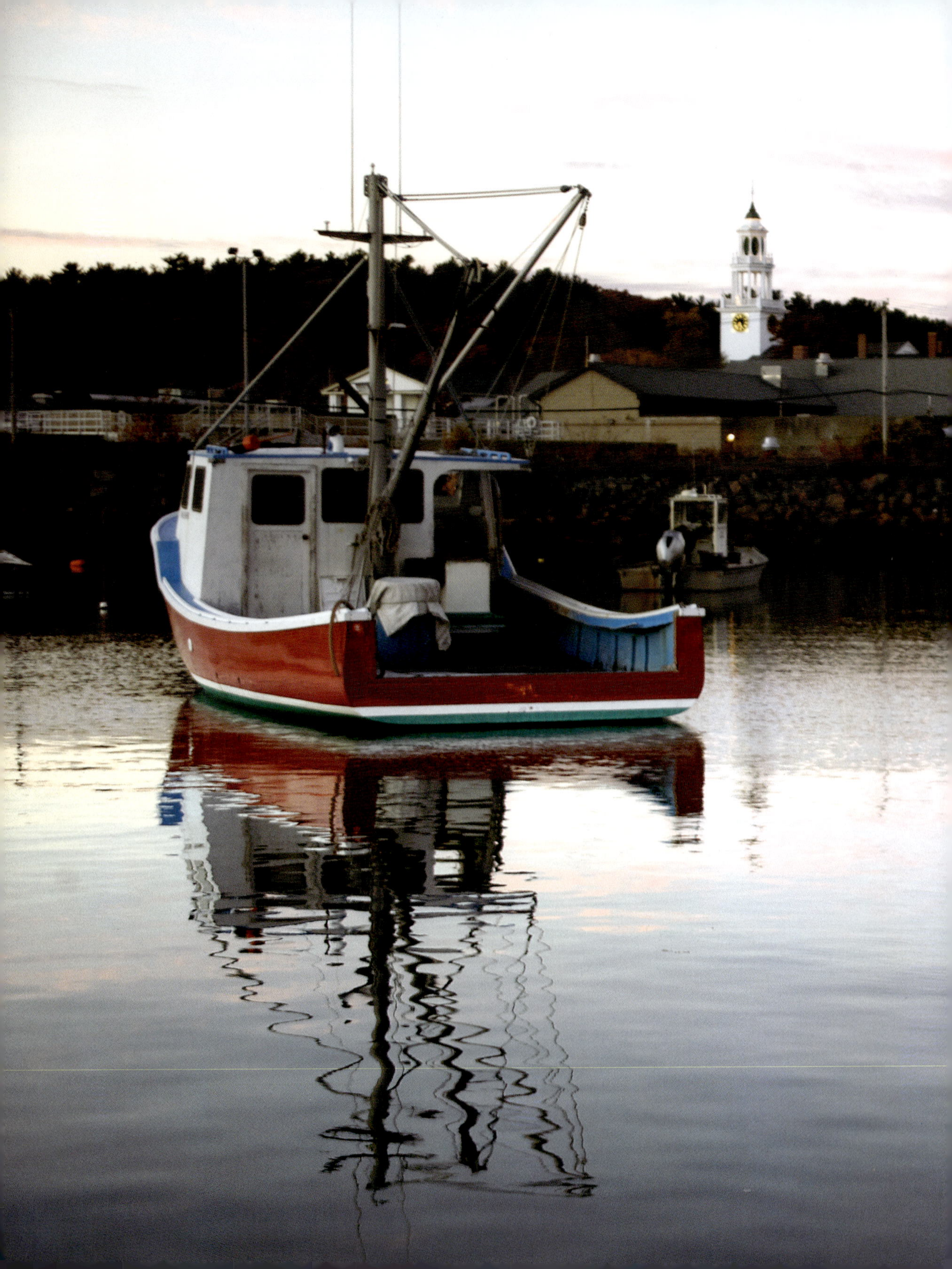

Manchester

Lobster boats moored in the tranquil waters of Manchester Harbor. There are full-service marinas and boat clubs here, and the area was used extensively for filming of the eponymous movie *Manchester by the Sea*.

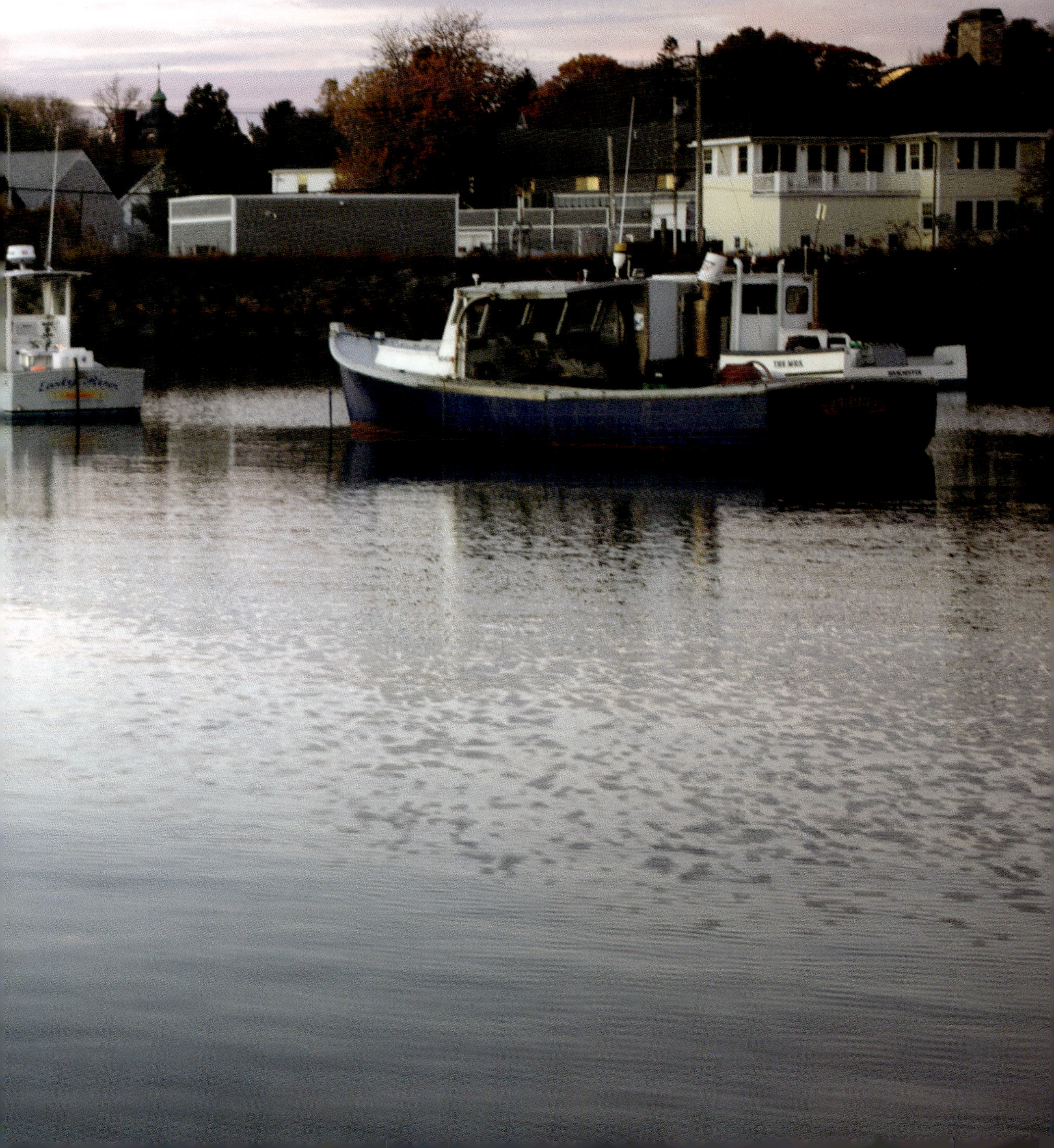

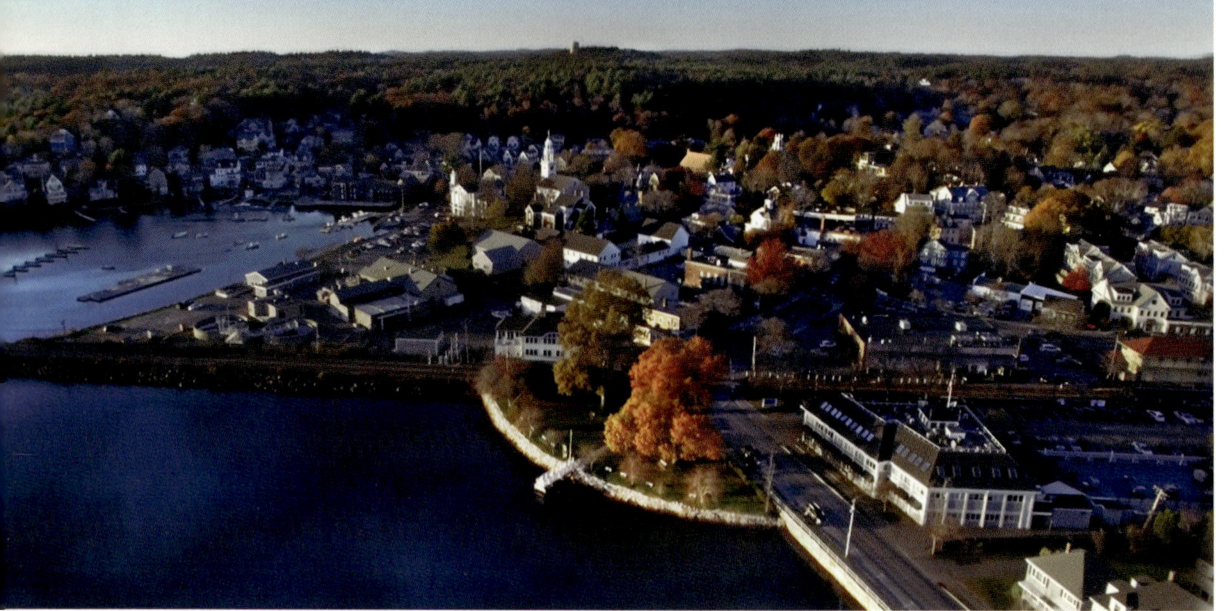

From above, a view of Manchester-by-the-Sea in November. A tree by the harbor clings to its autumn colors. Manchester was settled in 1629.

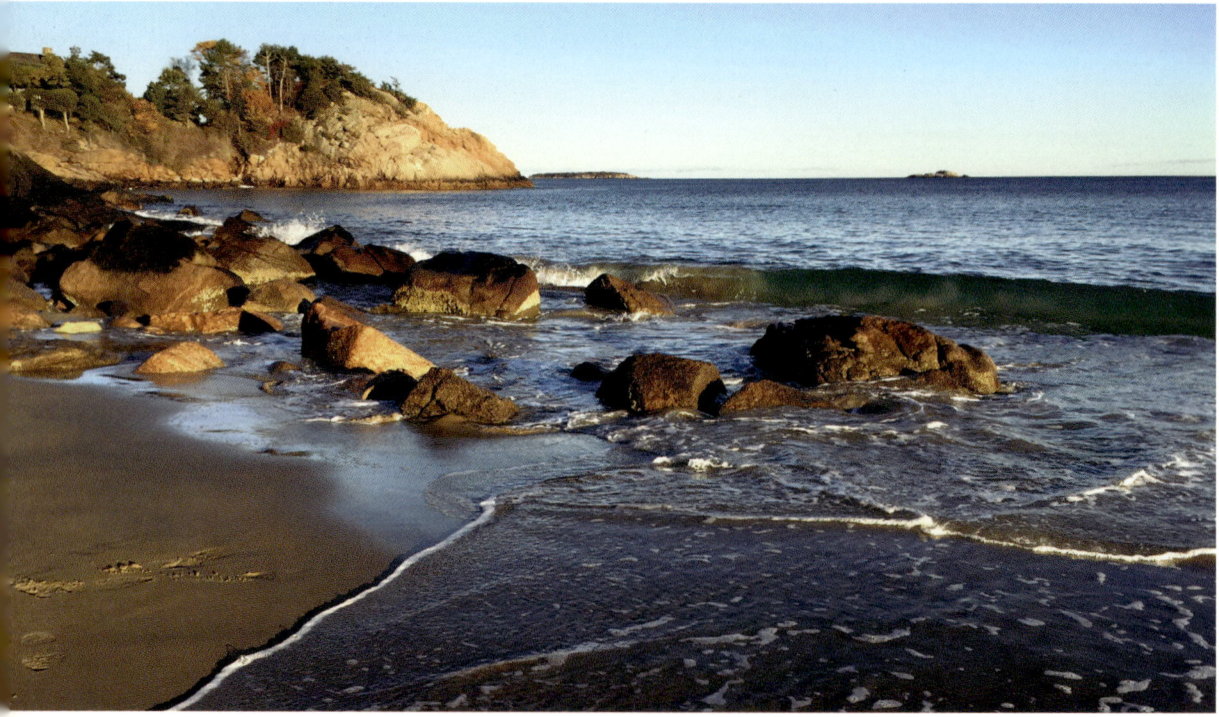

One of the more popular and curious beaches on the North Shore is Singing Beach. The most fascinating thing about the beach is that the sand squeaks every time you take a step. It's not exactly melodic, but it sure is fun.

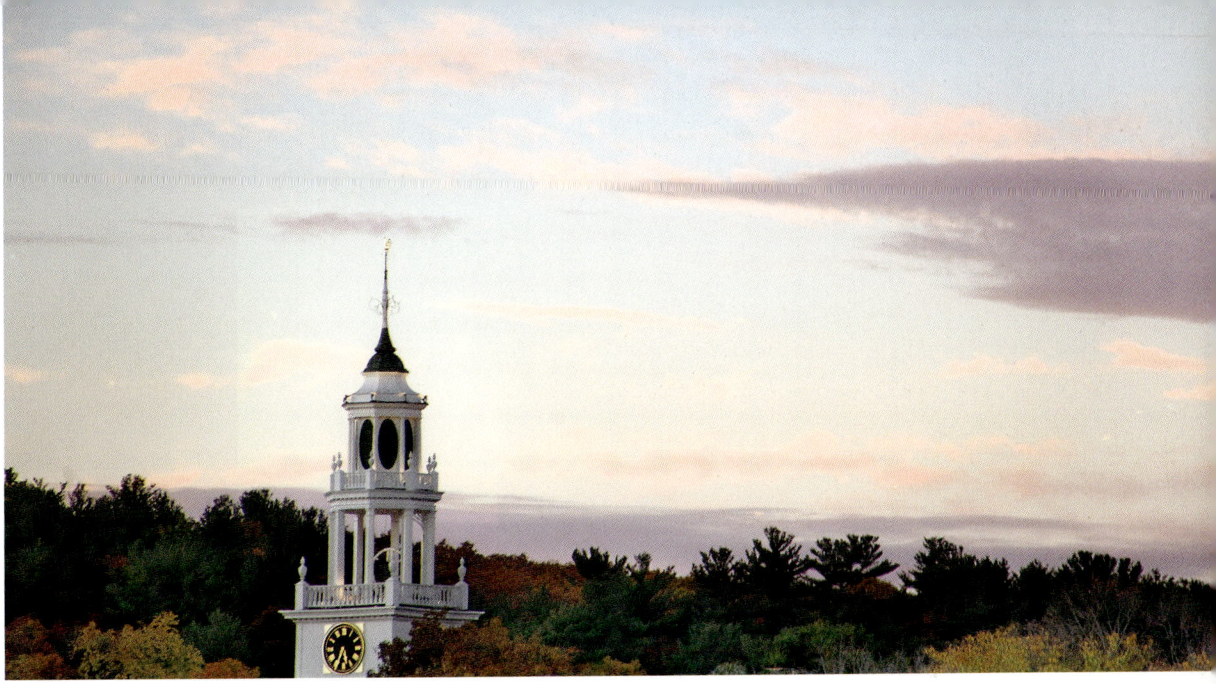

Pastel sunset clouds, as the First Parish Church ascends through the colorful fall canopy.

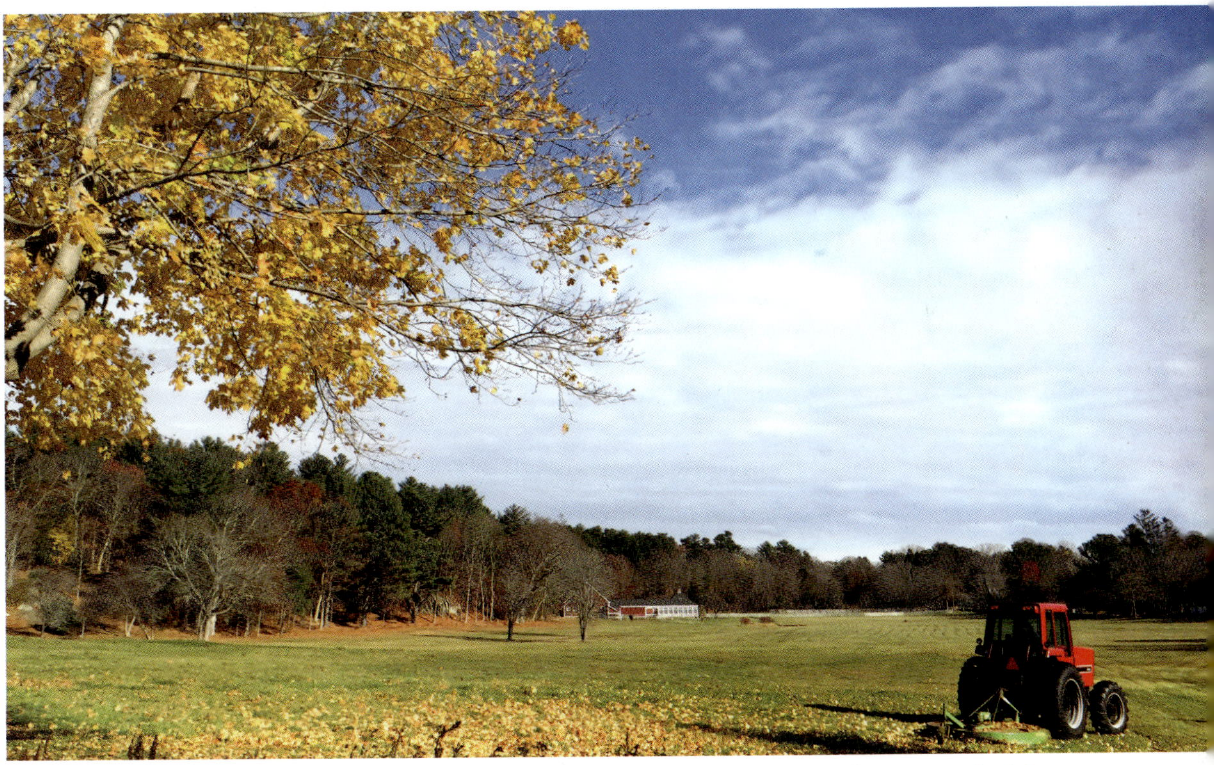

The primary colors are on display at this farm with a red tractor, yellow leaves, and a blue sky . . . a true New England classic!

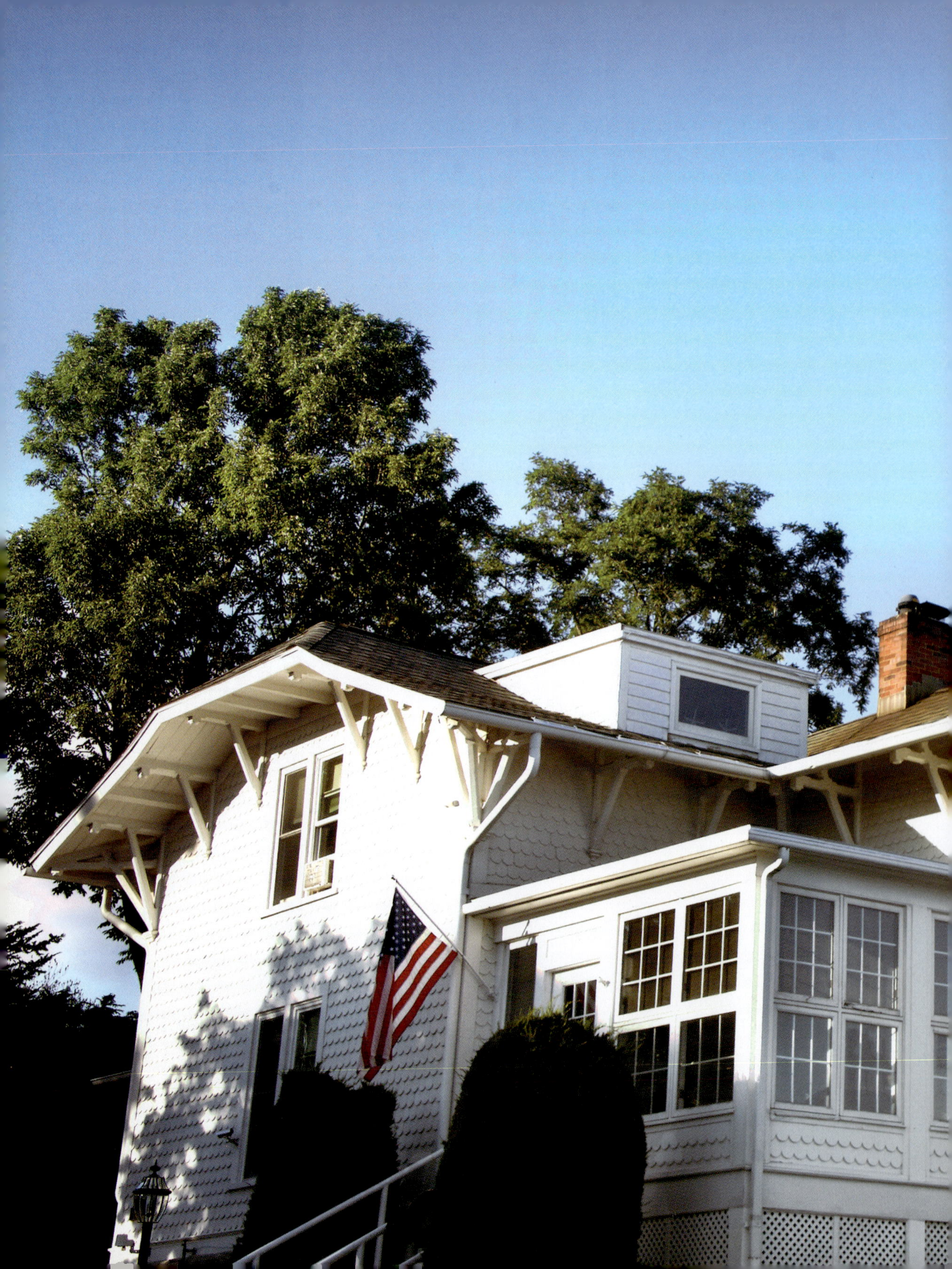

Beverly

Beverly was founded in 1626. The city played an important role in the birth of the United States Navy—although it is debated whether Beverly or Marblehead holds the official title as the "birthplace." The city includes the neighborhoods of Prides Crossing, Beverly Farms, and Ryal Side.

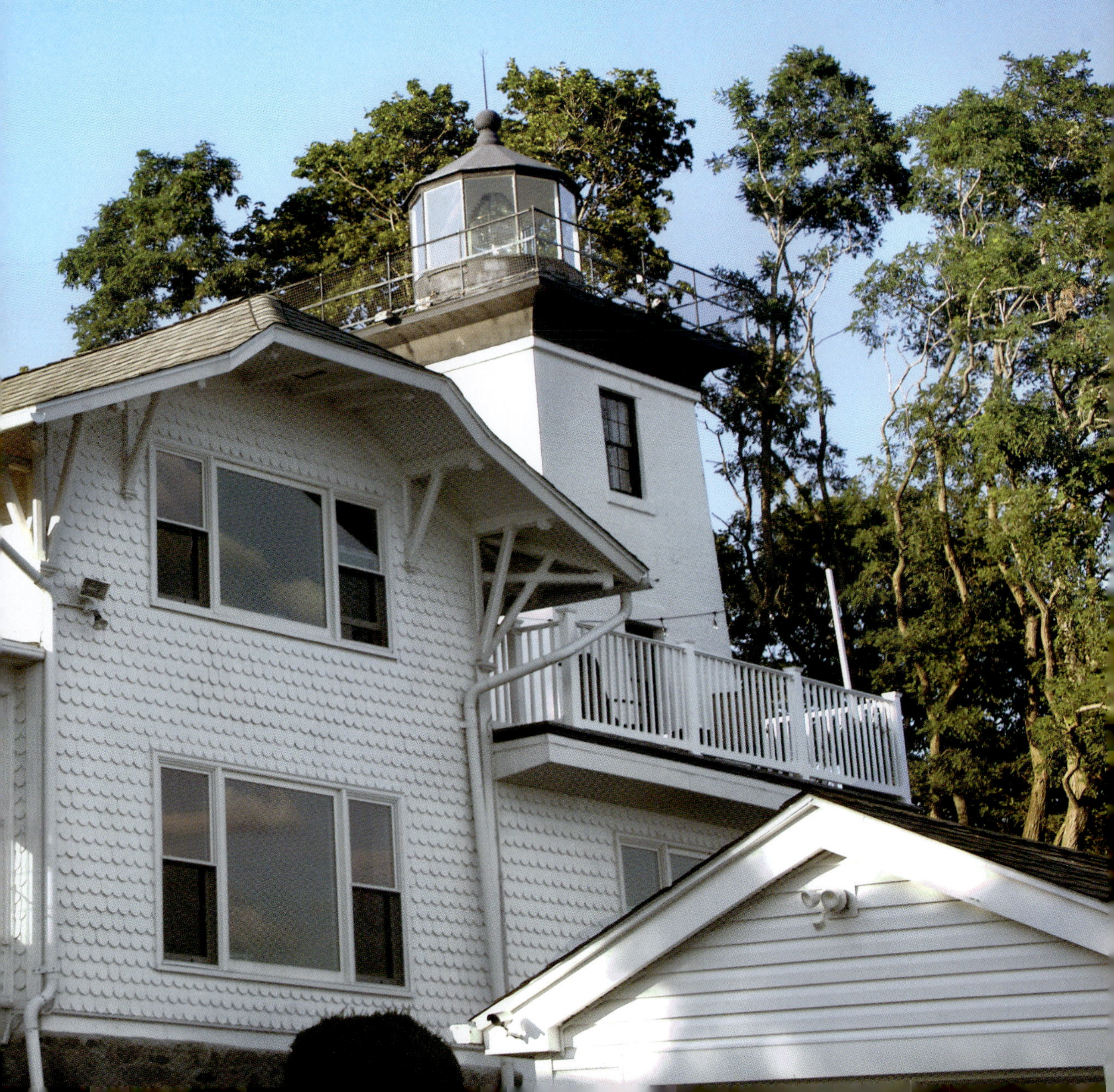

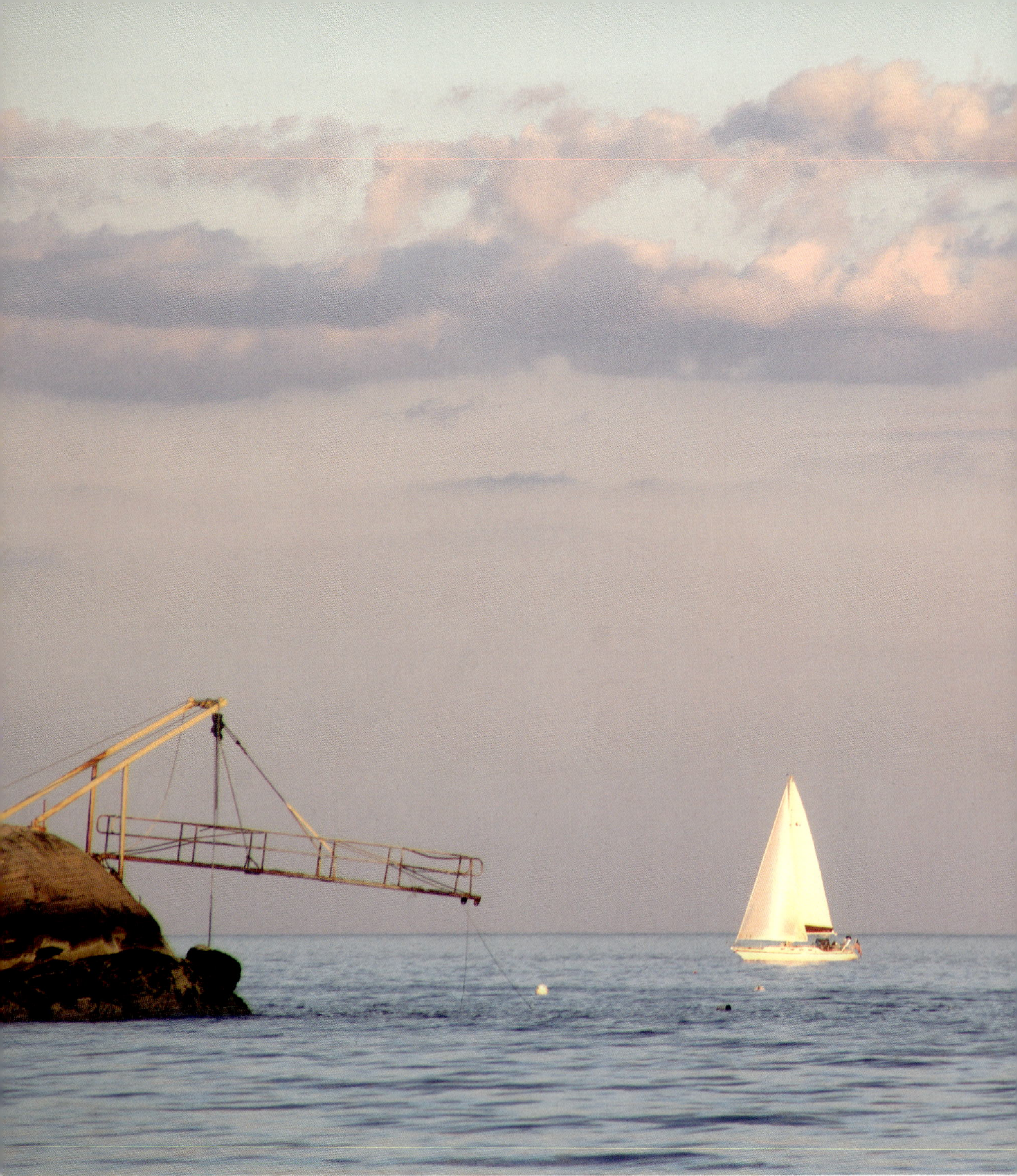

Helping guide vessels with a safe passage to Salem Harbor is Hospital Point Range Front Light in Beverly. The lighthouse was built in 1871, and is operated by the United States Coast Guard.

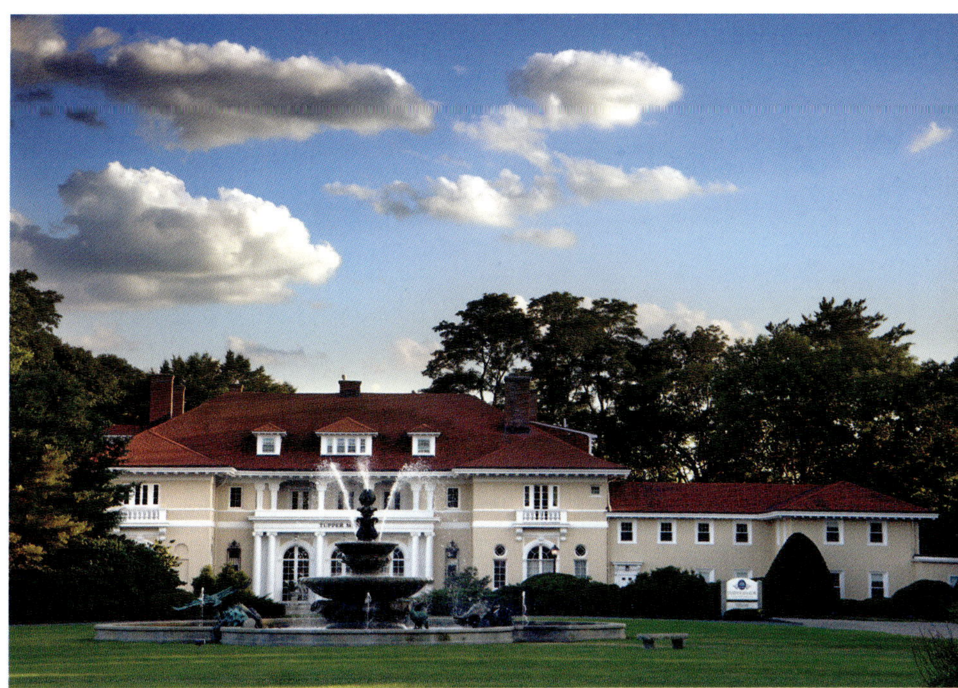

Tupper Manor at the Wylie Inn, on a dreamy late afternoon in July.

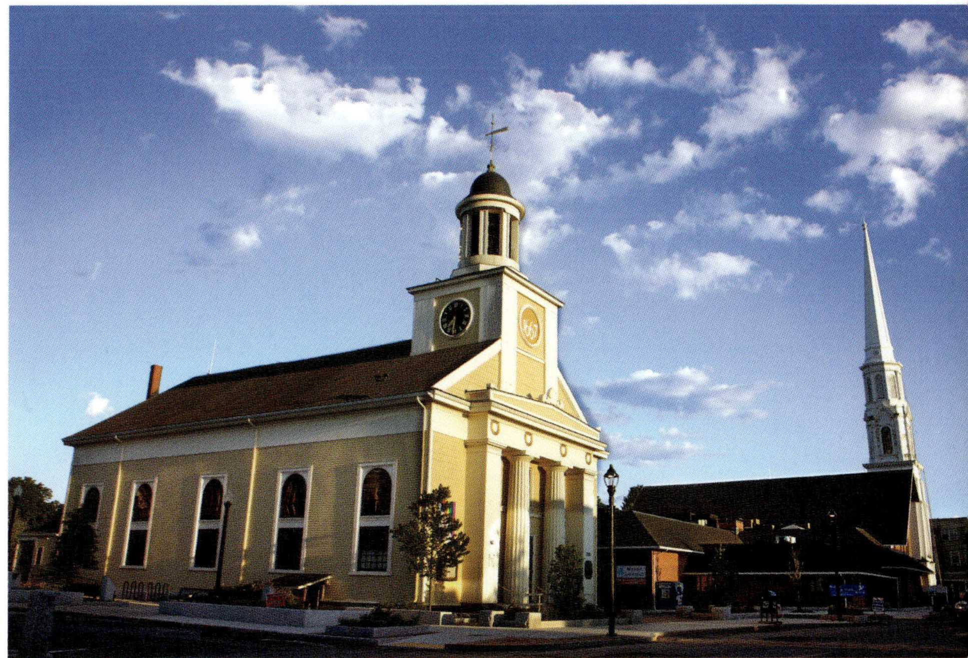

Golden sunlight hits a pair of steeples on Cabot Street under an indigo sky.

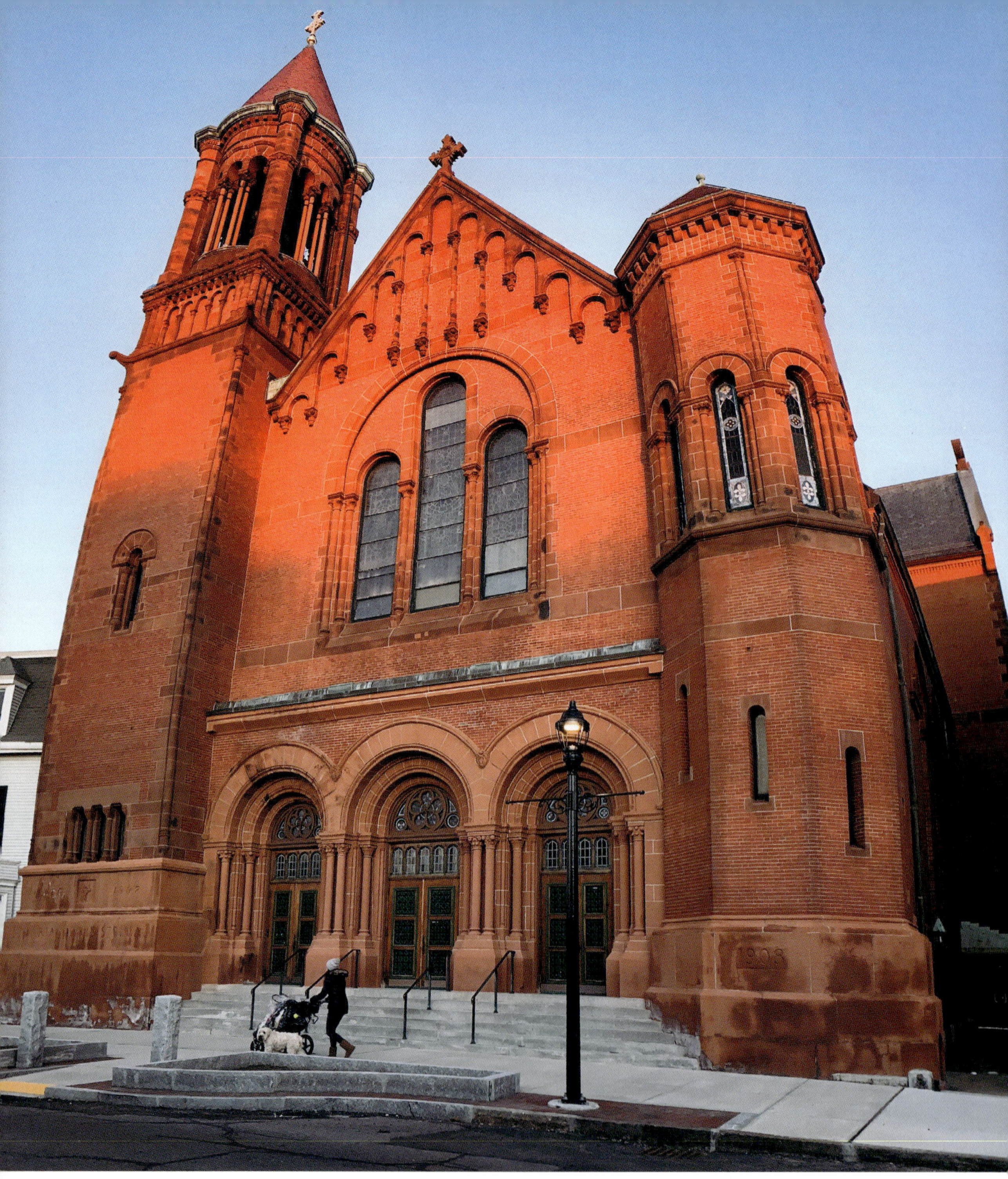

A mother has her infant bundled up in a stroller during a frigid winter sunset, as she walks by Saint Mary Star of the Sea Church.

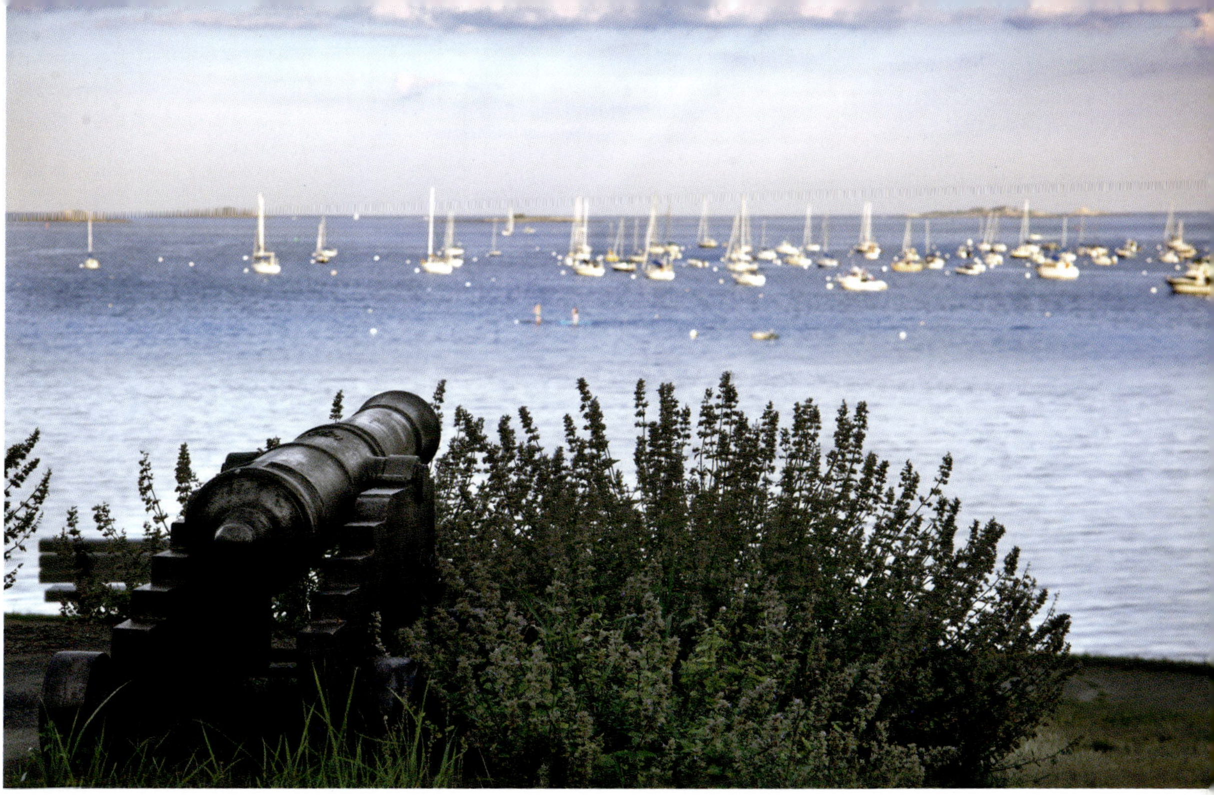

At historic Independence Park, a view towards sailboats, Salem Channel, and islands on the horizon.

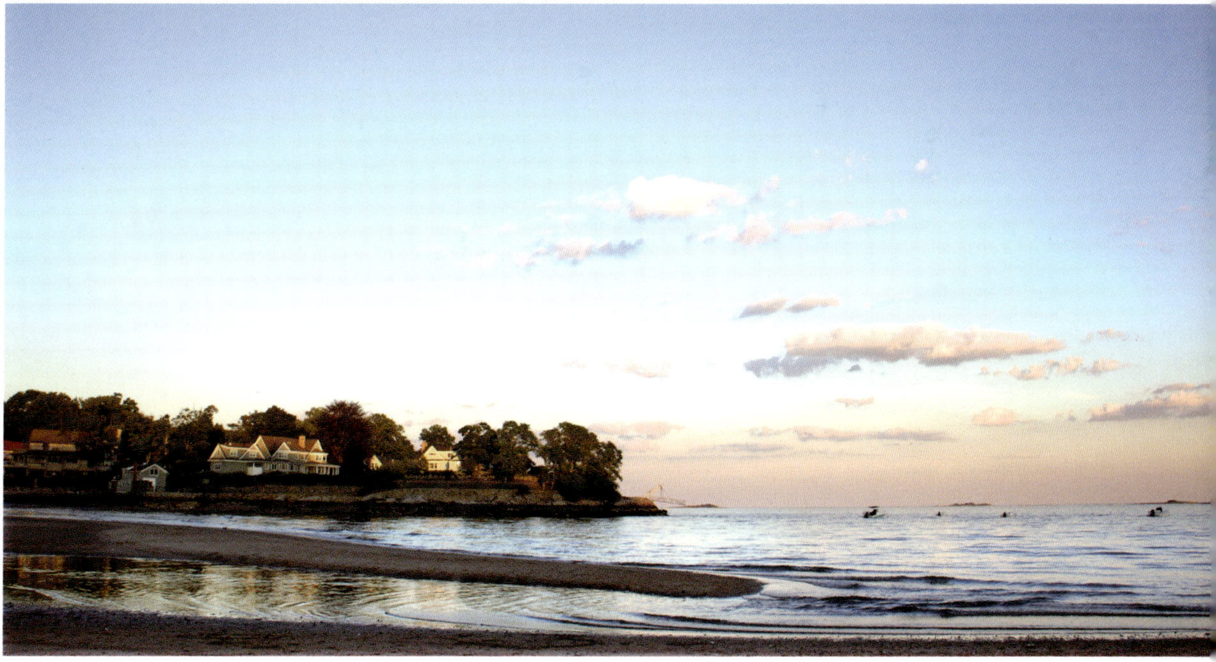

A twilight tide ripples in to the beach at Beverly Cove.

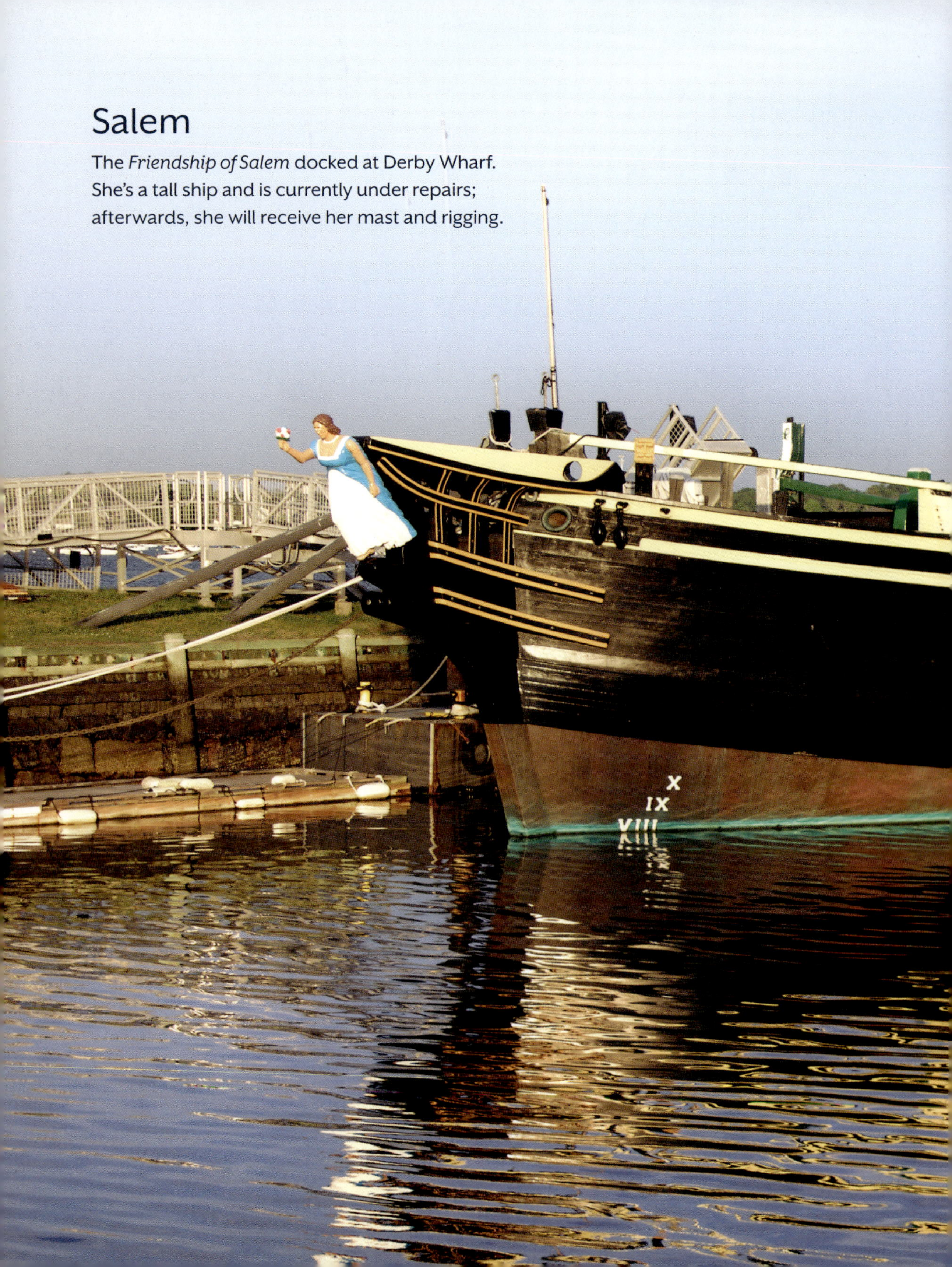

Salem

The *Friendship of Salem* docked at Derby Wharf.
She's a tall ship and is currently under repairs;
afterwards, she will receive her mast and rigging.

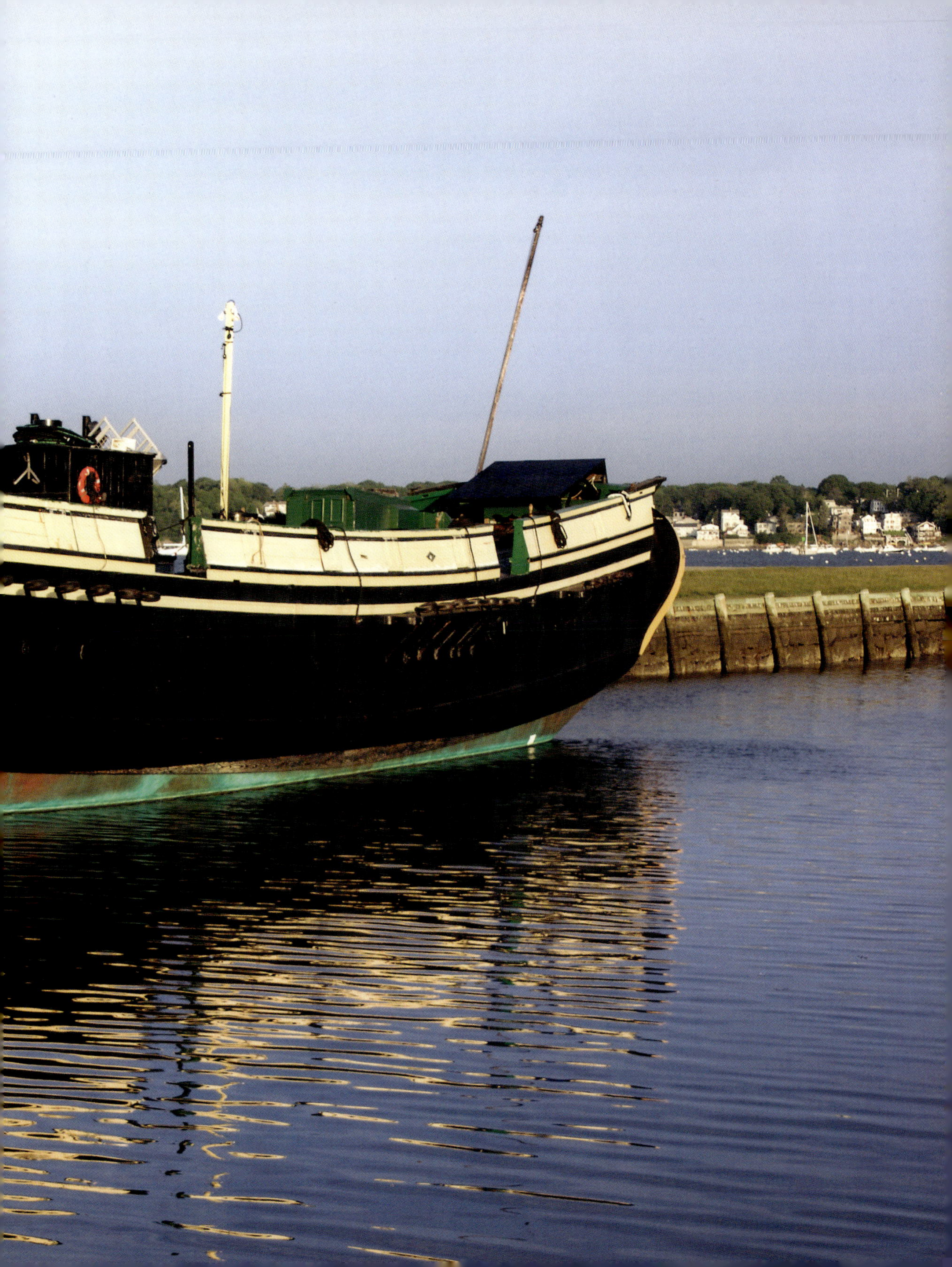

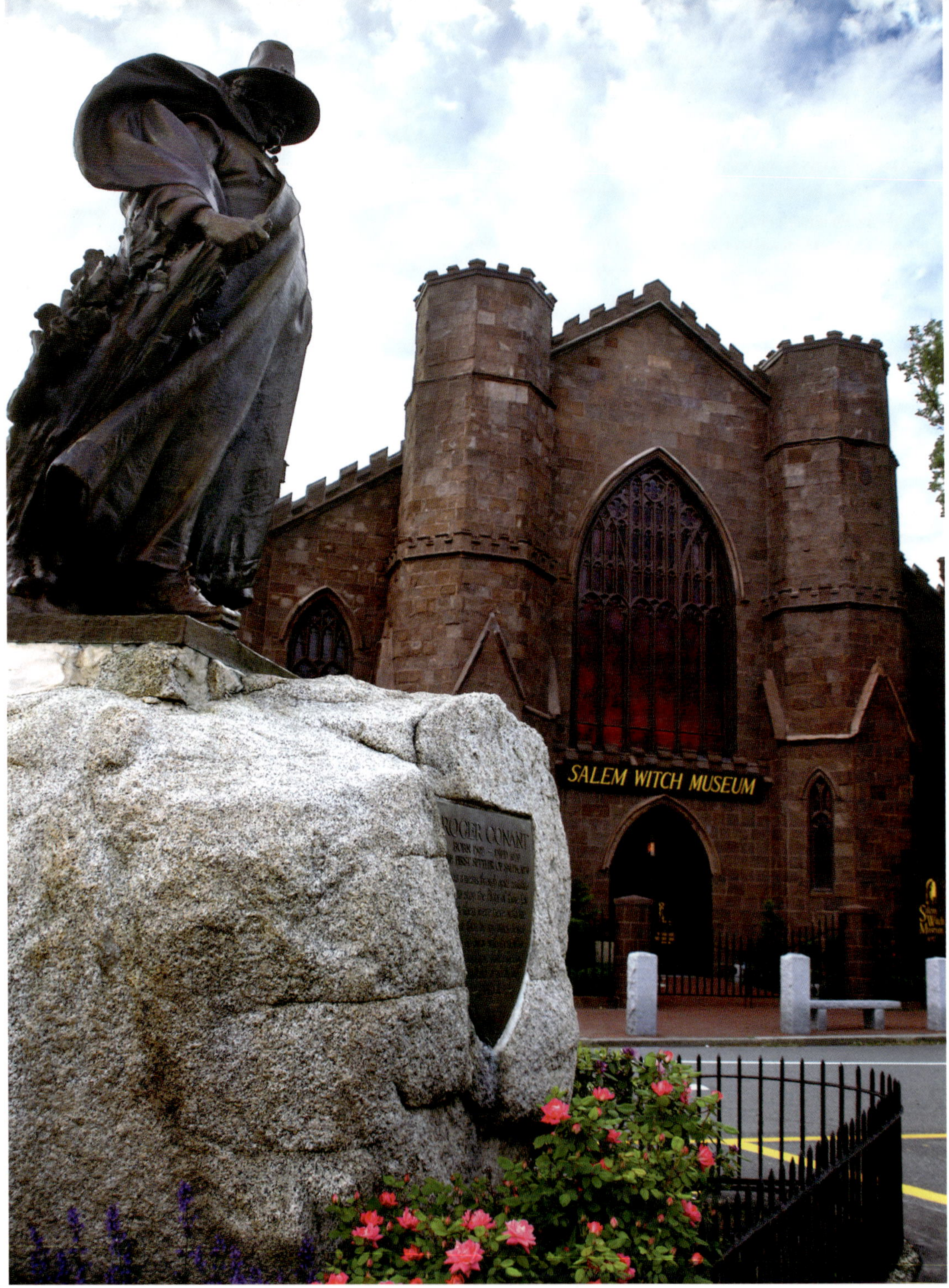

At the Salem Witch Museum, they illuminate the hysteria that lead to the Salem Witch Trials in the late 1600s. The statue is of Roger Conant, first settler of Salem.

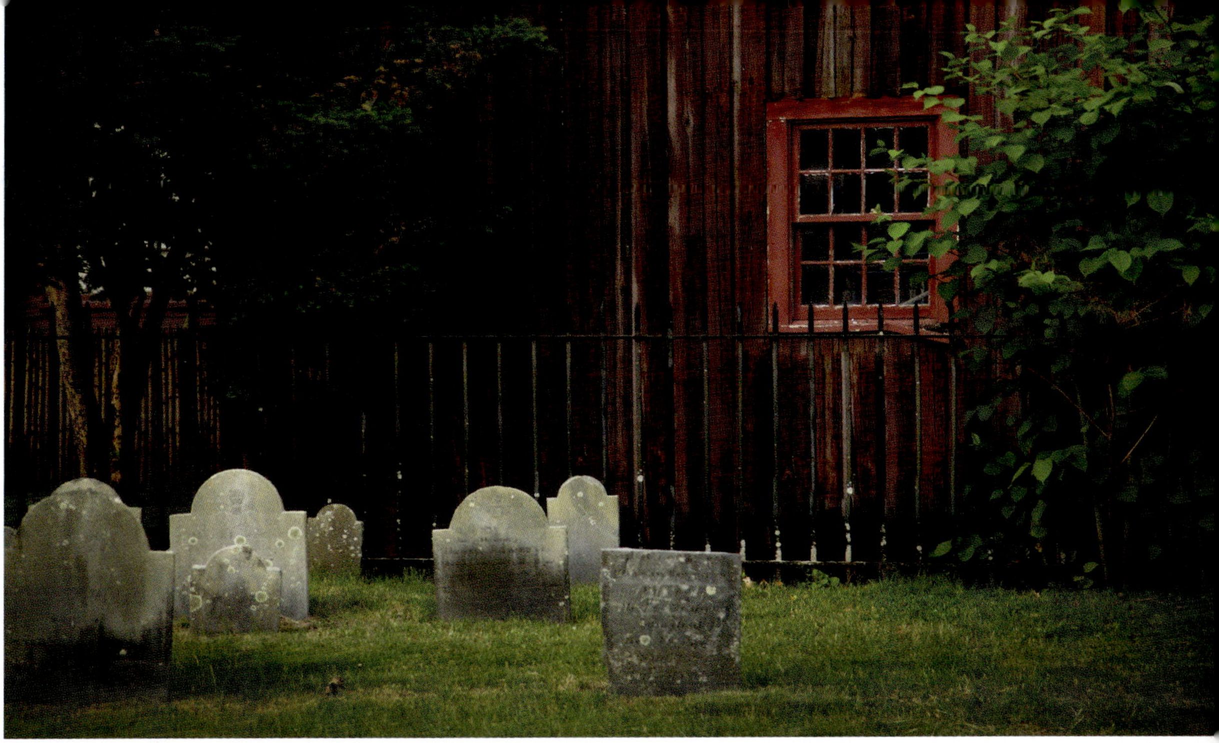

Headstones by moonlight at the Burying Point, circa 1637.

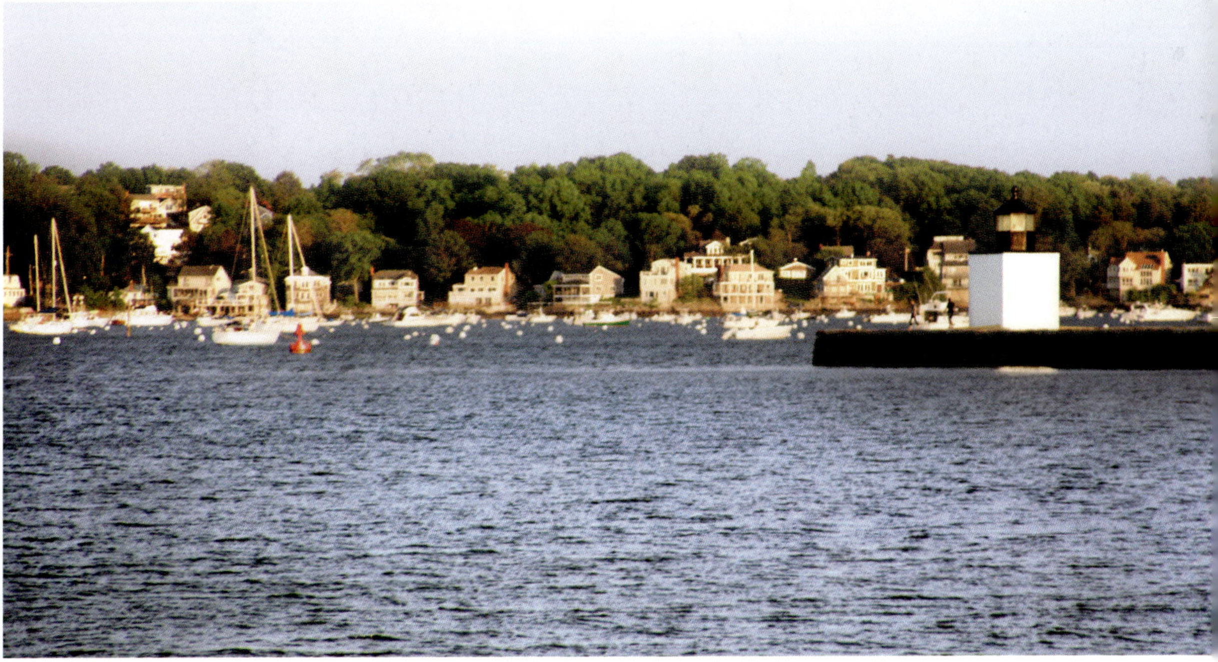

Derby Wharf Light Station assists vessels entering Salem Harbor. It's a square little lighthouse measuring in at a pugnacious 20 feet tall. Because of its crucial location, it's been a key resource for mariners since being built in 1871.

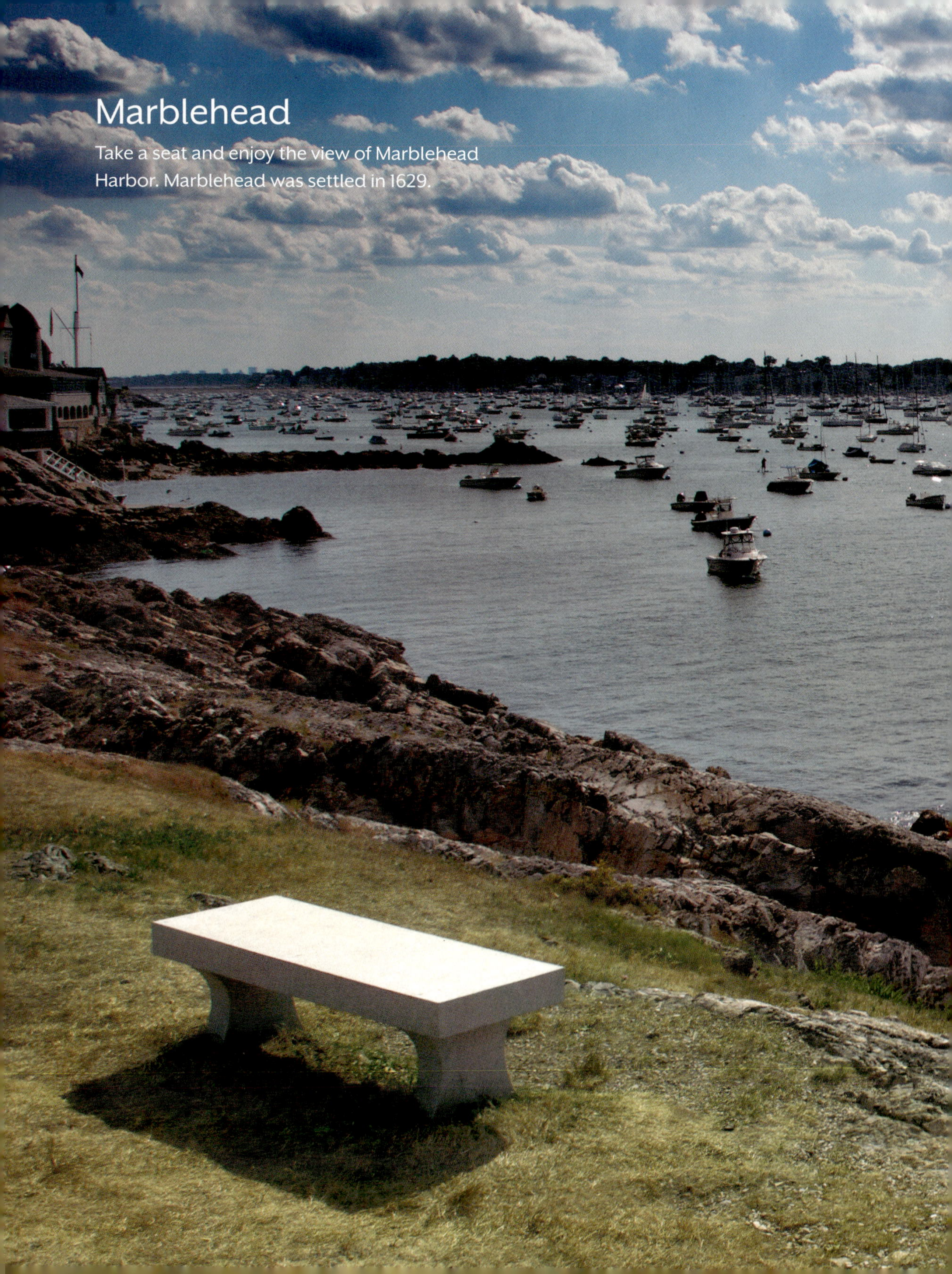

Marblehead
Take a seat and enjoy the view of Marblehead
Harbor. Marblehead was settled in 1629.

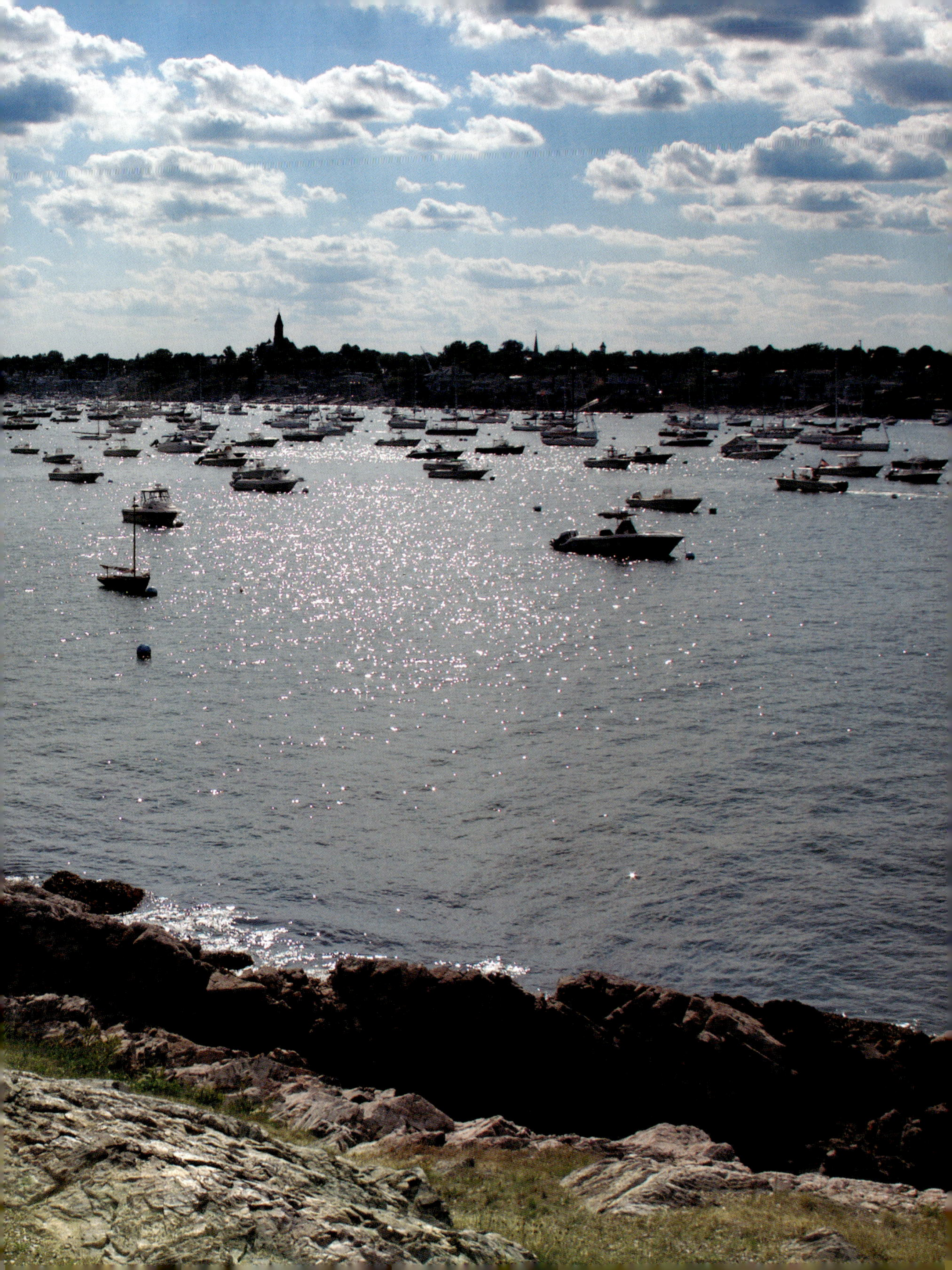

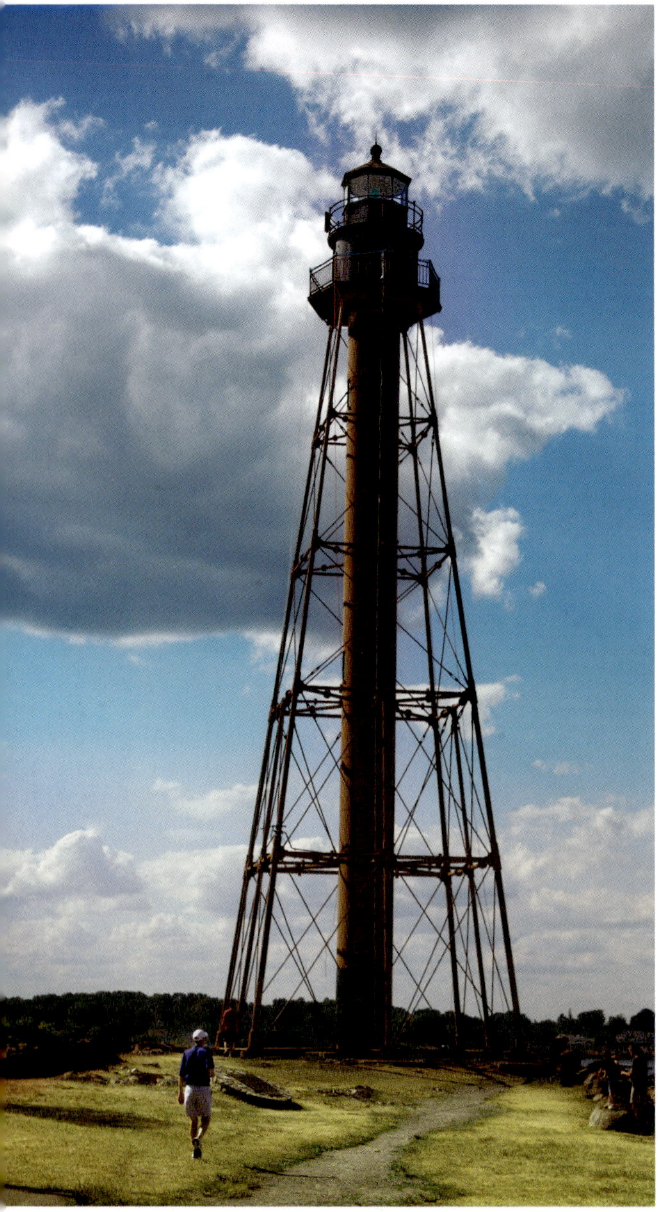

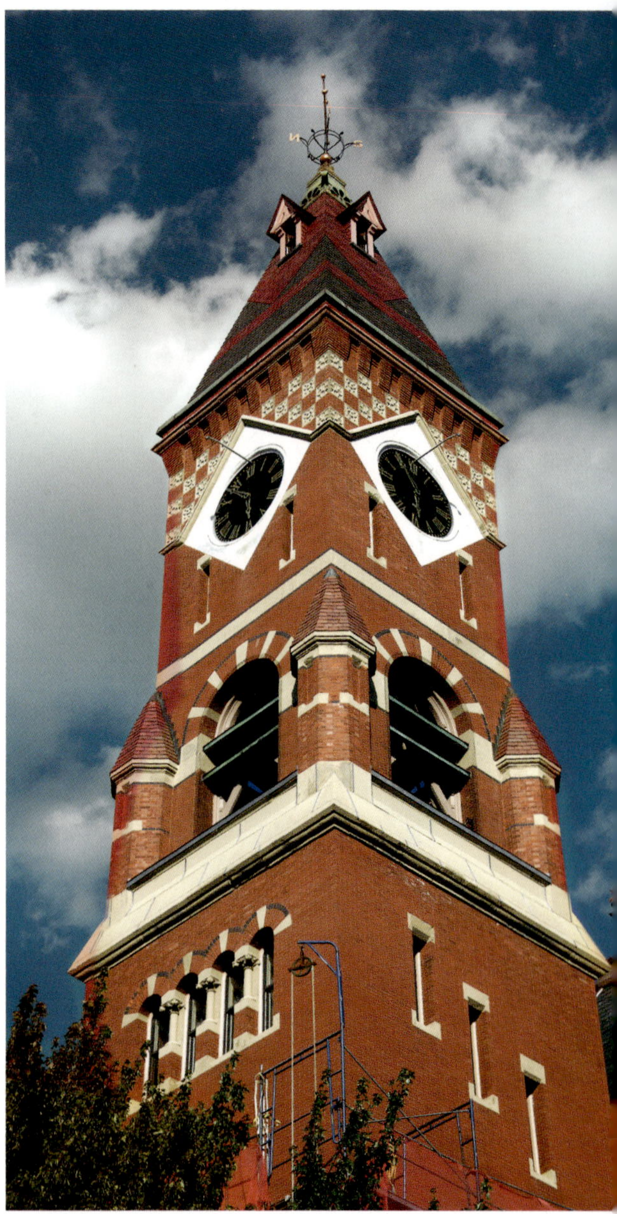

The skeletal Marblehead Light at Chandler Hovey Park. This lighthouse was built in 1895, to replace the original brick and wood tower from 1835.

The red-brick Abbot Hall against a blue sky. The Romanesque-style building was completed in 1877, and hosts the town offices and a maritime museum.

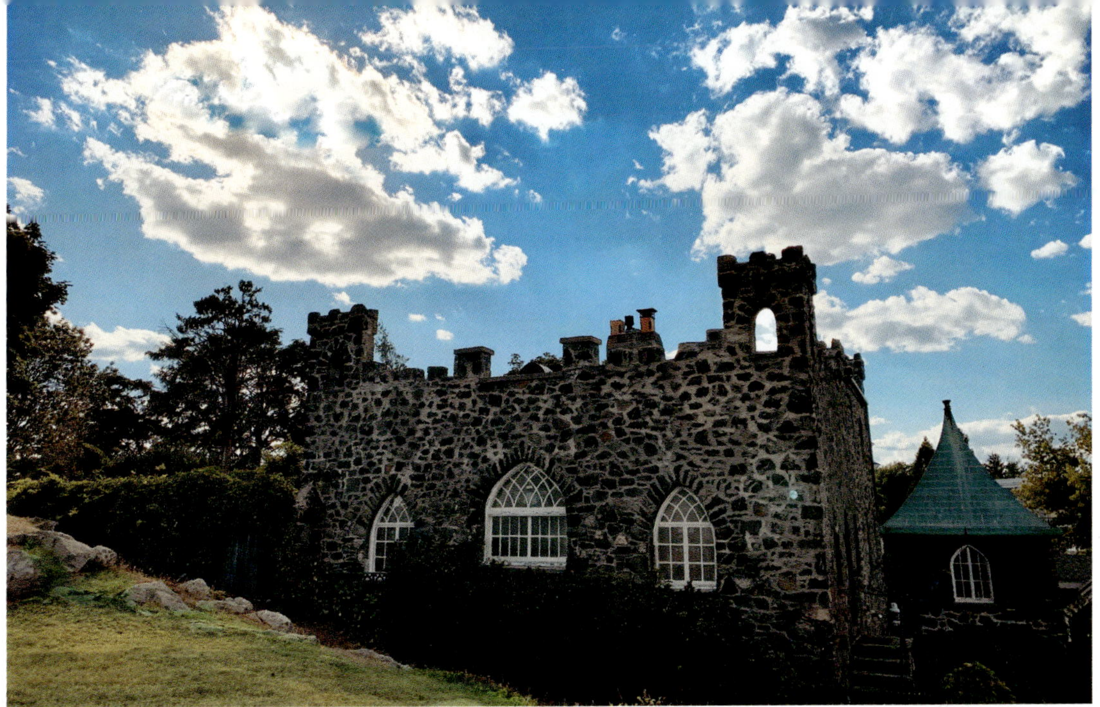

This castle-like home overlooks the harbor at Crocker Park.

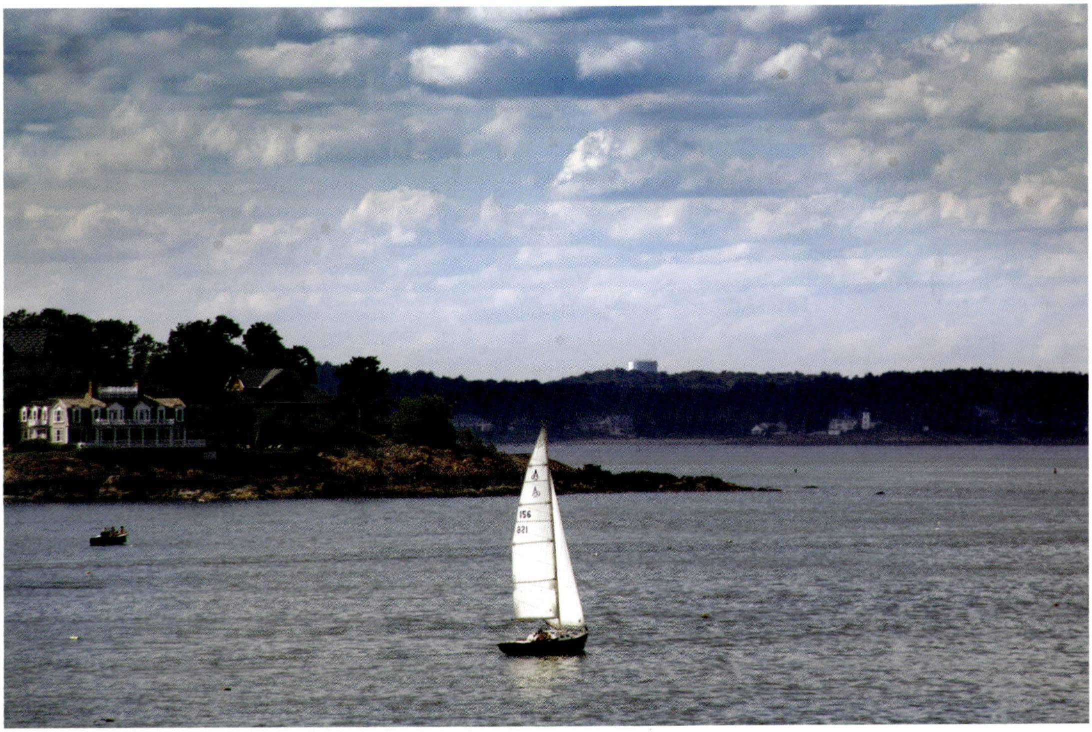

A steady breeze helps this sailboat make its way past Lighthouse Point, as it exits Marblehead Harbor.

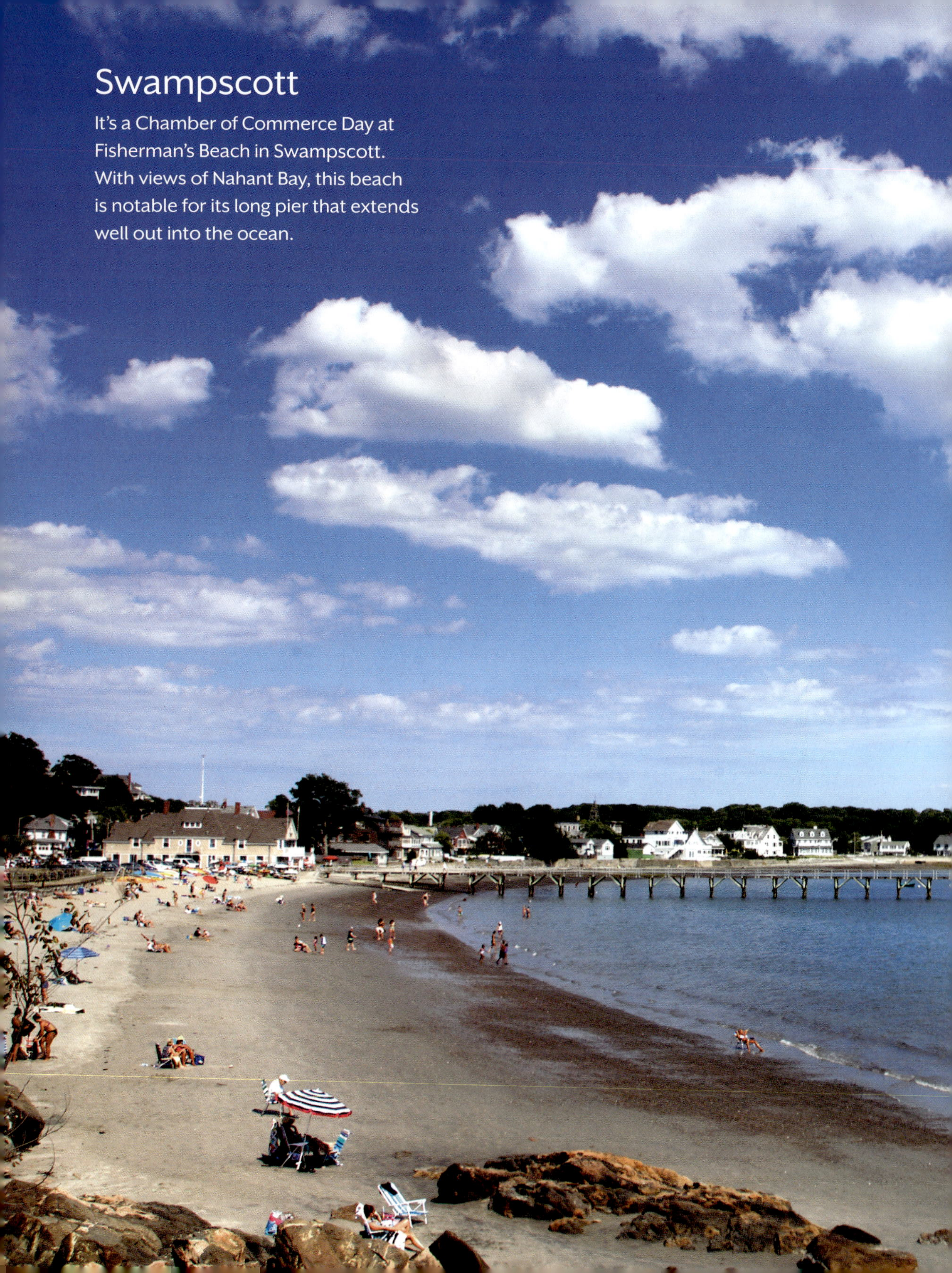

Swampscott

It's a Chamber of Commerce Day at
Fisherman's Beach in Swampscott.
With views of Nahant Bay, this beach
is notable for its long pier that extends
well out into the ocean.

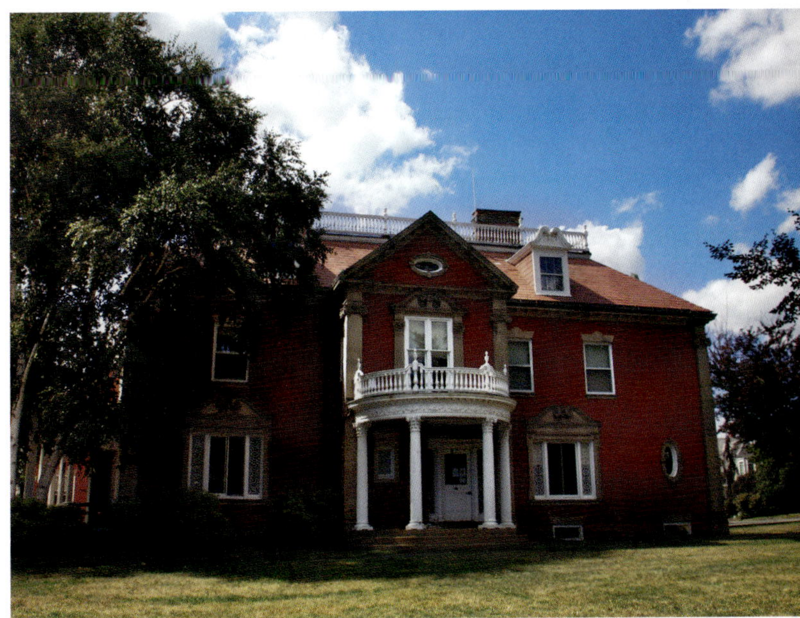

Architect James Kelley built Swampscott's historic Town Hall in 1889. Swampscott was settled in 1629.

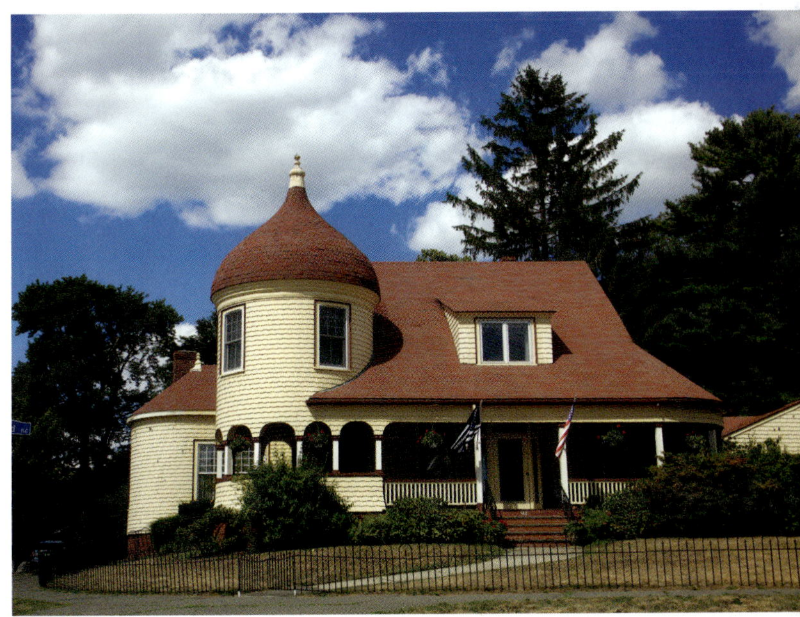

A beautiful yellow home with a conical architectural feature.

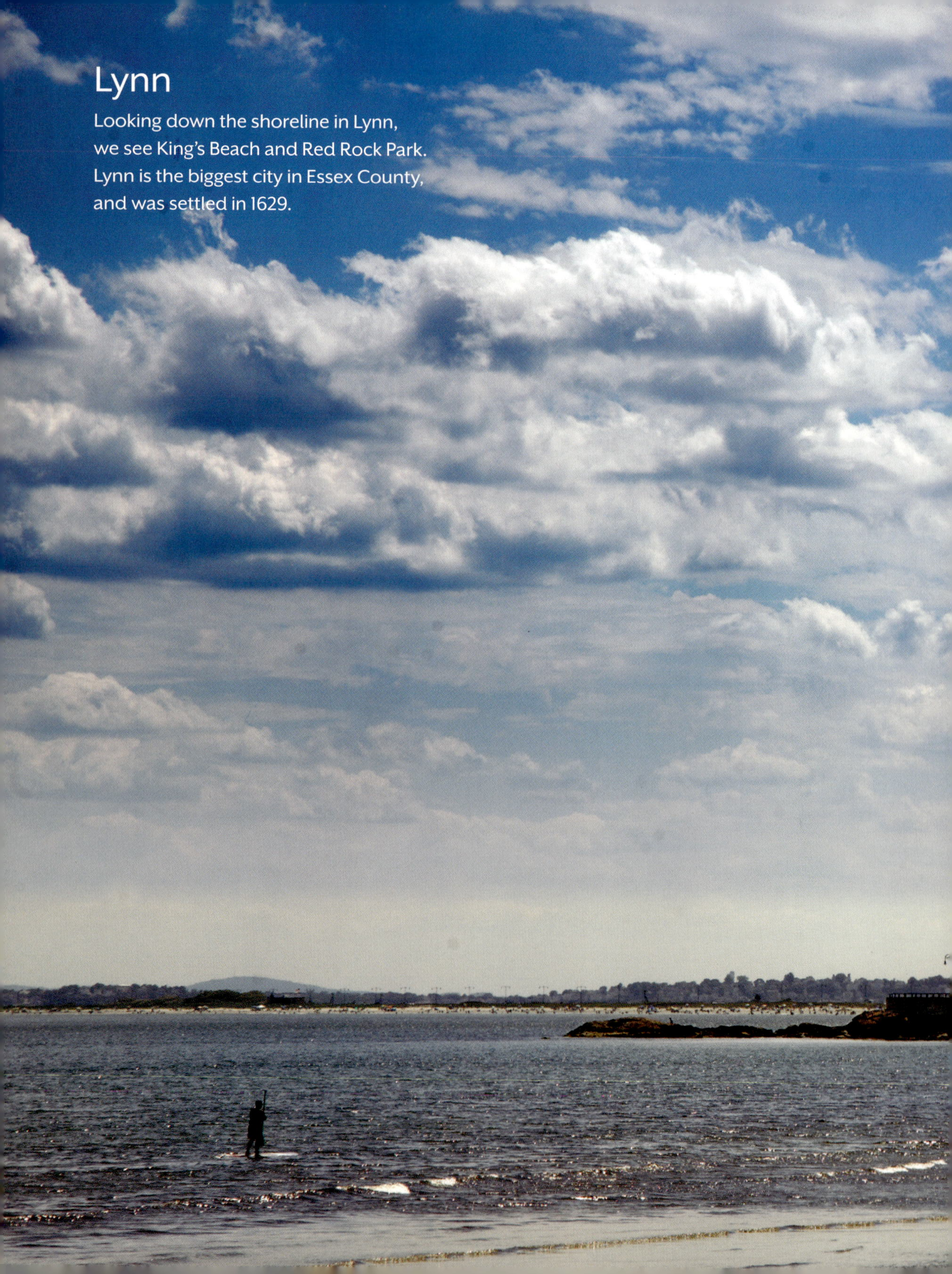
Lynn
Looking down the shoreline in Lynn,
we see King's Beach and Red Rock Park.
Lynn is the biggest city in Essex County,
and was settled in 1629.

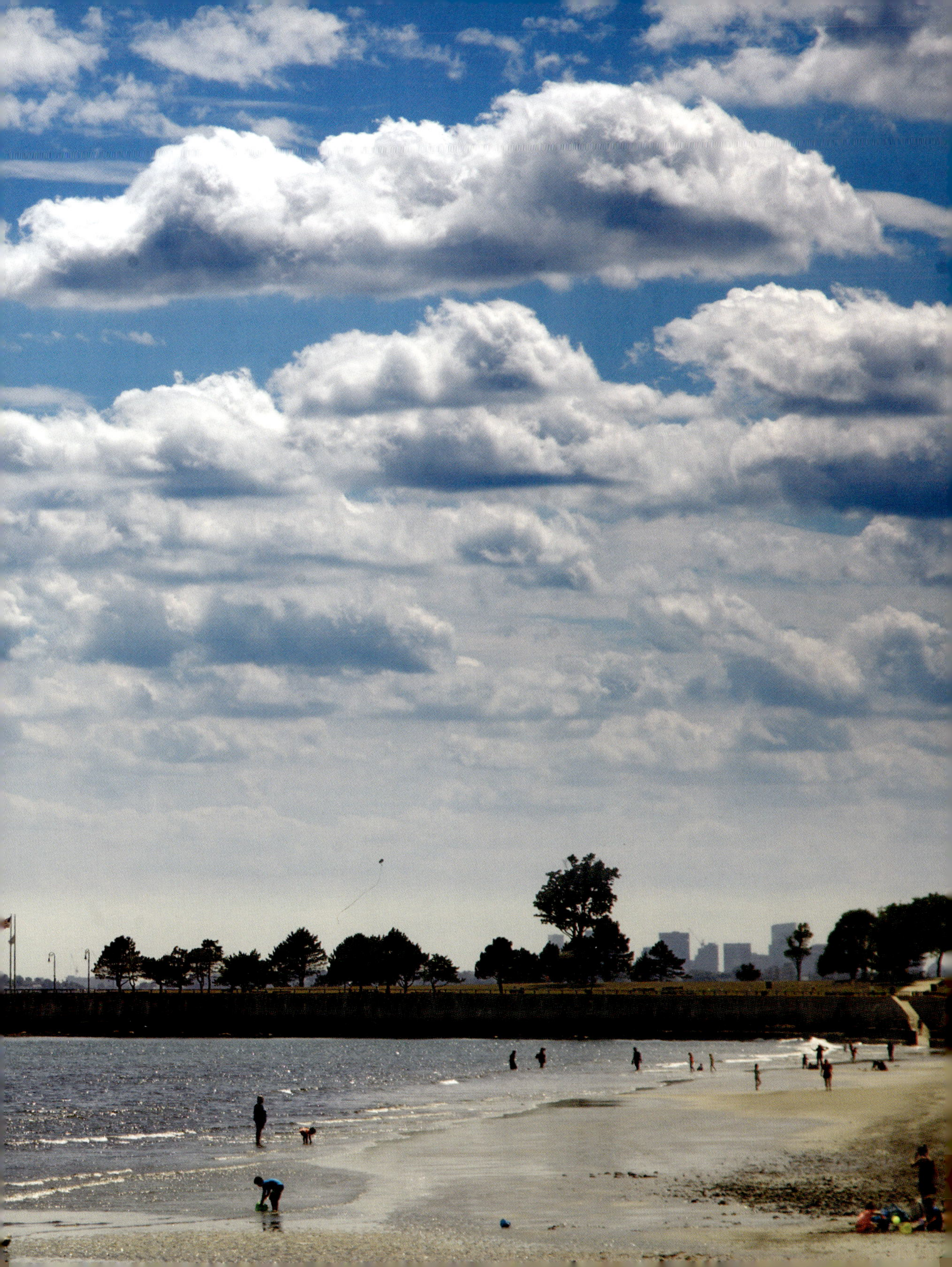

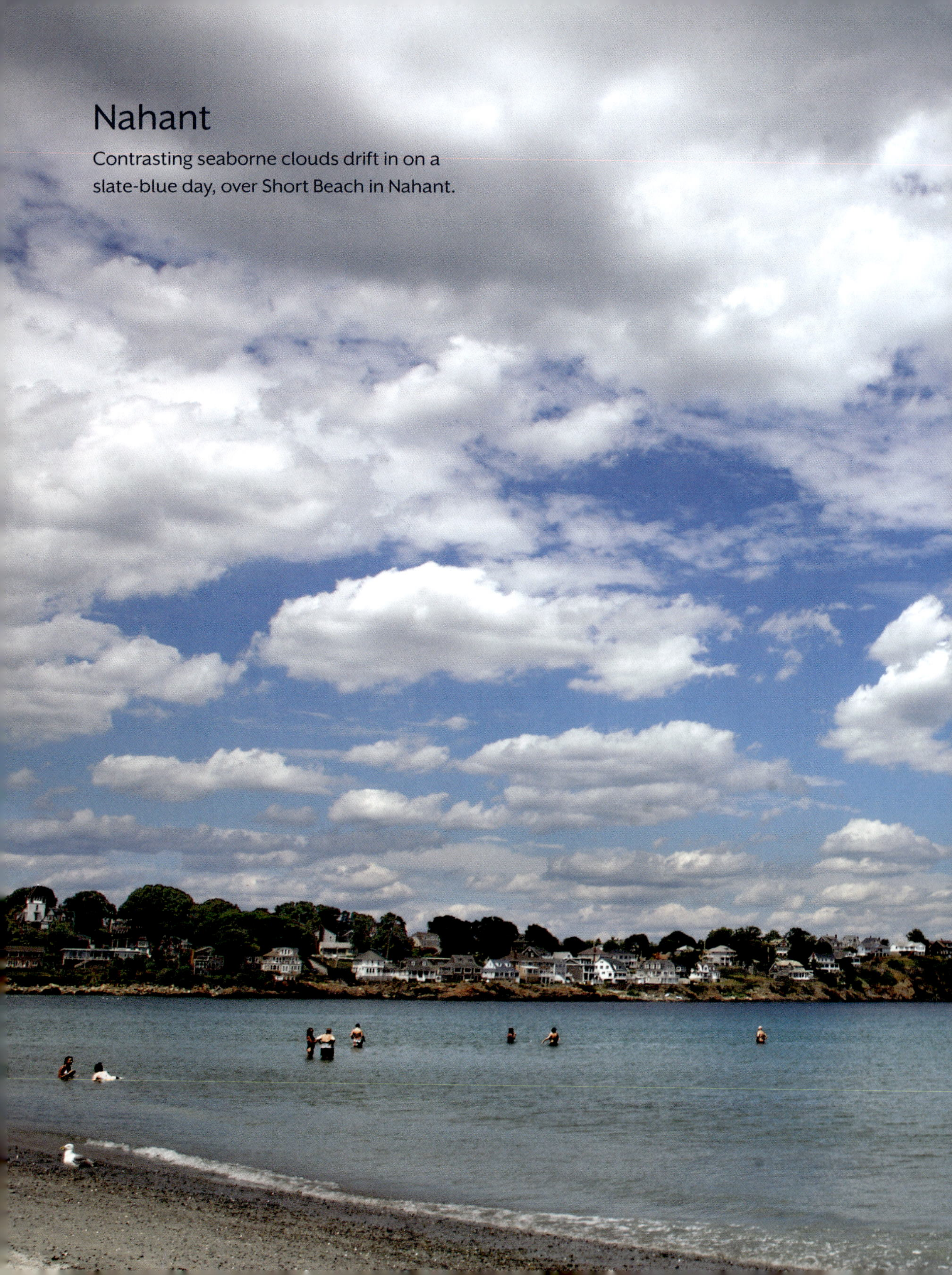

Nahant

Contrasting seaborne clouds drift in on a slate-blue day, over Short Beach in Nahant.

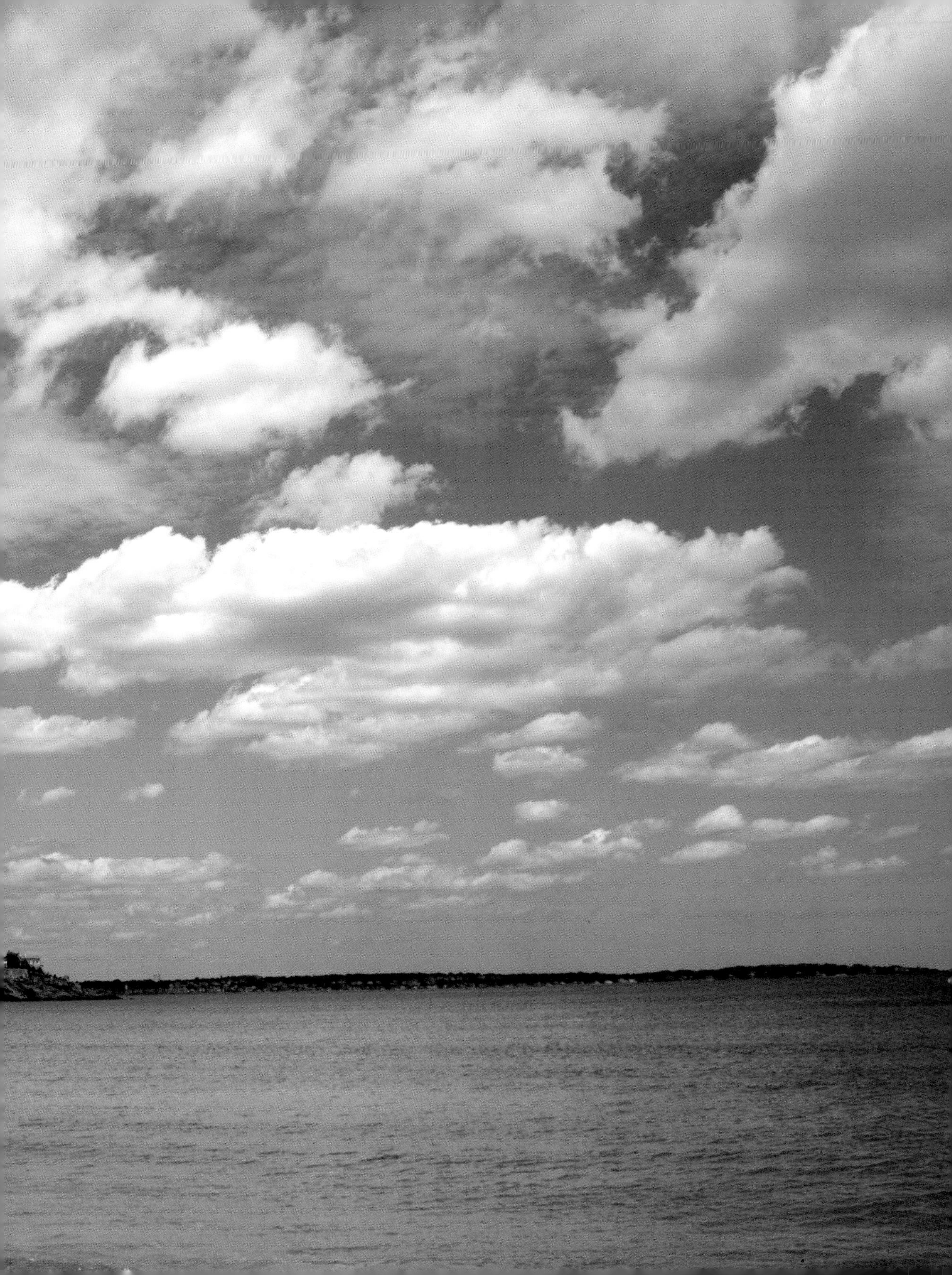

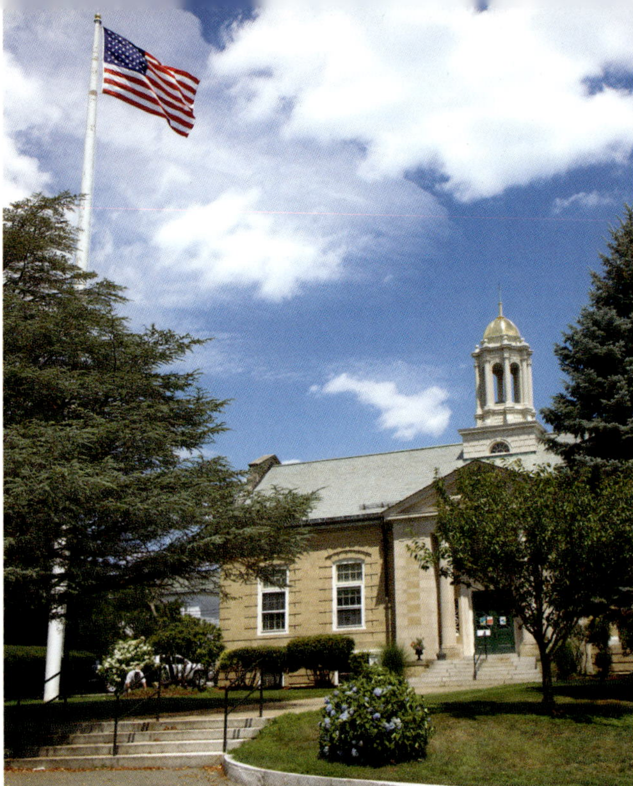

Old Glory flying high on a perfect summer day at Nahant Town Hall. The small residential town has only one square mile of land area, and it was settled in 1630.

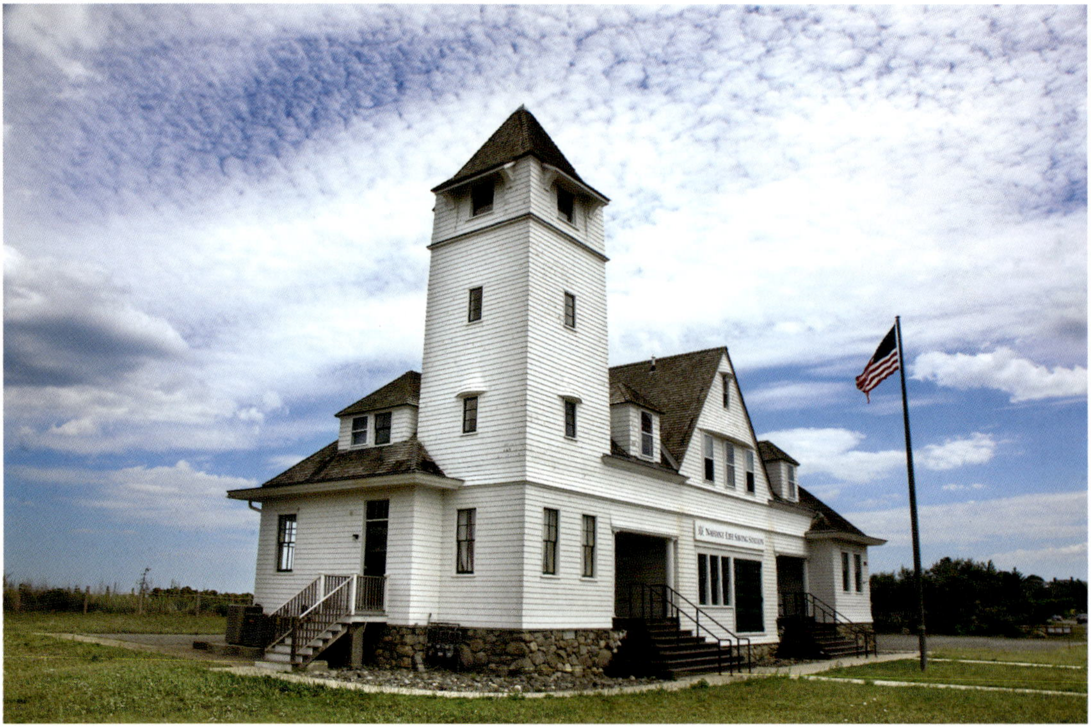

Built in 1900, the historic Nahant Life-Saving Station, under a dappled sky.

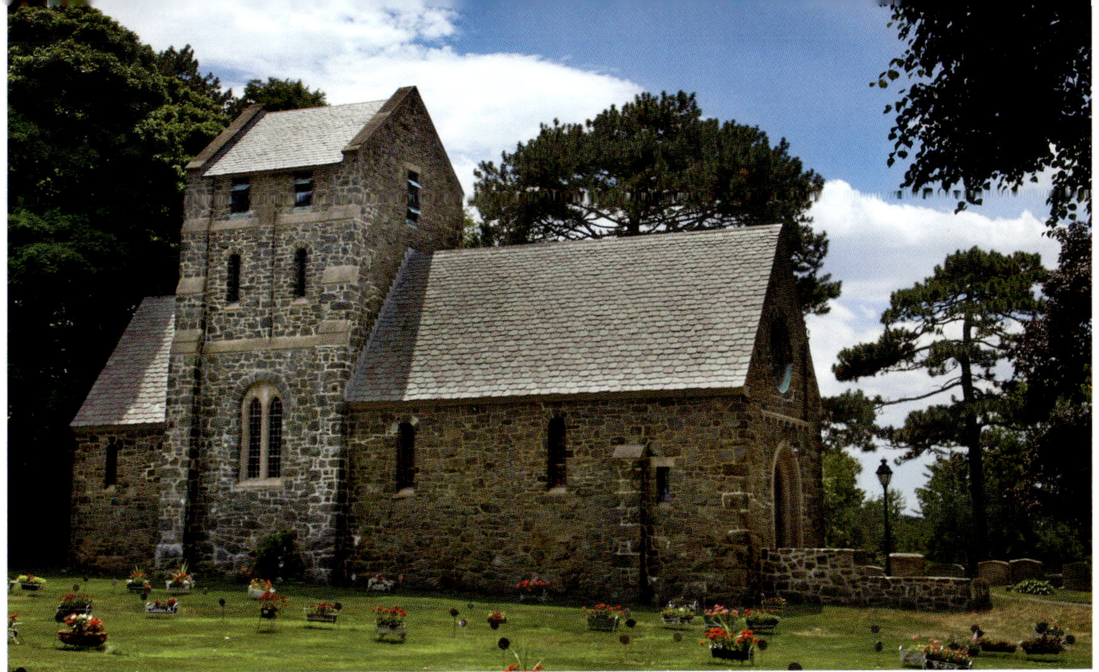

In Greenlaw Cemetery is this nice stone architecture called Elingwood Chapel, built in 1856.

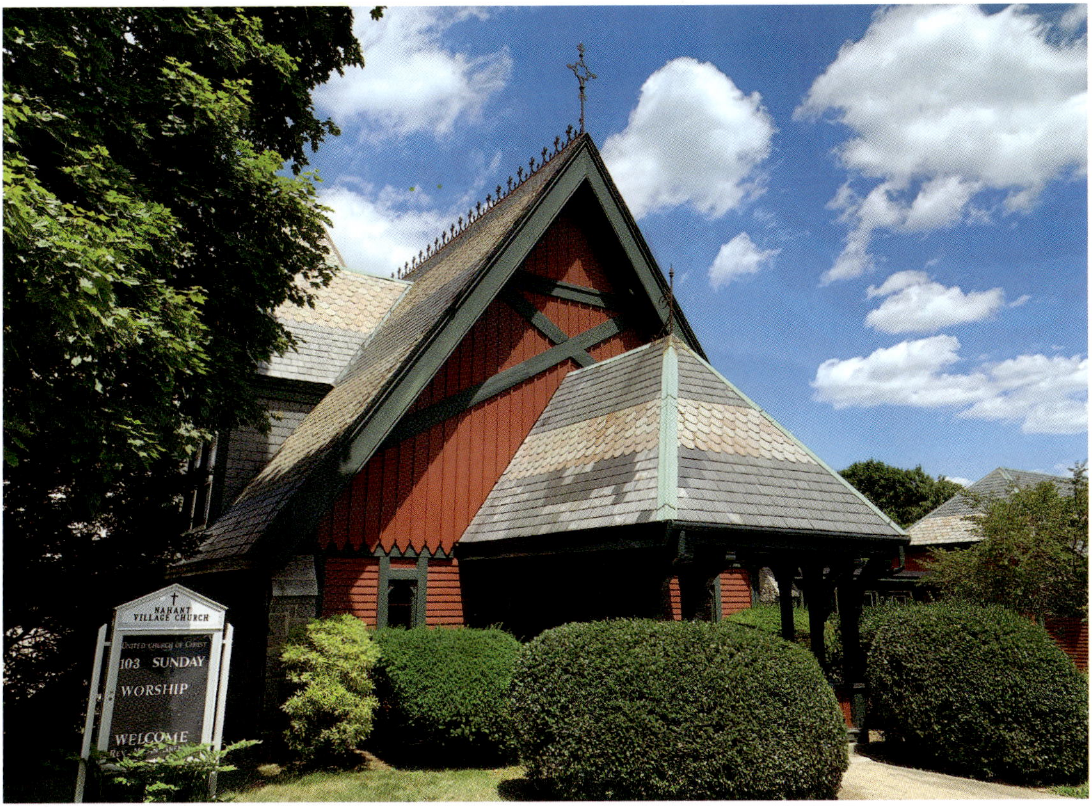

The Nahant Village Church, with its steep roof and decorative shingles.

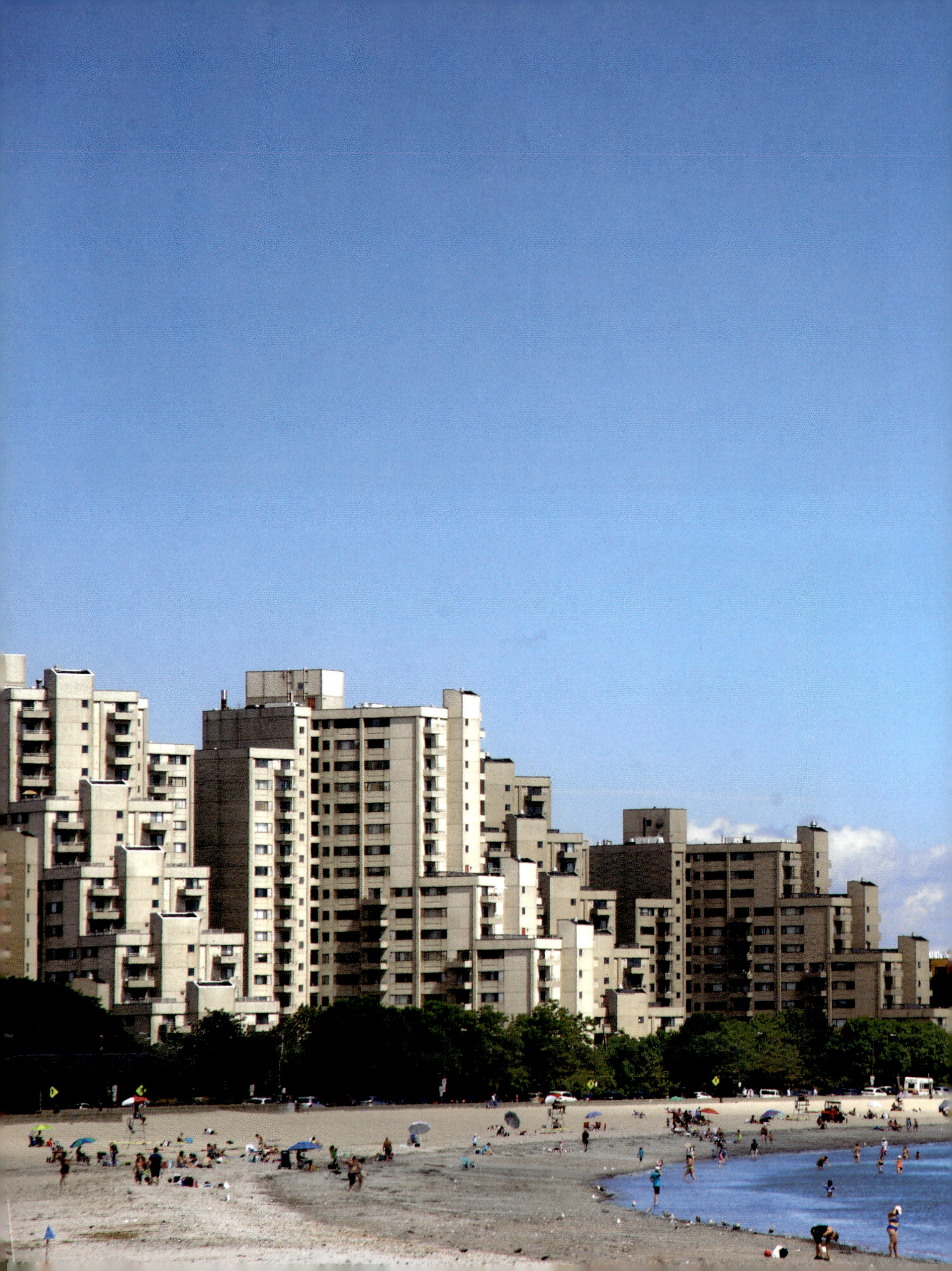

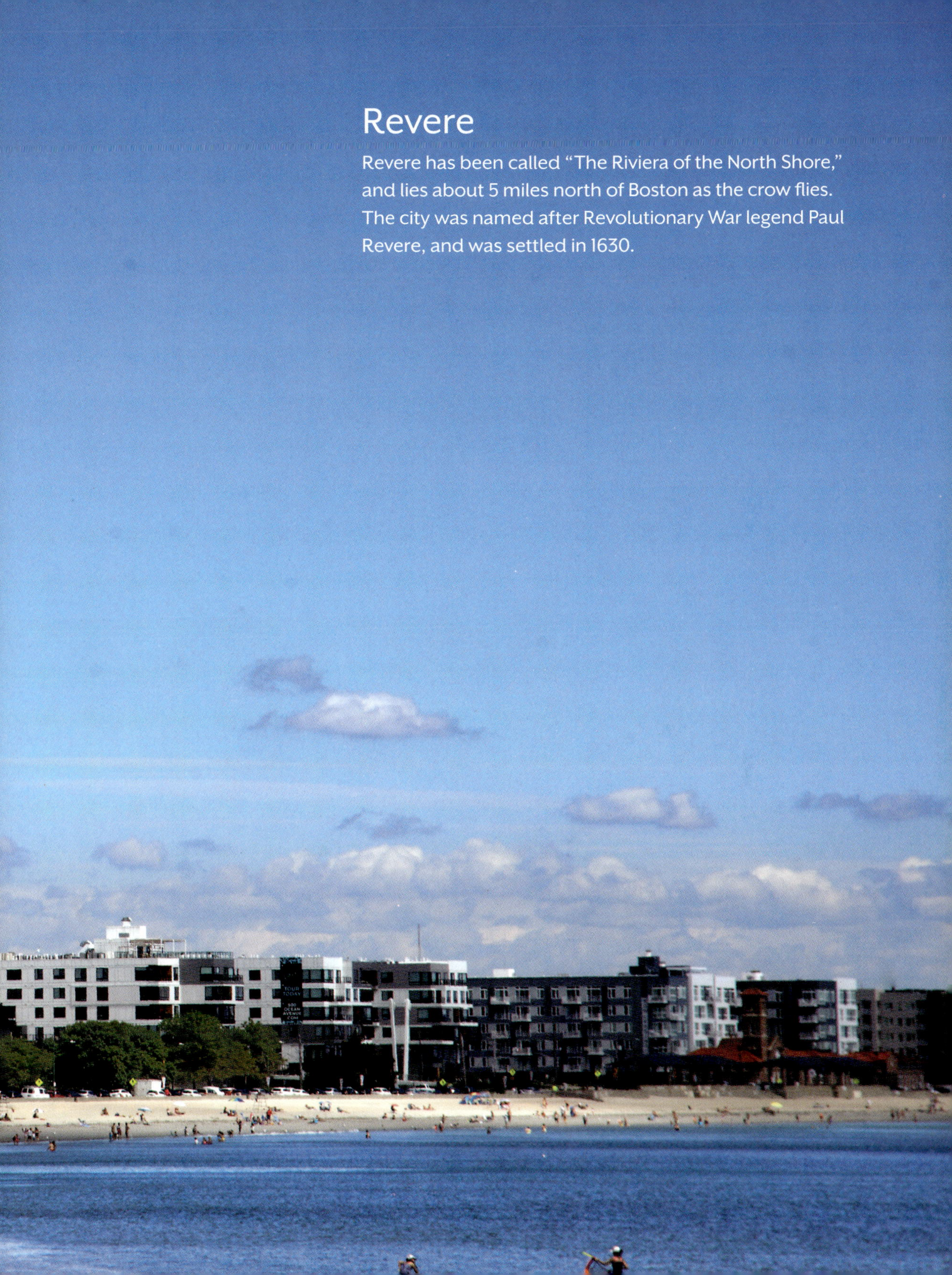

Revere

Revere has been called "The Riviera of the North Shore," and lies about 5 miles north of Boston as the crow flies. The city was named after Revolutionary War legend Paul Revere, and was settled in 1630.

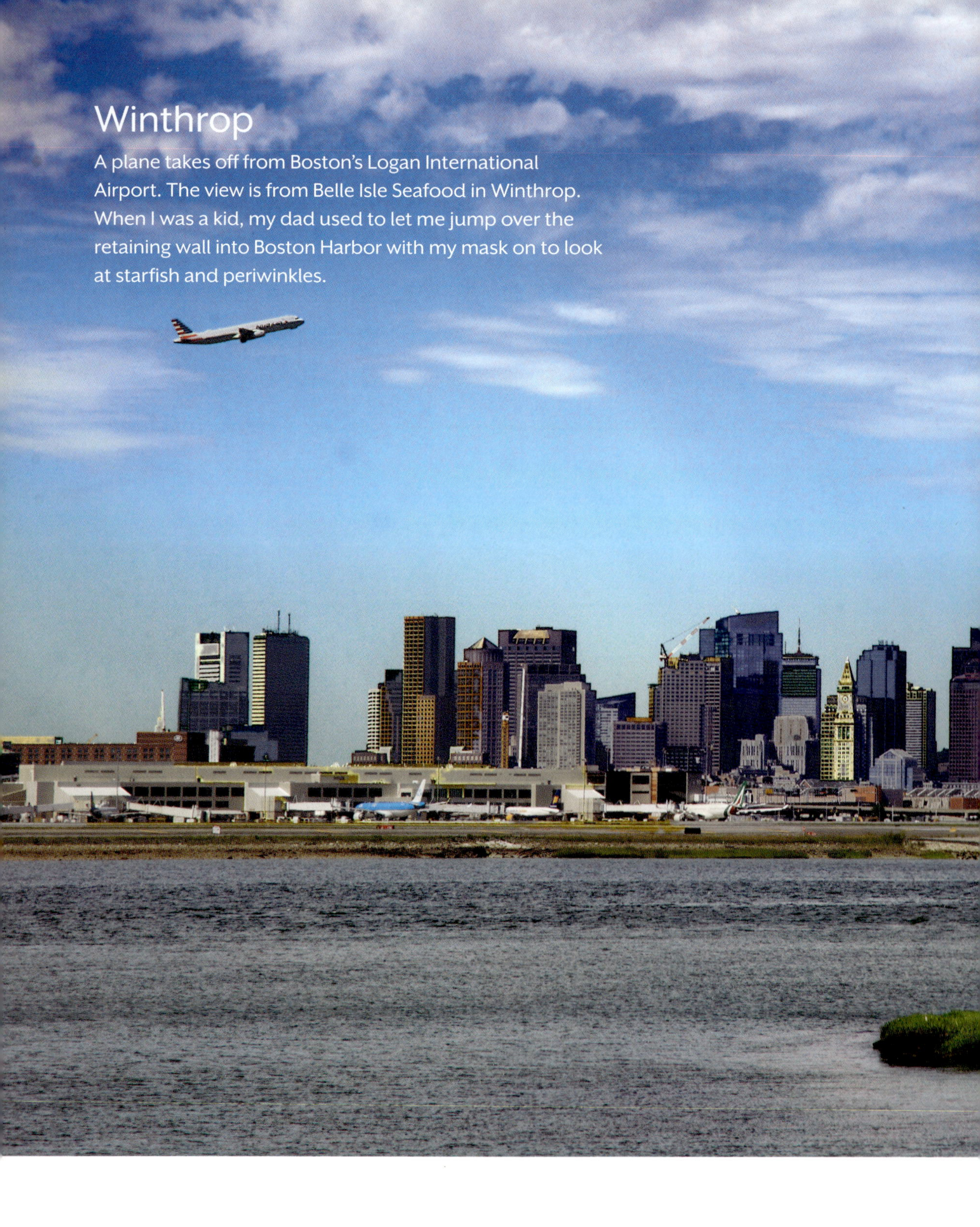
Winthrop
A plane takes off from Boston's Logan International Airport. The view is from Belle Isle Seafood in Winthrop. When I was a kid, my dad used to let me jump over the retaining wall into Boston Harbor with my mask on to look at starfish and periwinkles.

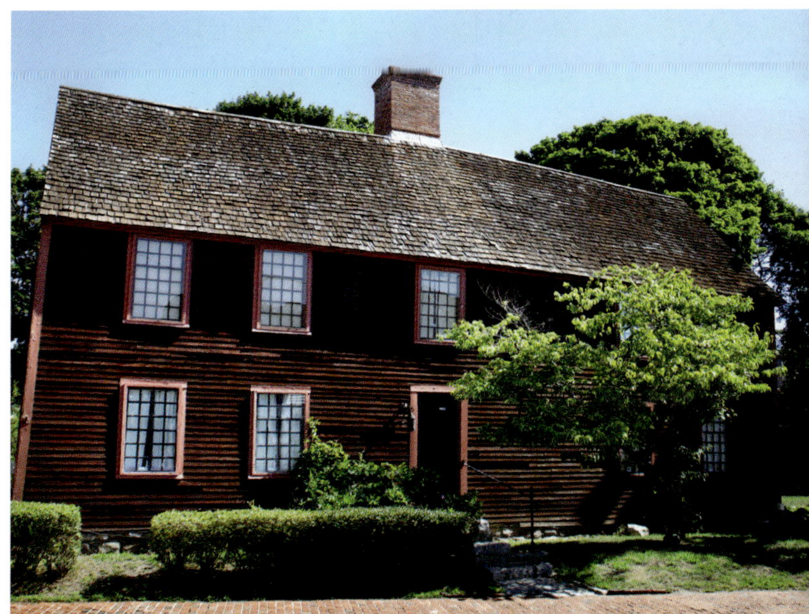

Authentic clapboards on the historic Deane Winthrop House, built in 1637. Governor John Winthrop's son Deane occupied the home from 1647 to 1703. Winthrop was settled in 1630.

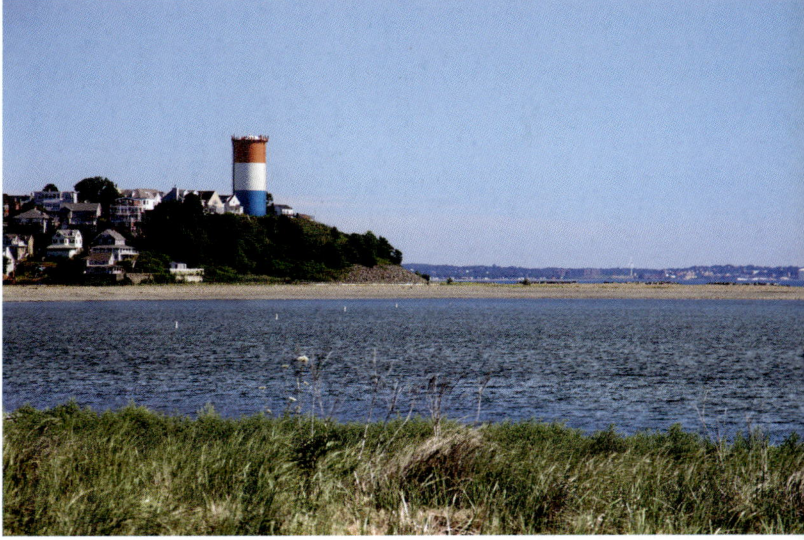

From Deer Island, the tri-colored water tower on a neighborhood hill.

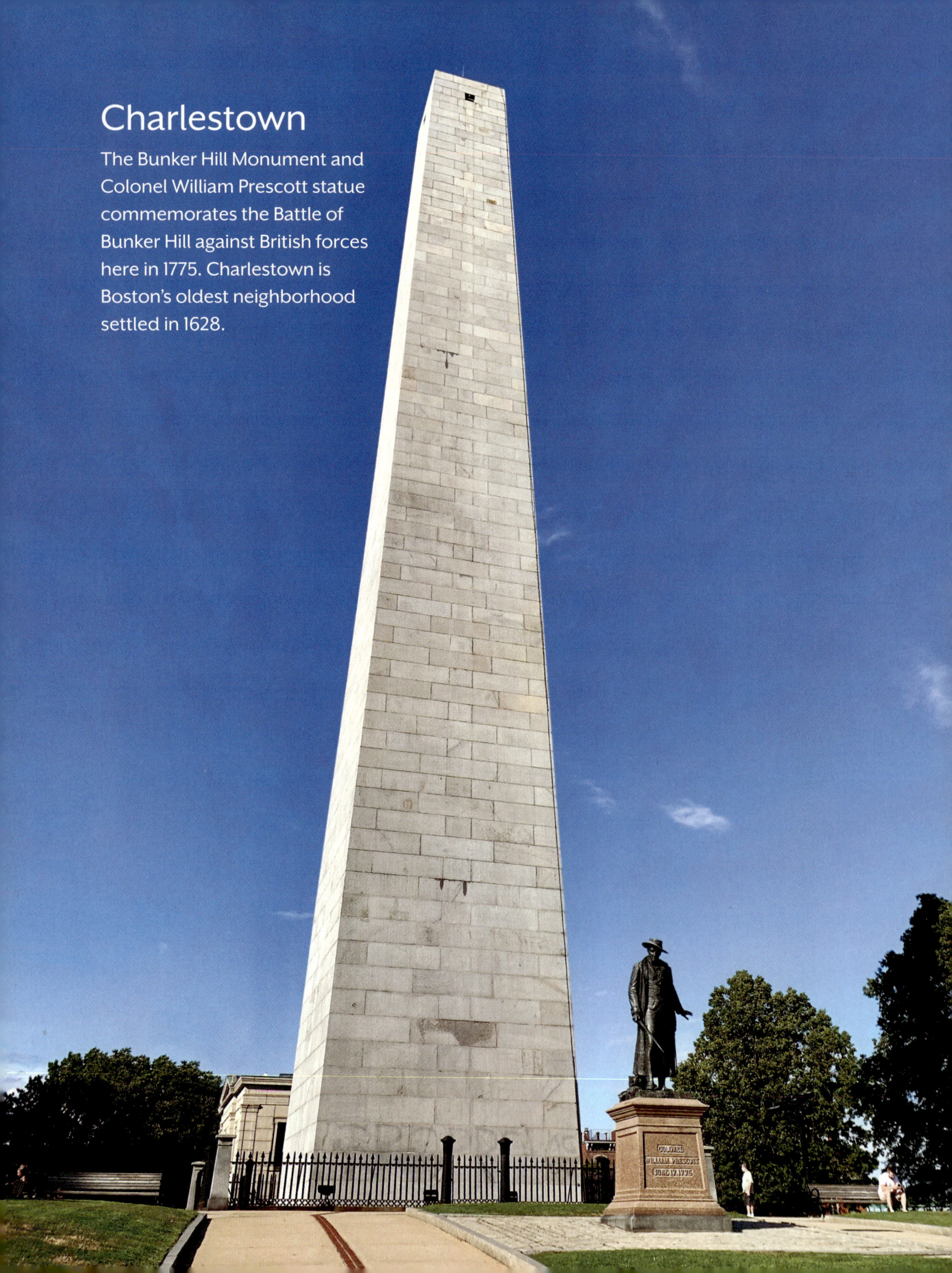

Charlestown

The Bunker Hill Monument and Colonel William Prescott statue commemorates the Battle of Bunker Hill against British forces here in 1775. Charlestown is Boston's oldest neighborhood settled in 1628.

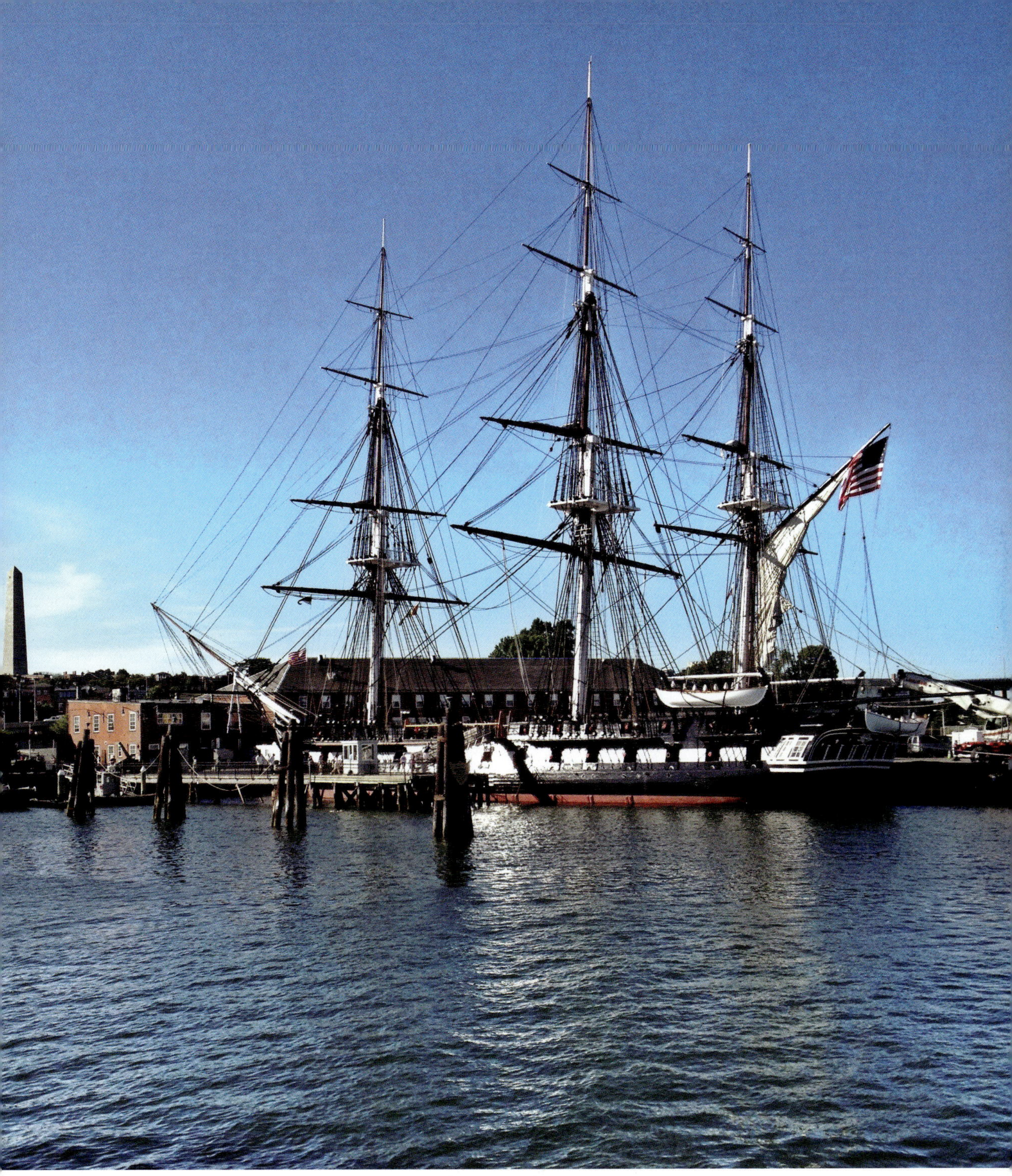

A view from across Boston Harbor of the USS *Constitution* in Charlestown Navy Yard. Known as "Old Ironsides," she's the oldest active ship in the US Navy.

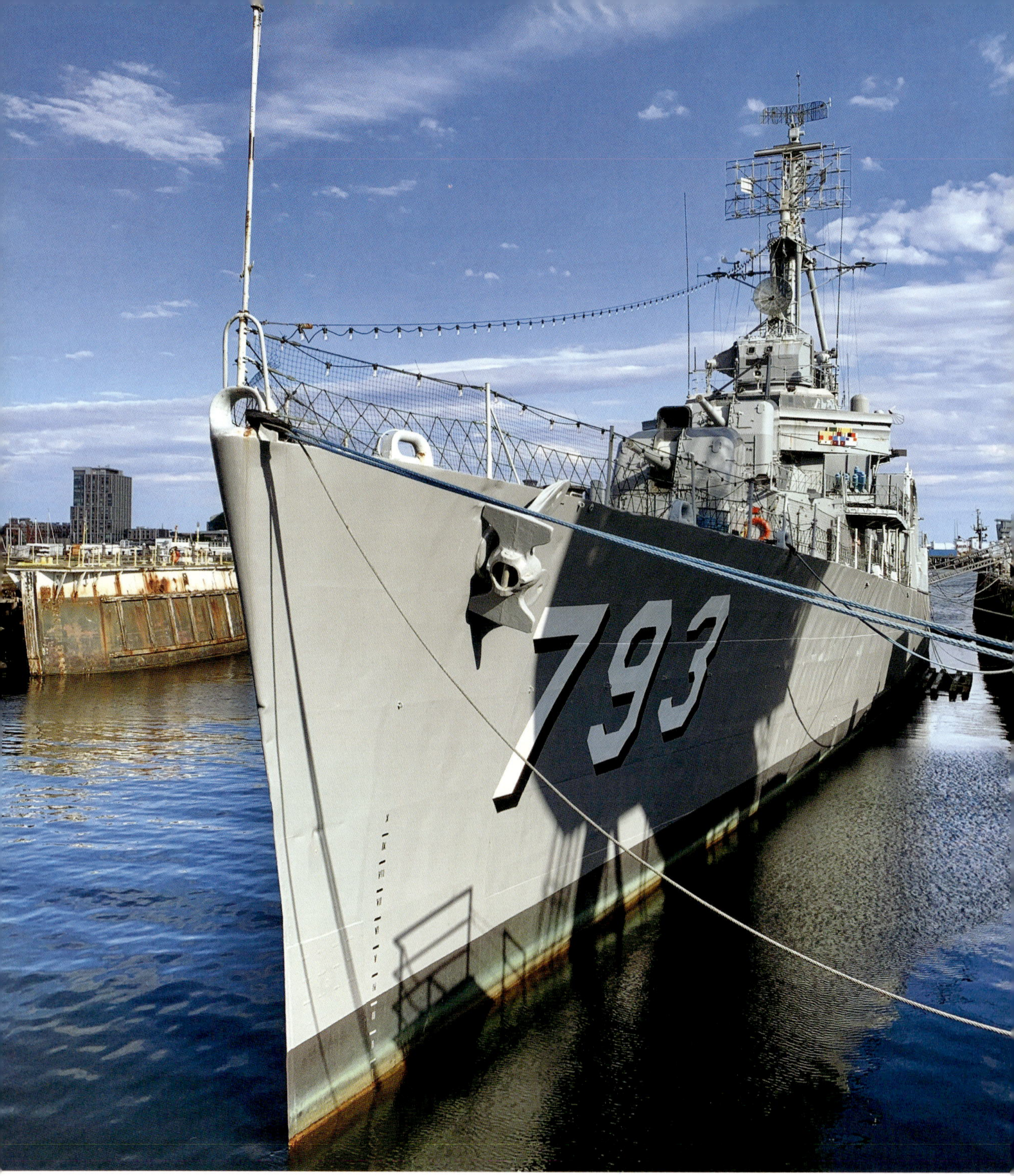

Also here is the naval destroyer USS *Cassin Young.* She was launched in 1943, and served in World War II and the Korean War.

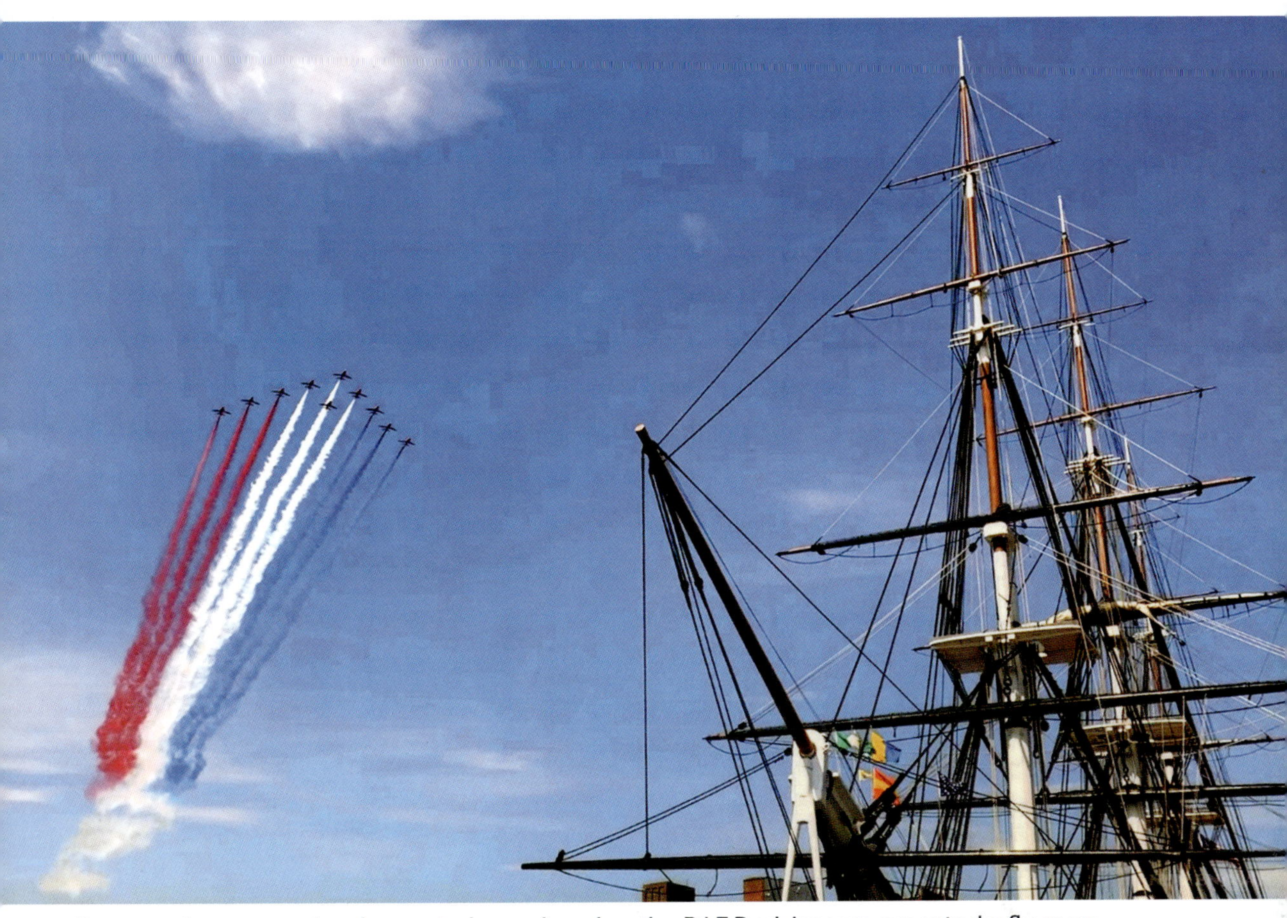

It was a pleasure and an honor to be on hand as the RAF Red Arrows executed a fly-over directly above the navy yard and *Old Ironsides.*

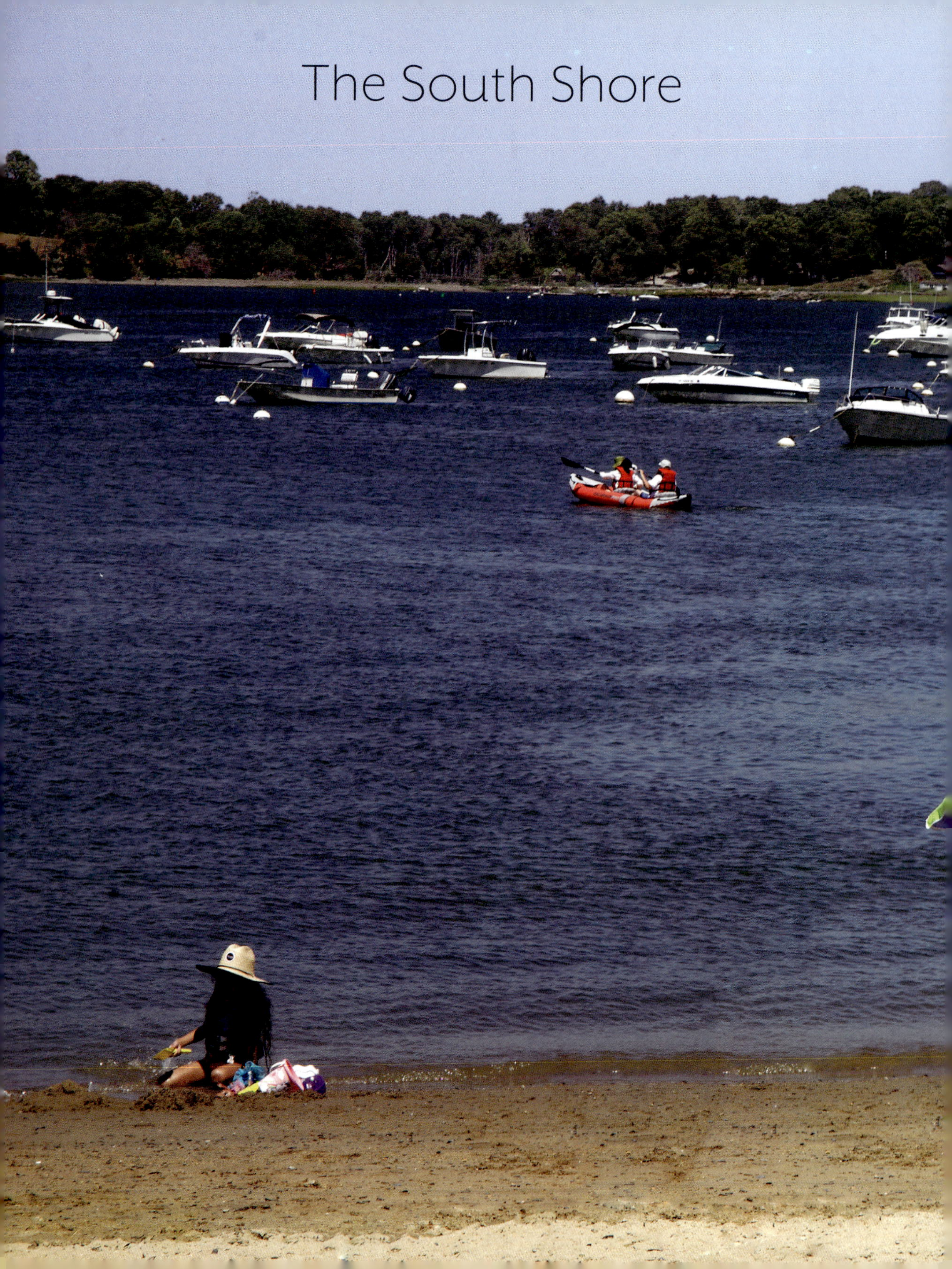

The South Shore

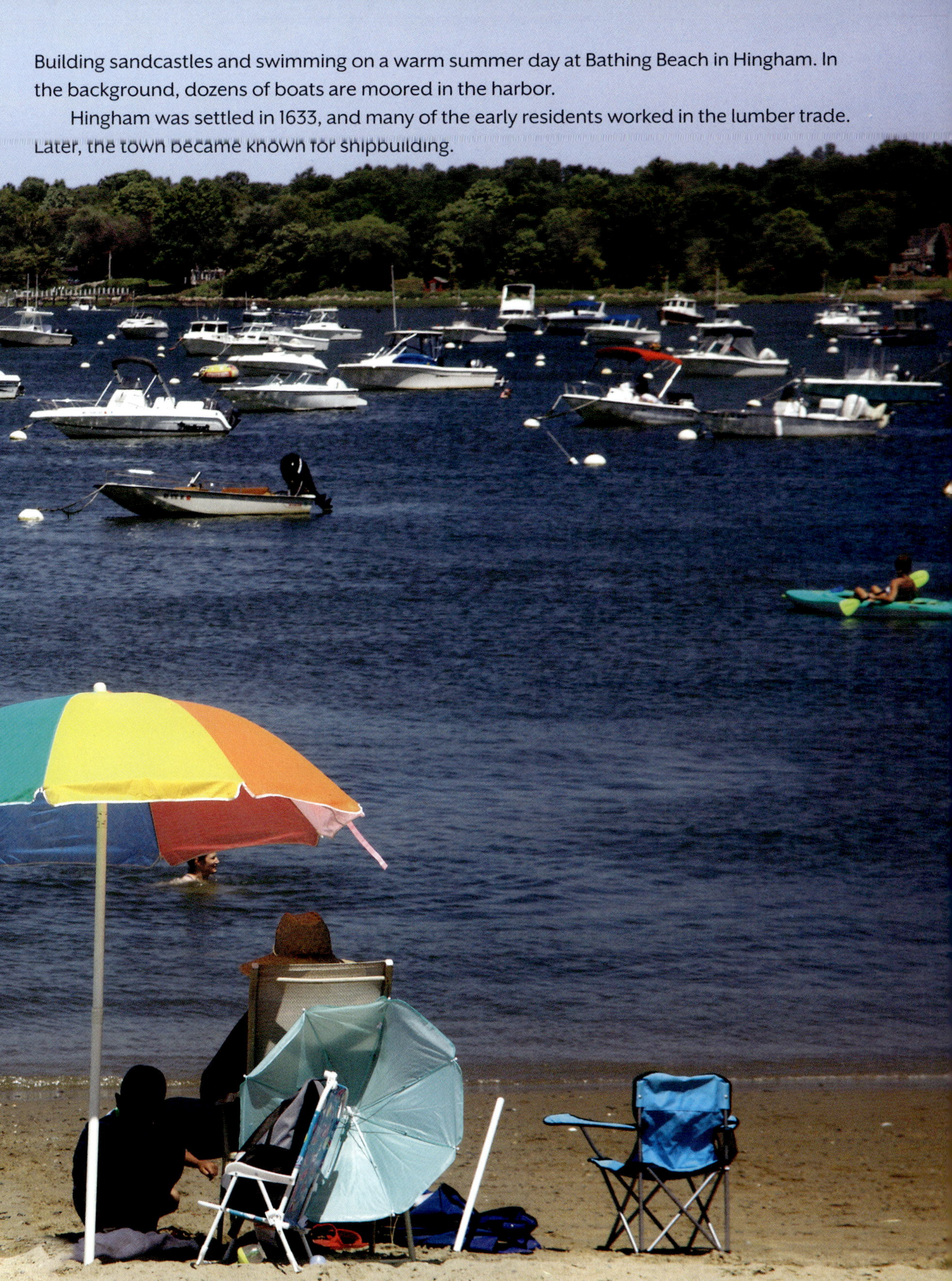

Building sandcastles and swimming on a warm summer day at Bathing Beach in Hingham. In the background, dozens of boats are moored in the harbor.

Hingham was settled in 1633, and many of the early residents worked in the lumber trade. Later, the town became known for shipbuilding.

Quincy

Situated on Wollaston Beach in Quincy Bay is the Squantum Yacht Club. The club was founded in 1890 to promote boating on the South Shore, and is operated and maintained by its members.

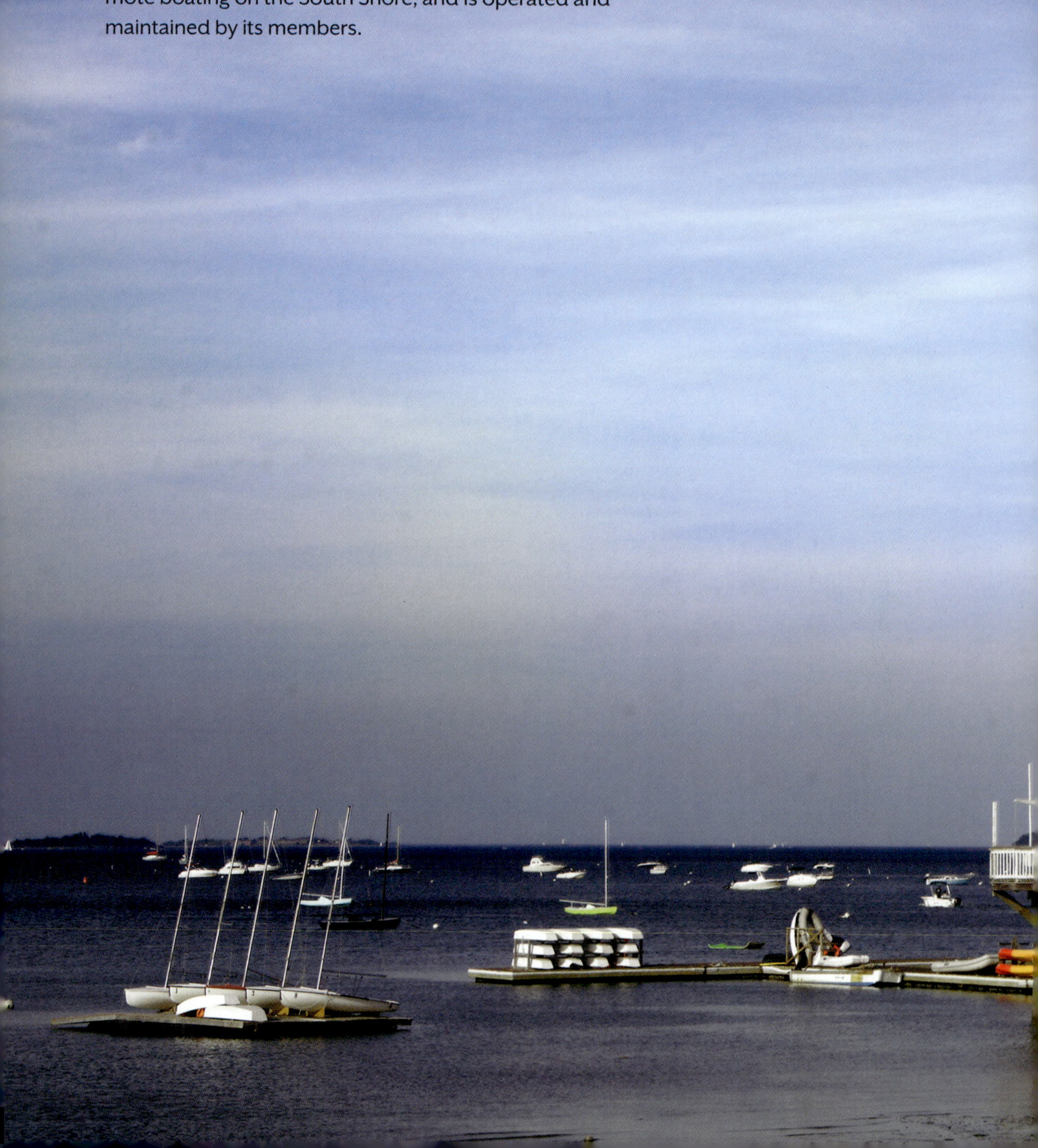

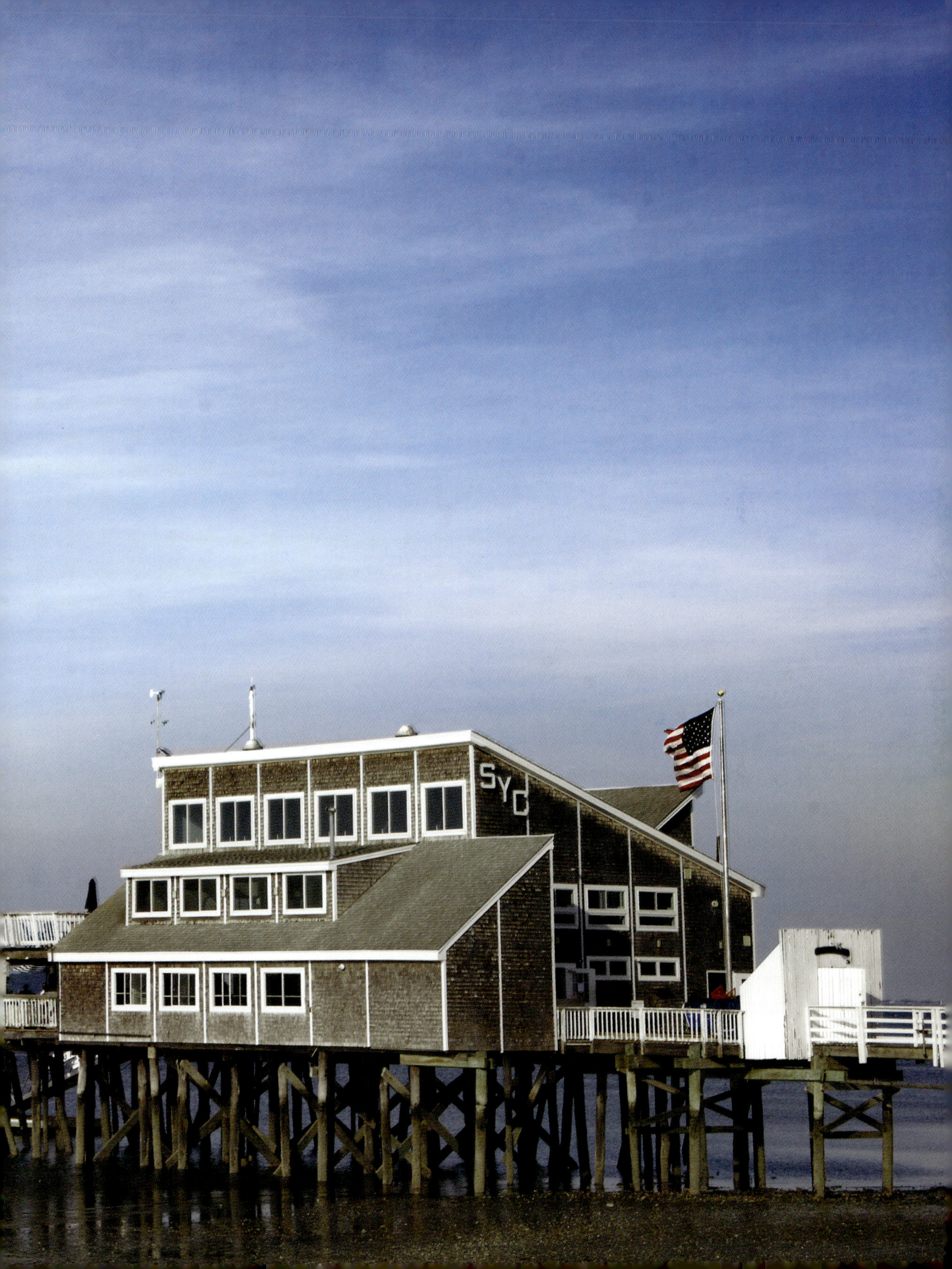

SYC

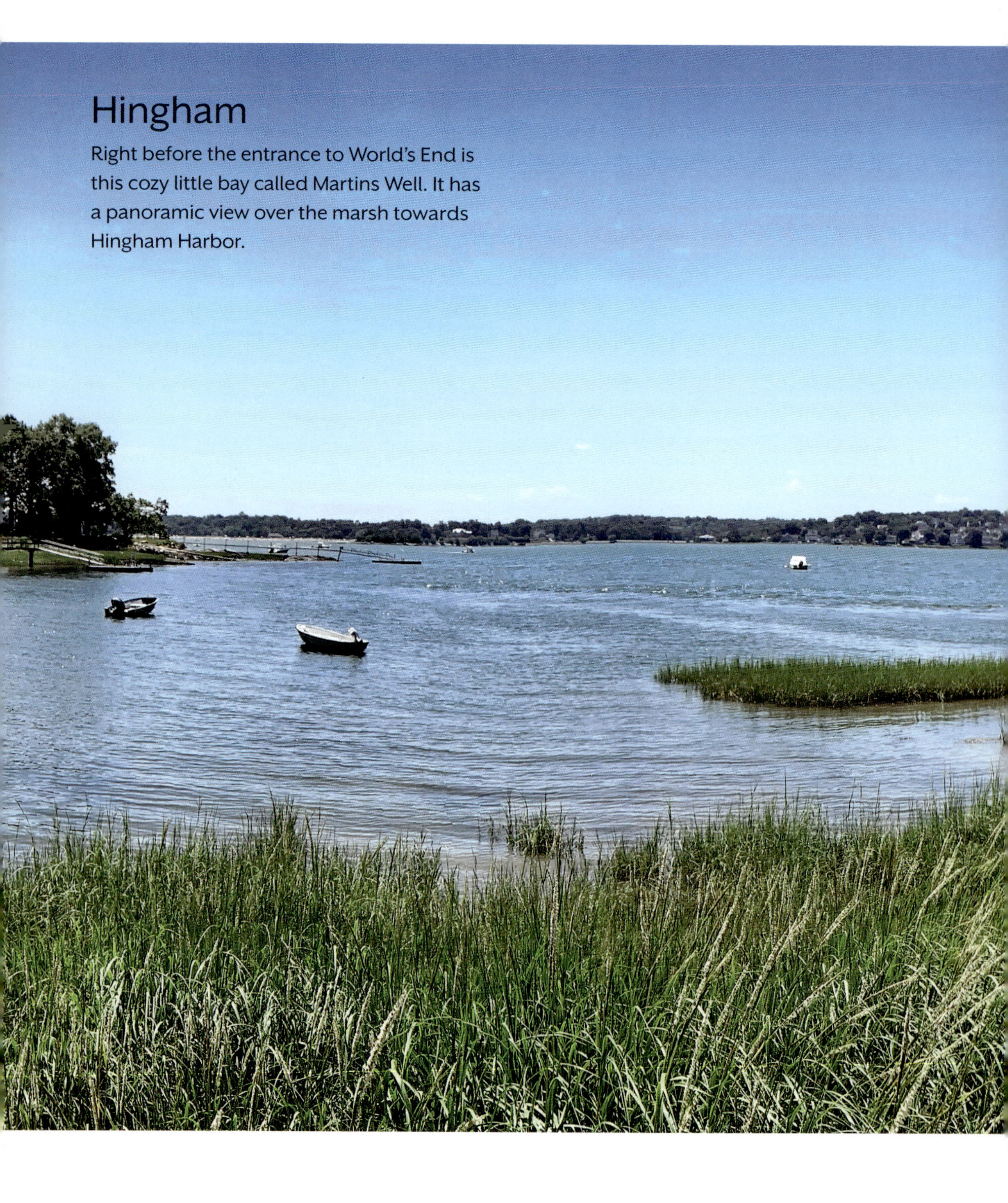

Hingham

Right before the entrance to World's End is this cozy little bay called Martins Well. It has a panoramic view over the marsh towards Hingham Harbor.

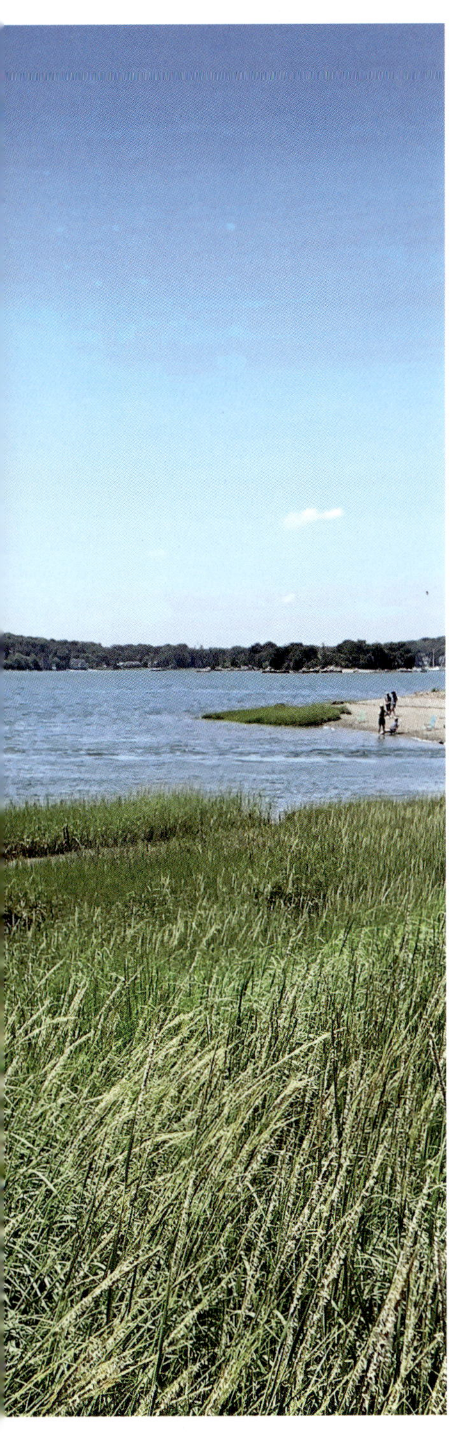

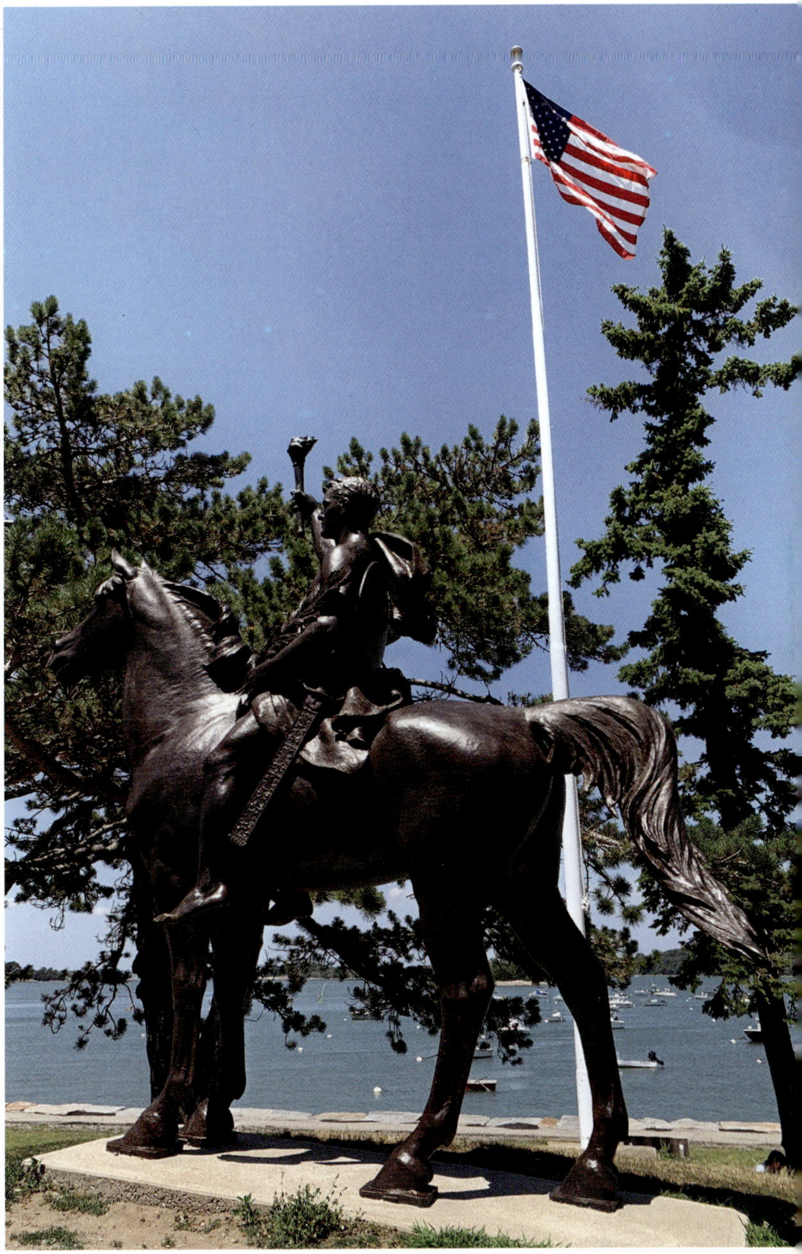

Walking along the waterfront of Hingham Harbor, there's a marina, boardwalk, and restaurants. At a park next to the beach is a memorial statue dedicated to soldiers from Hingham who served in war.

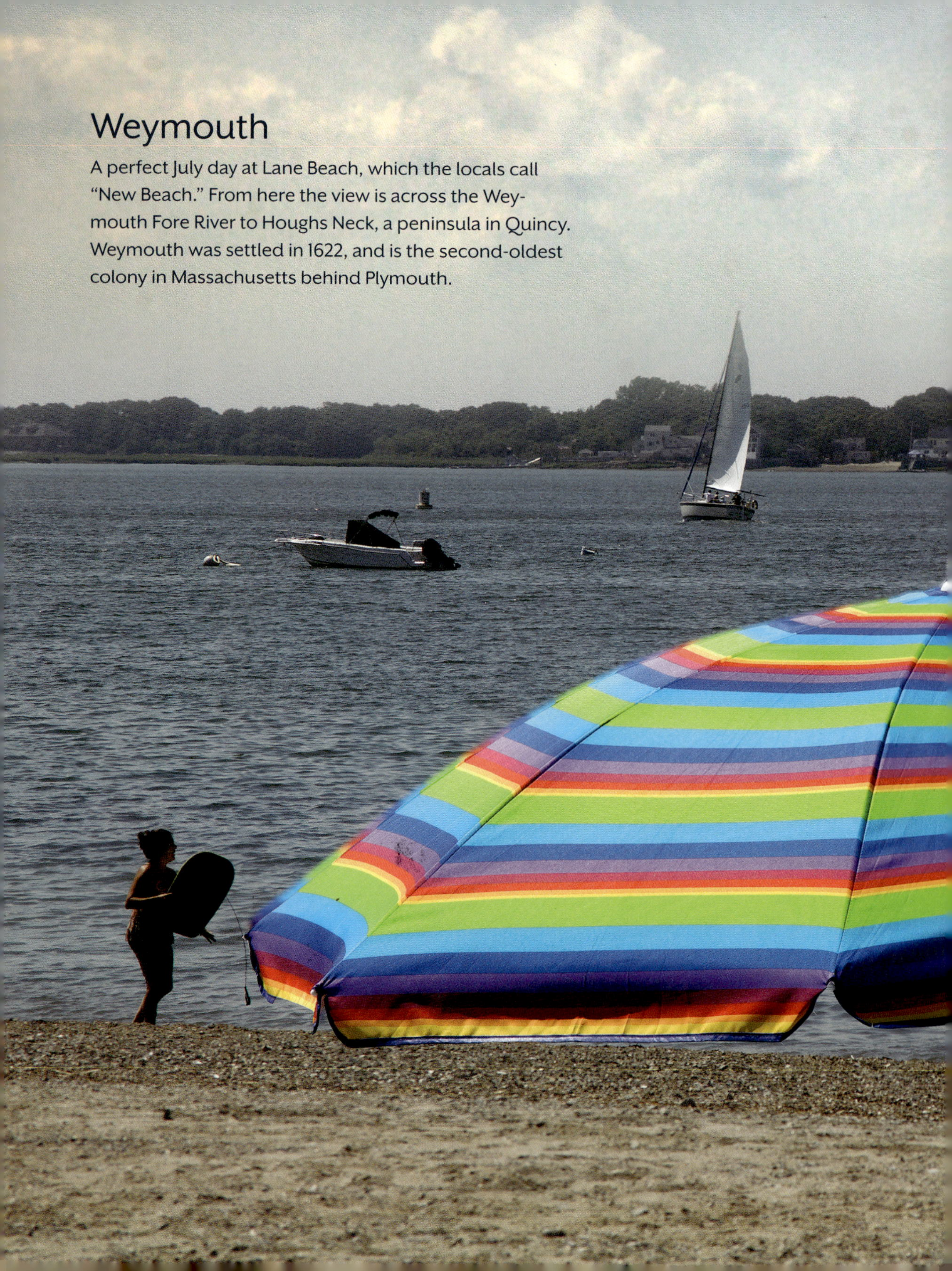

Weymouth

A perfect July day at Lane Beach, which the locals call "New Beach." From here the view is across the Weymouth Fore River to Houghs Neck, a peninsula in Quincy. Weymouth was settled in 1622, and is the second-oldest colony in Massachusetts behind Plymouth.

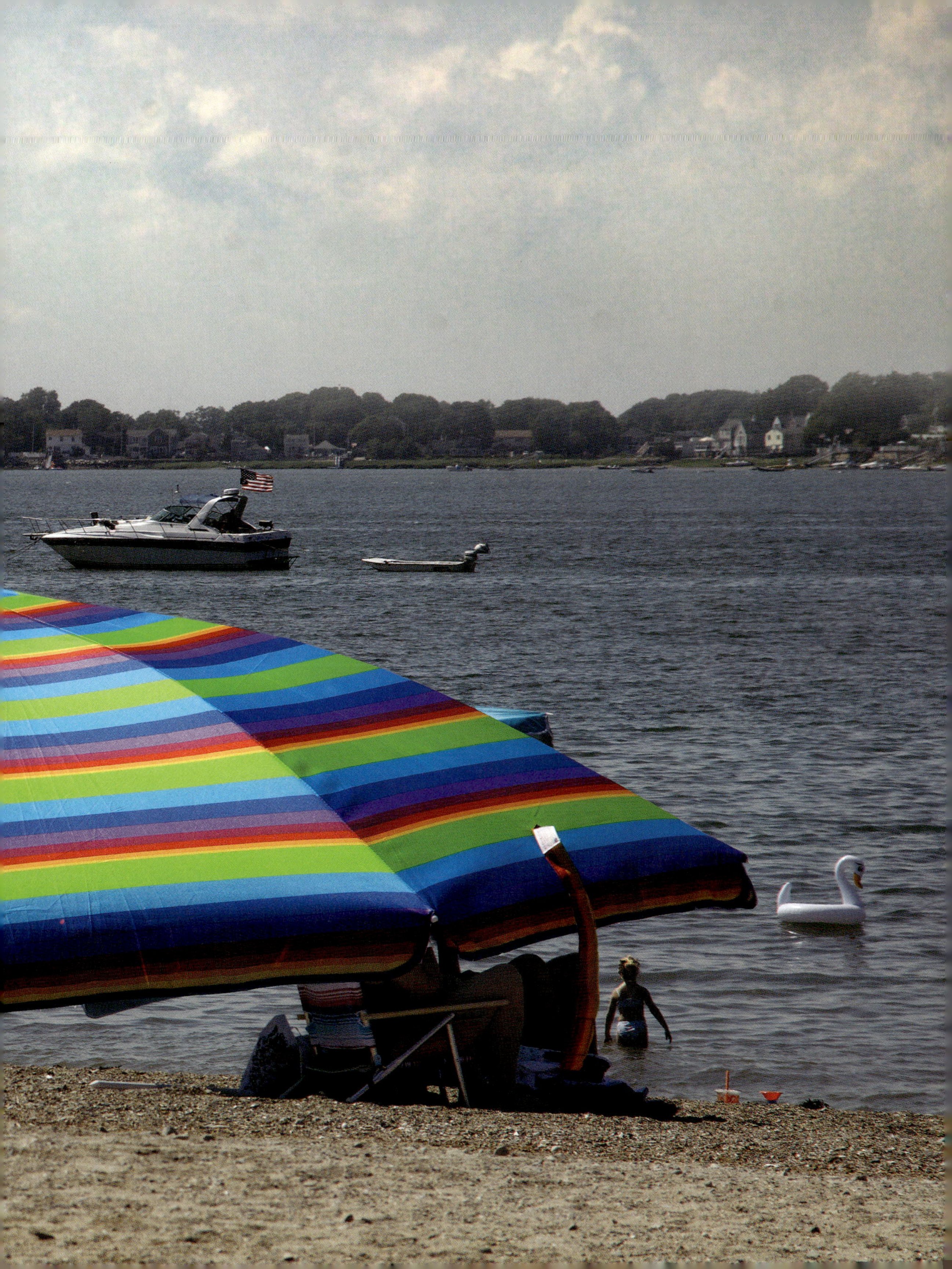

Hull

With its miles of fine sand, and countless tidal pools at low tide, Nantasket Beach is one of the most popular summer destinations in Massachusetts.

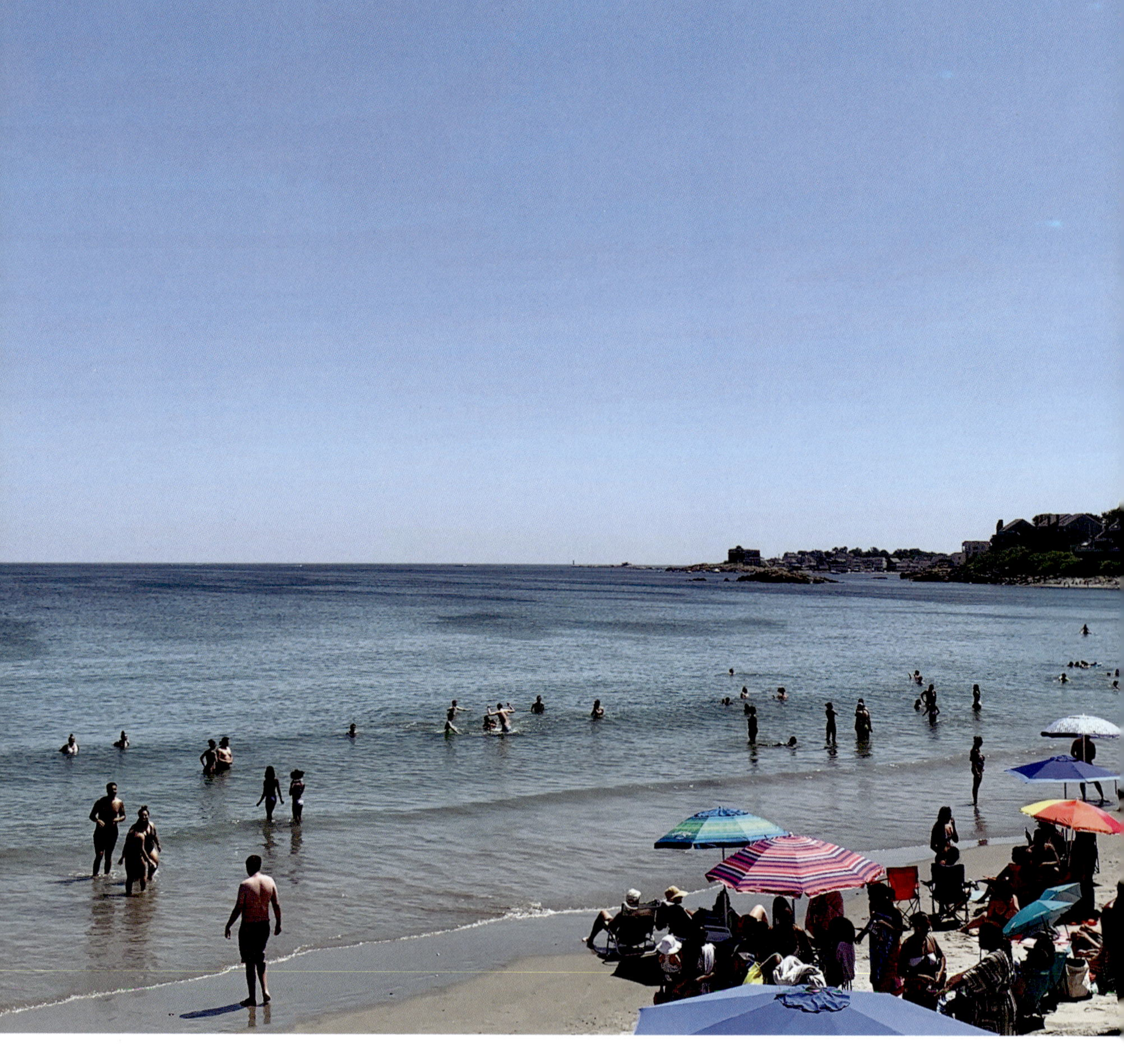

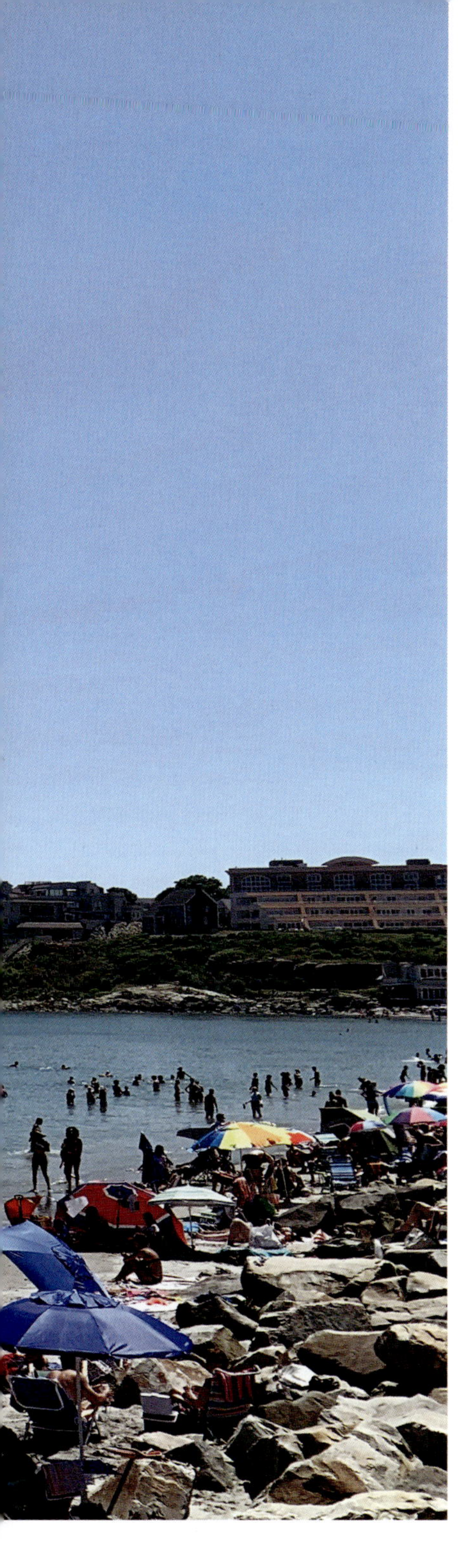

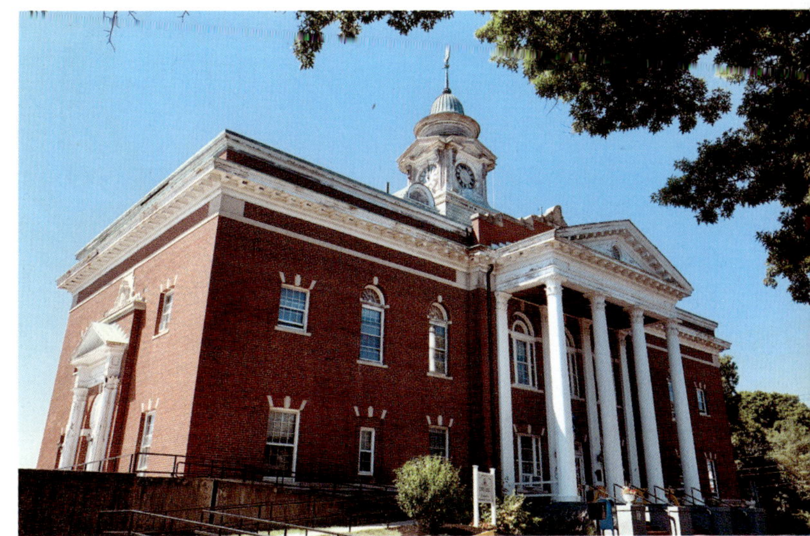

Hull Town Hall on Atlantic Ave. This little town is located on a long, thin peninsula in the southern portion of Boston Harbor. It's the smallest town in Plymouth County by land area.

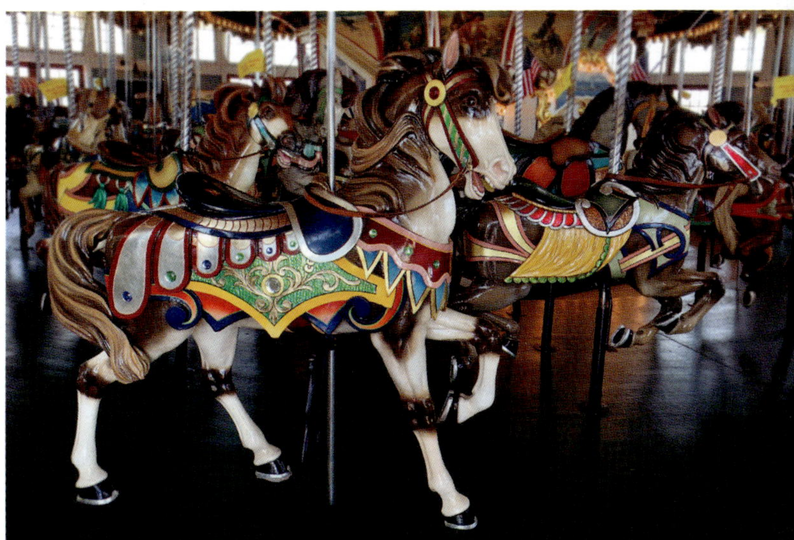

One of the most popular family attractions is the Paragon Carousel. Built in 1928, it has four rows of horses and two Roman chariots, so it's classified as a "grand carousel." It's one of only five left in the world with the rare Roman chariots.

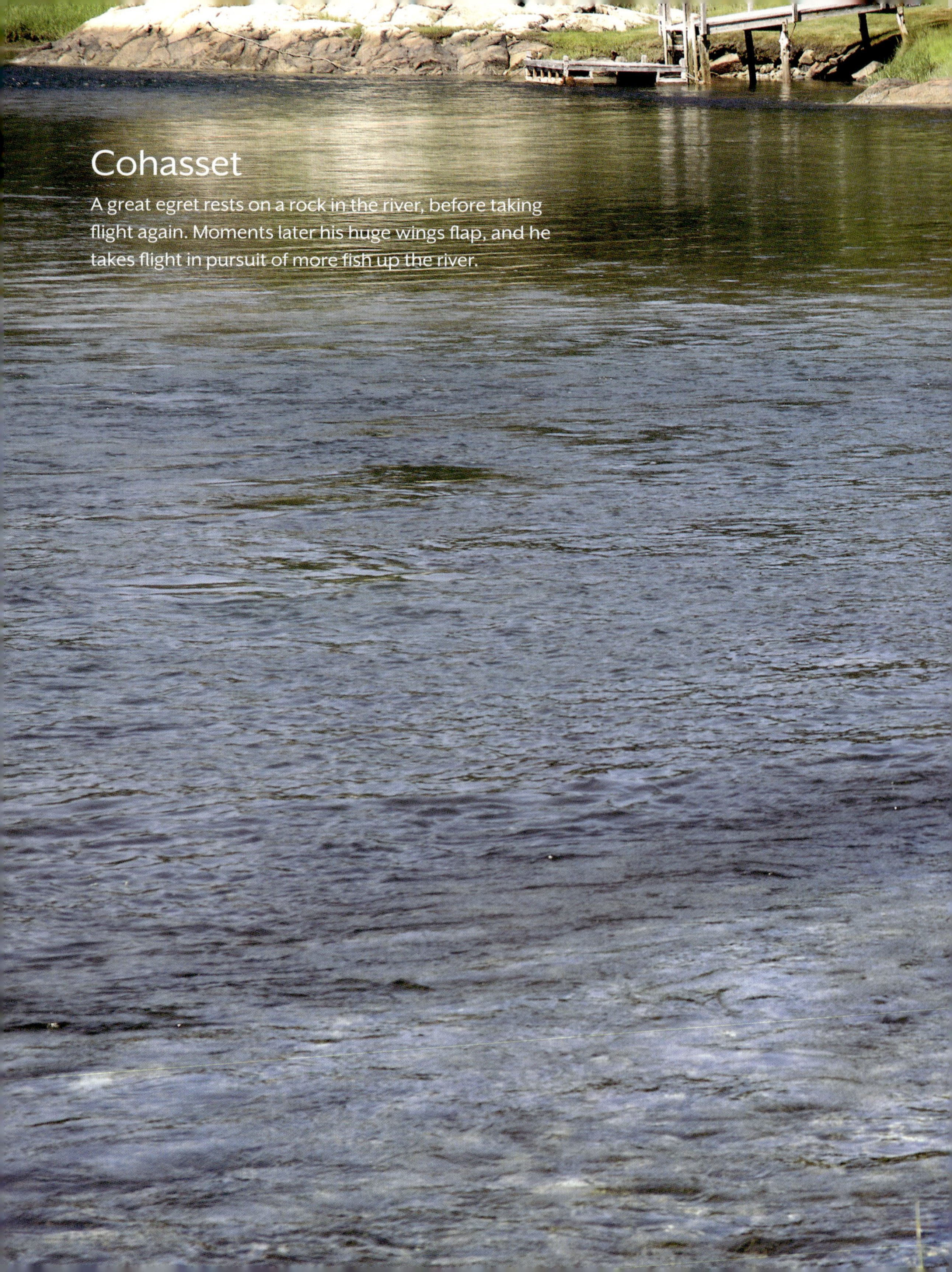

Cohasset
A great egret rests on a rock in the river, before taking flight again. Moments later his huge wings flap, and he takes flight in pursuit of more fish up the river.

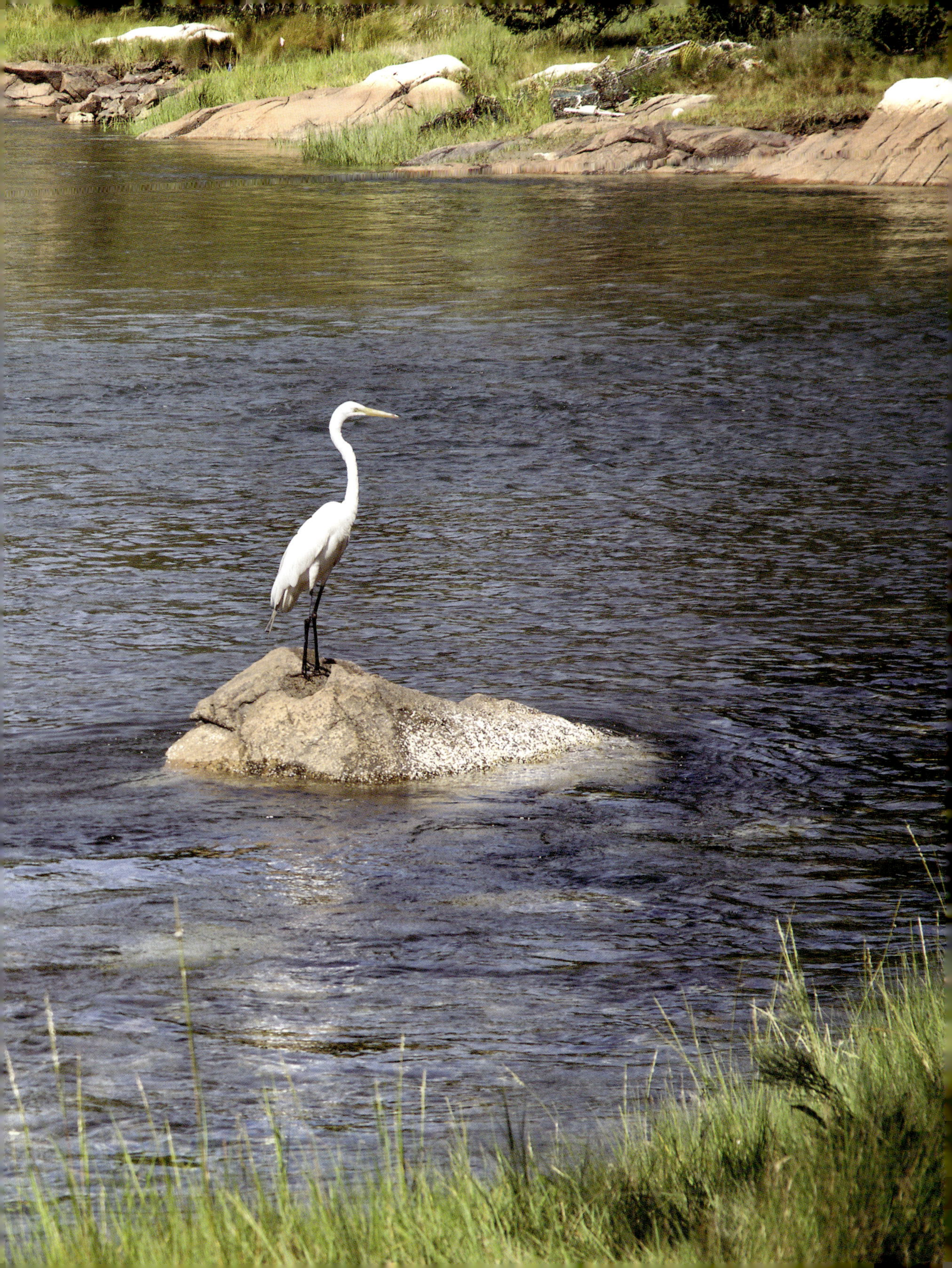

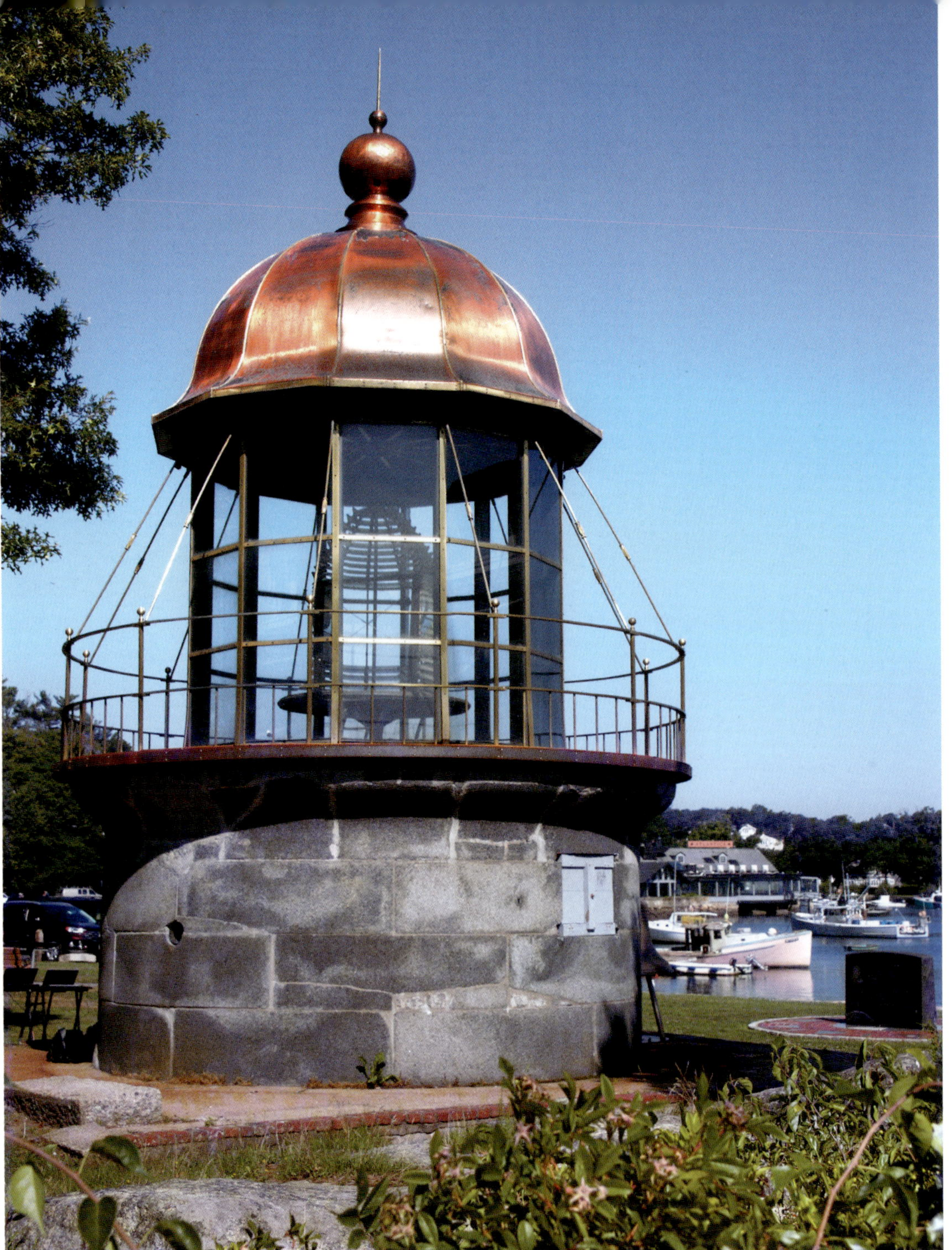

Also next to the harbor is this stunning homage to the Minot's Ledge Lighthouse. It's built on granite blocks that came from Minot's Lighthouse when it was under repair in 1987. It also contains a portion of the original Fresnel lens.

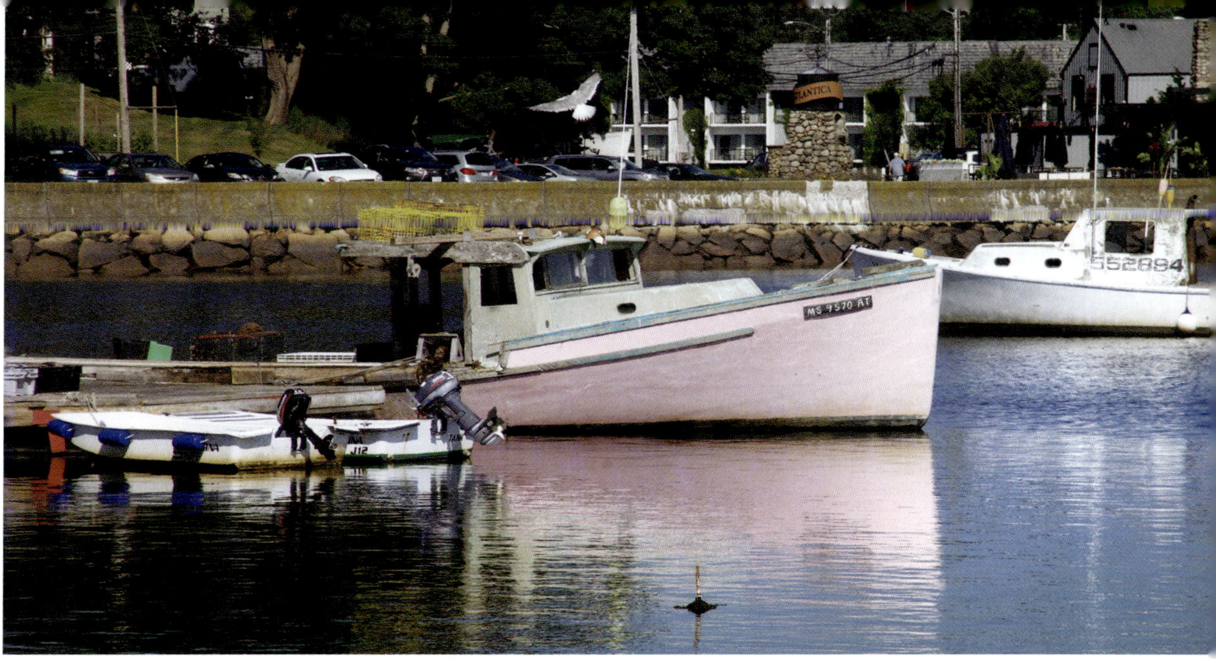

A seagull comes in for a landing on a pink lobster boat in the harbor in Cohasset. Settlers arrived here in the early 1600s. It officially became the town of Cohasset in 1770, when it separated from Hingham.

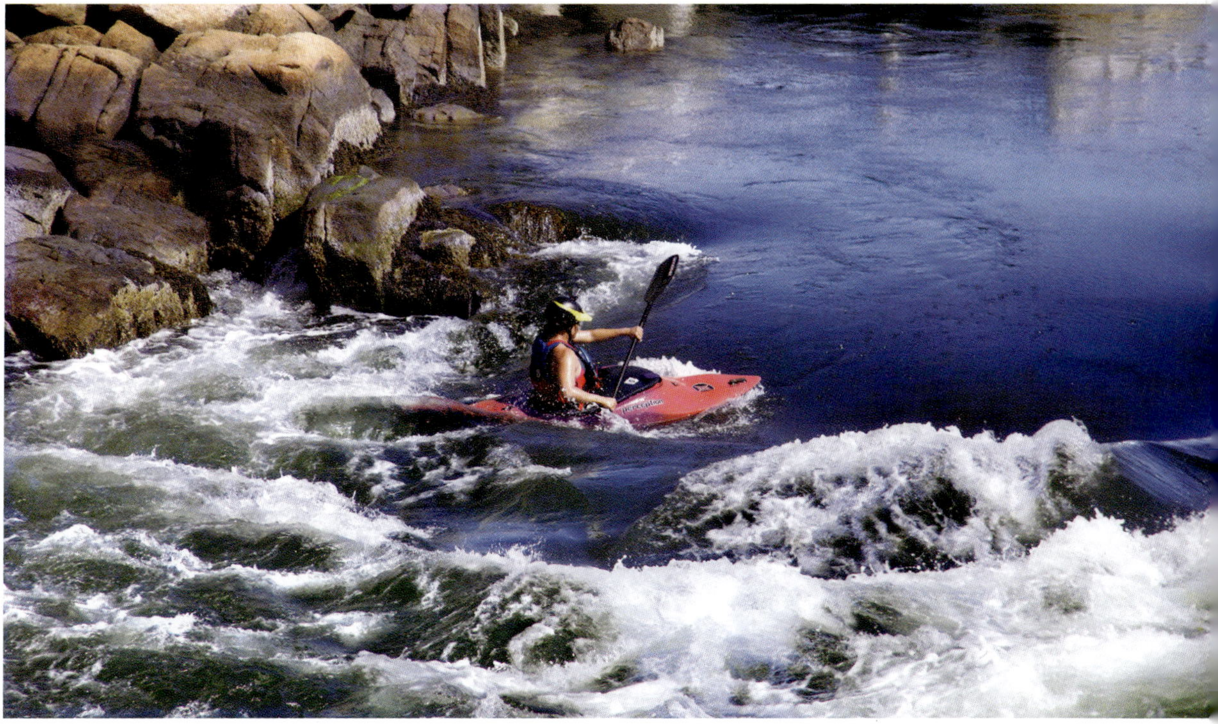

From the Border Street Bridge comes this view of a kayaker traversing the surge from the incoming tide.

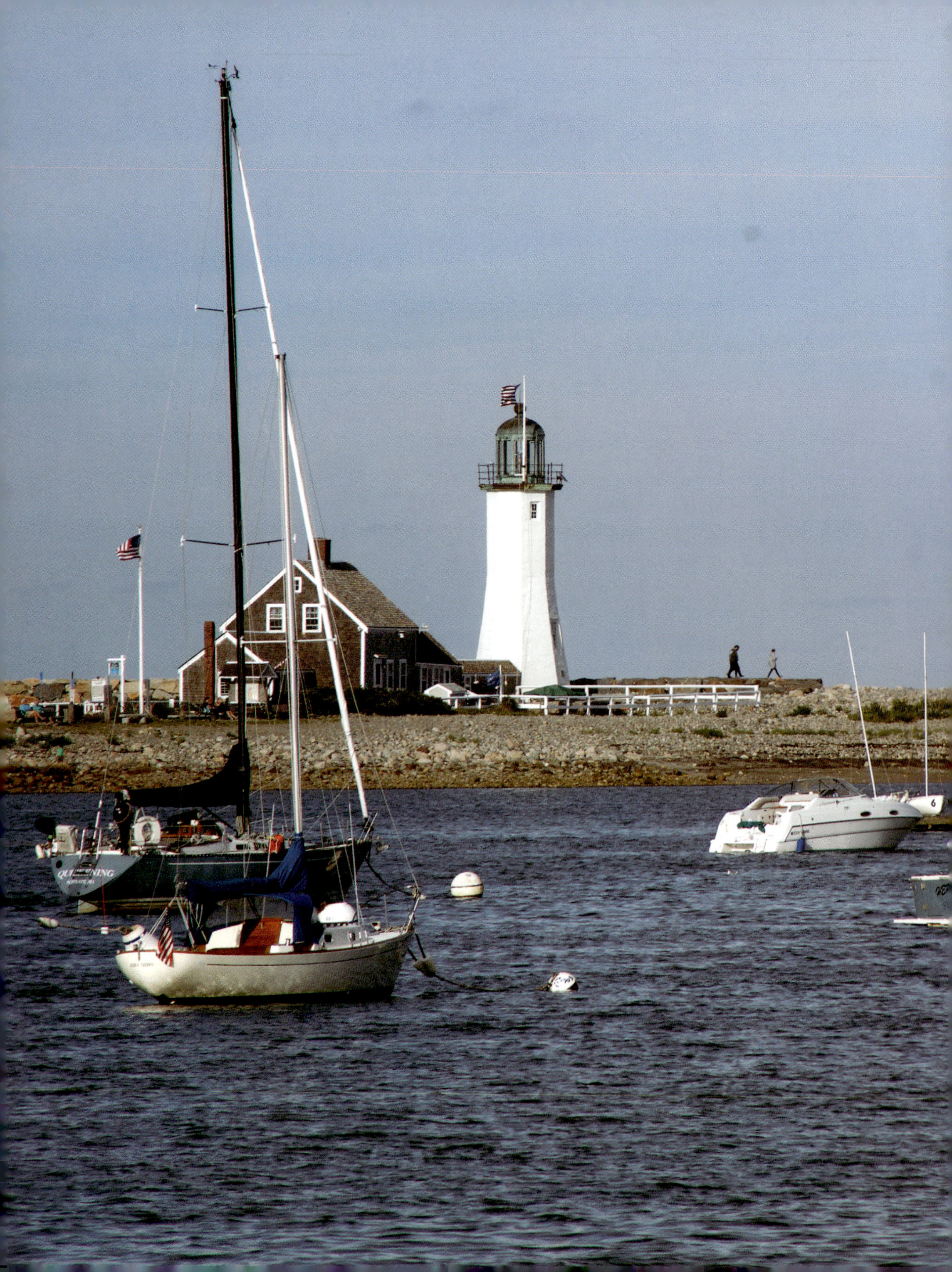

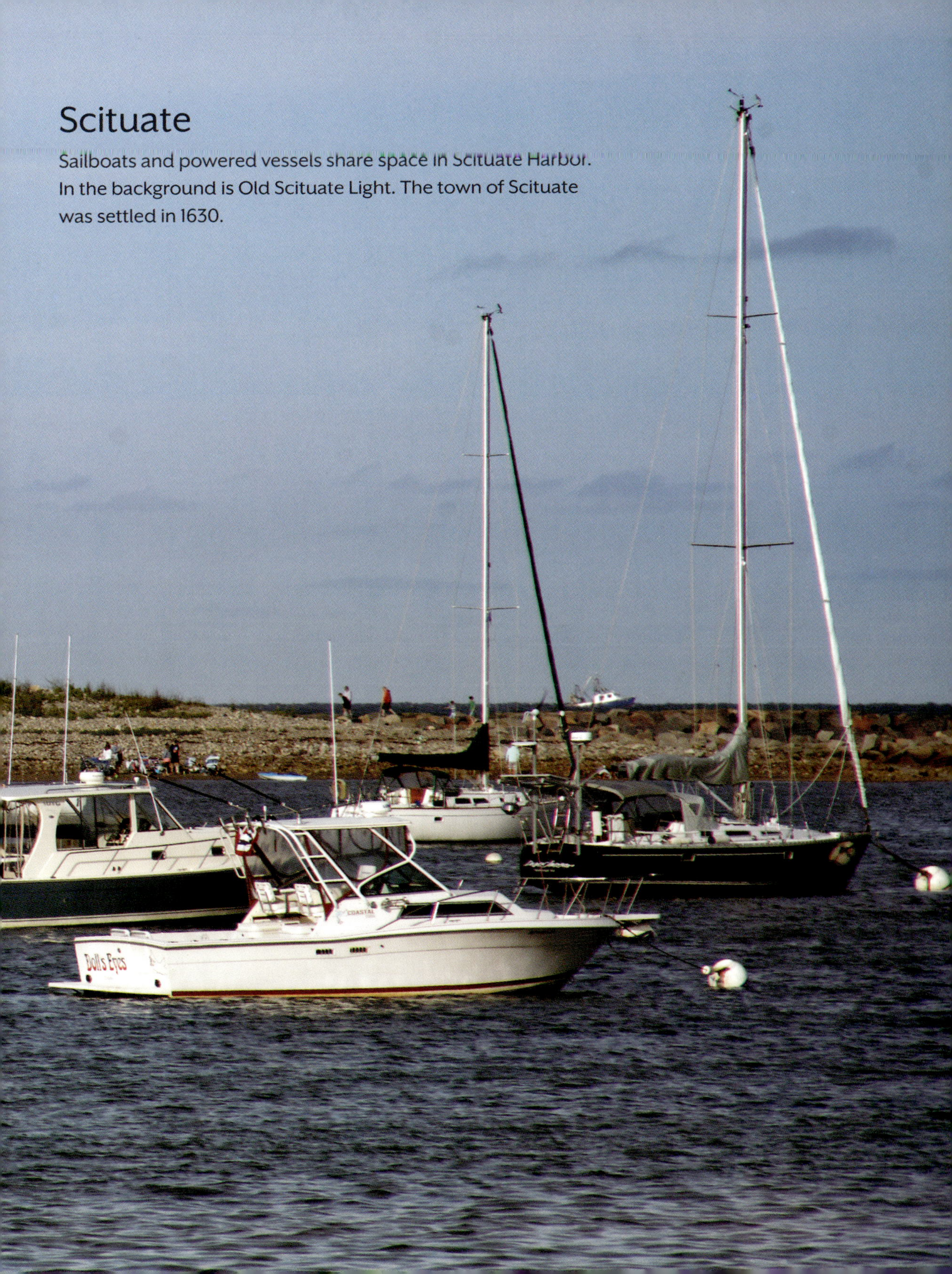

Scituate

Sailboats and powered vessels share space in Scituate Harbor.
In the background is Old Scituate Light. The town of Scituate
was settled in 1630.

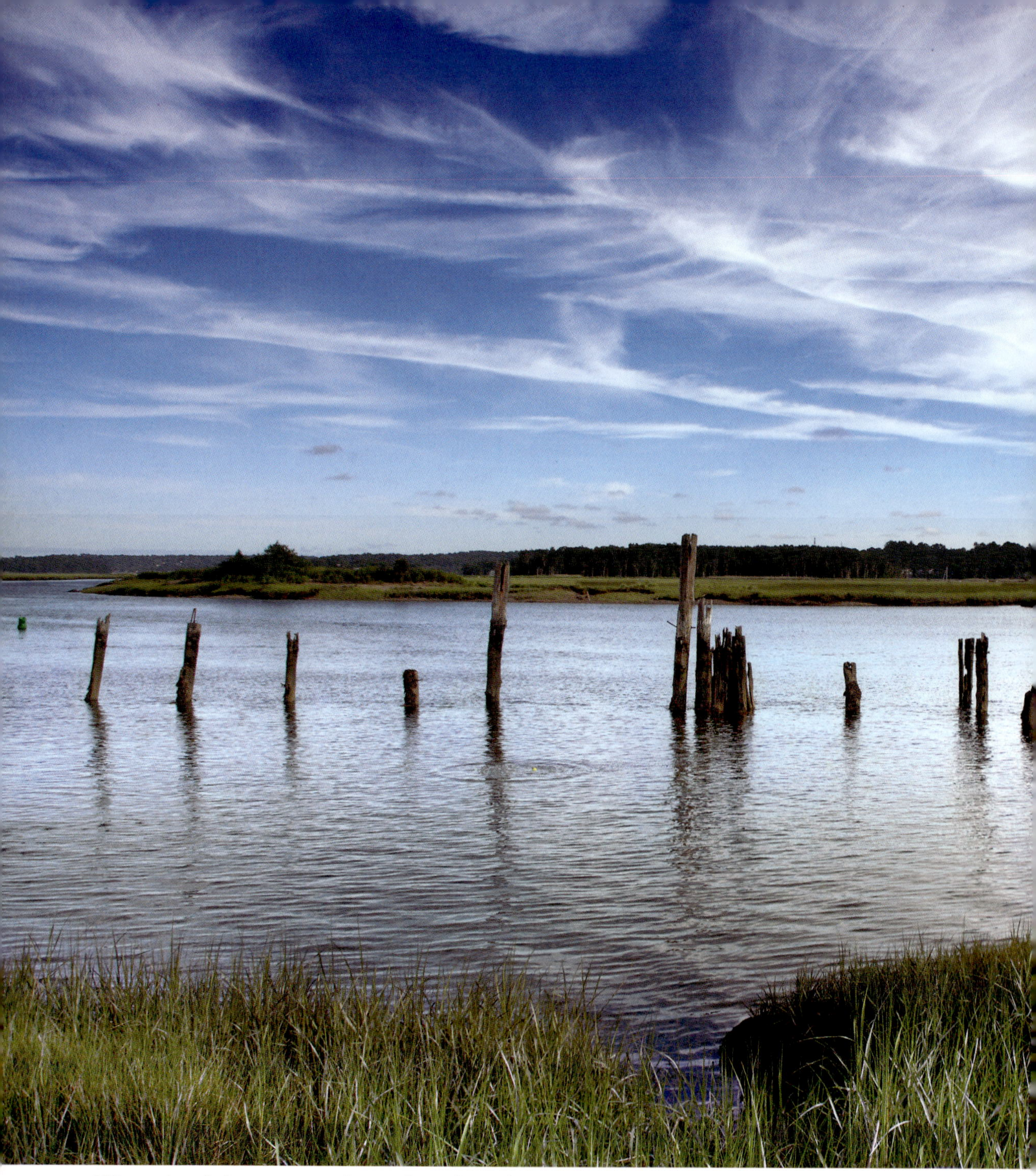

Wispy clouds linger over salt marshes along the Herring River at Conservation Park. Faded wood pilings are all that remain of an old wharf that was used to haul sand for construction in the 1930s.

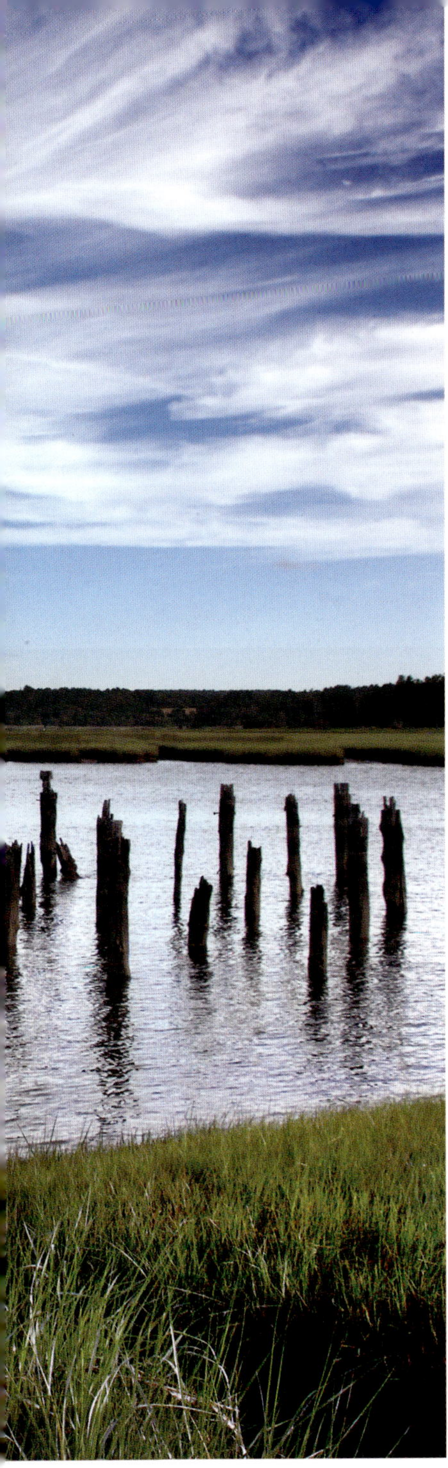

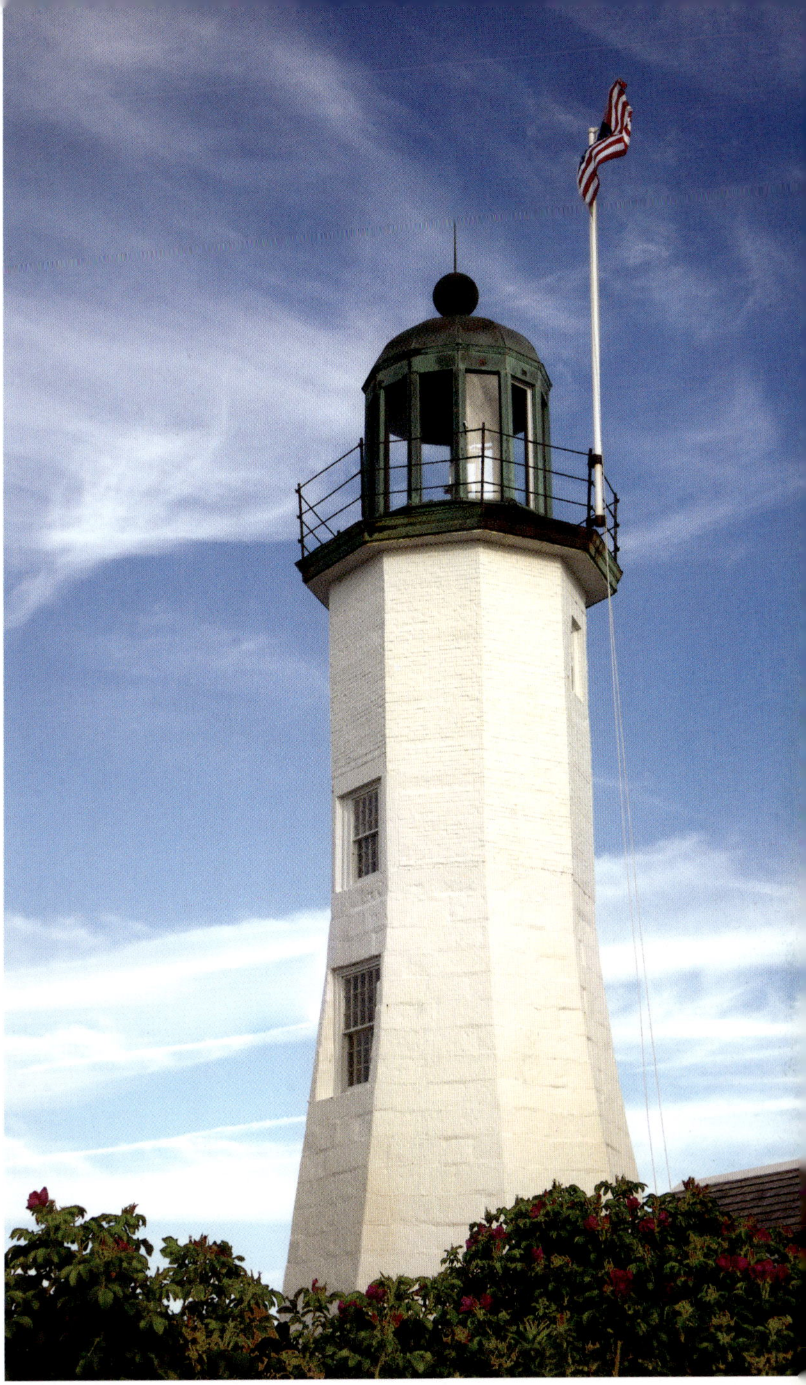

Scituate Light is located on Cedar Point near the mouth of Scituate Harbor. It was first lit in 1811, thanks to a vote granting $4,000 from Congress. It has a wonderful octagonal design, is built from brick and granite, and features a green lantern.

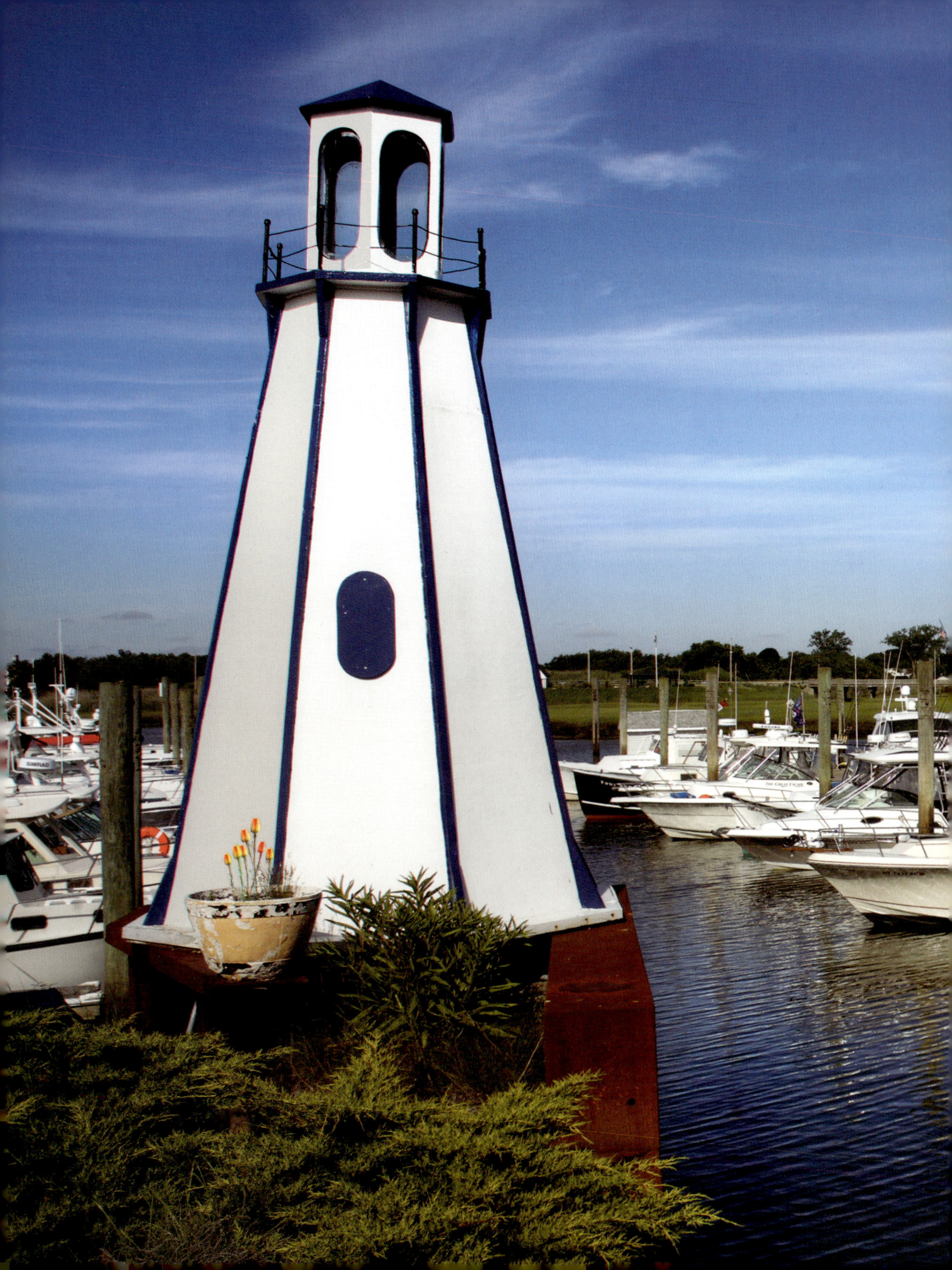

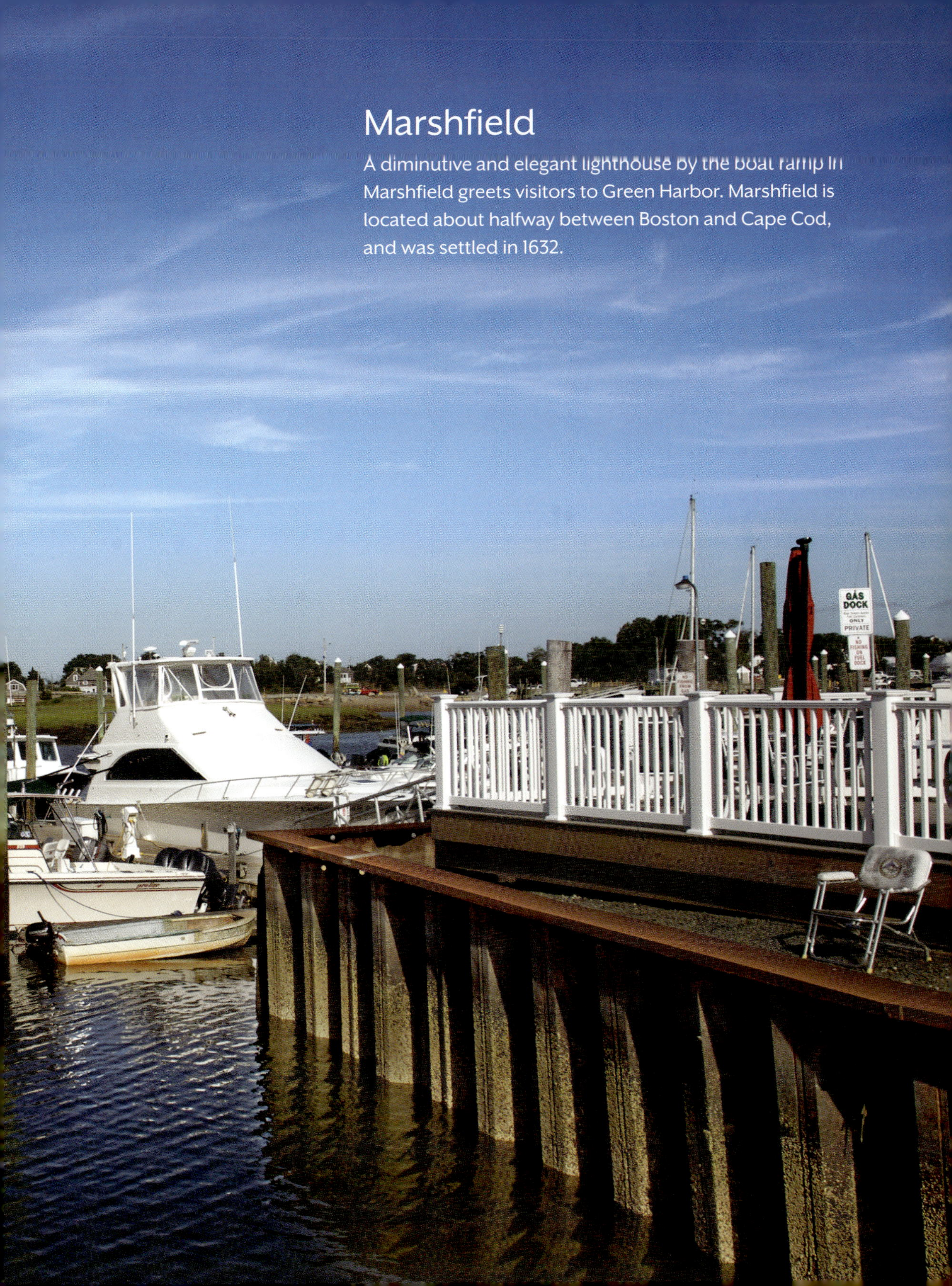

Marshfield
A diminutive and elegant lighthouse by the boat ramp in Marshfield greets visitors to Green Harbor. Marshfield is located about halfway between Boston and Cape Cod, and was settled in 1632.

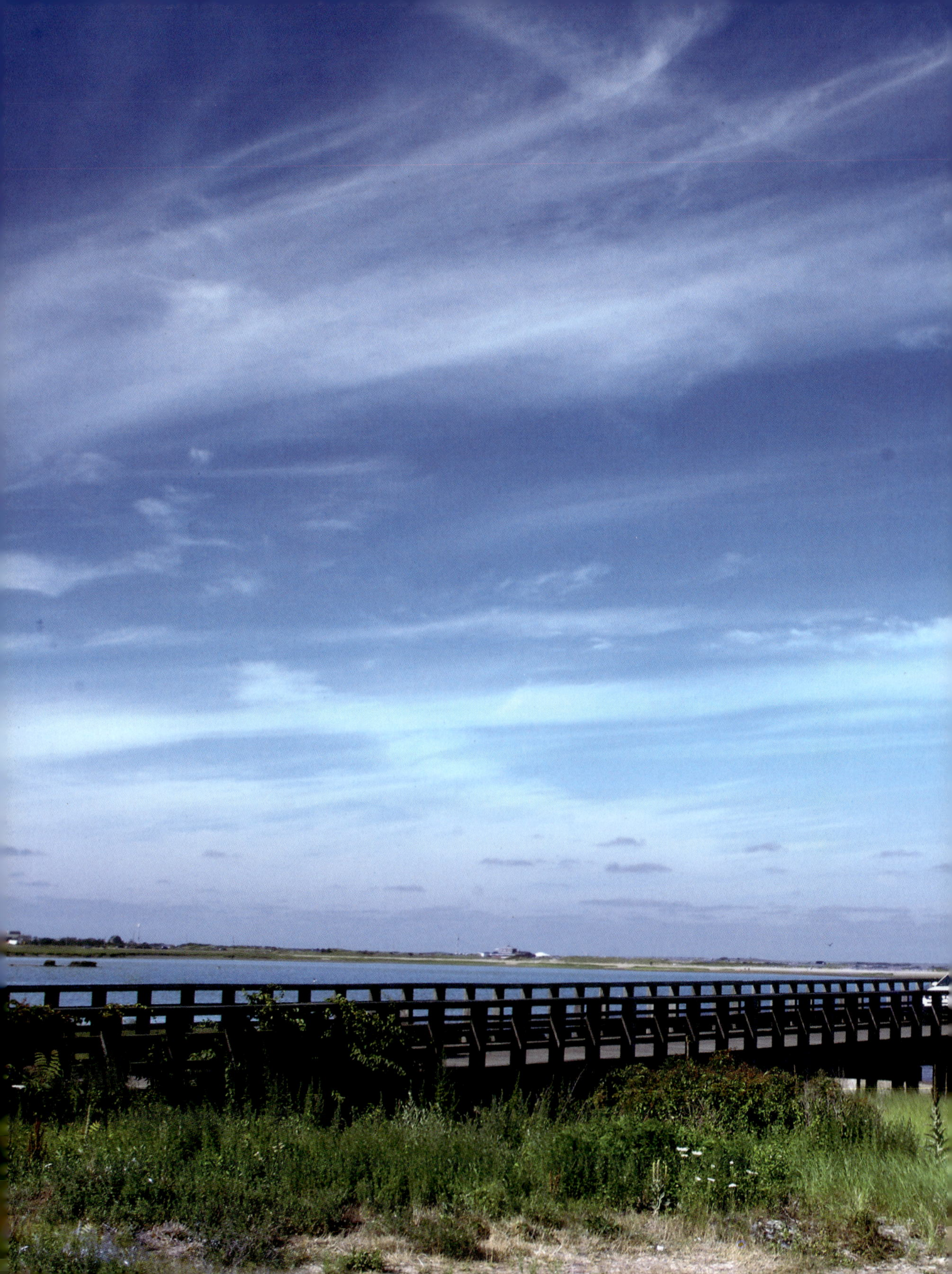

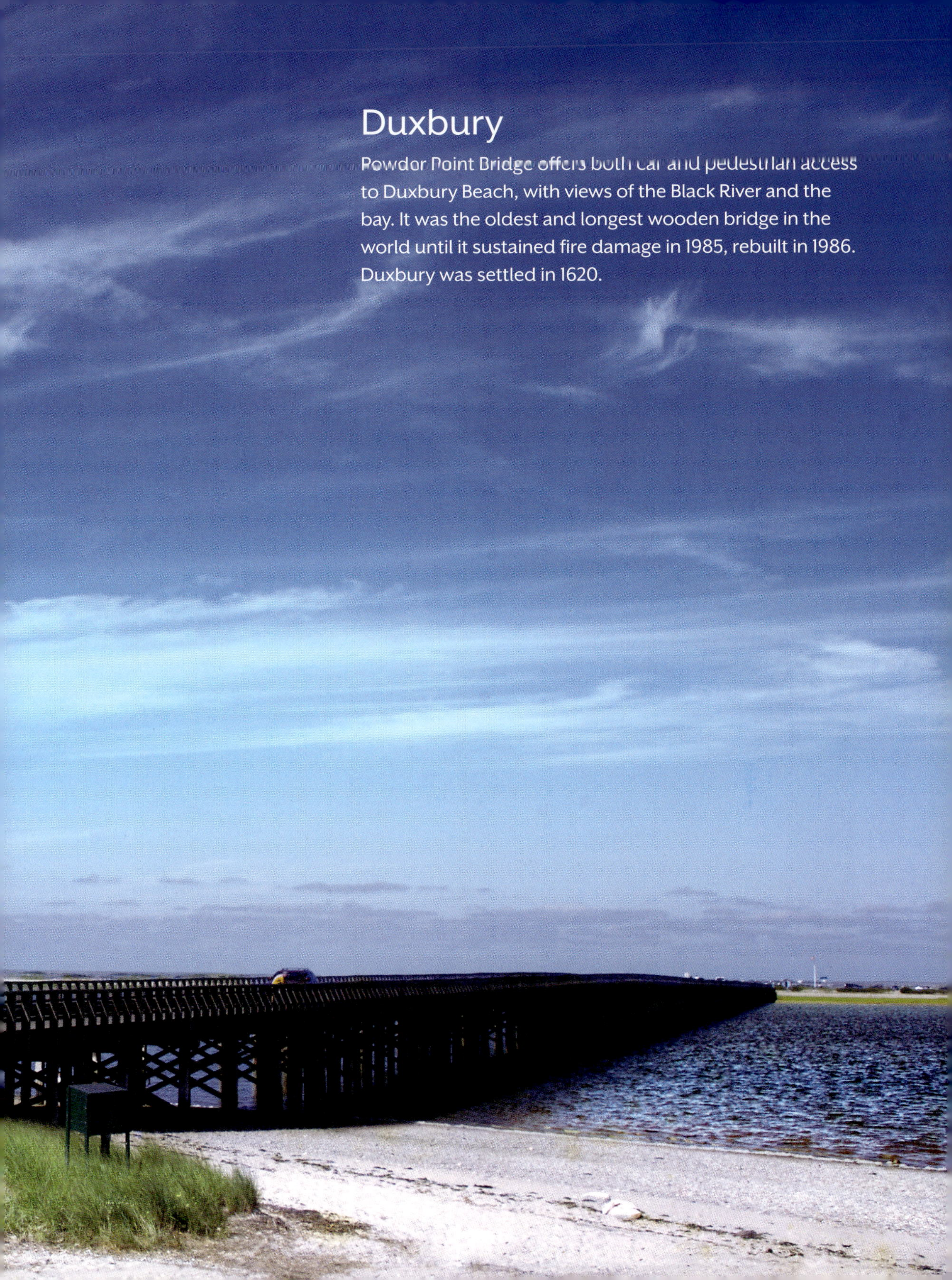

Duxbury

Powder Point Bridge offers both car and pedestrian access to Duxbury Beach, with views of the Black River and the bay. It was the oldest and longest wooden bridge in the world until it sustained fire damage in 1985, rebuilt in 1986. Duxbury was settled in 1620.

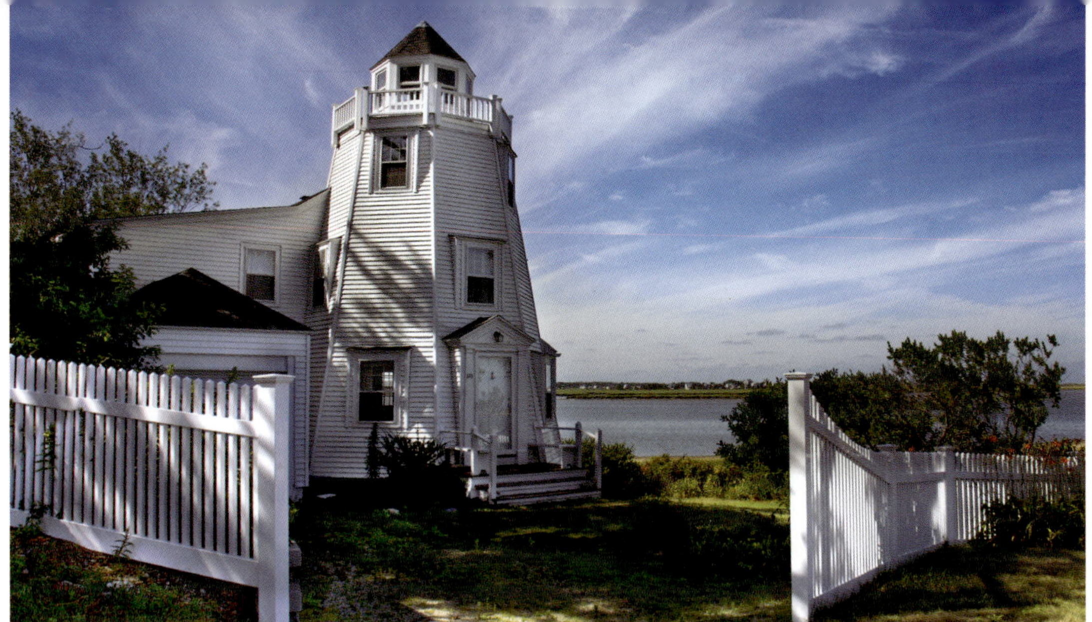

There are many homes in New England that feature lighthouse-like design. Some were lighthouses and became private homes. Others are a combination of a dwelling and a working lighthouse (including some Coast Guard Stations).

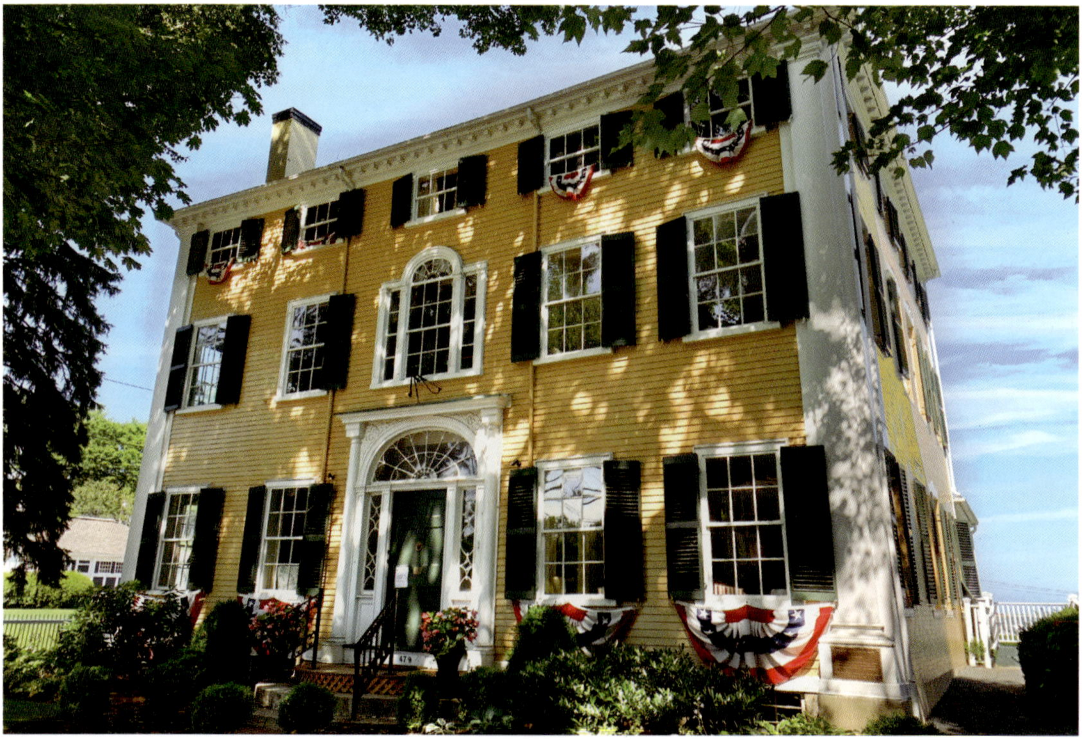

The Duxbury Rural and Historical Society is located at the beautiful Federal-style Nathaniel Winsor Jr. House, on Washington Street.

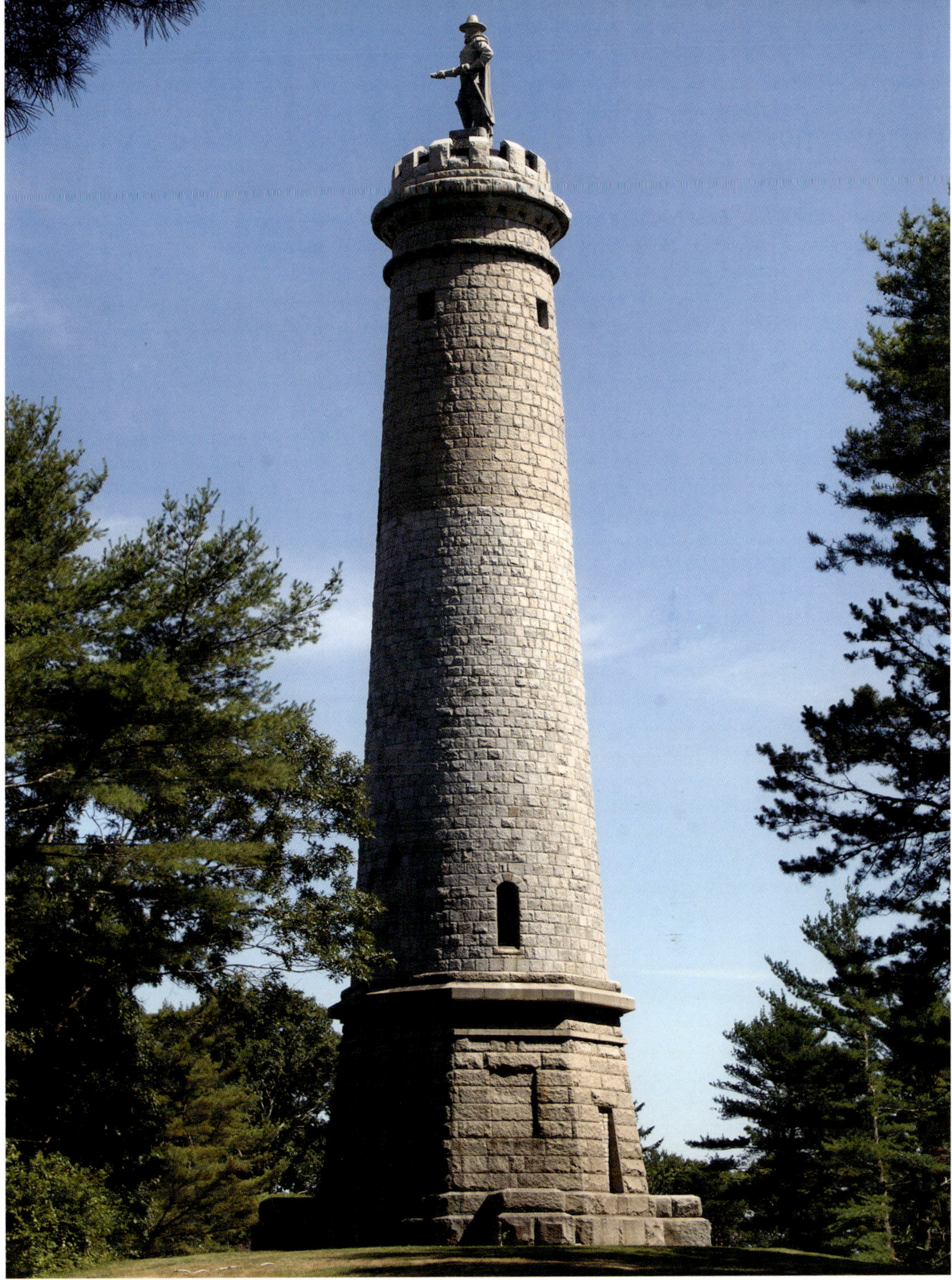

High atop Captain's Hill is the Myles Standish Monument and State Reservation. The monument was completed in 1898, and stands at a whopping 116 feet! It honors Myles Standish, who was military leader of the Plymouth Colony.

Kingston

Kingston was settled in 1622, originally part of Plymouth. An incoming tide fills the creek at Jones River Landing, a natural haven for wildlife.

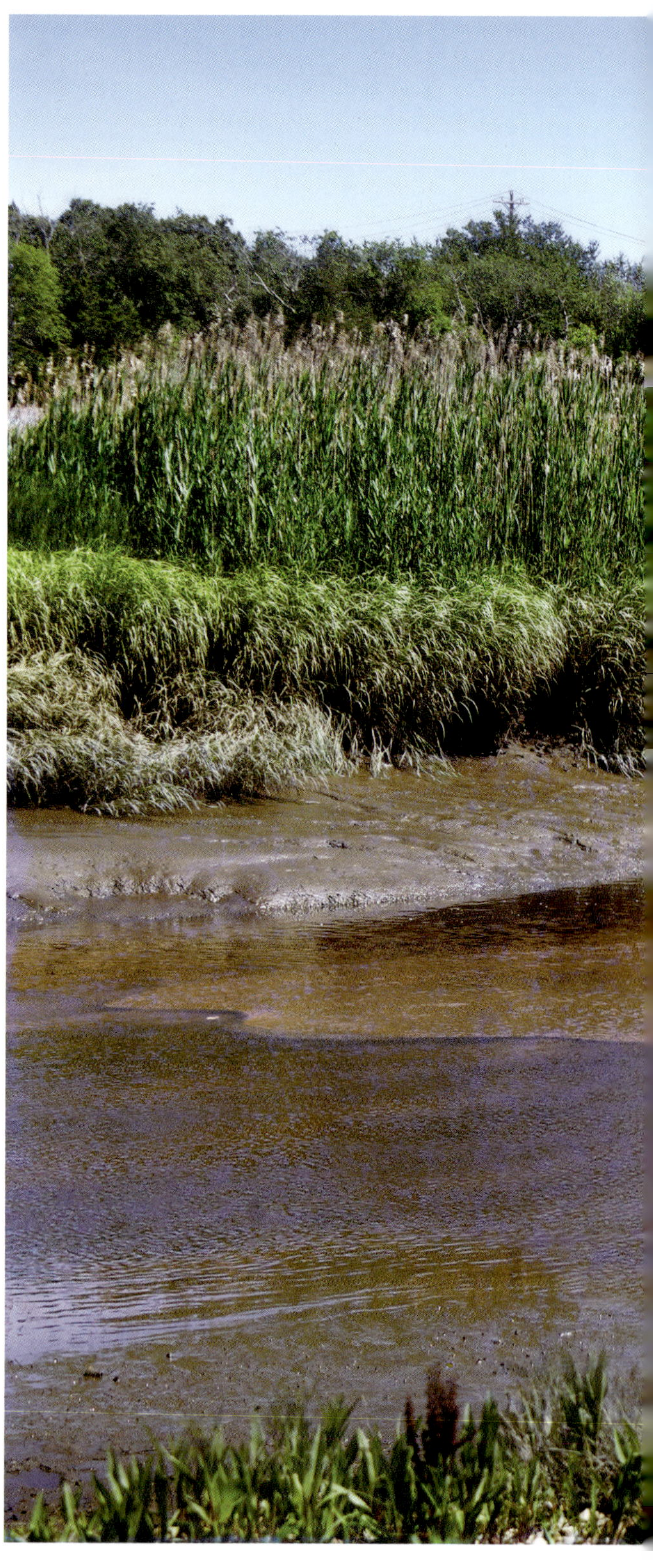

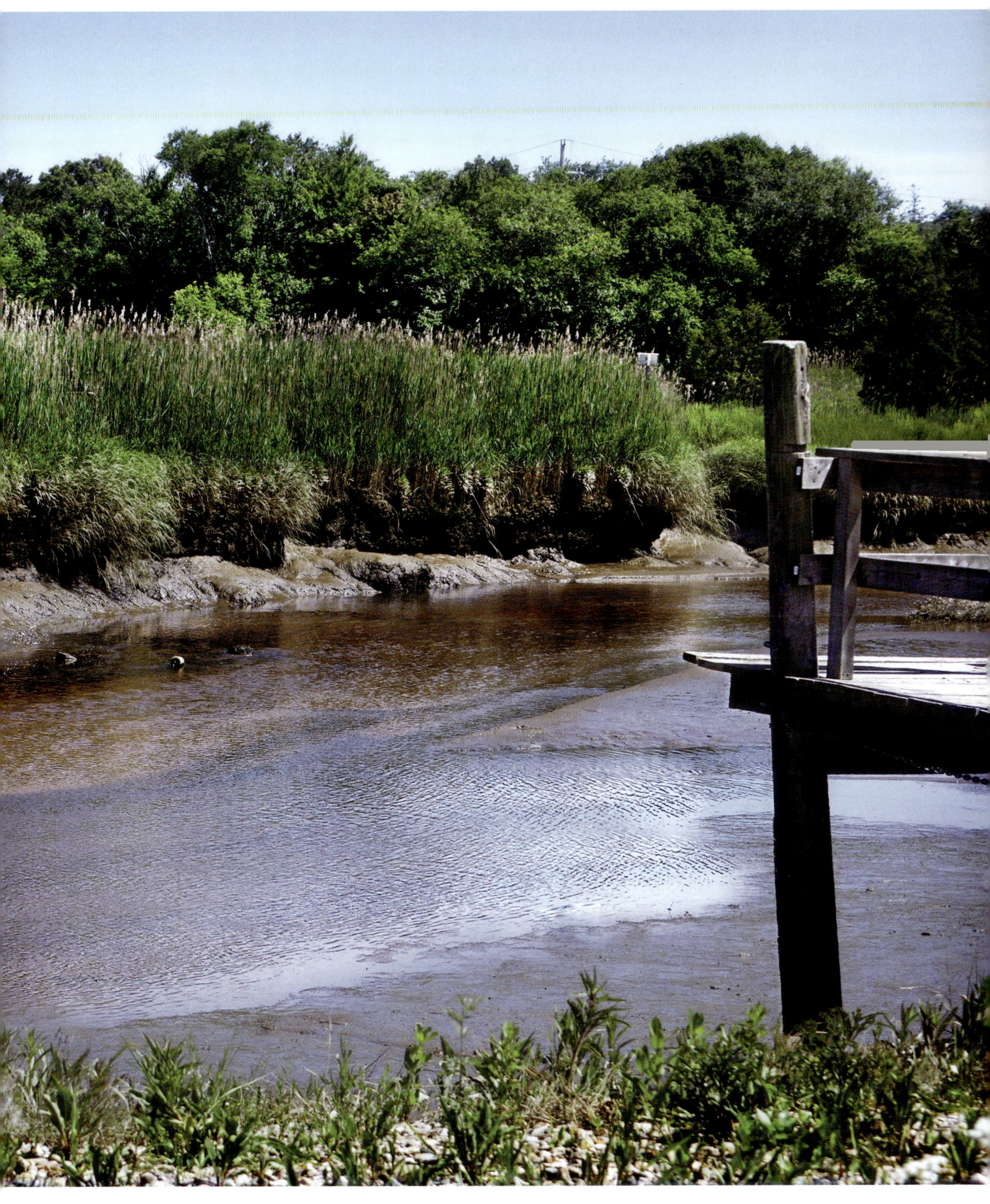

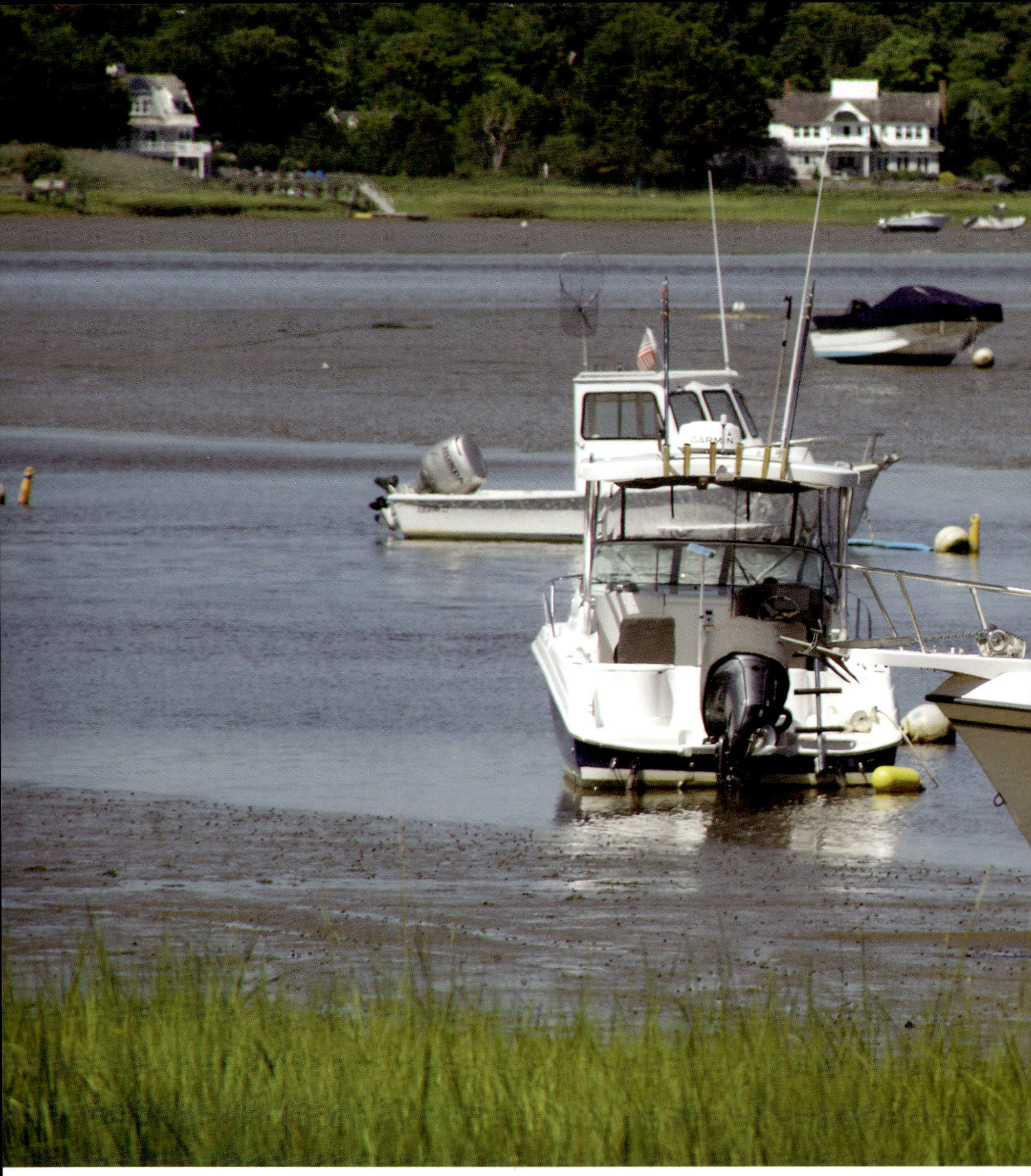

High and dry . . . or at least, muddy! Many coastal towns rely on tidal rivers and bays for ocean access. So the timing of a trip by boat is important. Time and tide wait for no one.

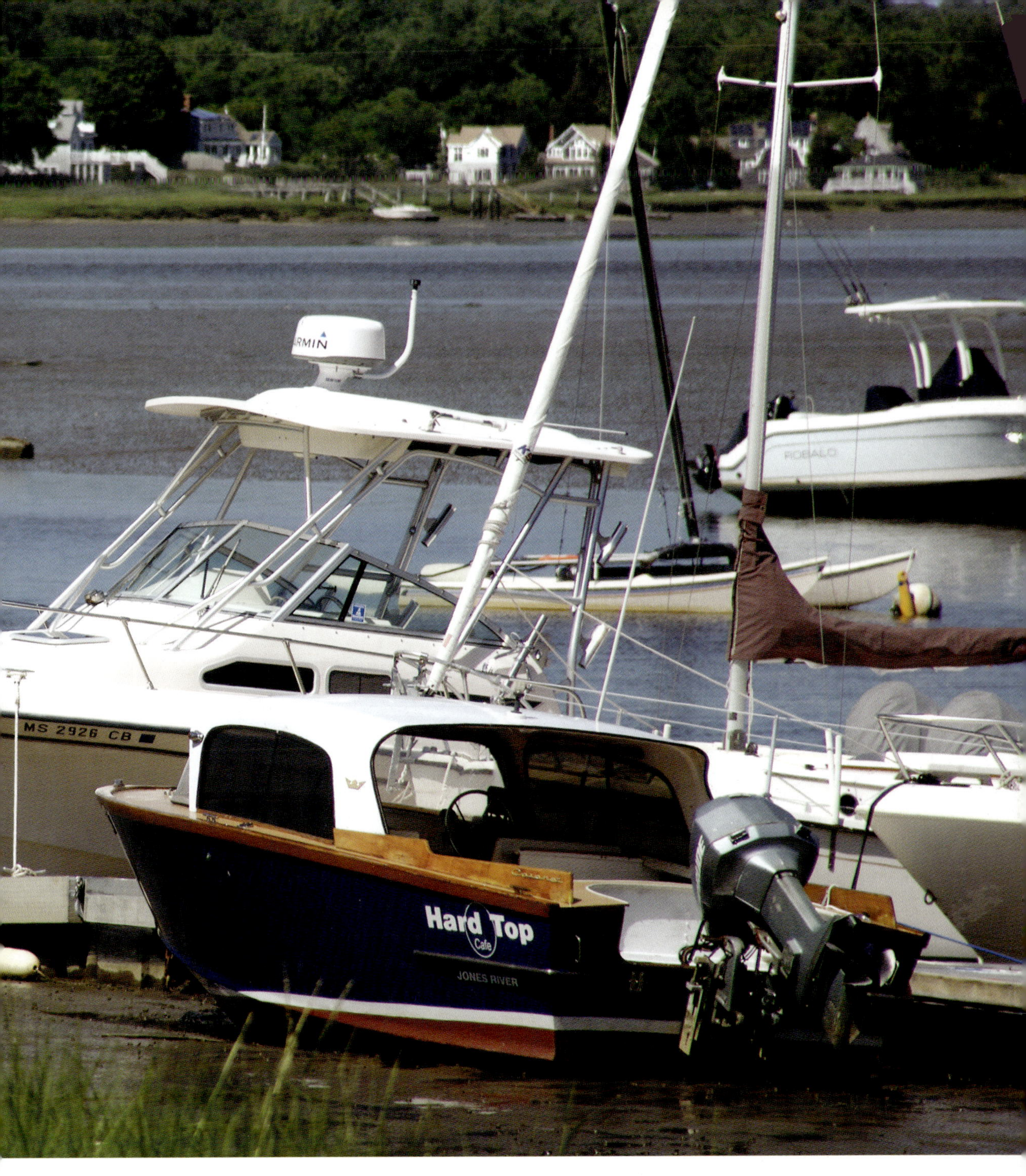

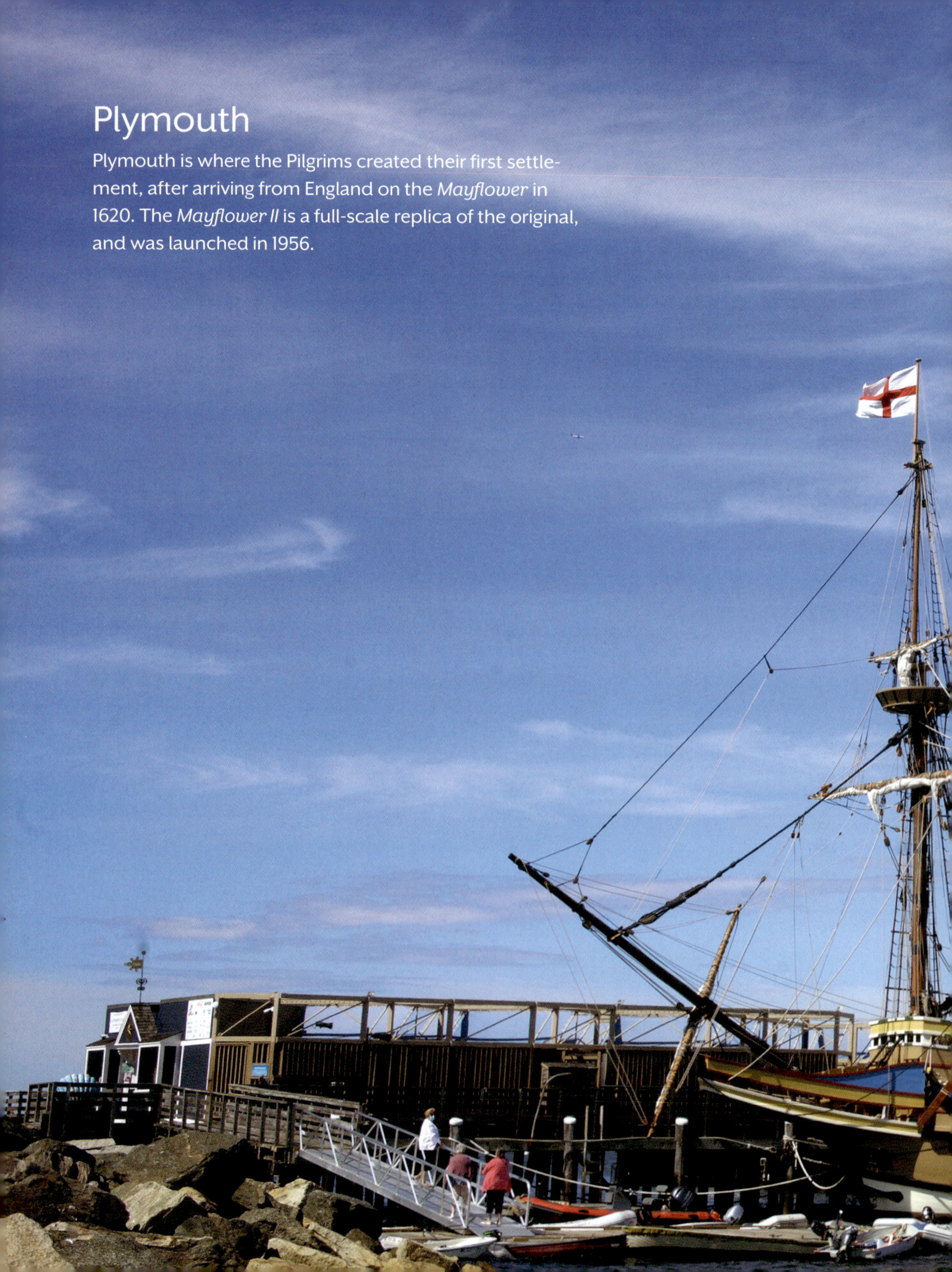

Plymouth

Plymouth is where the Pilgrims created their first settlement, after arriving from England on the *Mayflower* in 1620. The *Mayflower II* is a full-scale replica of the original, and was launched in 1956.

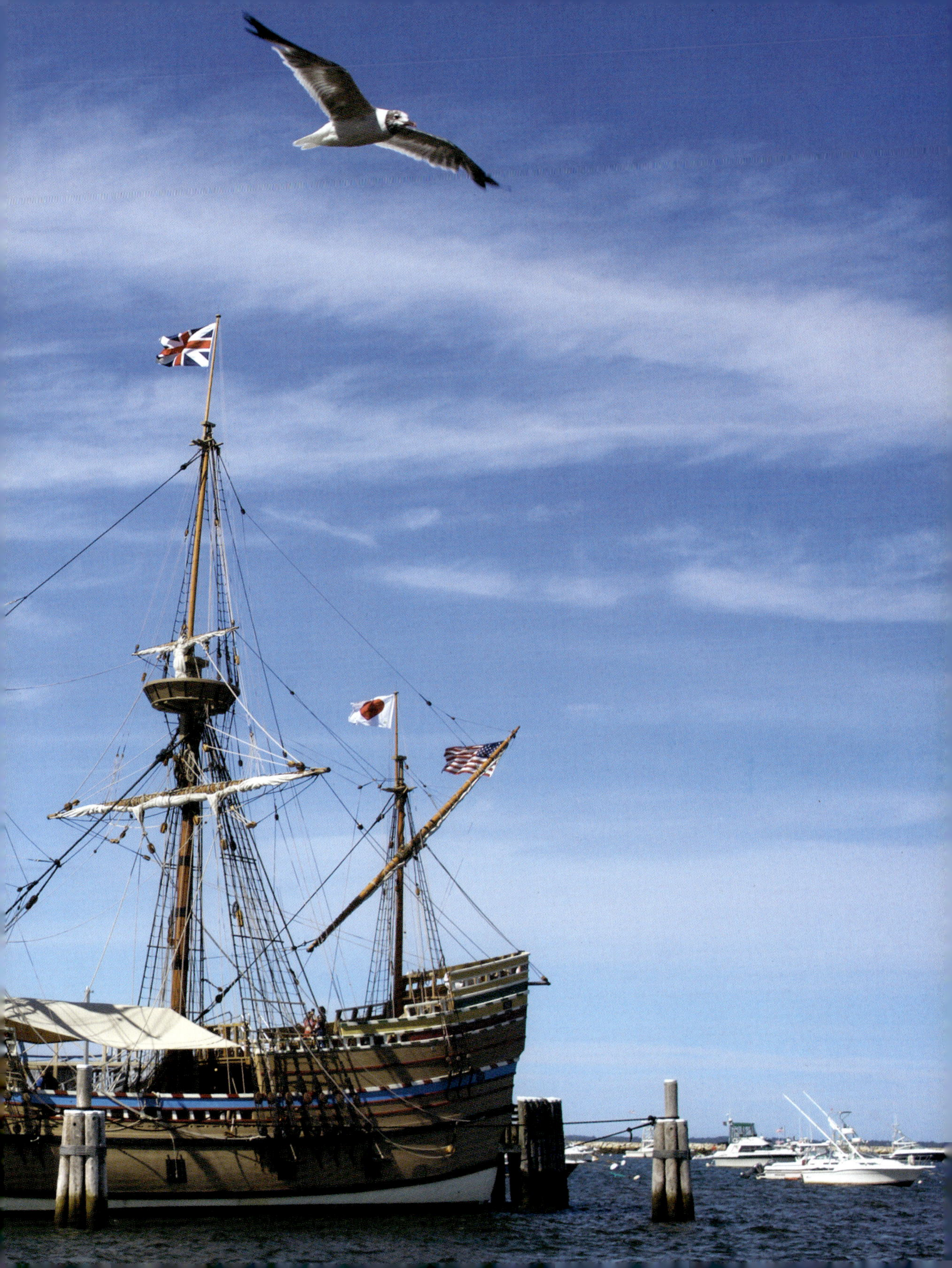

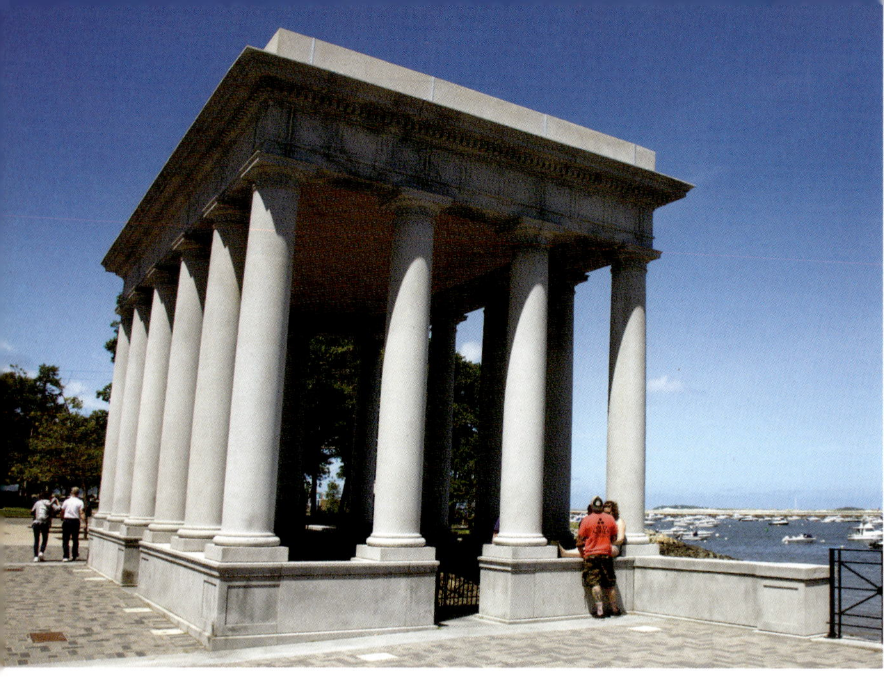

The structure with stone columns here at Pilgrim Memorial Park enshrines the boulder known as Plymouth Rock. It is believed that this is where the *Mayflower* landed, and the voyagers disembarked.

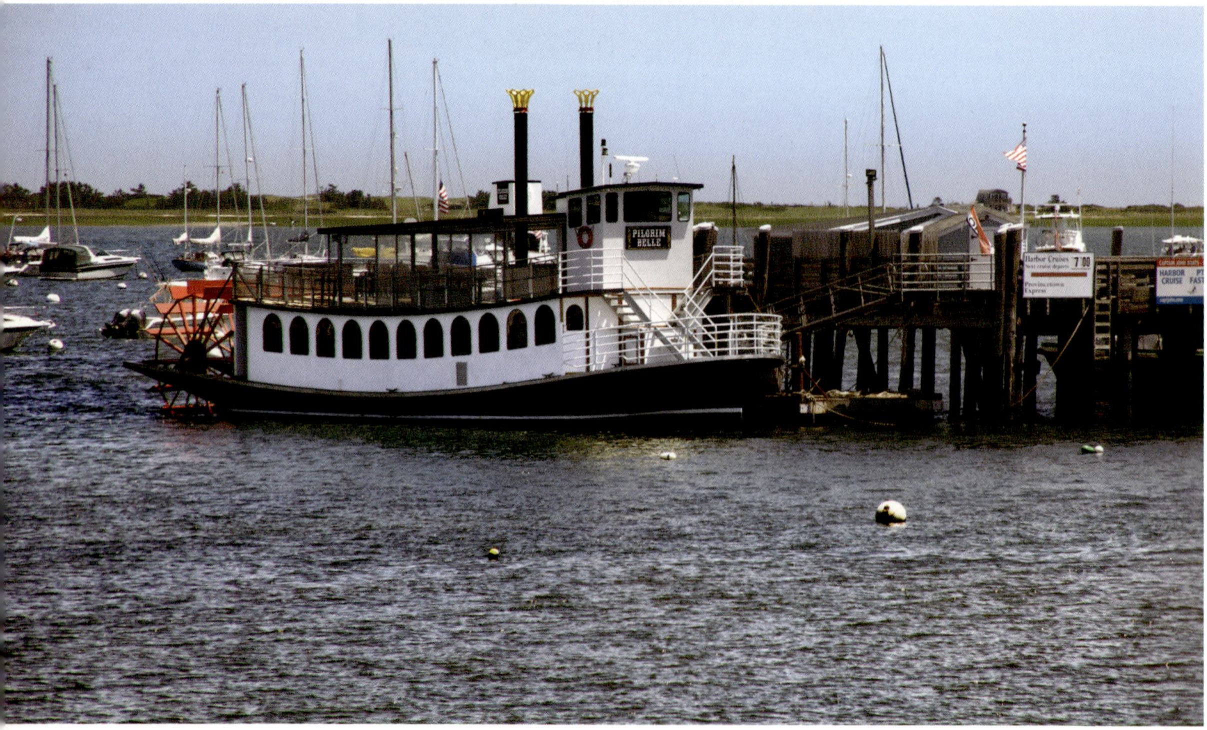

Traveling across the ocean by wooden ship in the 17th century was slow and dangerous. It took more than two months for the *Mayflower* to make her journey from Europe. You can take a tour and view Plymouth from the water on a classic paddlewheel boat called the *Pilgrim Belle.*

The sheep are just as curious as the guests at Plimoth Patuxet Museums. Here they have faithfully recreated the look and feel of the first settlements in New England. They also feature a look at the homeland of the Wampanoag People, who have inhabited the area for over 10,000 years.

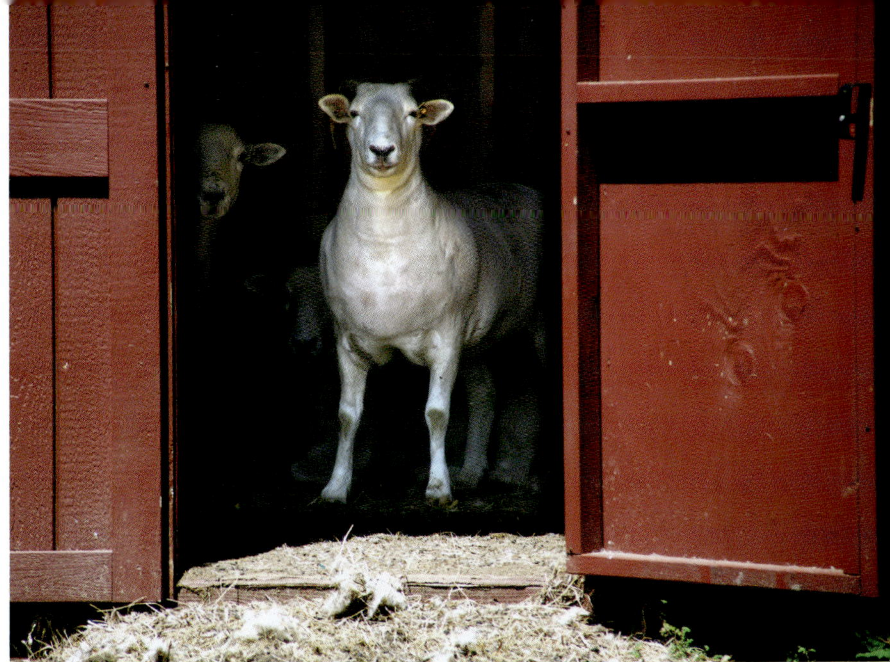

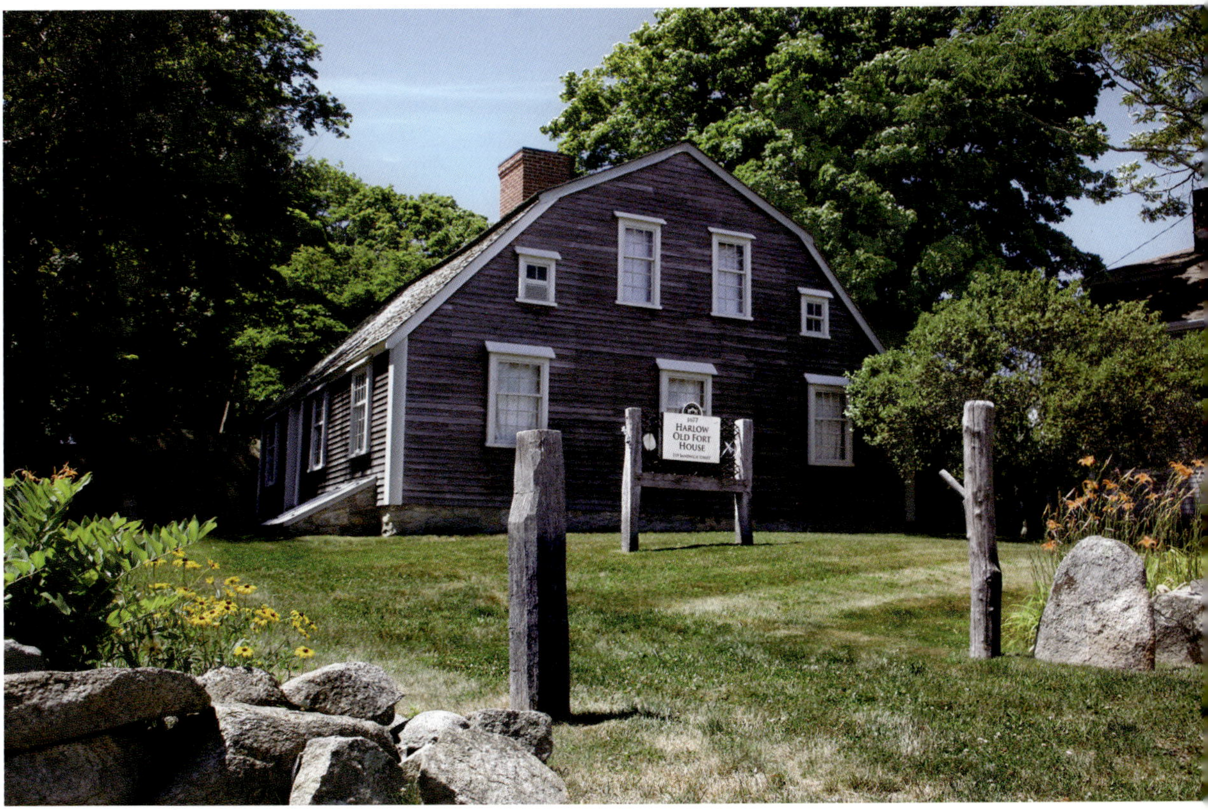

A ten-minute walk from the waterfront brings you to this First Period historic home located on Sandwich Street. It's known as the Harlow Old Fort House, and it was built in 1677.

The South Coast

Red umbrellas, a blue sky, and kids playing in the sand . . . what could be finer? The scene plays out at Mattapoisett Town Beach, a cozy little beach located a short walk from the village center.

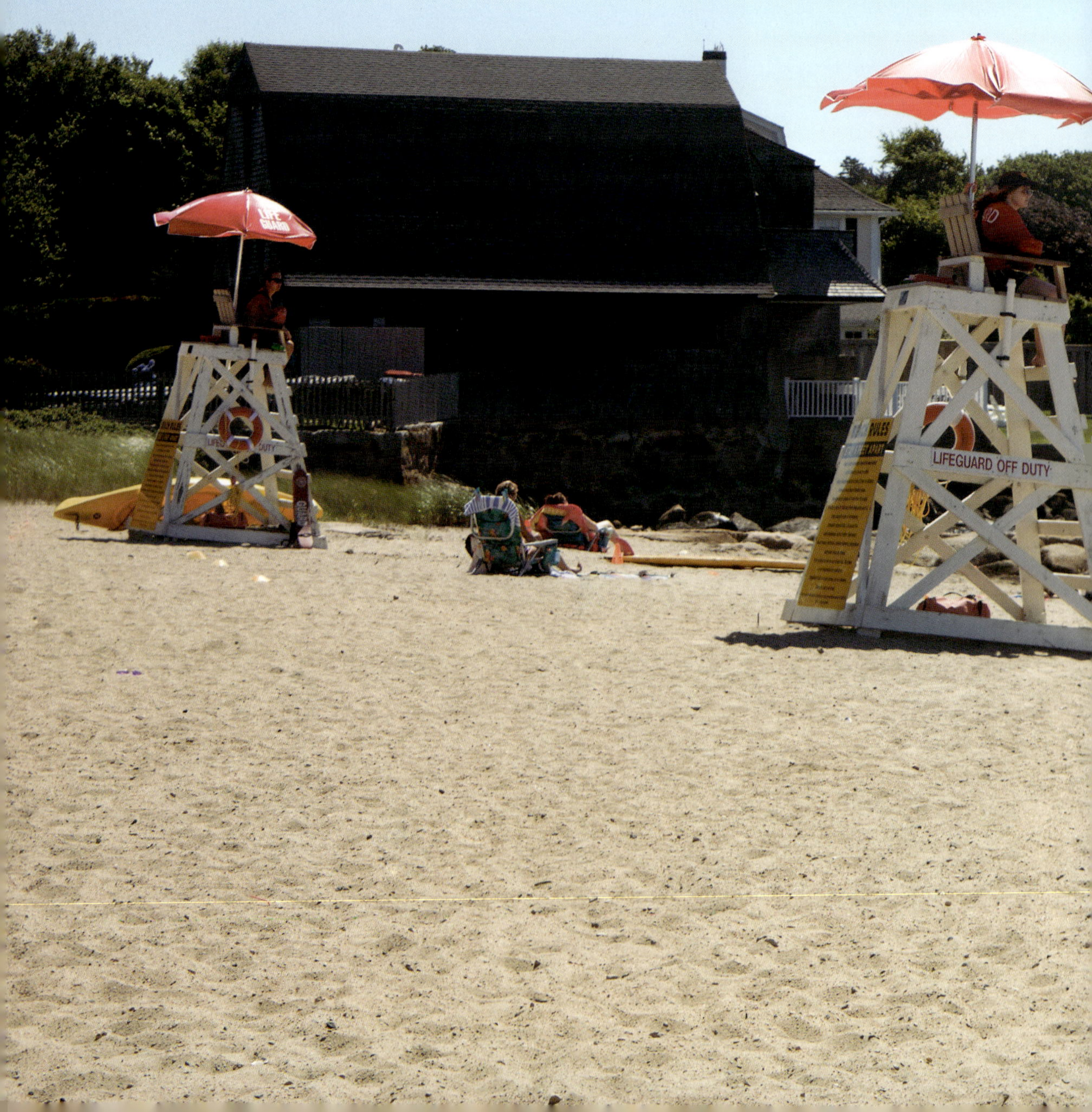

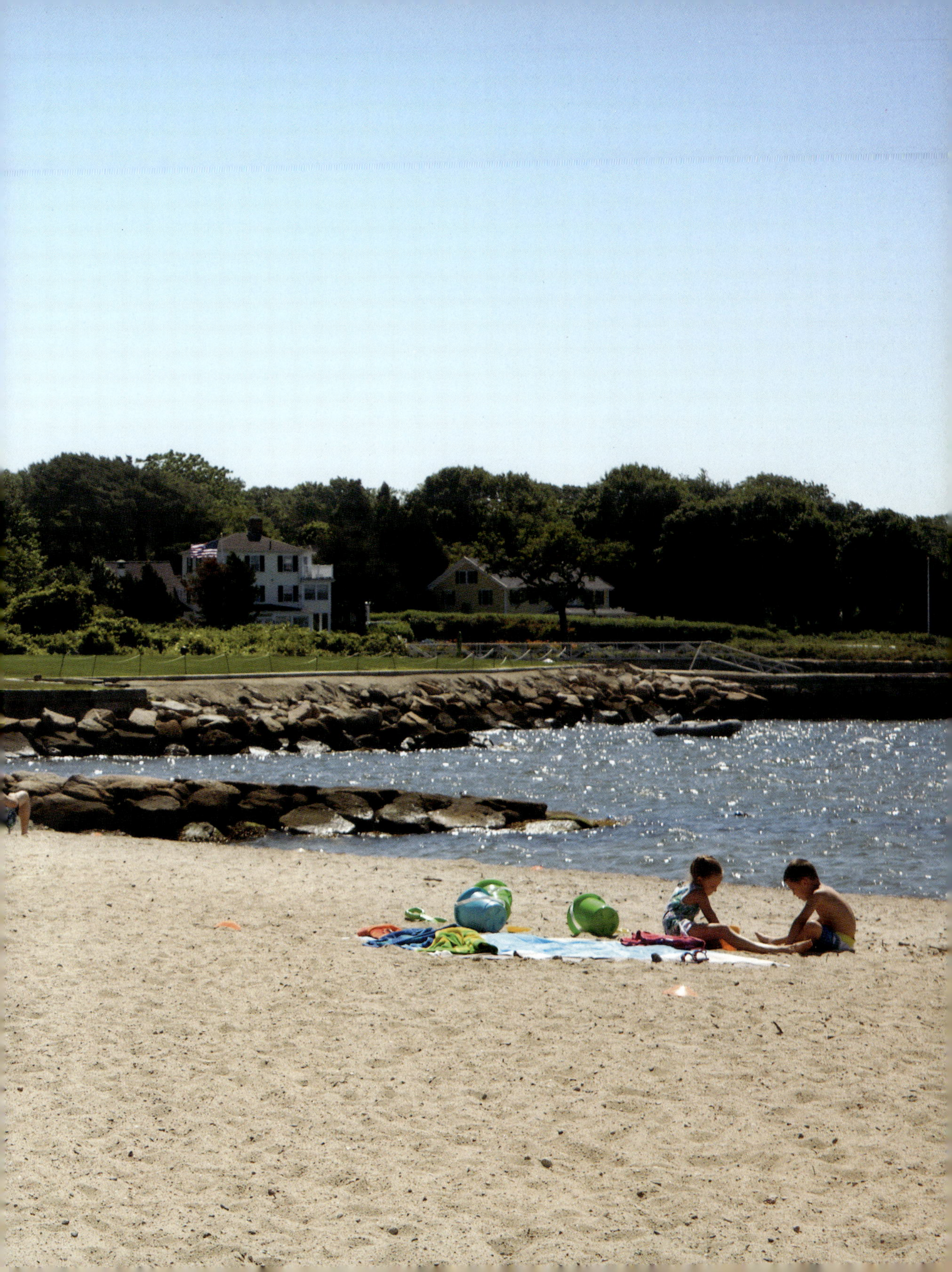

Wareham

Violet light pushes through the fog and shines down on
Wicket Island and Onset Harbor. Onset is a waterfront
village in the town of Wareham, which was settled in 1678.

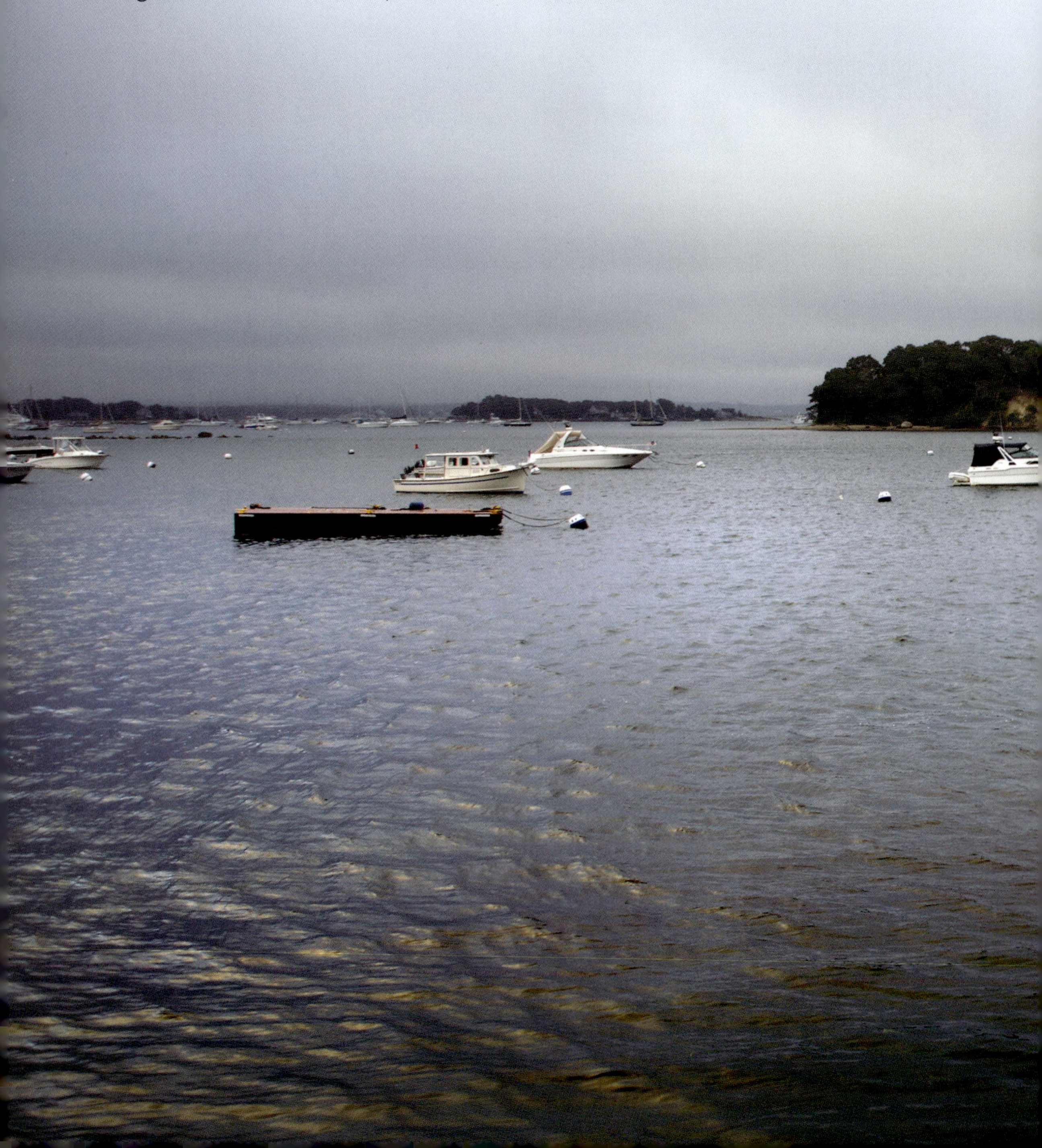

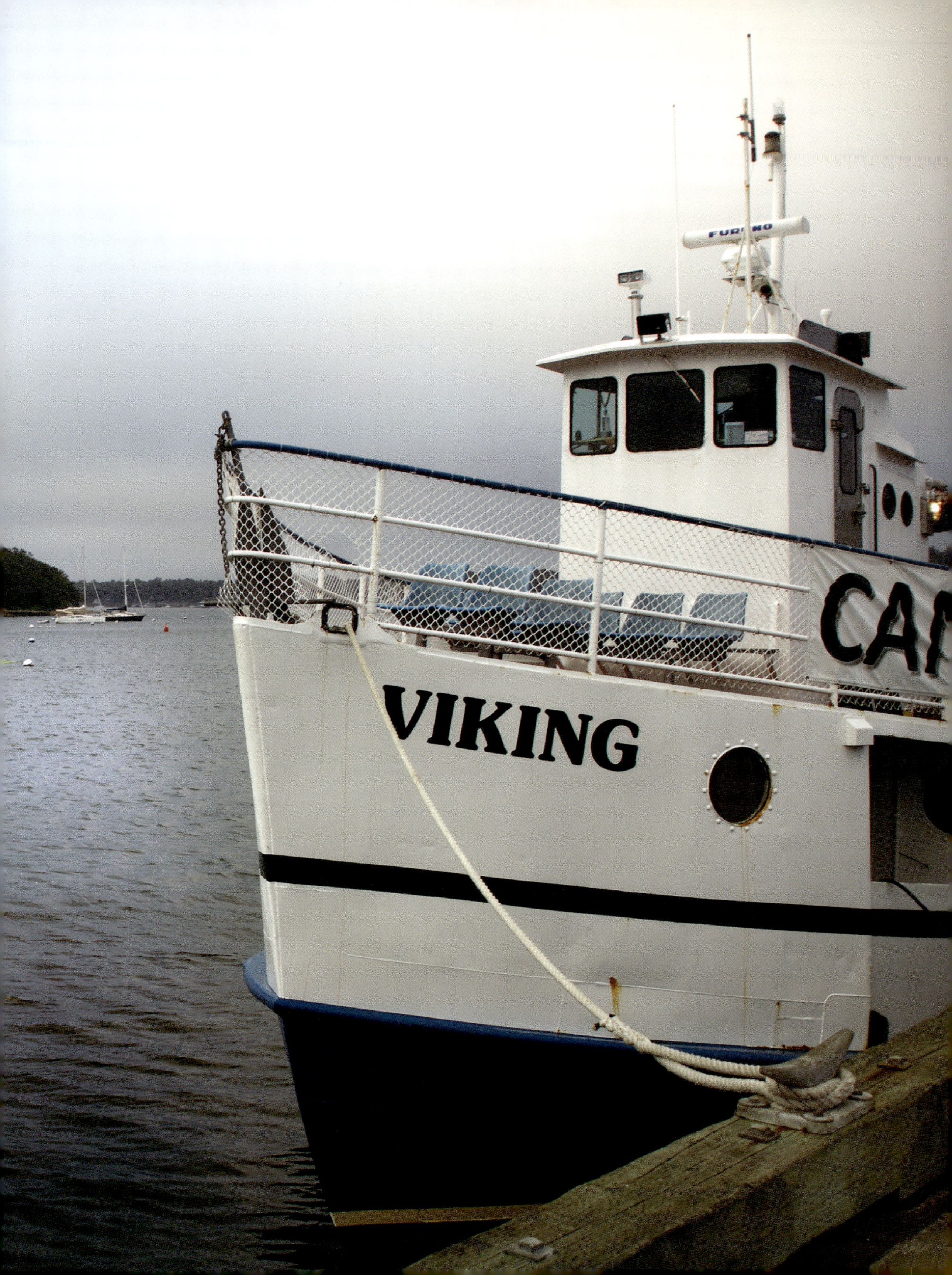

VIKING
CA

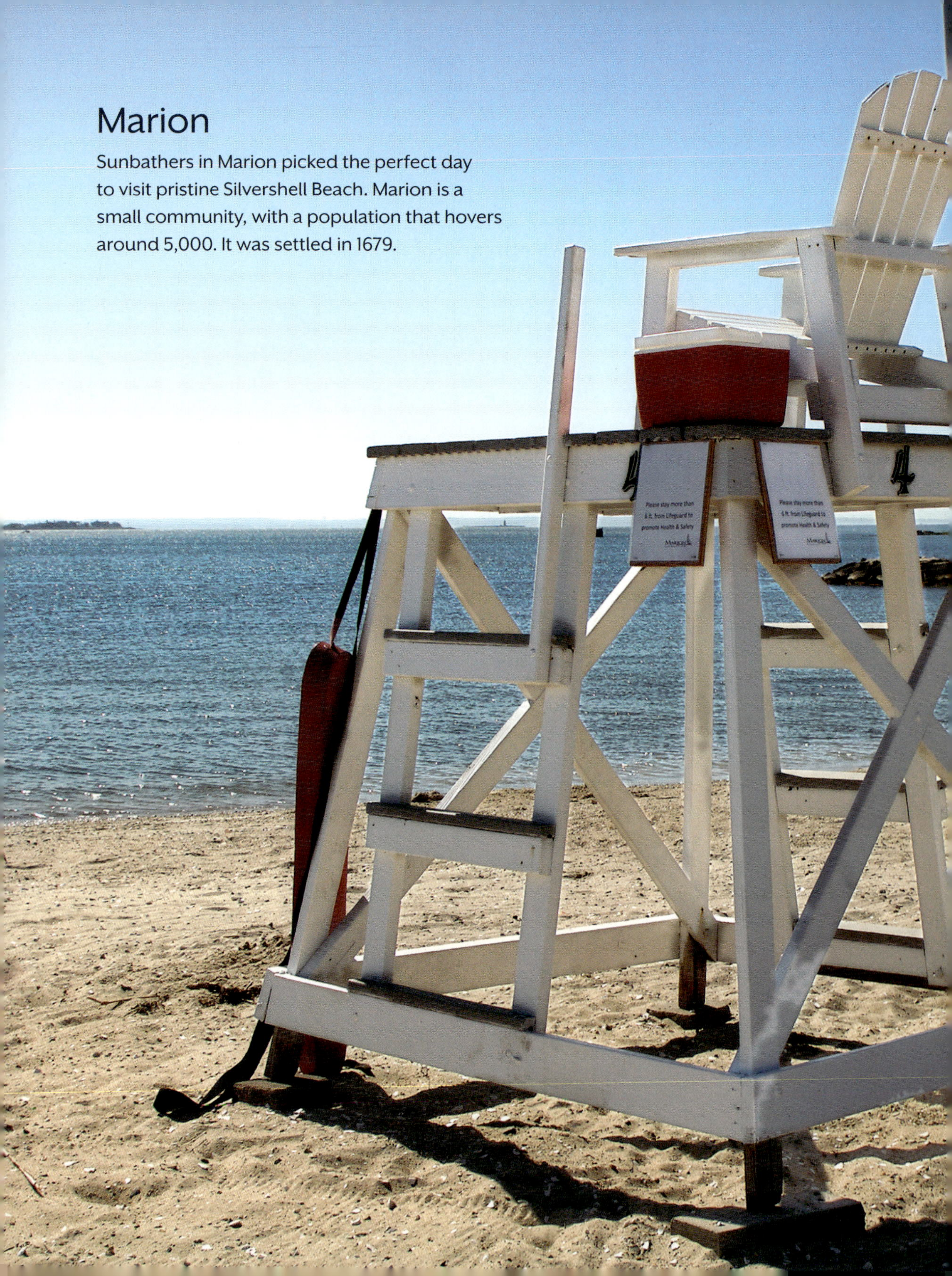

Marion

Sunbathers in Marion picked the perfect day to visit pristine Silvershell Beach. Marion is a small community, with a population that hovers around 5,000. It was settled in 1679.

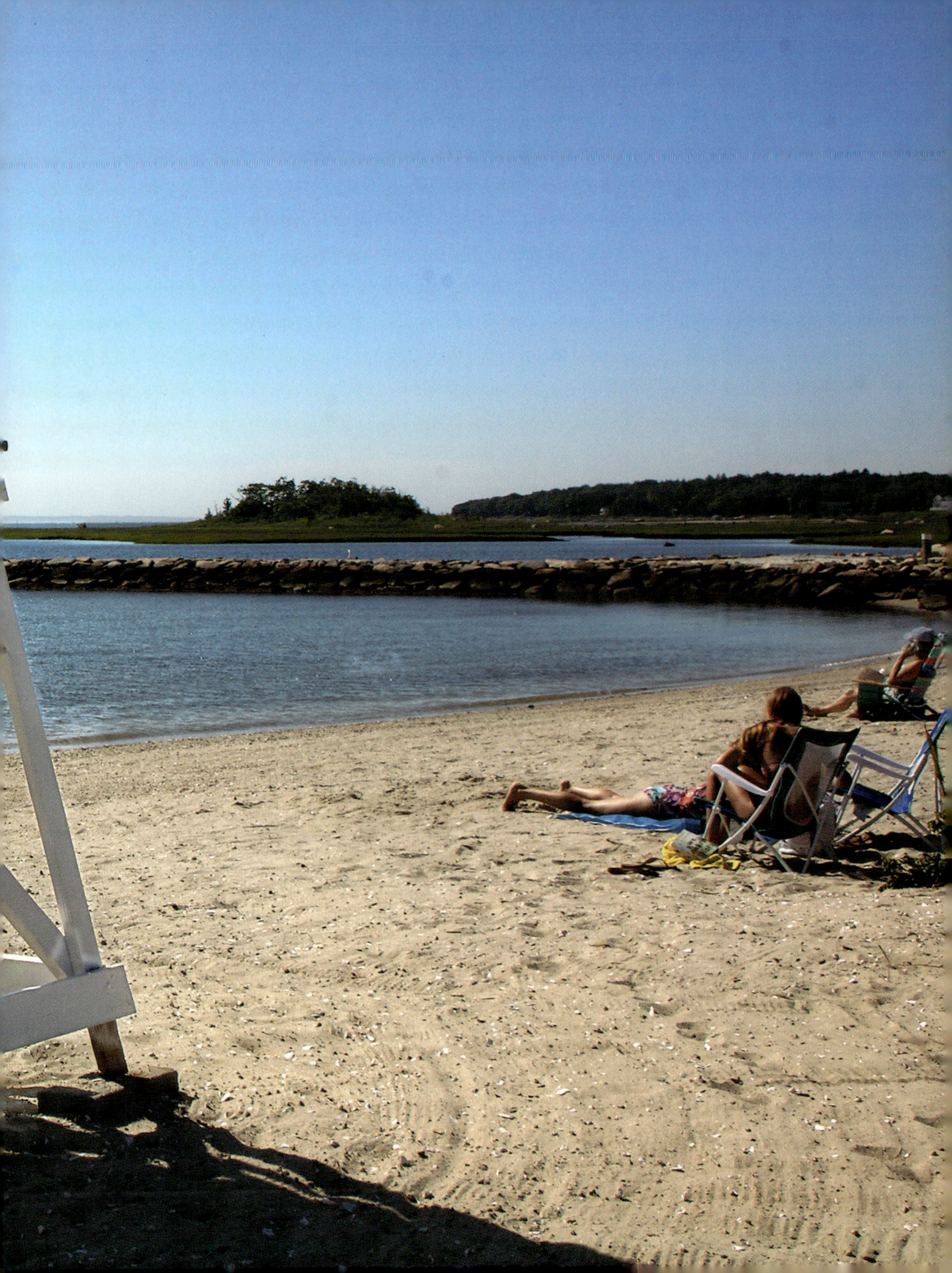

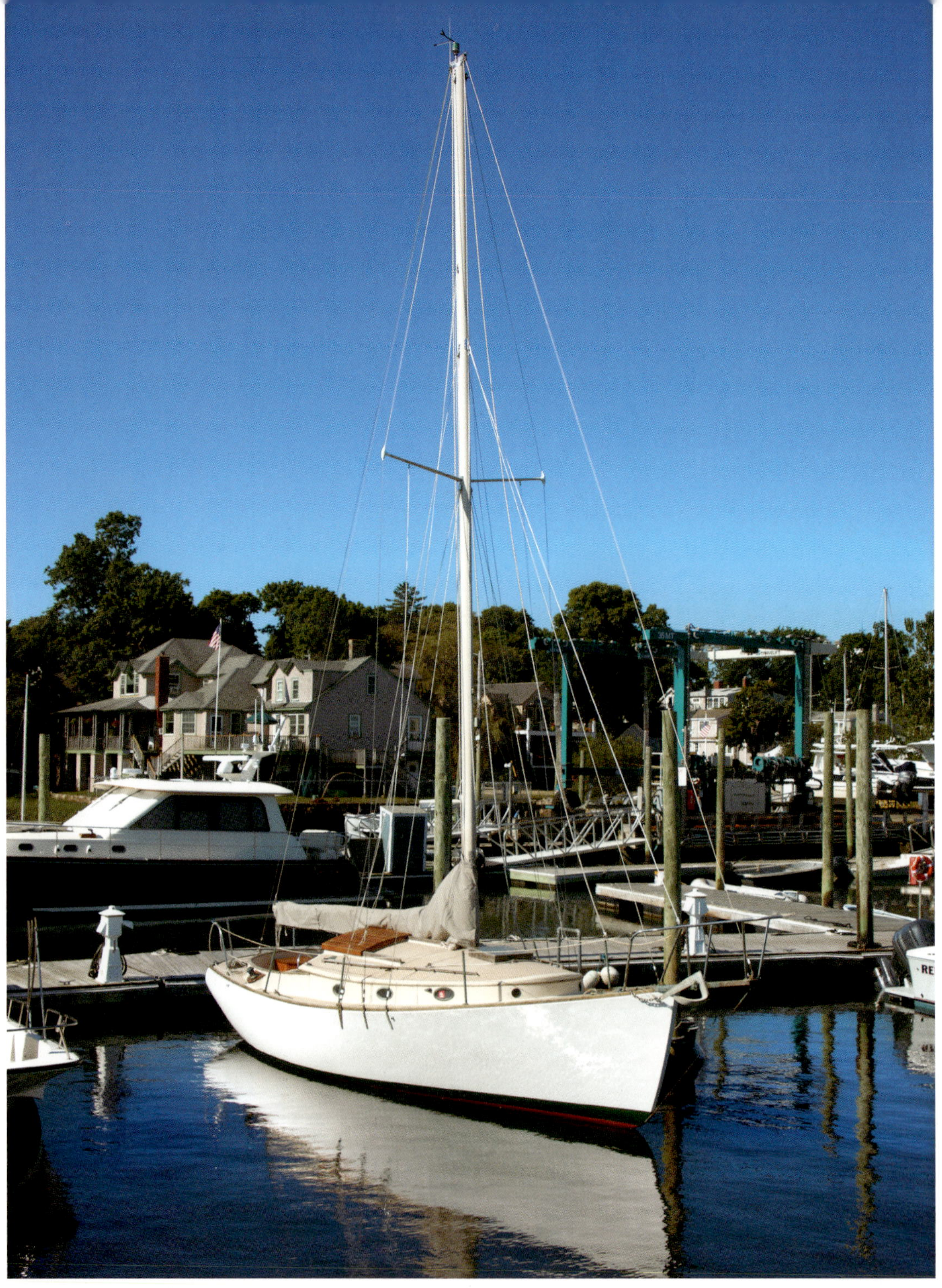

A sailboat and the deep blue sky are reflected in the mirror-like water at Barden's Boat Yard, in Sippican Harbor.

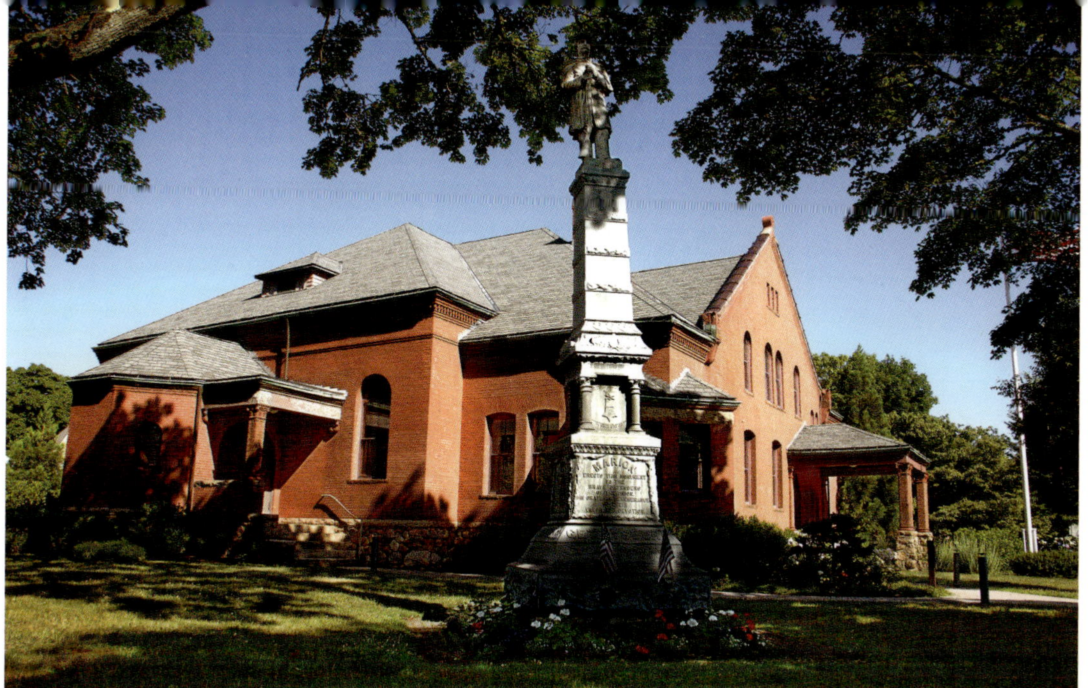

In the foreground is the Marion Civil War Memorial, which honors "the brave defenders of the Union in grateful remembrance of their valor and devotion." In the background is the Marion Music Hall.

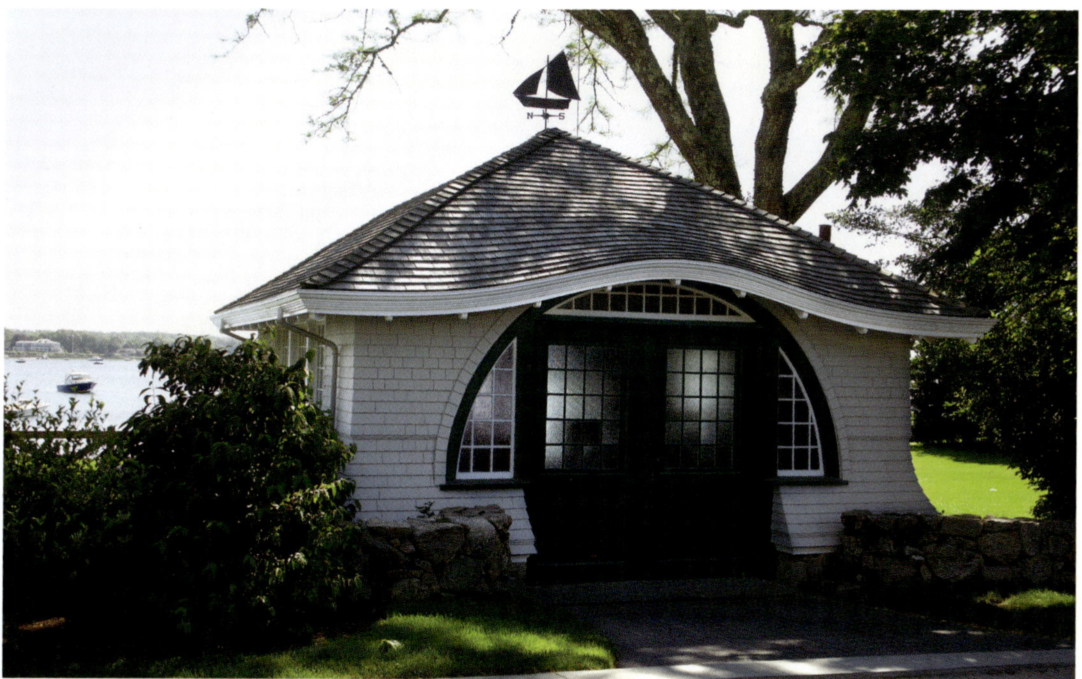

Morning sunlight filters through the frosted windowpanes of this nice bit of architecture. It also has a classic ship weathervane, which seems fitting for this idyllic coastal setting.

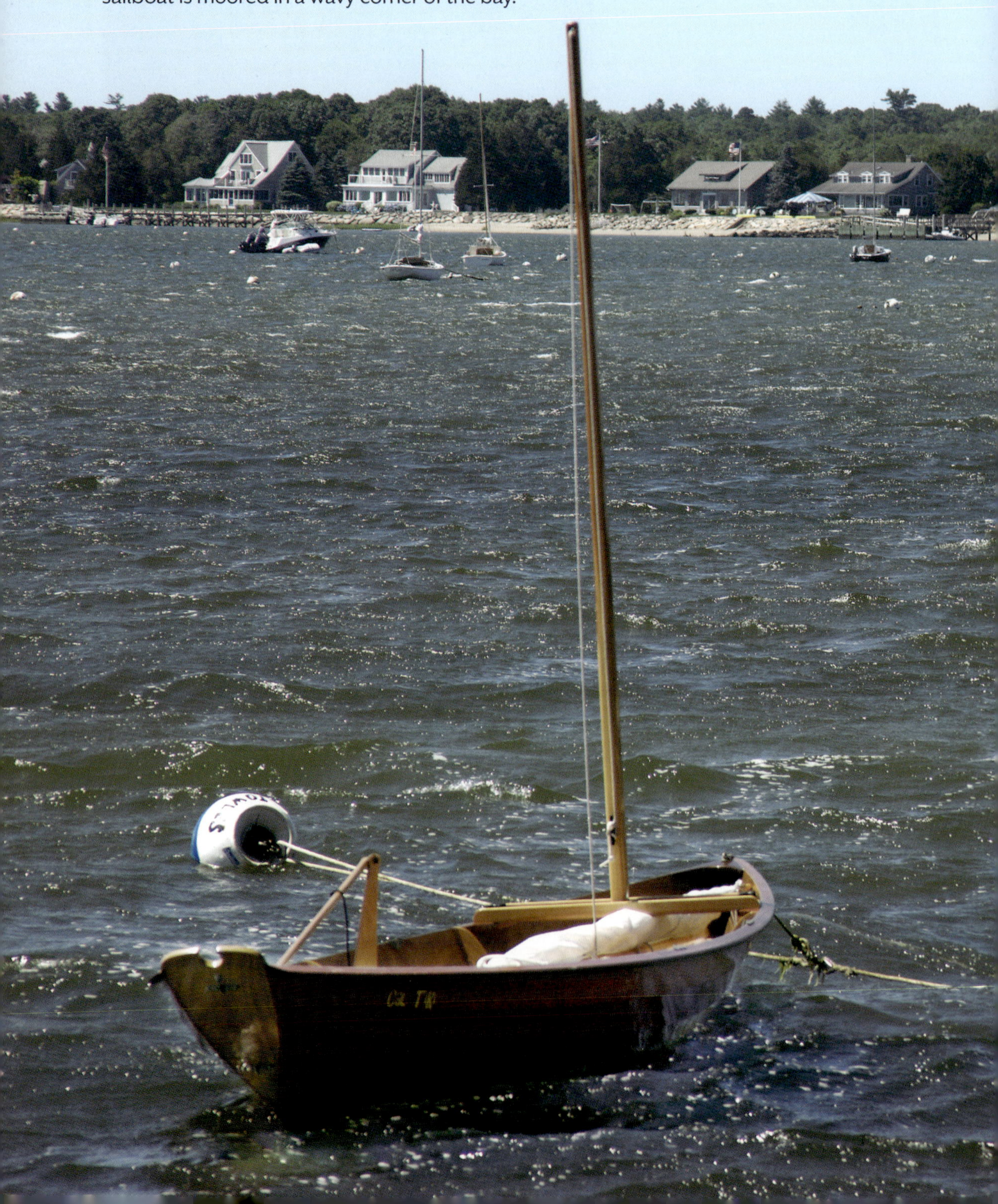

Mattapoisett

The view from Munro Waterfront Park, as a small wooden sailboat is moored in a wavy corner of the bay.

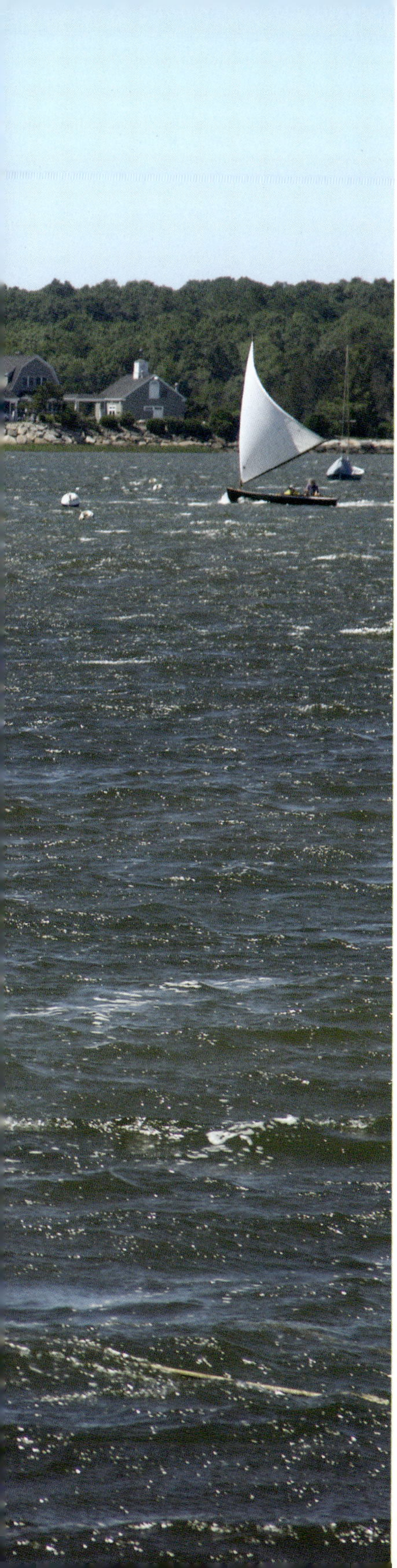

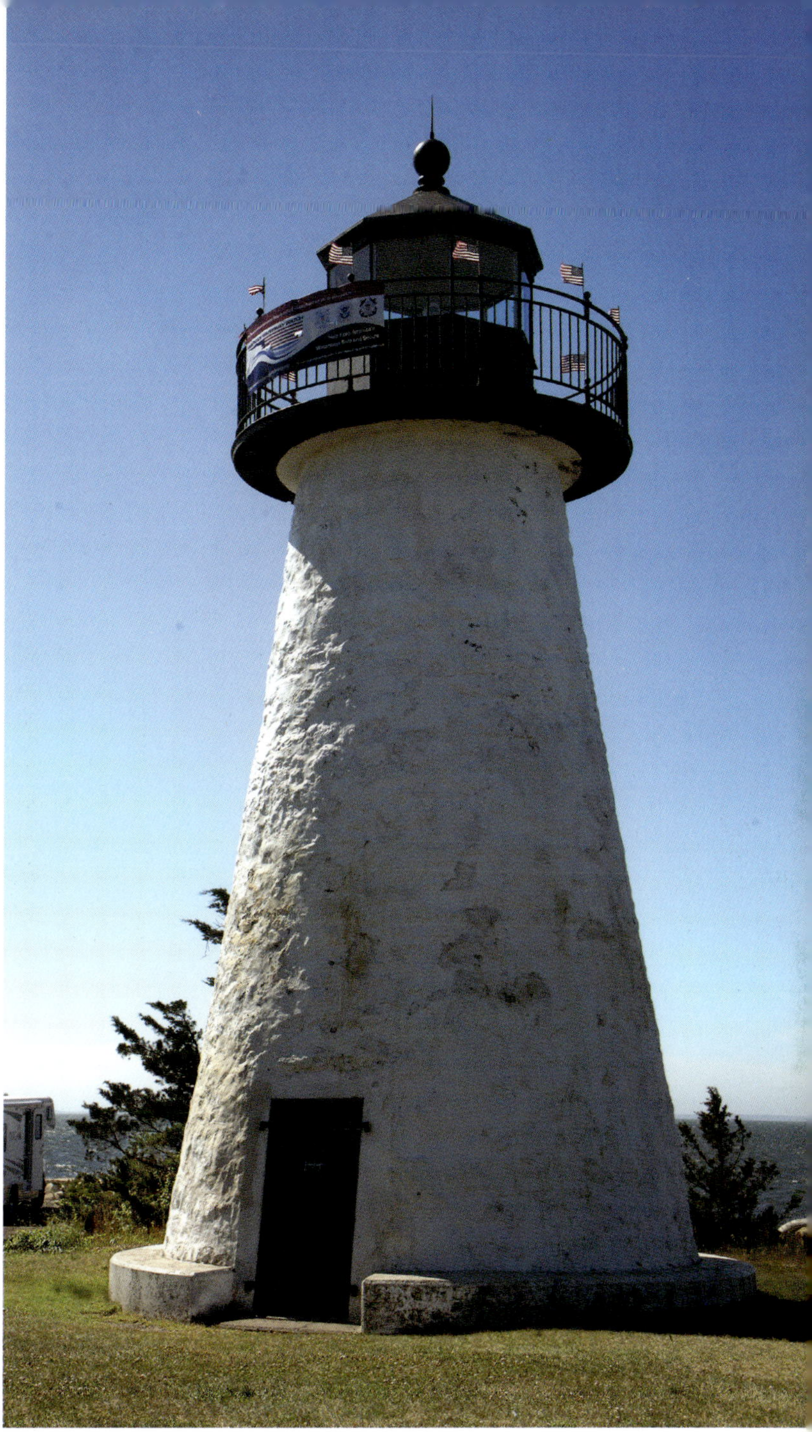

A popular stop for visitors to Mattapoisett is Ned Point Lighthouse. It was built in 1838, stands very close to sea level at 39 feet tall, and is accessible by Ned's Point Road. Mattapoisett was settled in 1750.

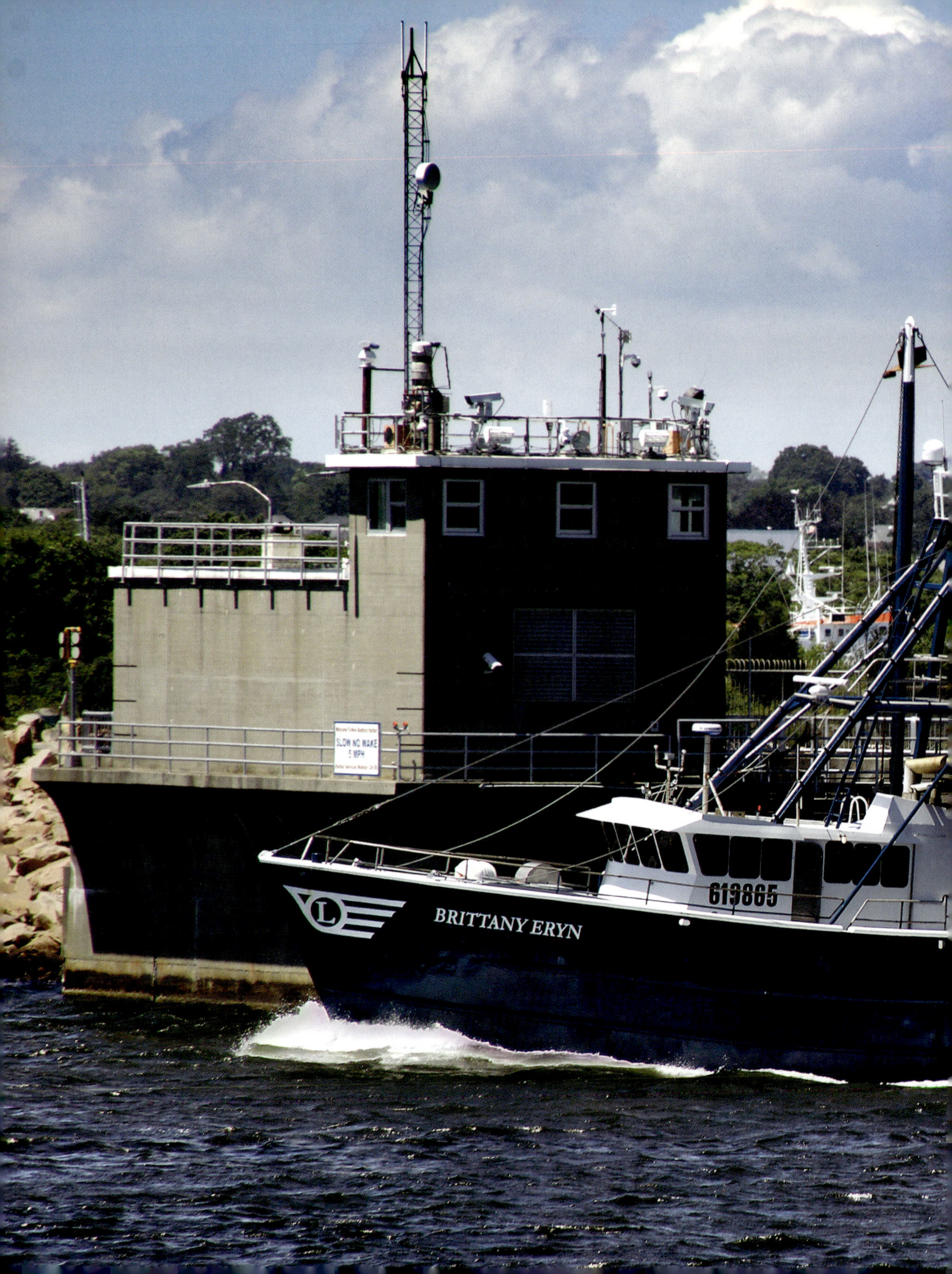

SLOW NO WAKE
5 MPH
L
BRITTANY ERYN
619865

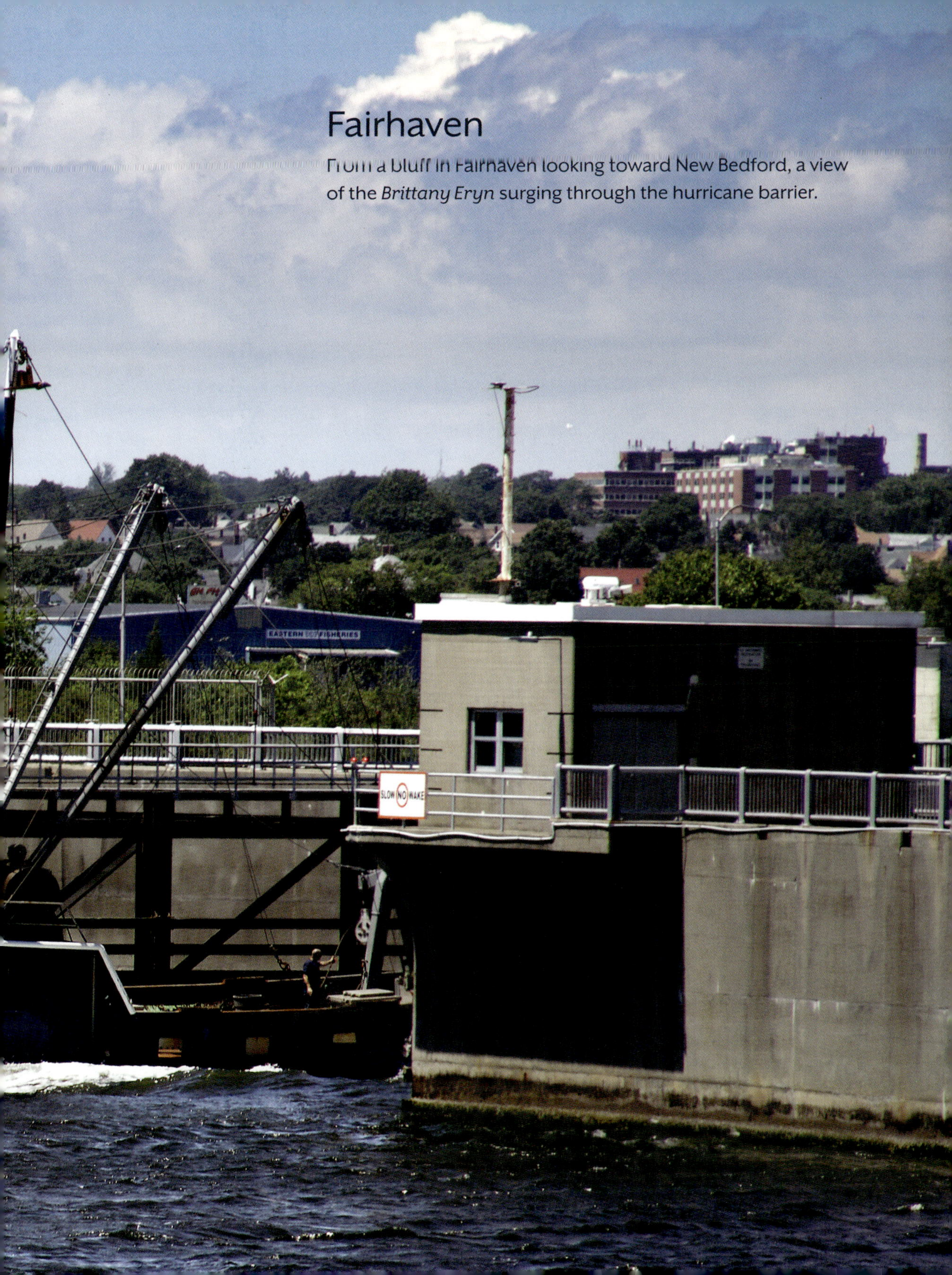

Fairhaven

From a bluff in Fairhaven looking toward New Bedford, a view of the *Brittany Eryn* surging through the hurricane barrier.

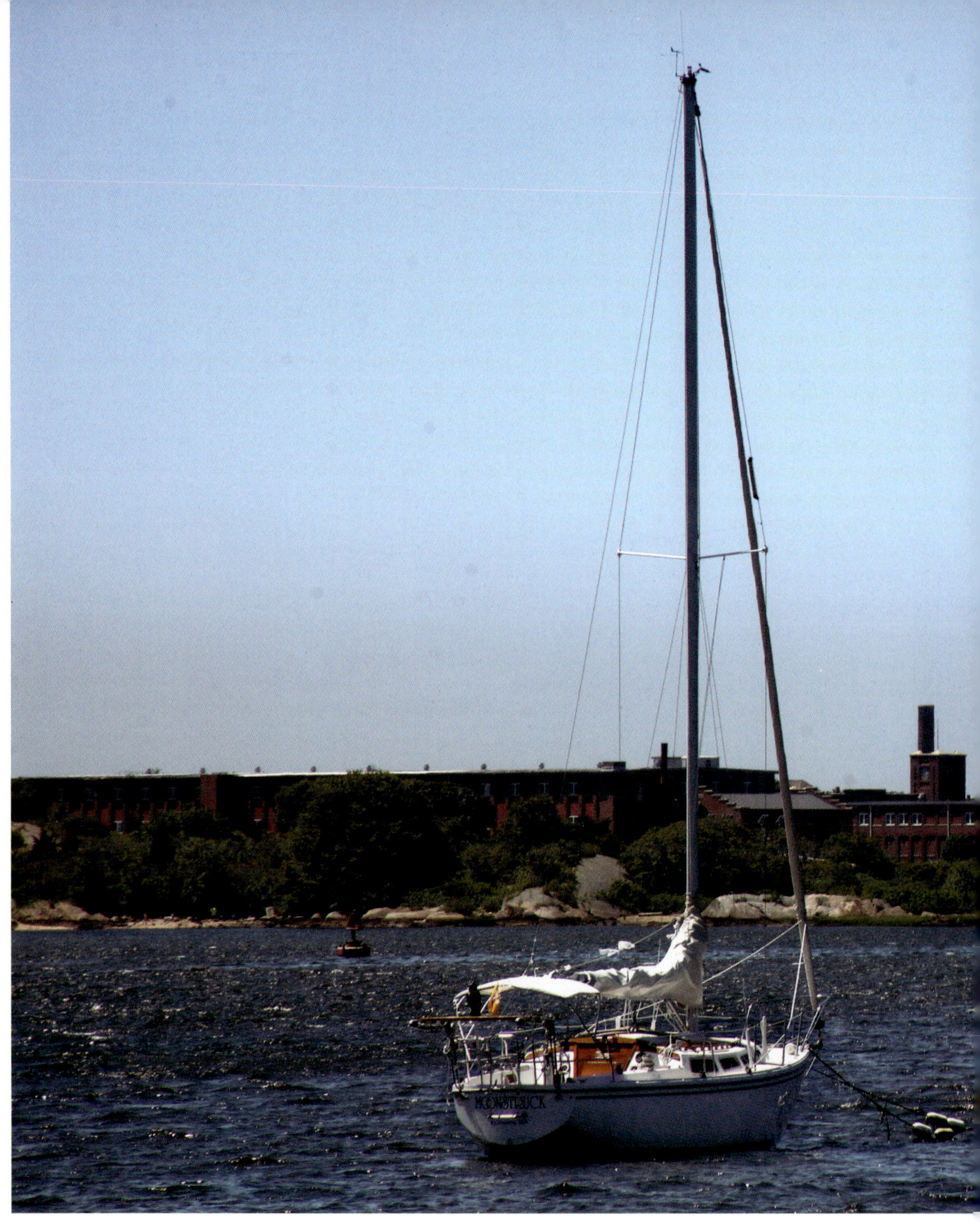

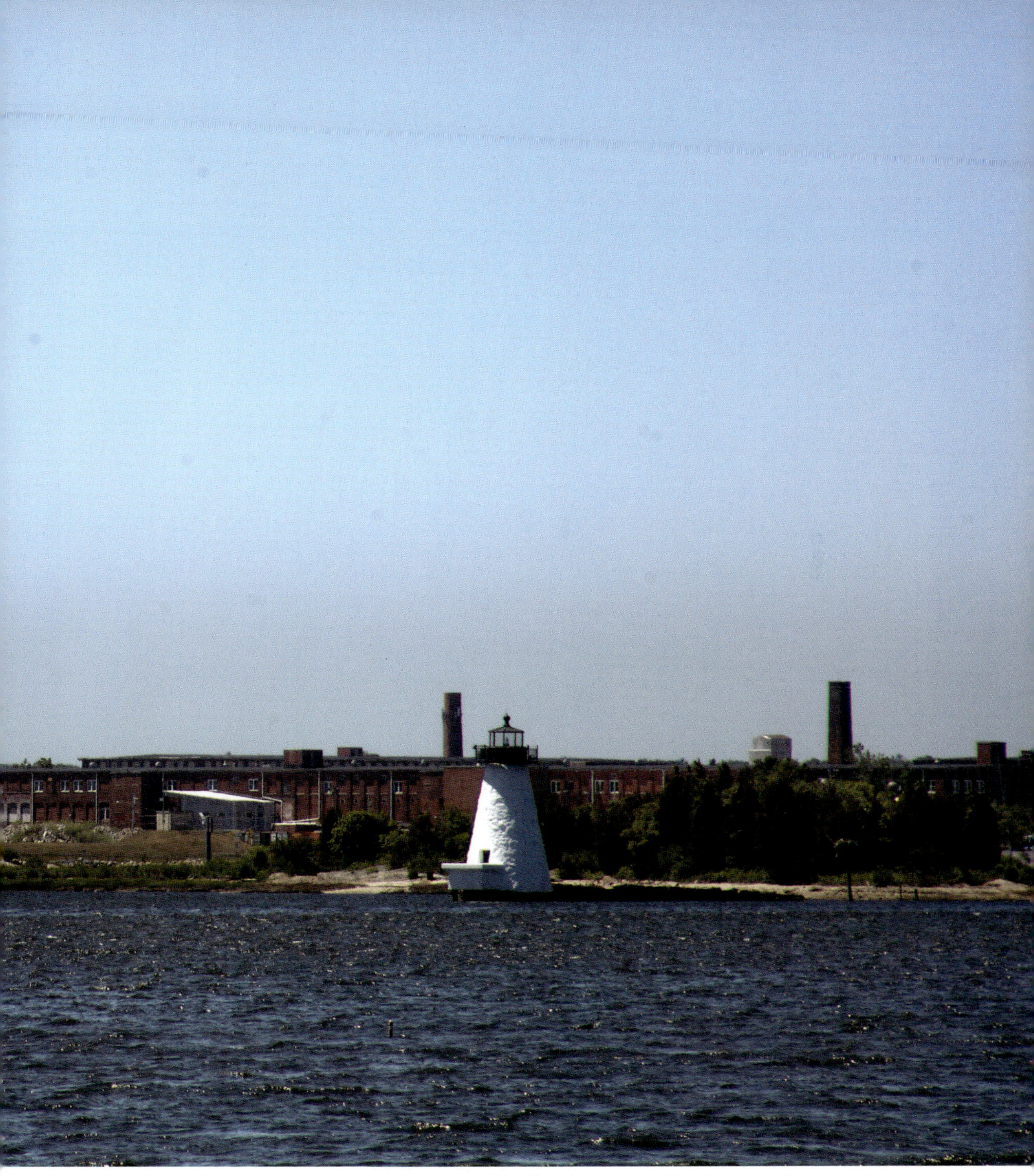

From a bluff in Fairhaven looking towards New Bedford, a view of the *Brittany Eryn* surging through the hurricane barrier.

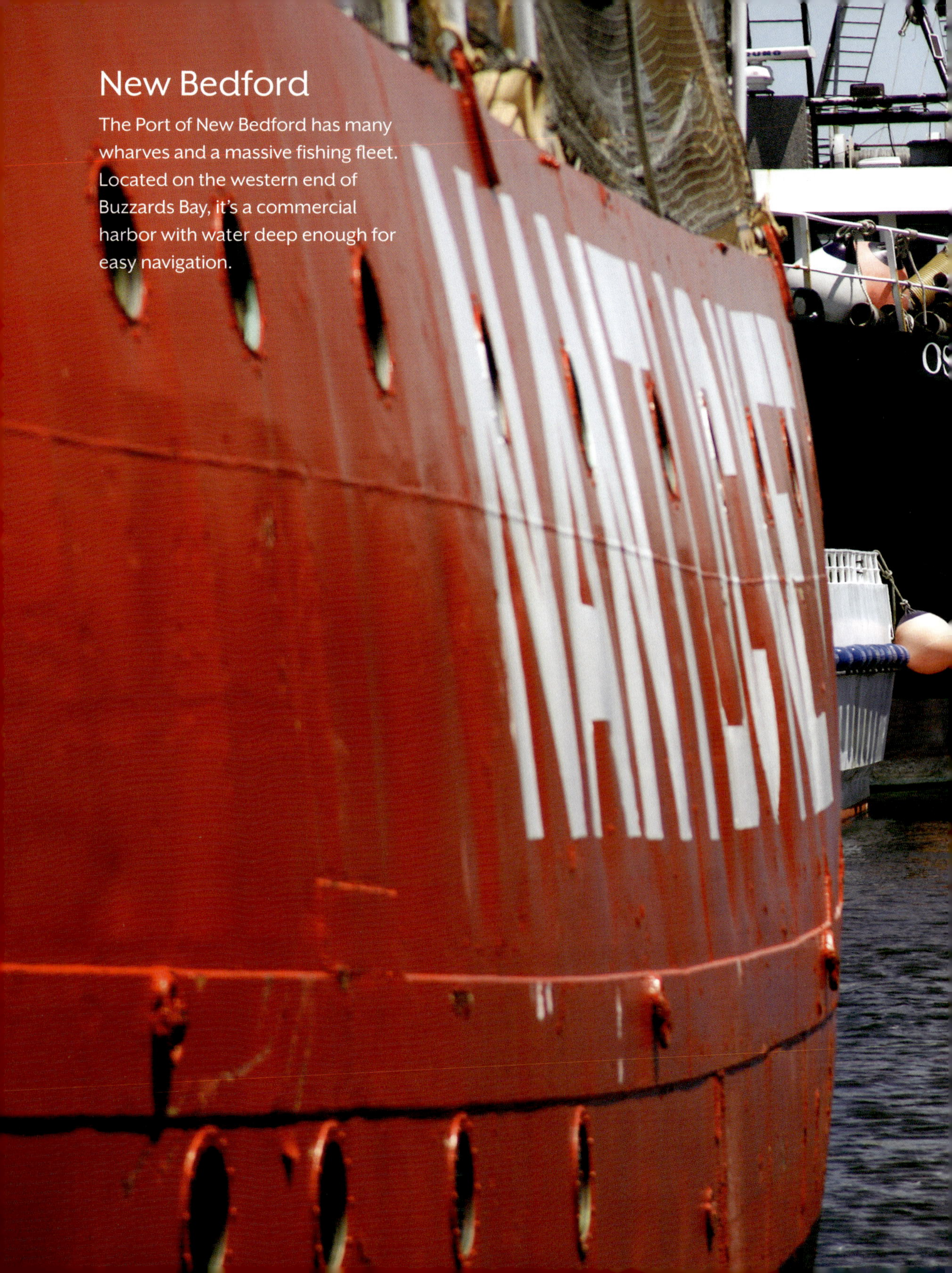

New Bedford

The Port of New Bedford has many
wharves and a massive fishing fleet.
Located on the western end of
Buzzards Bay, it's a commercial
harbor with water deep enough for
easy navigation.

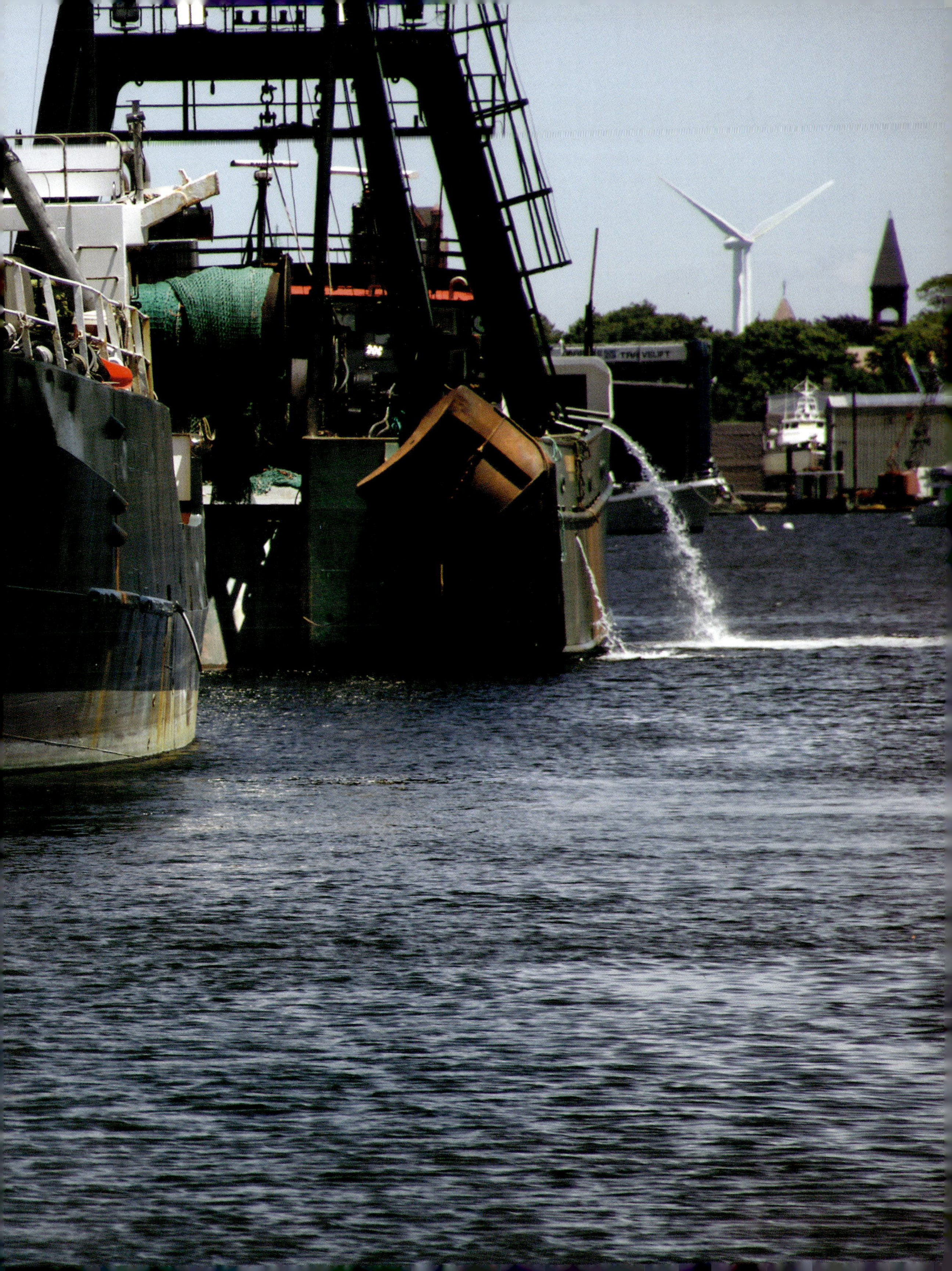

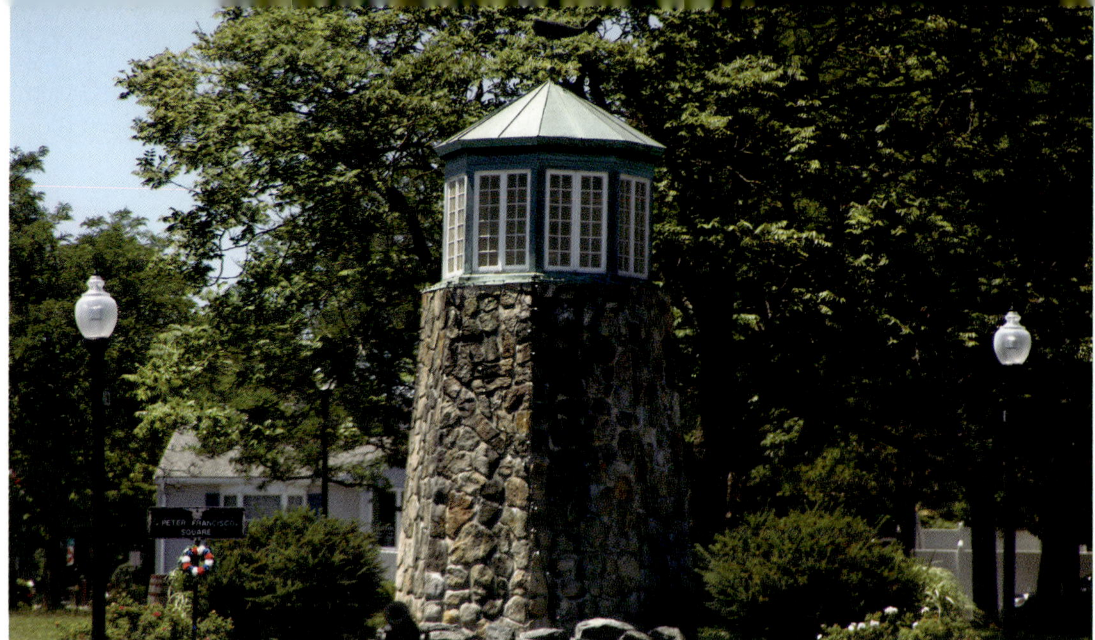

A small lighthouse in New Bedford welcomes visitors to Peter Francisco Square. New Bedford is one of the biggest and most historic fishing ports in America, with a history dating back to 1652.

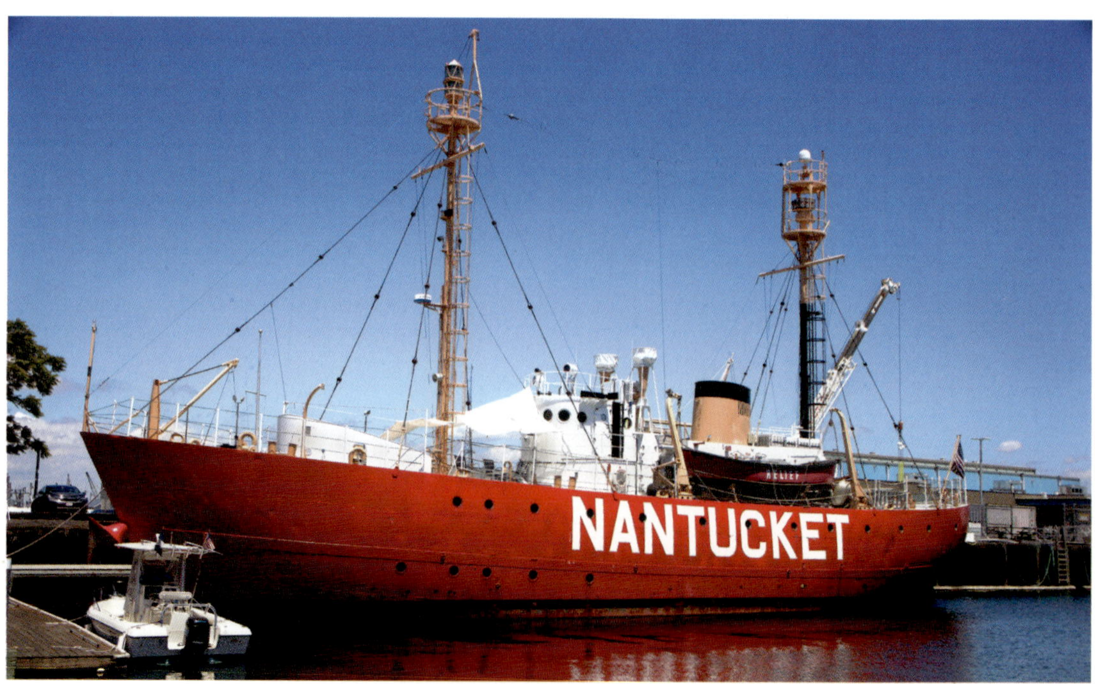

A view of the stunning United States Lightship *Nantucket* (WLV-612) from Merrill's Wharf. For decades the *Nantucket* helped vessels traverse some of the most difficult waters. She was launched in 1950, and decommissioned in 1985.

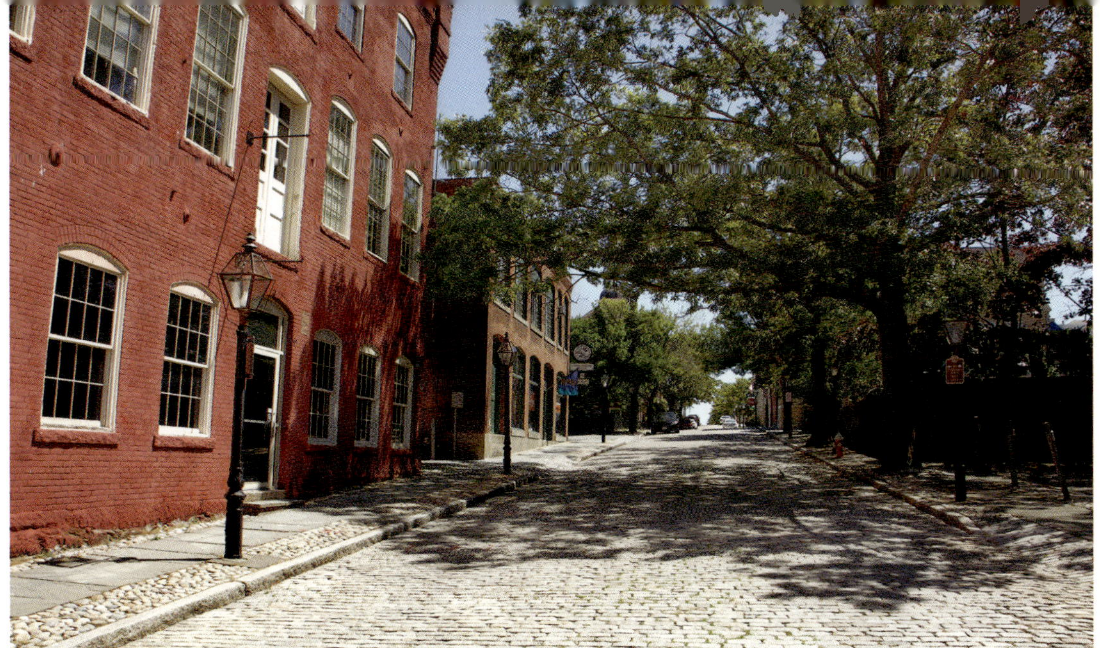

The inviting cobblestone-covered Bethel Street in the New Bedford Historic District. Cobblestones have been used for roads in New England since the 1600s.

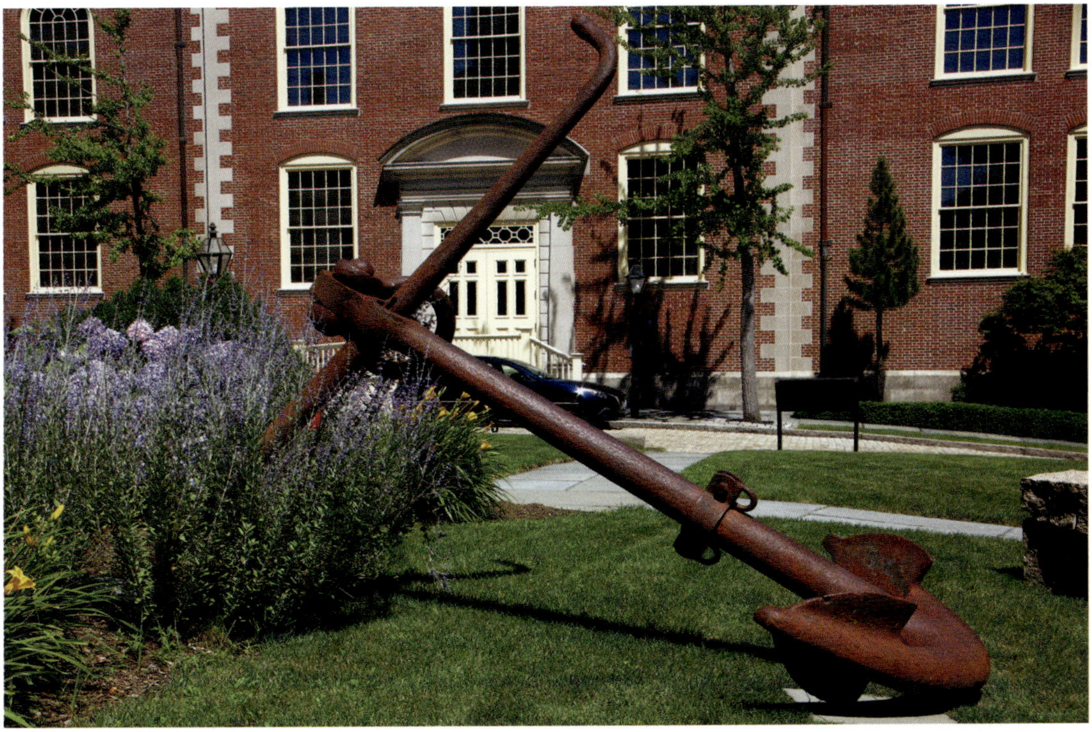

A large antique ship's anchor at the Seamen's Bethel & Mariner's Home. The brick building across the street is the New Bedford Whaling Museum.

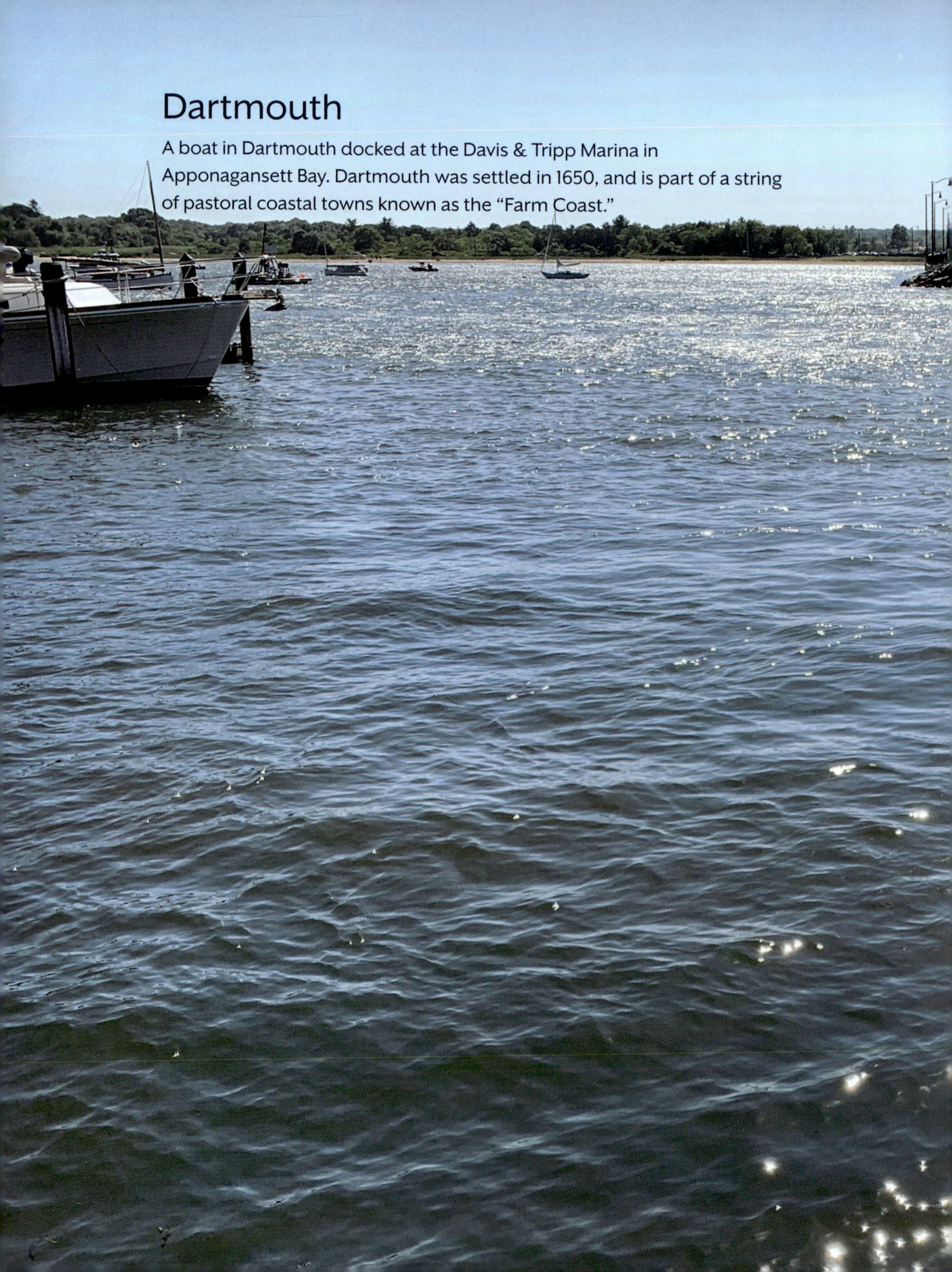

Dartmouth

A boat in Dartmouth docked at the Davis & Tripp Marina in Apponagansett Bay. Dartmouth was settled in 1650, and is part of a string of pastoral coastal towns known as the "Farm Coast."

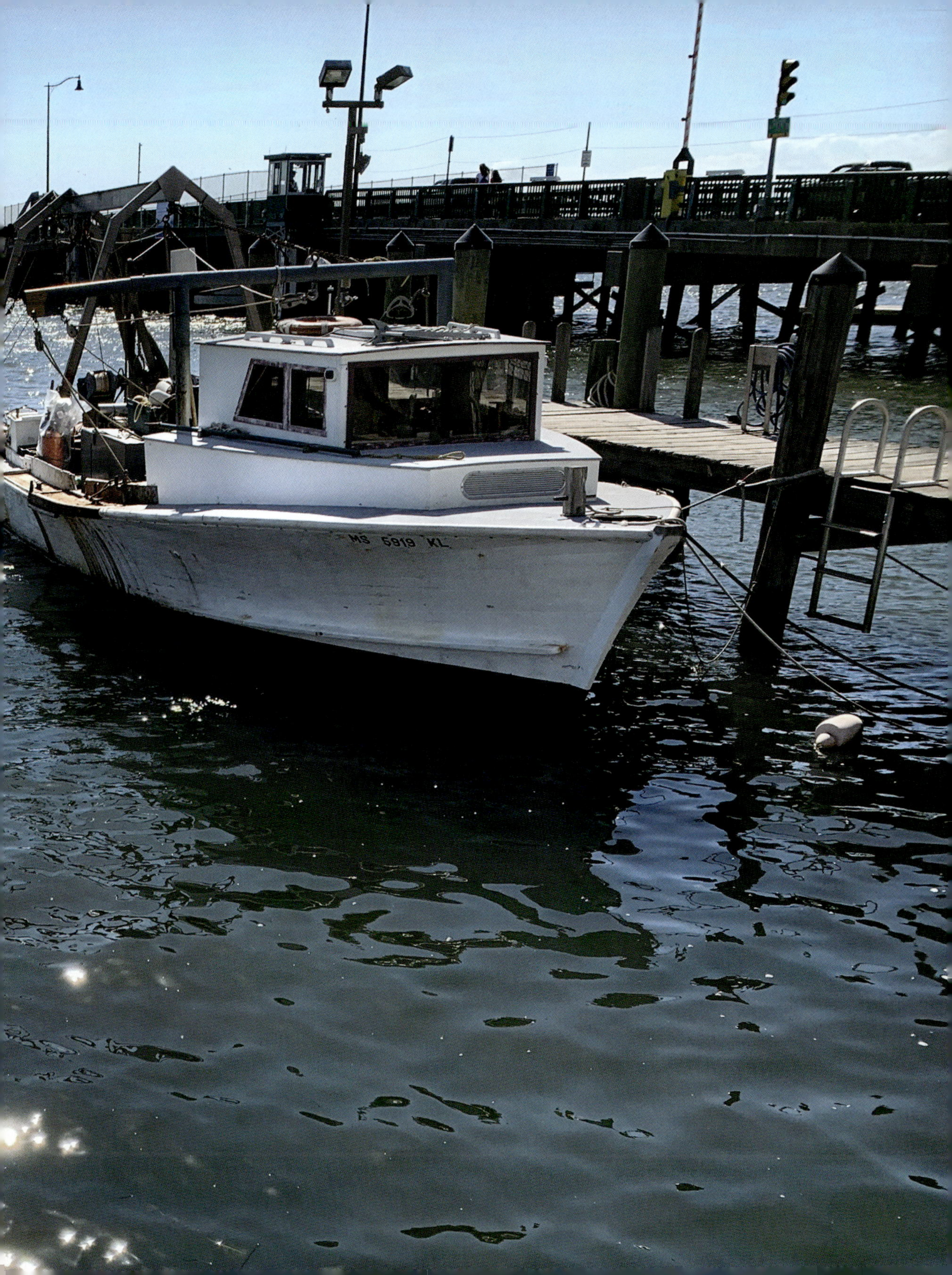
MS 5919 KL

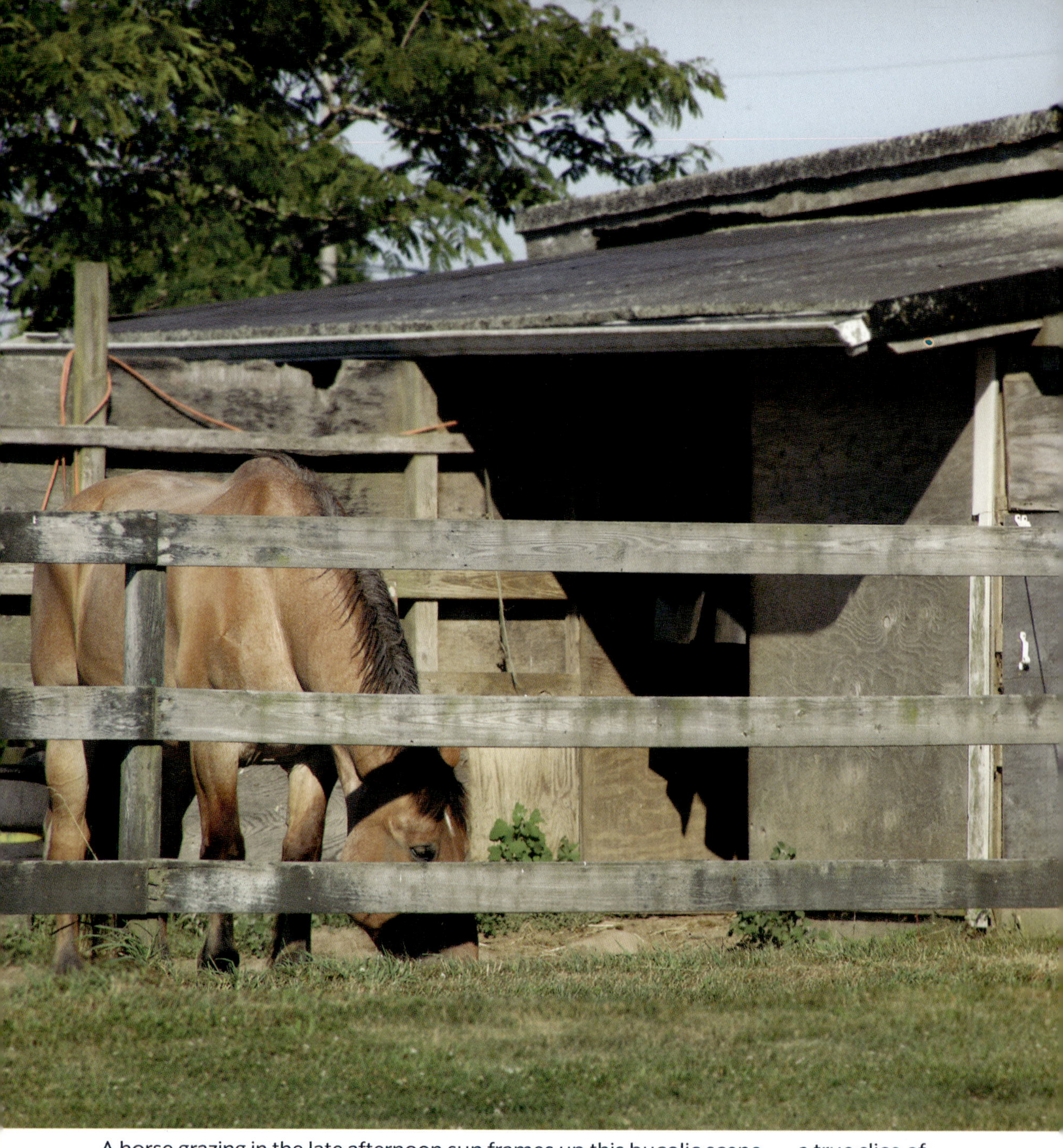

A horse grazing in the late afternoon sun frames up this bucolic scene . . . a true slice of Americana.

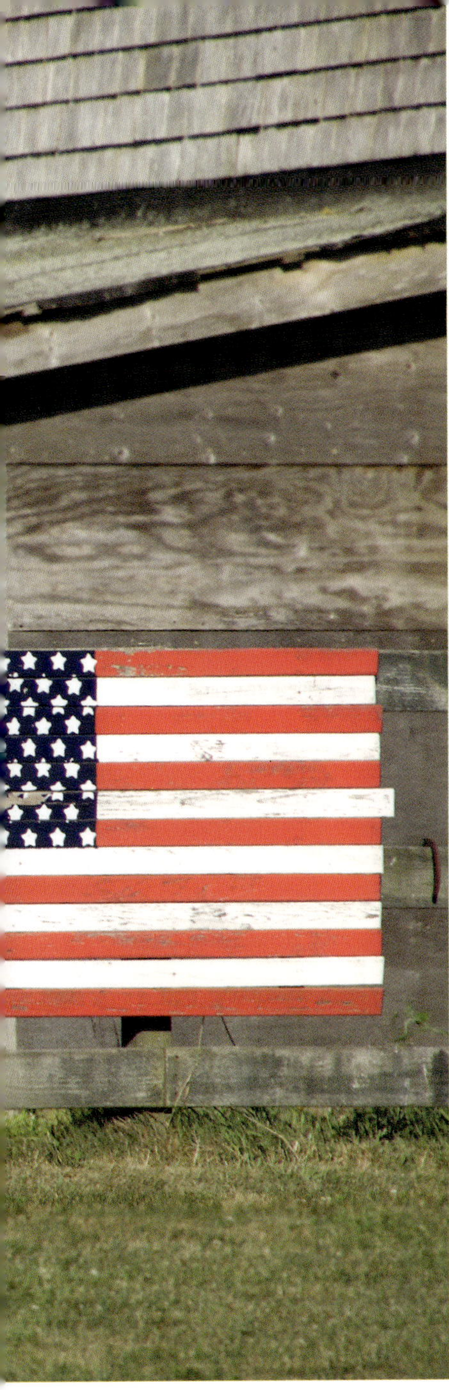

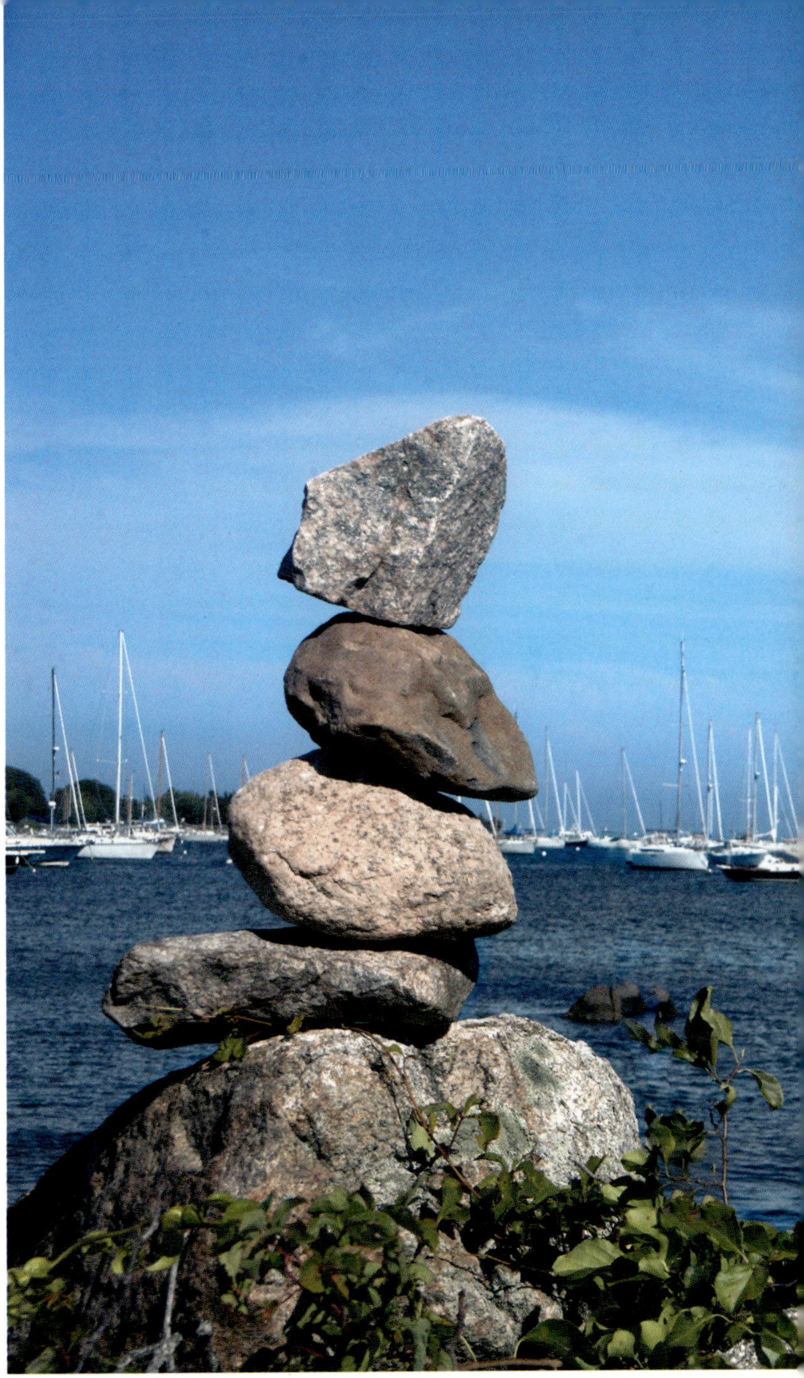

Cairn building is a time-honored art form and tradition dating back to prehistoric times. In early history, they were used as location markers, and also for ceremonial purposes like astronomy and burial monuments.

Westport

Sand dunes play a critical role in the ecosystem of coastal areas, offering a perfect habitat for mammals and birds, and barriers against heavy storm and flood damage.

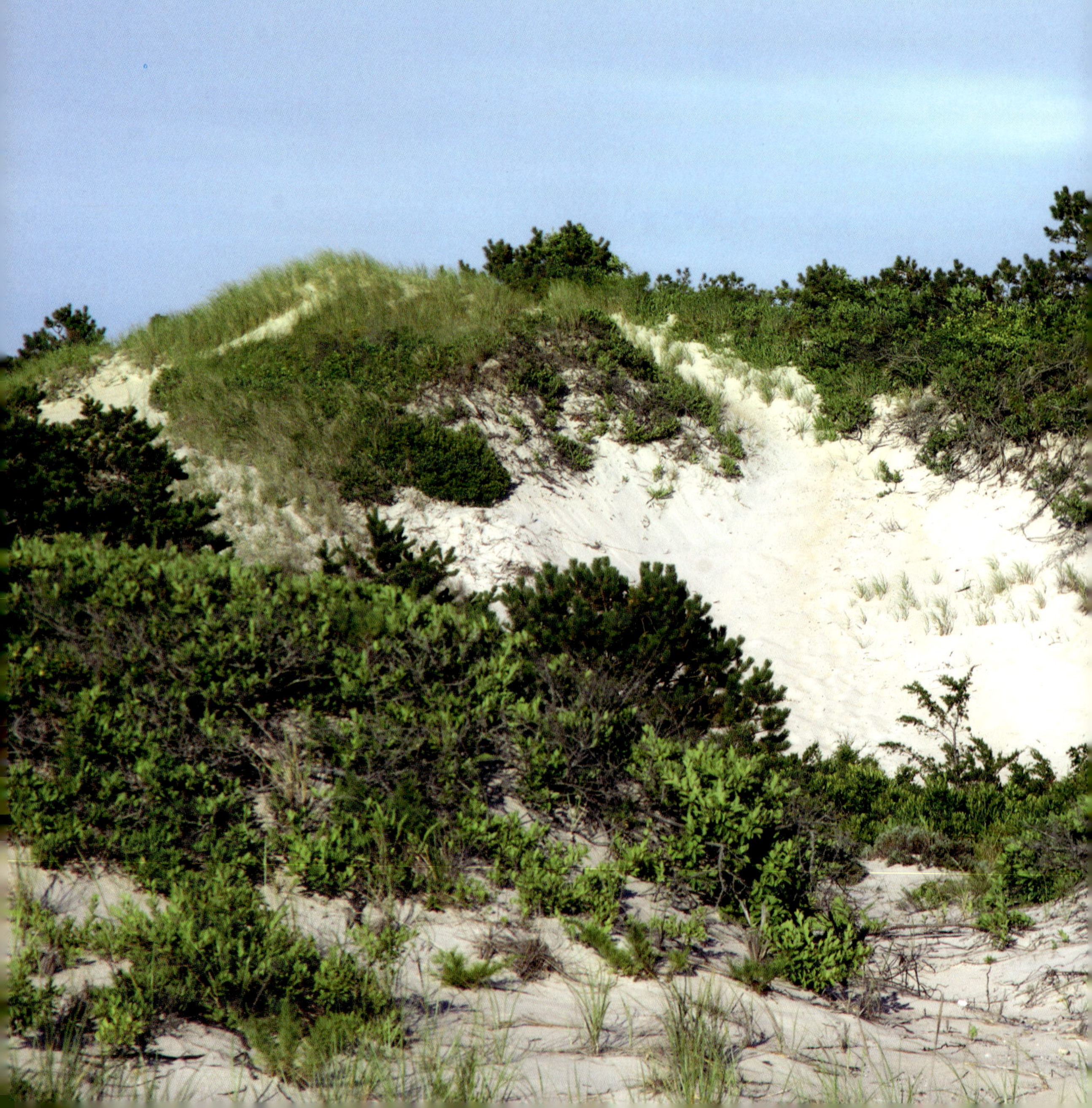

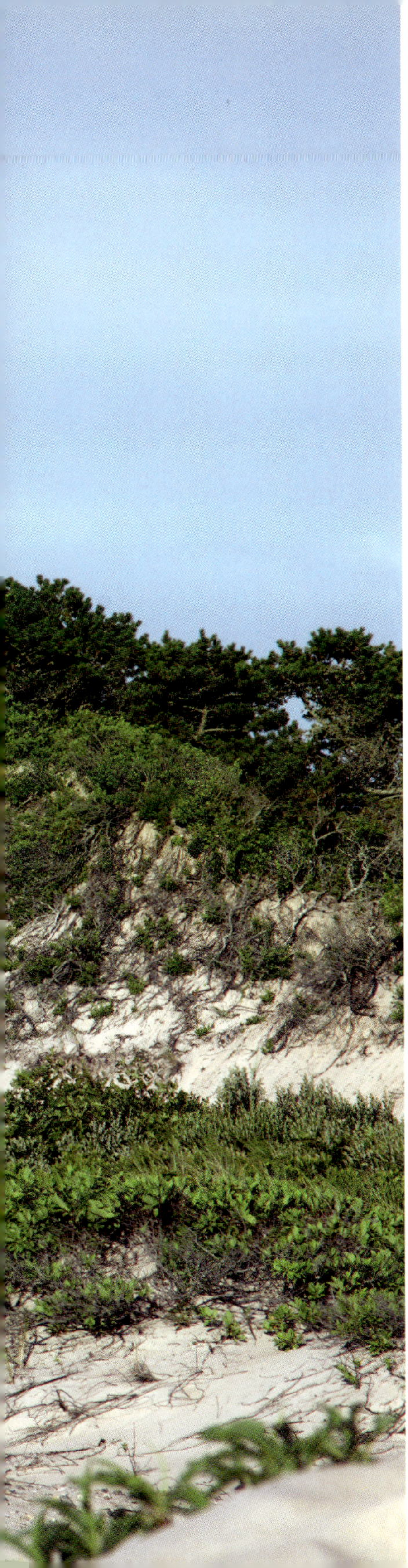

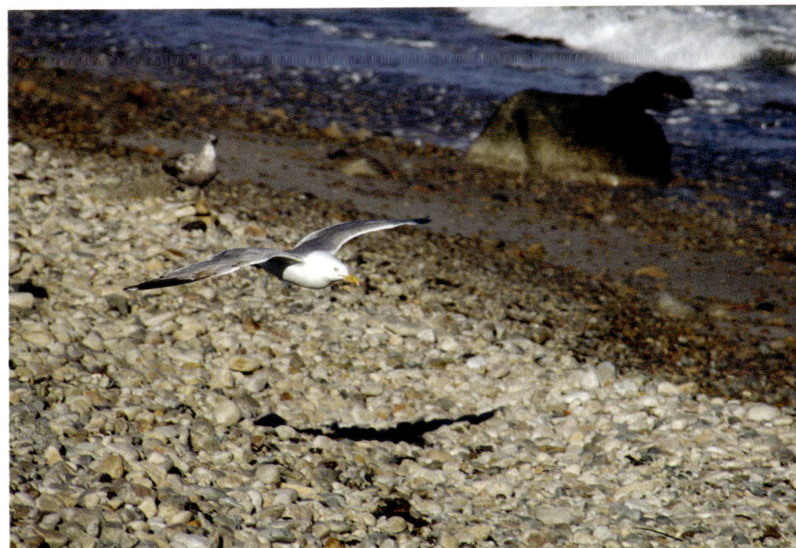

The way this seagull is eyeballing us, it's definitely thinking about stealing my hotdog—flying over the stone covered East Beach with impeccable panoramic views of the western Buzzards Bay.

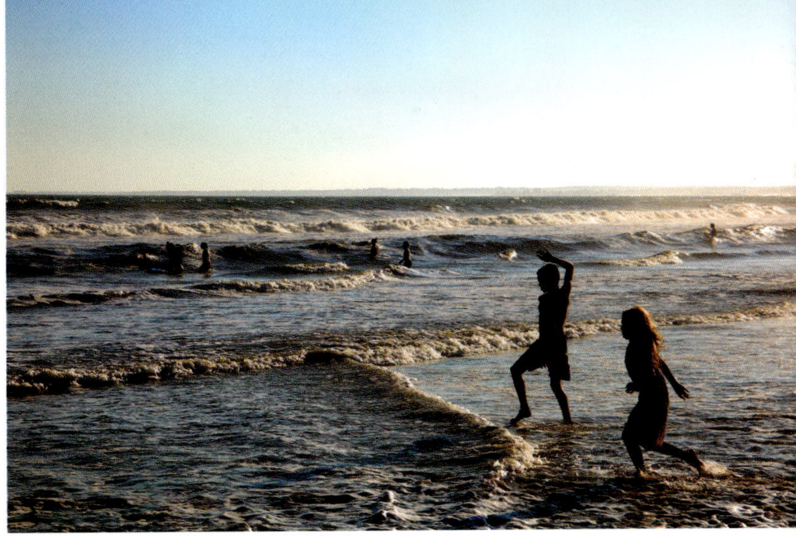

Kids making a dash for the waves at Horseneck Beach. My stepdad recommended coming here, as it was the first place his friends took him when he arrived in America by boat from Ireland as a young man. What a scenic and special place to get a first impression of the country.

Acknowledgments

Also sincere thanks and appreciation to Globe Pequot and Amy Lyons, friend and mentor Andy Borsari and his wife Elvira, friend and mentor Mark Wile, Philip Elliott Hopkins, Rockport High School and classmates, The Office of the Mayor of Gloucester, Captain Gussy Contrino and his wife Gretchen, Twin Lights soda proprietor Pierce Sears, The Cape Ann Museum, Rockport Inn & Suites, The Jimmy Fund and Dana-Farber, Saint Peter's Club, My coworkers at Daisy Buchanan's, DeeAnn Walker, Mary Beth from Salem, Christine Kostka Cohen, Geno Mondello, The Cape Ann Chamber of Commerce, Whale Cove crew, Allegra from Beverly, Wellfleet Harbormaster Will Sullivan, Chronicle TV host Ted Reinstein, and Paul Jackson.

About the Author

Mark Kanegis is an award-winning photographer who's made appearances on CNN and ABC and in the pages of *Yankee* magazine. His photography hangs in collections worldwide. He also hosts the travel-adventure show *New England Views* on YouTube. Mark started his photography career in his native Cape Ann, an area of quaint seaside villages on the North Shore of Massachusetts. He follows his passion with, at times, reckless abandon. Whether battling the heat to shoot a blazing bonfire, getting frostbite while photographing a frozen lighthouse, or balancing on the knife-edge of a cliff, he always challenges himself to capture the bold image.

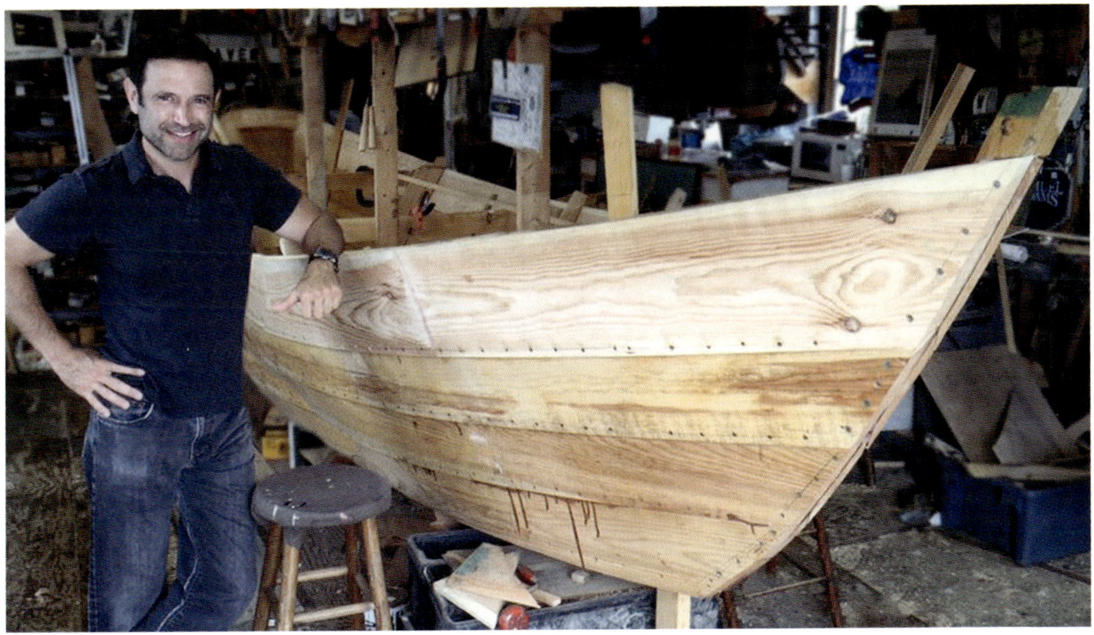